British consciousness and identity

The frontispiece to Michael Drayton's *Poly-Olbion*, 1610, depicting Great
Britain in the form of a woman enthroned in a triumphal arch and surrounded
by the figures of 'what Princes Time hath seene / Ambitious of her': Brutus,
Julius Caesar, Hengist, and William 'the Norman'.

British consciousness and identity

The making of Britain, 1533–1707

Edited by

Brendan Bradshaw

Queens' College, Cambridge

and

Peter Roberts

University of Kent at Canterbury

CAMBRIDGE
UNIVERSITY PRESS

PUBLISHED BY THE PRESS SYNDICATE OF THE UNIVERSITY OF CAMBRIDGE
The Pitt Building, Trumpington Street, Cambridge, United Kingdom

CAMBRIDGE UNIVERSITY PRESS
The Edinburgh Building, Cambridge CB2 2RU, UK
40 West 20th Street, New York NY 10011–4211, USA
477 Williamstown Road, Port Melbourne, VIC 3207, Australia
Ruiz de Alarcón 13, 28014 Madrid, Spain
Dock House, The Waterfront, Cape Town 8001, South Africa

http://www.cambridge.org

First published 1998, 2000
First paperback edition 2003

Typeface Plantin 10/12 pt.

A catalogue record for this book is available from the British Library

ISBN 0 521 43383 5 hardback
ISBN 0 521 89361 5 paperback

Contents

Contributors*

BRENDAN BRADSHAW is Director of Studies in History at Queens' College, Cambridge and is also a lecturer in early modern history at the University of Cambridge. He is a graduate of University College Dublin. His graduate studies on sixteenth-century Ireland were undertaken at Cambridge where he remained to teach.

KEITH M. BROWN now occupies a chair in History at St Andrews. He is a historian of Scotland and has previously taught history at a number of other Scottish universities.

MARC CABALL having completed a doctorate in Celtic studies and history at Jesus College, Oxford, is currently director of Ireland Literature Exchange, the state-supported agency for the international promotion of Irish writers. A former research scholar at the Dublin Institute for Advanced Studies, he is a graduate of Trinity College, Dublin.

JANE DAWSON, originally specialising in early modern English history at Durham, moved to St Andrews and became increasingly interested in Anglo-Irish, Anglo-Scottish, Highland Scottish and also British history. She now lectures in Ecclesiastical History at the University of Edinburgh.

ALAN FORD lectures in history at the Department of Theology of the University of Durham. He is a graduate of Trinity College, Dublin and conducted his doctoral research on the Reformation in Ireland at Cambridge.

* These brief profiles outlining the background from which the contributors approach British history are offered in the hope that the plurality of nationalities which they indicate may help to dispel ill-informed charges of 'anglocentrism under another name' now being levelled by critics of the new British history.

ANDREW HADFIELD is a student of early modern English literature. Having completed his doctoral studies at the University of Ulster, Coleraine, he moved to the Department of English of the University of Wales at Aberystwyth.

PHILIP JENKINS Welsh by background and education, he undertook graduate studies at Cambridge since when he has taught history at Pennsylvania State University.

COLIN KIDD a Scot, read history as an undergraduate at Cambridge and completed his doctoral studies at Oxford where he became a Fellow of All Souls before returning to Scotland to teach in the Department of Scottish History at Glasgow.

WILLY MALEY is Glasgow-Irish by background. Educated at the Universities of Strathclyde and Cambridge, he has taught at Goldsmiths and Queen Mary and Westfield Colleges in London, and is currently lecturer in English Literature at the University of Glasgow. Having worked extensively on English views of Ireland in the early modern period, he is turning his attention to Scottish and, inevitably, 'British' matters.

PETER ROBERTS undertook research at Cambridge on the Tudor union of Wales and England, and has since then taught at the University of Kent at Canterbury. As an honorary fellow of the University of Wales Centre for Advanced Welsh and Celtic Studies, he has contributed to the project on the social and cultural history of the Welsh language. He is the editor of *The Transactions of the Honourable Society of Cymmrodorion*.

JIM SMYTH went to Trinity College, Dublin from Belfast to take a B.A. in history. He then moved to Cambridge as a research student. He undertook post-doctoral studies at the Institute for Irish Studies attached to The Queen's University of Belfast and at Trinity Hall in Cambridge. Having briefly occupied a position as a lecturer at Robinson College in Cambridge he moved to the Department of History at the University of Notre Dame, Indiana.

Preface

As the multinational states of Eastern Europe crumble, and the longer established ones to the west continue to be vulnerable to militant agitation for secession on the part of minority nationalities comprehended within them, the historic stability of the United Kingdom begins to seem something of a phenomenon. By reason of the particular perspective which it adopts – on which see the Introduction – the collection of essays presented here is offered in the belief that it sheds light upon the secret of the remarkable stability of the British multinational conglomerate. At the same time it also points up the fragility of the Union, not least in the form of its historic and ongoing Irish problem. Finally in terms of a contribution to the 'new subject' of British history it aims to fill a niche not hitherto adequately provided for so far as the early modern period is concerned – on which also see the Introduction. In that respect it may perhaps be claimed that with its appearance the pioneering phase in the development of the new subject has been brought to completion at least so far as concerns the early modern period.

Some debts remain to be gratefully acknowledged. First the editors wish to thank the young historians who comprise their co-contributors. Their ready response to the invitation to join the project and their cooperation at all stages has been a continuing source of encouragement to the editors in overcoming unanticipated difficulties. In that regard Brendan Bradshaw wishes to record a special debt of thanks to his fellow editor and to the other contributors for their forbearance and assistance in a period of special personal difficulties which delayed the completion of the volume for rather longer than might have seemed reasonable. He also wishes to thank the publishers for similar forbearance particularly on the part of the editor, William Davies, without whose understanding and encouragement the project might have foundered. Lastly but by no means least – the expression is no less heartfelt for being clichéd – Brendan Bradshaw wishes to record his special indebtedness to Mrs Teresa Hodgson of the Cambridge History Faculty's General Office staff. She produced several drafts of his contribution with unflappable efficiency and cheerfulness. She also acted as a highly efficient factotum in assembling the volume and in preparing it for submission to the publishers.

BRENDAN BRADSHAW and PETER ROBERTS

Introduction

Brendan Bradshaw and Peter Roberts

British history as a 'new subject' may be said to have been launched by John Pocock in a series of path-breaking studies charting the conceptual contours that define its unique territory which appeared over the two decades from 1974.[1] So far as concerns the chronological span to which the present volume is devoted, the early modern period, the subject was 'brought down to earth', to adopt the phrase of Rees Davies, the distinguished practitioner of the genre for an earlier period, in the mid nineteen nineties. In the last few years a series of studies has appeared in print firmly grounded in documentary sources which explore the possibility of a political history of the Atlantic Archipelago as a coherent entity, not just as the sum of its national constituents, much less as a history of England with occasional glances towards the Celtic fringes as they intruded themselves into domestic politics.[2] The agenda which emerged from these pioneering explorations largely relates to the implications of political developments on the two islands over the period for an emergent British state. One item they address is the extent to which the constitutional unions between England and Scotland in 1707, and between the United Kingdom thus constituted and Ireland in 1800, were pre-conditioned by moves towards greater integration between the relevant polities in the sixteenth and seventeenth centuries. More particularly they discuss the significance that is to be attached in a British context to the state-building in which successive English monarchs engaged in this period, notably the incorporation of Wales within the English kingdom under Henry VIII in the 1530s, the conquest of

[1] J. G. A. Pocock, 'British history: a plea for a new subject', *Journal of Modern History*, 4 (1975); Pocock, 'The limits and divisions of British history', *American Historical Review*, 87 (1982); Pocock, 'Conclusion: contingency, identity, sovereignty', in A. Grant and K. J. Stringer (eds.), *Uniting the Kingdom? The making of British history* (London and New York, 1995).

[2] Among the most important of these are the following collections of essays: Ronald G. Asch (ed.), *Three Nations – a common history?* (Bochum, 1993); Steven G. Ellis and Sarah Barber (eds.), *Conquest and Union* (London, 1995); Brendan Bradshaw and John Morrill (eds.), *The British Problem, c. 1534–1707* (London, 1996).

1

Ireland under Elizabeth, the various attempts of the Tudors to reassert suzerainty over the Scottish monarch, the abortive attempt of James VI and I to translate the union of crowns in 1603 into a union of the kingdoms, and the short-lived Cromwellian archipelagic republic. Then, changing the focus from the centre to the constituent territories of the multiple kingdom, these studies raise a further series of issues. What insights are to be gained on historical developments in Ireland, Scotland and Wales by attending to their status as national entities within a state-system centrally governed by a sedentary English monarch? More particularly, how did the increasing assertiveness of government from the centre over the period impinge on internal political developments? That last question presents itself most arrestingly perhaps in the context of what historians, alerted to its British context, have come to call the War of the Three Kingdoms in the 1640s. However, the most historically and complex question remains the contrariety of Ireland. In contrast to Wales, and to Scotland after a spate of 'teething problems' in the seventeenth and eighteenth centuries, Ireland alone has persisted, from the outset of the Tudor period of imperial state-building, in constituting a seriously destablising element within the multinational polity governed by the crown of England.

The collection of essays assembled here continues the exploration of such issues. Its special claim as a contribution to the new subject rests on the historical categories in which they are investigated. The effect, we modestly suggest, is to add valuably to the scope of the discussion and to the agenda to which British historians of the new ilk address themselves. The special concern of the volume, then, is with the intellectual, cultural, linguistic and ideological dimensions of British history in this period. These are brought to bear in discussions that focus on that essential concomitant of territorial integration in the successful forma-tion of a nation-state: a matching sense among the communities comprehended within the new state-system of a shared political identity. In a word, a main object of enquiry of the studies that follow is that elusive and altogether too much taken for granted phenomenon, 'Brit-ishness'.

When, where and in what circumstances is such a sentiment discern-ible among the people of the two islands at this period? Did it pre-exist the embarkation of the Tudors on a policy of territorial consolidation? Did it therefore constitute a dynamic of the process for the formation of the British multinational state or was it generated in the process? What was the content of this notoriously unanalysed sentiment? Did the content vary in accordance with the predilections of the national communities that responded to it? How was it moulded by the unionist

ideologues who manipulated it to win support for the various projects
for the formation of an integrated archipelagic British state? Was it
adequate as a political concept and in its historical resonances to fulfil
the ideological demands made upon it by the constitutional union of
which it became the rhetorical referent?

Much of the discussion that follows is preoccupied with such considerations. However, many of the contributors rightly devote themselves to investigating *in tandem* or even exclusively an associated
question relating to the political mentality that conditioned the response
of the communities of the two islands to the project for an integrated
archipelagic state over the two centuries. That is the much-controverted
one of the existence or otherwise of a sense of national identity,
specifically as such, within the various territorial entities that formed the
patrimony of the English crown. For to raise the question of a British
sensibility as a feature of the mind-set of the relevant communities is to
beg the question of whether an English, Irish, Scottish and Welsh
sensibility had taken hold at this period in any case. The relevance of
that consideration to the preoccupations of the British historian need
hardly be emphasised. For instance, one of the issues to which a good
deal of space is devoted in the studies that follow is whether and, if so to
what effect, the communities of the regional dominions resisted cultural
anglicisation over these centuries given their increasing exposure to an
English, imperial and metropolitan public culture; given further the
insidious attraction to the elites of the regions within the new state-
system of the ambience and the patronage benefits of court and
metropolis. In that regard a British paradox of no little long-term
historical significance is explored in these pages: the vigorous survival of
a distinctive national cultural ethos, both 'high' and 'popular', within
the communities of Scotland and Wales despite the failure of national
sentiment to express itself, as it did with apparent ineluctability in the
case of Ireland, in political agitation for secession from the union or
indeed for a form of devolved self-government. The resolution of the
paradox as it emerges here lies at least in part precisely in the vagueness
of the notion of Britishness referred to earlier. Its genius as an ideological concept is found in its capaciousness: its capacity to seem to
buttress the self-esteem of each of the constituent nationalities of the
British conglomerate – apart significantly from that of the Irish – while
at the same time subsuming these identities under a more comprehensive category of nationality.

Such then is the conceptual frame and the agenda which the essays
that follow adopt under the rubric of the new British history. The
chronological range of the volume also requires a word of explanation.

No doubt the *terminus a quo* reflects the influence of the late Sir Geoffrey Elton, an influence which the two editors as research students of his would by no means wish to repudiate. His major interpretative contribution as a Tudor historian was the thesis, powerfully argued for throughout his distinguished career, of a Tudor 'revolution' in church and state conducted under the auspices of Henry VIII's chief minister and a group of radically minded Erastian reformers in the 1530s. These, he maintained, availed of the opportunity of the crisis precipitated by Henry VIII's unavailing quest for a papal annulment of his marriage to Catherine of Aragon, to launch a programme of reform by statute, which moulded the English crown's medieval patrimony into a more integrated and centralised unit, governed under the absolute sovereignty of the 'king in parliament' in accordance with the Renaissance imperial principle 'rex est imperator in regno suo'.[3] Whatever the present status of Sir Geoffrey's thesis – certain features of his original formula concerning the bureaucratisation of the central administration undoubtedly require modification[4] – it cannot be doubted that the 1530s mark a point of discontinuity in the crown's approach to the government of the English localities and to the constituents of its multinational medieval patrimony. In the former case the late medieval system of delegating responsibility and thereby royal authority to a local magnate was effectively terminated by means of the statute 'for liberties and franchises' and the extension of the shire system virtually uniformly throughout the realm.[5] At the same time a series of statutes incorporated Wales within the English realm and clinched the union by the shiring of the country on the English model.[6] The imperial programme for Ireland did not entail a constitutional union of the Lordship with the English kingdom in the Welsh manner. Nevertheless the form of government now set in place involved a hardly less radical break with the medieval past. The system of so-called 'aristocratic home-rule', in effect the devolution of crown government to the colonial political elite, and in particular to its most powerful magnate dynasty, the Kildare Fitzgeralds, was abandoned. Henceforth the central administration in Dublin was

---

[3] The classic statement of the thesis is contained in G. R. Elton, *England under the Tudors* (London, rev. edn. 1974), ch. 7. It is more fully elaborated, developed and modified in the light of later research in Elton, *Reform and Reformation* (London, 1977), chs. 7, 9.

[4] See especially D. Starkey and C. Coleman (eds.), *Revolution Reassessed* (London, 1986). The consolidation of the realm in the 1530s is one aspect of the Elton thesis which is not addressed in this critique. The essays are generally well balanced and probing apart from Starkey's overheated and overstated introductory essay.

[5] Elton, *Reform and Reformation*, 201–2.

[6] Glanmor Williams, *Recovery, Reorientation and Reformation: Wales c. 1415–1642* (Oxford and Cardiff, 1987), ch. 11. P. R. Roberts, 'The act of union in Welsh history', *Transactions of the Honourable Society of Cymmrodorion* (1974), 49–72.

headed by an English administrator, often an experienced military commander. Increasingly the key administrative posts went to New English officials, not to the old colonists according to the disposition of the Fitzgerald lord deputy. Meanwhile provision was made for the protection of the colonial territory from marauding Irish borderers by the establishment of a garrison force as a substitute for the entourage of the colonial satrap.[7] Here is found the origins of the system by which Ireland was to be governed down to the establishment of the Free State in the 1920s. More immediately the effect of the programme of reform was to destabilise Anglo-Irish relations and to embroil the crown in a process of increased militarisation in governing Ireland that terminated in the conquest of the 1590s. One further significant alteration of the medieval system in relation to Ireland needs finally to be noted. This was the elevation of the status of the Lordship to that of a sovereign kingdom in consequence of the statute of 1542 ostensibly designed simply to affirm the English ruler's sovereign authority throughout the island.[8] Succeeding generations of Irish patriots were to argue steadfastly from this point forward that Ireland in virtue of its sovereign status was not subordinate to English institutions of government, most especially to English law and to the English parliament, but only to its king whose sovereignty in Ireland resided in the Irish parliament, and in the laws there enacted or consented to. Finally it is relevant to the significance of the later reign of Henry VIII as an historic turning point in British history properly so-called, to bear in mind that the 'rough-wooing' of Scotland embarked on in 1542 was accompanied by a propaganda campaign in which the English king's claim to suzerainty over his Scottish counterpart as the senior British monarch, first entered by Edward I, was revived, and in consequence a British 'rhetoric' was reintroduced into English political discourse.[9]

As to the *terminus ad quem*, the turn of the seventeenth century may be taken to mark also a turning point in British history as decisive as that of the later reign of Henry VIII. The process of state-building that got under way in the 1530s now reached a certain completion. Wales was firmly and unproblematically committed to political union; yet its survival as a geographical and cultural entity, contrary to the imperialistic design announced in the so-called statute of union of 1536, was also assured. The Welsh had ingeniously resisted total anglicisation.

[7] Elton, *Reform and Reformation*, 206–11; Brendan Bradshaw, *The Irish Constitutional Revolution of the Sixteenth Century* (Cambridge, 1970), chs. 4–6.
[8] Bradshaw, *Irish Constitutional Revolution*, chs. 7–9.
[9] Roger A. Mason, 'Scotching the brut: politics, history and national myth in sixteenth-century Britain', in *Scotland and England, 1286–1815*, ed. Roger A. Mason (Edinburgh, 1987), 60–84.

They retained a strong sense of a Welsh national identity which found expression in the protestant faith, in antiquarian scholarship and in various forms of high and popular culture. Traditional accounts of the early-modern history of the polity of 'England and Wales' which was created in 1536 have done scant justice to the complexity of the relationship. By means of the acts for the union of the kingdoms of England and Scotland passed by the respective parliaments of both kingdoms in 1707, the union of the crowns effected by the accession of James VI of Scotland to the English throne was brought to the consummation so ardently desired by that monarch, though perhaps not quite in the form he had envisaged. The island of Britain, historically so called, now for the first time comprised a single constitutional entity, governed from the capital of the sedentary British monarchy in London. The last of the dynastic wars for the British throne had yet to be fought in 1745 but the union of the three national territories within a single British state was never again to be seriously challenged. Meanwhile Ireland had emerged as *the* British Problem, the main problem that was to destabilise the state internally in the course of the modern period. The contours of the Irish problem had by now also become evident. In the aftermath of the Treaty of Limerick in 1691 which concluded the 'War of the Two Kings' – James II and William III – many of the remaining Catholic landowners availed of the opportunity to seek their fortunes in the service of the Catholic monarchs of Europe. The opportunity was thus offered to the New English, Scottish and Cromwellian planters to undermine both the guarantees of security of tenure extended to Catholics under the treaty and that of toleration for the private practice of the Catholic religion. The protestant Ascendancy had begun. It would seem that, in practice, Ireland had been reduced, uniquely within the amalgam of territories that comprised the United British Kingdom, to the status of a colony. Its traditional Catholic elite had been dispossessed, their lands now being occupied by protestant planters. Henceforth Catholics who formed the majority of the island's population were to be systematically discriminated against by means of the penal laws, a code not dissimilar to that from which the legislation of 1536–43 had released the Welsh.[10] The Catholics in Ireland were thus subjected to a form of 'social apartheid' more selective than that which affected their co-religionists in other parts of the British state.[11] Government relied upon substantial assis-

[10] The Lancastrian penal laws against the Welsh, which became a dead letter in 1536, were not formally repealed until 1624, while parliament had rescinded hostile English laws against the Scots in 1607. Stats. 4 & 5 James I, c. 1; 21 James I, cc. 10, 28 section 11: *Statutes of the Realm* (London, 1819), vol. iv, pp. 1134–7, 1219, 1239.

[11] J. G. Simms, 'The establishment of protestant ascendancy, 1691–1714', in T. W. Moody and W. E. Vaughan (eds.), *A New History of Ireland* (Oxford, 1986), iv, 1–30 at

tance from an occupying garrison force.[12] The issues that were to render Ireland an unassimilable element within the British state and to fuel Irish nationalism into the twentieth century were now in place: land, religion and the garrison.

The curtain had come down upon the early modern phase of British history. The stage was set on which the history of modern Britain would be enacted.

16–21; David Dickson, *New Foundations: Ireland 1660–1800* (Dublin, 1987), 40–52; Thomas Bartlett, *The Fall and Rise of the Irish Nation: The Catholic Question, 1690–1830* (Dublin, 1992), chs. 2, 3, 4.

[12] Thomas Bartlett and Keith Jeffery (eds.), *A Military History of Ireland* (Cambridge, 1996), chs. 6 (Ellis), 10 (Guy), 11 (Connolly), 12 (Bartlett), 16 (Crossman), 17 (Fitzpatrick).

1   Tudor Wales, national identity and the British inheritance

Peter Roberts

The concept of Britain which dominated the history of Wales in the Tudor period was the long-held belief that the Welsh were the descendants of the ancient Britons and that they spoke 'the British tongue'. The consciousness of this inheritance, heightened by the perception that the dynasty was of Welsh name and descent, was to have a transformative impact on the sense of a national identity which survived the constitutional union with England. Indeed Wales and Welsh identity emerged from the imperial programme of the Tudors strengthened rather than undermined. The explanation of this paradox is central to the agenda for the new British history in its Welsh dimension. It has long been evident from the anglocentric character of the traditional accounts of early modern England that the most persistent 'British Problem' is one of historiography. The call to revision invites a discussion of the extent to which the *old* British History – including the *Historia Regum Britanniae* of Geoffrey of Monmouth, as it was manipulated by Welsh historians and other writers in the post-union period – shaped not only dynastic propaganda but national identity and British consciousness. Some of these commentators even aspired to exercise a formative influence on Tudor and early Stuart policy or statecraft.

I

The so-called Act of Union of 1536 (27 Henry VIII, c. 26), formed part of Cromwell's legislative programme for the integration of the realm. The dissolution of the marcher lordships in this act was complemented by the abolition of liberties and franchises within the realm in a contemporaneous act (27 Henry VIII, c. 24). In that both statutes gave the quietus to surviving feudal enclaves, they represented an extension of the concept of empire enunciated in the preamble to the Act of Appeals (1533) in the sense of territory as well as jurisdiction. The novelty was disguised in a conservative statement in the preamble to the Act of Union, that Wales was already 'incorporated, annexed, united and subject to and under the imperial crown of this realm', which misrepresented the true constitutional position. In conveying the impression that the country formed a coherent and integrated entity, the rhetoric conveniently ignored the history of the Marches which were now abolished. Edward I's Statute of Wales of 1284 had legislated for the lands conquered from the last native prince, and the annexation it effected had been of those lands to the crown and not to the realm of England. With the provision in 1536 for the conversion of the marcher lordships into shires, the whole of Wales was incorporated with England. Most revolutionary of all, every distinction in legal status between the king's subjects in England and Wales was to be removed in recognition of his 'singular zeal, love and favour' towards the Welsh. This equivocal statement is the nearest any of the Tudors ever came to acknowledging the special regard for the nation which later Welsh commentators came to claim on their behalf.

Although the union legislated in 1536 was a unilateral measure passed by a parliament in which there were as yet no elected representatives from Wales, it was based in part on petitions for the introduction of English law as well as proposals for administrative reform which had been advanced since the early 1530s by Welsh landowners and English officials in Wales. Parliamentary representation was granted in the act itself and by the time the consolidating statute of 1543 was passed, members from these new constituencies had been returned to the Commons to participate in the final formulation of the settlement. In the preamble to this act (34 & 35 Henry VIII, c. 26) it was declared that the king, 'of his tender zeal and affection that he beareth towards his loving and obedient subjects' of Wales, had devised ordinances which, in response to their 'humble suit and petition', he is pleased to have enacted in parliament.

The legislators had good reason to suppose that the generality of Welsh landowners would be well disposed to the new dispensation and could meet the qualifications for holding judicial and administrative offices. There were also clear indications (as there were not in the case of the native Irish) that the attachment of this class to the indigenous culture would prove to be no barrier to the reception of English law and all that it entailed.[1] The need to secure the western coastline against the threat of invasion may have been a key factor in the timing of the

[1] P. R. Roberts, 'The union with England and the identity of "Anglican" Wales', *Transactions of the Royal Historical Society*, 5 ser., 22 (1972), 61–4; Roberts, 'The Welsh language, English law and Tudor legislation', *Transactions of the Honourable Society of Cymmrodorion* (1989), 26–8.

reforms, but it is evident that the whole of Wales was no longer regarded by the king and his council as an intractable border area. Two years after inaugurating the rigorous regime of Bishop Rowland Lee, lord president of the Council in the Marches, to curb lawlessness in the lordships, Cromwell judged it was safe to adopt a less coercive approach to the problems of Welsh government.

In 1536 Wales became an integral part of the kingdom instead of a collection of disparate territories comprising the crown dominion, already administered as shires in the north and west, and since 1301 known as the Principality, and the private jurisdictions of feudal lordships. With this enlargement of the kingdom and of the composition of parliament, the new polity of England *and* Wales was created as a unitary state which was sufficiently flexible in its constitution to allow for future contingencies. The 'Principality and Dominion of Wales' was not legislated out of existence but extended to cover the whole country, which was now united internally as never before. The rights of a future heir to the throne who might be created prince of Wales were probably taken into account when the legislation was framed. Prince Edward was born in 1537 and before the settlement was completed contingency plans were drawn up for the revival of the Principality as an institution which could be invested in the prince at the king's pleasure. This apanage for the heir apparent was to be endowed with a more comprehensive and coherent jurisdiction under royal authority than any prince had enjoyed in the past. To accommodate this eventuality, the king was given powers in the second 'Act of Union' in 1543 to alter the legislative provisions at his discretion without further parliamentary sanction.[2] The 'Union with England' was therefore a very provisional one which could be altered to suit changing dynastic circumstances, and the imperial sovereignty it envisaged had not entirely lost its associations with suzerainty.[3] No such creation or investiture followed in this reign to qualify the constitutional union or the unity of the realm, and there was not to be another Tudor prince for whom a patrimony co-terminous with the whole of Wales could be revived. Nevertheless, the special relationship between the crown and the Principality was perpetuated beyond the union, and the enabling clause in the act of 1543 remained

---

[2] P. R. Roberts, 'The "Henry VIII Clause": delegated legislation and the Tudor Principality of Wales', in T. G. Watkin (ed.), *Legal Record and Historical Reality* (London, 1989), 37–49.

[3] After bestowing the Dominion on the prince, the king was to reserve the right to pardon treasons and the general authority to revise and reform the settlement at his discretion. 'A Breviat of the Effectes devised for Wales', ed. P. R. Roberts, *Camden Miscellany*, 26, Camden 4th ser., 14 (1975), 31–47, esp. 43.

on the statute book until it was repealed in 1624.[4] This was what the sovereignty of 'the king-in-parliament' meant in the case of Wales, a contiguity but not a complete merger of royal prerogative and the composite authority of the king, lords and commons assembled in parliament. The significance of the distinction between these powers has remained obscure because the discretion was never exercised in the event, for subsequent Tudor parliaments would continue to legislate for what was still called the 'dominion, principality and country of Wales', though it was no longer described as 'the king's dominion'. It would be governed along with the English border shires by the revamped provincial council based at Ludlow, but even without a definite border to replace the Marches and in the absence of a prince, the twelve shires formed an entity with a distinct legal personality. The Tudor union had thus a constitutional as well as a cultural significance in the history of Welsh national consciousness, for it redefined the identity of Wales as well as of Welshness.

The general assimilation of Welsh to English law and administration had a levelling effect within Wales itself with the removal of old jurisdictional boundaries. Not only did the border between the Principality and the Marches disappear, but within the lordships the distinctive enclaves of 'Englishries' (areas where the law of the March prevailed) and 'Welshries' (where native customs were observed) were absorbed into the shire system. With the removal of these differences the association of Welshness with only parts of the country disappeared as well. The union released the Welsh from the sense of occupying only sections of their own country (they had previously held the status of 'foreign inhabitants' in the northern principality) and they could now be said to inhabit a land united for the first time in history. The towns, like the former 'Englishries', were to become increasingly Welsh in character, though some anglicised pockets remained in the Vale of Glamorgan and in some marcher boroughs. In contrast to this internal process of cymricisation, the hundreds transferred to English border shires after 1536 contained rural communities in which the Welsh language flourished. These were to survive intact for three centuries and more as outliers of Welshness in England and reminders that the boundary between the two countries had been artificially drawn.

---

[4] 21 James I, c. 10. Ivor Bowen (ed.), *The Statutes of Wales* (London, 1908), 165–6. P. R. Roberts, 'Wales and England after the Tudor "Union": crown, Principality and parliament, 1543–1624', in C. Cross *et al.* (eds.), *Law and Government under the Tudors: essays presented to Sir Geoffrey Elton on his retirement* (Cambridge, 1988), 111–38.

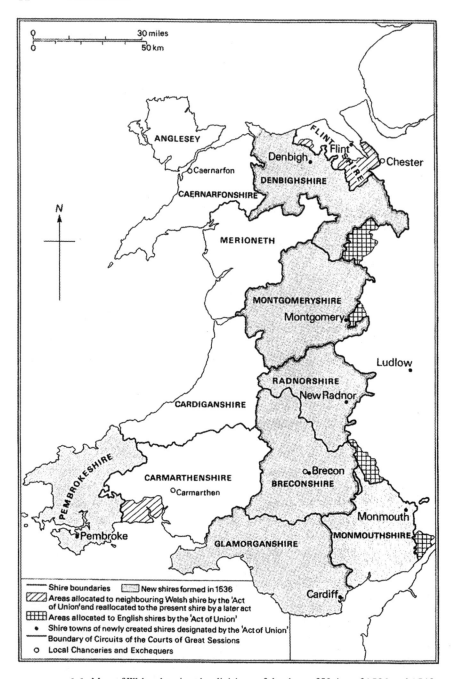

1.1 Map of Wales showing the divisions of the Acts of Union of 1536 and 1543

II

The distinctive national ethos of Wales, which hinged on the integrity of the language and the memory of past glory, had survived without the benefit of national institutions since the loss of independence in 1282. With the decline after the conquest of the institutional framework provided by a comprehensive system of native law, the language in which the law had been enshrined had remained as the most potent palladium of nationhood. Indeed the word *iaith*, which signified both 'language' and 'nation', encapsulated the sense of national identity all the more effectively in the absence of a single territorial entity called Wales. While the Tudor union brought an unprecedented degree of internal unity to Wales, the native language suffered a loss of status. In these circumstances Welsh national consciousness was to confront as great a challenge as it had experienced in the period of conquest and oppression.

The crisis was surmounted because the unitary realm which came into being after 1536 was not monolithic: there was to be a common language for all the king's subjects, but a certain cultural pluralism was tolerated in practice. What historians have termed 'Tudor imperialism' was a complex phenomenon as far as Wales was concerned. In 1536 it involved a far less draconian approach to the indigenous language than was applied in the case of Ireland and Calais, the other dominions of the crown on the periphery of the realm.[5] In a measure designed to remove all invidious distinctions between the king's subjects of England and Wales, Welsh and marcher laws and customs were abolished and England was made the official language of law and administration. The declared legislative intention was to bring the king's subjects in England and Wales to 'an amicable Concord and Unity' commensurate with equality before the law of England, and 'utterly to extirp all and singular the sinister usages and customs differing from the same'. The language itself is evidently not intended to be included in this category of usages and customs. The common law of England was to be administered in the new courts exclusively through the English language; no Welshman who was not proficient in it could hold judicial or fee-bearing office under the crown. Although Welsh was left in a precarious position, it was not proscribed. Welshmen ambitious for office were encouraged to become bilingual, and there was no shortage of candidates already deemed to be eligible on these terms.[6]

---

[5] Roberts, 'The union with England', 61–2.
[6] The wholesale eradication of customs intimated in the preamble was not realised in the act itself: partible inheritance was abolished in the second enacting clause and partially

There was enough ambiguity in the phrasing of the preamble and the relevant enacting clause to permit contemporary and later commentators to construe the language provision, and on occasion to represent the very premises of the act, in the light of their own preoccupations. The interpretations of churchmen, humanists and antiquaries are as revealing of contemporary values as those of lawyers and litigants, and what these perspectives suggest is that from the outset there was no real consensus on the cultural implications of the union.[7]

The ending of the medieval 'colonial' phase in Anglo-Welsh relations was marked by the emergence of a protestant form of English cultural imperialism. William Barlow, the English bishop of St Davids, complained to Cromwell late in 1536 that English was 'nothing preferred after the acte of parleamente' and he proposed that a grammar school be set up in his diocese in which knowledge of Scriptures would also be taught, whereby 'the Welsche rudenesse wolde sone be framed to English cyvilitie and their corrupte capacyties easely reformed with godly intelligens'. Barlow achieved his aim with the foundation of Christ's College, Brecon, in 1541, the charter of which explains the urgent need for a grammar school in south Wales. Because of their ignorance of the English language, both clergy and laity were not only ignorant of their duties to God and the king but unable to understand their obligations under the law.[8] For Barlow and other advanced protestants the conditions for the establishing of 'English civility' – a combination of the rule of law, the reformation of manners and a common language – were also the prerequisites for the reception of the true faith.

Barlowe's missionary zeal may be compared with the responses of Welsh protestant humanists to the challenges posed by the Reformation and the union to the preservation of the language and a distinctive national ethos. In 1546-7 the first printed books in Welsh made their appearance, with the approval of the king: Sir John Price's religious miscellany, *Yn y llyvyr hwnn* (In this book . . .), and William Salesbury's Welsh–English *Dictionary*. The compilers of these books as well as the writers of works produced in English in the 1540s cultivated a strong sense of Welsh/British consciousness even as they expressed an unqualified loyalty to the regime and the concept of the unitary state. The tension between the rival demands of 'English civility' and the identification of the Welsh as the survivors of the ancient Britons was to be a creative one for the survival of the distinctive sense of nationhood. Just

reprieved in one of the provisos later added in a schedule to the original bill. *Statutes of Wales*, 75–6, 87, 81.
[7] Roberts, 'The Welsh language', 26–44.   [8] *Ibid.*, 41–2.

as the descent of the Tudors from British kings had been exploited in dynastic propaganda, their Welsh connection was now invoked in printed literature in support of religious and secular reform. The royal patronage enjoyed by these writers played as important a part as did the distribution of crown offices and church lands to the gentry in ensuring the untroubled reception in the country of both union and Reformation.

In his *Yn y llyvyr hwnn* (1546), which included translated extracts from the Scriptures, Sir John Price paid tribute to the king's temporal gifts to the Welsh nation which were to be complemented by spiritual blessings. Price was a man of affairs as well as of letters and, as secretary of the Council in the Marches from 1540, he was a key figure in supervising the enforcement of the legislation of union. His close association with Cromwell (they became brothers-in-law in 1533) makes it highly probably that he was consulted at an earlier stage. Price also helped to shore up the defences of the British History against the scepticism of Renaissance historiography. His *Historiae Britanniae Defensio*, a riposte to the attack on Geoffrey of Monmouth by Polydore Vergil, which had so offended the susceptibilities of the Welsh, was drafted before 1545 and circulated in manuscript before it was printed in 1572.[9]

However, the first Welshman (at least an honorary Welshman, for he seems to have identified himself with the nation) to answer Polydore Vergil in print was Arthur Kelton of Shrewsbury. In *A comendacion of welshmen* (1546) Kelton celebrated the imperial lineage of the Welsh Tudors, especially Henry VII 'of Cadwaladers line rightfull kyng of Britayne called Englond'.

> Thus maye ye se
> That welshmen be of the blood imperiall
> Of nature fre
> Cosyns in degre
> To the goddes immortall.

Kelton reminded his Welsh readers not only of their glorious British heritage but of Henry VIII's bounty to them:

> What he hath deuised
> Onlie for youe
> Statutes made newe
>   And lawes wholy commysed
> To that intente

---

[9] The work is dedicated to Sir Brian Tuke, who died in 1545. Neil Ker, 'Sir John Prise', *The Library*, 5 ser., 10 (1955), 3–12. E. D. Jones, 'Llyfr Amrywiaeth Syr Sion Prys', *Brycheiniog*, 8 (1962), 97–104.

> You shulde assent
>   To your ciuilitie
> One lawe one loue
> One god aboue
>   And one prencely magestie.[10]

In the following year he developed his British theme in *A chronycle* in verse, in which Vergil was resoundingly trounced:

> We Welshmen saie for our defence
> That ye Romayns, surmountyng in pride
> With your Imperiall magnificence
> Supposyng therby, the hevens to devide
> Came long after, our noble tribe
> So that we maie, write of your estate
> Not ye of us, ye came all to late.[11]

With this rehearsal of the virtues of the unitary realm and Henry VIII's imperial kingship the Welsh were invited to reconcile themselves to the union with England in a celebration of the distinctive British inheritance of a nation which also enjoyed a special relationship with the ruling dynasty. Kelton's accessible doggerel may well have been more effective in popularising the claims to imperial status advanced for Henry VIII than the most ambitious of the printed propaganda sponsored by Cromwell. However, the message could have reached only a limited readership among the literate Welsh, most of whom were monoglot. Ideas of Tudor imperial grandeur would have been propagated more widely in Wales through the poetry declaimed by the bards in praise of the prowess of the king and the Welsh lords in the military campaigns in France.[12] After 1536 the only bard to comment on affairs of state with any regularity was Lewys Morgannwg, who as an unofficial poet laureate continued to praise Henry for his imperial qualities as the heir of Brutus and a second Charlemagne,[13] and (in an allusion to the laws of 1534) for disciplining the unruly Welsh for their own good. The opportunistic poet who before the break with Rome had honoured the monastic vocation in an ode to the abbot of Neath now commended the king for

---

[10] A. H. Dodd, 'A commendacion of Welshmen', *Bulletin of the Board of Celtic Studies*, 19 (1961), 235–49.

[11] *A chronycle with a Genealogie declaryng that the Brittons and Welshemen are lineally dyscended from Brute*, sig. Ciii.

[12] E. J. Rowlands, 'Terwyn a Thwrnai', *National Library of Wales Journal*, 9 (1955–6), 295–300.

[13] Lewys's ode to King Henry is inscribed in John Price's Welsh commonplace book, together with an ode to Price himself. The former contains the lines 'Emperial Brutys dalaith / Emprwr fydd mab Harri'r saith' and allusions to the king as protector of the faith, king of France, lord of Ireland and the 'lion of Great Britain'. Bodleian Library, Oxford, Balliol College MS 353, fos. 20–1.

suppressing the corrupt monasteries, and yet he did not entirely abandon his attachment to the traditional faith. After the fall of Ann Boleyn, who is held responsible for promoting the 'new religion', Lewys denounced her as a second Alice Rowena, whose corruption had betrayed the kingdom of the Britons in 'the treachery of the long knives'. In the same poem the king is urged to prefer local men before Englishmen of low breeding to high offices, for the sake of the security and contentment of the realm. This appears to be the only allusion to any aspect of the legislation of 1536 in the poetry of the age.[14]

There is a more specific reference to the act 27 Henry VIII, c. 26, in the dedication to the king of Salesbury's *Dictionary*. A section of the preamble is paraphrased in the comment that it was fitting and convenient that all the subjects of the king and supreme head should use a common language, for this conduced to harmony and obedience. That the Welsh should learn English was the ostensible purpose of the *Dictionary*, for which Salesbury had obtained a special royal licence in December 1545, and with it a monopoly for another seven years for the printing of translations. He seized the opportunity to print religious books in Welsh and to raise the collective consciousness of the nation about the fate of the mother tongue. As he explained in his Welsh prefaces to his publications, this was in danger of degenerating into a patois unless it could be rehabilitated as a learned language and a suitable vehicle for the Scriptures. In 1550 Salesbury published a guide to learning Welsh for the use of Englishmen, foreign scholars and, not least, those Welshmen settled in England who wished to make contact with their families in Wales, '& moost chiefely to edifie them as well in civyle institutions and in godly doctryne'. Salesbury thus accepted the necessity of English 'civility' as well as the desirability of a common language for all the subjects 'under the obeysaunce of the imperiall diademe, and triumphante Sceptre of Englande'. He recognised the importance of English as a worthy medium for learning and the Scriptures, but he argued the case for the Scriptures in the vernacular of Wales on the grounds that the spiritual needs of the Welsh were too urgent to wait until they acquired a knowledge of English. He was determined that what he insisted on calling 'the British tongue', which 'by continuall misnomer the recorder of the aunciente hostilitie is called Welshe', should attain a commensurate status with English by

---

[14] Lewys was the chief herald-bard of Wales, who claimed to have a royal commission to oversee the bardic order. Some of the early copyists of his verse claimed that he received payment from the king. E. J. Saunders, 'Gweithiau Lewys Morgannwg' (University of Wales M.A. thesis, 4 vols., 1922), i, 64; G. J. Williams, *Traddodiad Llenyddol Morgannwg* (Cardiff, 1948), 65–71.

recovering a lost inheritance. The Scriptures which the ancient Britons had possessed in their own language had disappeared without trace, whereas the codices of the obsolete laws of Hywel Dda, he adds with pointed irony, had survived intact.[15]

Not all the protestant reformers in Wales shared the confidence expressed by Barlow and Salesbury in the benefits of 'English civility'. The former's successor as bishop of St David's, Robert Ferrar, got into trouble in the diocese for suggesting that the Welsh were more civil than the English – or so his enemies in Carmarthen maintained in 1551-2. Behind the attack on the bishop lay his dispute with the chapter at St David's, but the complaints which were brought against him reveal the latent ethnic as well as religious tensions to be found in Edward VI's reign among the inhabitants of the largest town in the Principality. Ferrar was accused of contravening the tenor of the legislation of union which had conferred many benefits on the Welsh who had prospered in the peace established 'under feare and obedience, which evermore they do most thankfullye embrace as aperteynith'. The gloss which the complainants placed on the wording of the preamble to the act of 1536 contrasts with that of William Salesbury. The union is interpreted as having imposed a kind of contract on the Welsh, who were granted the benefits of English law, 'and to all purposes be as meere Englissmen', on condition that they abjured their 'olde and ylle customes'. Among these customs were vain prophecies, the utterers of which were liable to punishment according to English law. The bishop had offended the more zealous protestants in his flock by his preaching, which they judged to be subversive when it was not inadequate, and they delated him to the Privy Council on a charge, among many others, of having ingratiated himself with the Welsh by denigrating the English. In a sermon preached after Easter 1551 in St Peter's Church, Carmarthen, Ferrar had commended the warmth of the welcome extended to strangers by the native inhabitants, among whom the Christian precept of hospitality was more diligently observed than in other parts of the realm. It was in vain that Ferrar protested that his words had been travestied in the depositions so as to read: 'But heere yn Wales ye ar more gentle, and not without cawse, for ye wer the Brytans sumtyme, and had this Realme yn governaunce, and yf the prophecye of Merlyn be true, ye shall be Brytaynes ageyne, and this lande shal be called grete Brytayne.'

The bishop had been moved to appeal to the national pride of the congregation by his preference for a gradualist approach to religious

---

[15] Roberts, 'The Welsh language', 45-6; R. Brinley Jones, *William Salesbury* (Cardiff, 1994), 23-6.

change but this had led the radical reformers in the town to accuse him of inciting 'envite and hatred betwixt the two peoples'. His opponents criticised his reluctance to remove all traces of 'superstition' in the church. Ferrar pleaded in his defence that he was apprehensive lest sudden innovation provoke the 'grudge of the people' and lead to such tumult as had disturbed the west country in 1549.[16]

III

There was no rebellion in Tudor Wales, for Welsh allegiance to the dynasty was never seriously put to the test in any reign. After the pilgrimage of grace had been suppressed Rowland Lee reported to Cromwell that Wales was quiet, for few Welshmen 'conceived of the matters in Englande, fforasmoche their language doth not agree to the advauncement thereof'.[17] The Welsh publications of the protestant humanists surmounted the language barrier to ensure that the Henrician religious and secular reforms were advanced in their own country. At the same time the reorganisation of law and government went ahead without serious incident despite Rowland Lee's misgivings. These structural changes were consolidated under Edward and Mary but the campaigns for church services to be held in the vernacular faltered in the extreme religious settlements of both reigns. Early in Elizabeth's reign it was decided that the exigencies of the church settlement required a revision of the policy of uniformity in language. The cause of the vernacular Scriptures which William Salesbury had promoted in his publications finally prevailed with the passing of the act of 1563 to authorise the translation of the Bible and the Book of Common Prayer.[18] With the official recognition of Welsh as a language of worship came a relaxation of the pressures for cultural as well as administrative assimilation to England. The peaceful reception of the Elizabethan reformation was a measure of the success of the protestant humanists

---

[16] Ferrar had thus incited not only 'envite and hatred betwixt the two people' but the uttering of pernicious prophecies and the emblazoning of arms by idle rhymesters. This was but one of 56 charges levelled against him by 127 witnesses; in some of the 9 depositions describing the prophecy uttered in the sermon, he is alleged to have concluded: 'ye shall so have it agayne'. The bishop denied that he had made any such sinister claims or invidious comparisons. In preaching on hospitality (his text was apparently taken from 1 Peter 4), he had approved the Welshmen's friendship to strangers, for they had received the lesson of loving-kindness 'originalye from Goddes people' (an allusion perhaps to the belief in the British mission of Joseph of Arimathea). BL Harleian MS 420, fos. 80–178. Glanmor Williams, 'Carmarthen and the Reformation, 1536–1558', in *The Welsh and their Religion* (Cardiff, 1991), 132–5.

[17] 15 Jan. [1537], BL Cotton MSS, Cleo. E v, fo. 414.

[18] 5 Elizabeth, c. 18. *Statutes of Wales*, 149–51; Roberts, 'The Welsh language', 56–9.

and historians in naturalising the reform movement in the native tradition.

Salesbury collaborated with Bishop Richard Davies of St David's on the translation of the Prayer Book and the New Testament, both of which duly appeared in 1567. In an address to the Welsh people which prefaced the New Testament, Davies urged them to embrace the reformed faith by appealing to the traditions of the early Celtic church. In a direct identification of the sense of nationality with British consciousness, he apostrophised his fellow countrymen: 'do not denationalize yourselves, do not be indifferent, do not look down but gaze upwards to the place where you belong . . .'[19] It was a rallying cry to the Welsh to remember their unique spiritual heritage: their ancestors the ancient Britons had been converted to the pure faith whereas the Saxons had espoused the impurities of Rome through the mission of Augustine of Canterbury. After the treachery of Vortigern and the defeat of the Britons, a dark age had descended in which the latter had lost the Scriptures which they had originally possessed in their own language.[20] The Reformation was thus represented as the recovery of a lost inheritance which was restored to the Welsh through the beneficence of a dynasty to their own nation. For Salesbury the queen's gift surpassed the temporal boons granted to the nation by her father and grandfather as the soul does the body, for it was the Gospel 'translated into the British language, which is our vulgare tongue'.[21] With the publication of William Morgan's translation of the complete Bible in 1588, religious worship in Welsh was finally established in the churches in Wales. Even as they achieved their ends, both Salesbury and Bishop Morgan went out of their way to commend to their readers that there should be one uniform language for all the realm. Their translations laid the basis for a revolution in the religious culture of Wales which helped to win the country for protestantism and to save the language from disintegration and decline. The Elizabethan protestant commitment to the principle of the vernacular Scriptures revivified the ethos of a distinctive nationality despite, even perhaps because of, the closer ties with England.[22]

[19] 'Paid ath ddigenhedlu, paid ath ddifrawy, paid ac edrych ir llawr, tremia i vyny tu ar lle ich hanyw . . .' (Aiii); translation in A. O. Evans, *A Memorandum on the Legality of the Welsh Bible and the Welsh Versions of the Book of Common Prayer* (Cardiff, 1925), 83–4.
[20] In expounding this theory of the precedence of the British race over the Saxons in the espousing of the true faith, Davies elaborated on the writings of John Leland and John Foxe. Glanmor Williams, 'Some Protestant views of early British church history', *Welsh Reformation Essays* (Cardiff, 1967), 207–19.
[21] Salesbury's dedication to Elizabeth of *Testament Newydd*, 1567: Aj–Aij v.
[22] P. R. Roberts, 'The union with England', 49, 70.

The 'amicable concord and unitie' between the English and the Welsh which, according to the rhetoric of its preamble, the act of 1536 sought to establish, was in the event advanced not so much by the process of assimilation as by the accommodation which the Elizabethan church and the protestant establishment made with the traditional culture of Wales. The old faith persisted in sheltered communities in Snowdonia and in the border country, but the violent resistance to religious change which Bishop Ferrar had feared did not materialise. The greater harmony which characterised Anglo-Welsh relations within the newly united realm was not to be found among the Elizabethan Catholic exiles in Italy as they prepared for the 'enterprise of England'. Just as the 'nations' had conflicted as discrete groups in the medieval universities, especially in Oxford, so they formed exclusive factions among the students in the English College at Rome after its formation by Dr Owen Lewis in 1578. The English students threatened to withdraw altogether from the College at Rome in protest at the favouritism which they alleged the rector, Morris Clynnog, showed to his fellow countrymen. On hearing of this threat Hugh Gruffydd, the unruly nephew of Dr Lewis, 'gave a leap in the College hall, and shouted "Who now but a Welshman?"' Alarmed at the prospect of the defection of the English students, the pope intervened in their support, and when reconciliation failed Clynnog was forced to resign and the Jesuits were given control of the College. Fr Robert Parsons commented to Cardinal William Allen: 'Thus you see when national dissension is once raised how hard it is to appease it.' Allen was exercised as to 'how I might deal to save and salve that great sore and exulceration of minds betwixt the two parties, English and Welsh ... for the good of our common country'. But conciliation between the nations was more difficult to achieve in the conditions of exile than in England and Wales. 'By which disorder', Allen lamented, 'I perceive the Scottish nation begin to put in for it ...' Lewis was criticised by Allen for his partisanship in making common cause with the Scots, for he was alleged to have once said to the Bishop of Ross: 'My Lord, let us stick together, for we are the old and true inhabiters and owners of the isle of Britanny [sc. Britain]; these others be but usurpers and mere possessors.'[23]

<hr />

[23] *The Letters and Memorials of William Allen: Records of English Catholics*, ii (ed.), T. F. Knox (London, 1882), 74, 78–85. The quarrel involved not only clashes of incompatible temperaments among the leaders of the two groups but a fundamental difference in religious attitude. There was also a generation gap: according to their opponents, the Welsh were older and less well trained in post-Tridentine theology. They were accused of being more interested in filling offices in Rome than in preparing for the missionary campaign.

This was the begir ›ing of the rift in the Catholic orders between the Jesuits and the secular clergy, and as Fr Augustine Baker later put it, the 'division had its deplored effects both in the Colledges, and in the mission itselfe of England'. Fr Baker was himself a Welsh-speaker from Monmouthshire, but in his exile on the continent after 1603 he identified himself with 'our nation', the English. The loss of face at the dismissal of Clynnog may have been traumatic for the sense of distinctiveness which the Welsh Catholics had sought to preserve in exile, while the subsequent controversy over rival Welsh and English interpretations of the British History was to add salt to the wound.[24]

Between 1580 and 1584 a disagreement arose between the English and Welsh at the College in Rome over the inscription on a tomb recently discovered in the Vatican. This had been variously read as denoting either Cadwallas, king of Wessex, or Cadwaladrus, the last king of the Britons, and it led to a dispute between the factions as to whether to follow the authority of Geoffrey of Monmouth or that of Bede. Owen Lewis, Robert Owen and Richard White, later rector of the College at Douai, were among the Welshmen who took an active part in the controversy. It became so heated that papal arbitration had to be sought again, and the task was delegated to the Vatican librarian, Cardinal Sirleto. Robert Owen, one of two brothers from Plas-du, Caernarfonshire, who had gone into exile in 1584, tried to impress Sirleto with his researches in support of Geoffrey of Monmouth's account of Cadwaladr's pilgrimage to Rome in the time of Pope Sergius.[25] The reading 'Cadwalla' was finally accepted by the authorities, which implied a rejection of the Galfridian correction to Bede. Robert Owen added ruefully that he could have presented further arguments for his case had he not been prevented from returning to his own country, which was occupied by heretics.[26] Presumably he had quitted the realm before acquiring a copy of David Powel's *Historie of Cambria, now called Wales*, published in the same year.

---

[24] W. Llywelyn Williams, 'Welsh Catholics on the Continent', *Transactions of the Honourable Society of Cymmrodorion* (1901–2), 61–87; 'The memoirs of Fr Robert Persons', in J. H. Pollen (ed.), *Catholic Record Society: Miscellanea, II* (London, 1906), 83–162, *passim*.

[25] There is a confusion of identity here, as in many other accounts, between Cadwaladr, the 'last king of the Britons', and St Cadwaladr: see *The Dictionary of Welsh Biography*, ed. R. T. Jenkins *et al.* (London, 1959), *s.v.* [hereafter *DWB*.]

[26] Among the authorities which Owen listed in support of the Roman pilgrimage of St Cadwaladr were Leland and Bale. Anthony Munday, *The English Romayne Life* (London, 1582); W. Ll. Williams, 'Welsh Catholics on the Continent', 33–4. Geraint Bowen, 'Apêl at y Pab ynghylch dilysrwydd *Historia Regum*, Sieffre o Fynwy', *National Library of Wales Journal*, 15 (1967–8), 127–46.

IV

While Welshmen of both religious persuasions were at one in championing the British History against the sceptics, the Elizabethan protestant
publicists such as Lhuyd and Powel mounted a far more effective
defence in the tradition of Sir John Price. They turned their reading of
the Welsh past to account as propaganda for a nascent Welsh protestant
patriotism as well as for a resurgent dynasticism. By the second half of
the century, however, the antiquaries had succeeded the bards as the
chief memorialists of the nation, and it was they who now developed the
loyalist and imperial themes. For Humphrey Lluyd, David Powel, Rice
Merrick and George Owen, as for Sion Tudur the poet and the
translators of the Bible, the blessings conferred by the Tudors had been
cumulative: Henry VII had delivered the Welsh from servitude, Henry
VIII had completed their enfranchisement by making them equal with
the English before the common law, while Elizabeth was to present
them with the Scriptures in their own tongue.[27] This interpretation of
recent Anglo-Welsh history was accepted by English chroniclers like
William Harrison.[28] In the Welsh, English and Latin prose of these
Elizabethan protestant writers, the benevolence of the Tudors to the
Welsh nation is consistently linked with the British inheritance. In
affirming the identity of the Welsh as the descendants of the ancient
Britons, this antiquarian literature fortified the distinctive sense of
nationality which had survived the union and which was now better
placed to withstand its anglicising tendencies. With their Tudor, protestant and 'British' sympathies, the antiquaries also contributed to the
processes of dynasticism and state-formation in Elizabethan England,
just as the repertory of historical arguments used by the humanist
reformers served to vindicate the established church against the charge
of new-fangledness.

Humphrey Lhuyd's *Commentarioli Britannicae Descriptionis Frag-
mentum*, an apologia for the Brut tradition, was published by Ortelius in
Cologne in 1572 and englished by Thomas Twyne in 1573 as *The
Breviary of Britayne*. Lhuyd's partisan erudition was not appreciated by

---

[27] *Rice Merrick, Morganiae Archaiographia: A Book of the Antiquities of Glamorganshire*, ed.
B. Ll. James. South Wales Record Society, i (1983), 67. George Owen, 'The dialogue
of the government of Wales', in H. Owen (ed.), *The Description of Penbrokshire*, part 3
(London, 1906), 38–9, 56–7.

[28] In his MS 'Chronology' Harrison acknowledges the Tudor rehabilitation of Wales and
the Welsh, though he confuses the actions of Henry VIII with those his father, who
'coming of the race of Cadwallader made the Welshmenne or Britons equall in
condicion with the English in every respect & use of lawes', BL Add. MS 70984, fo.
213v.

Hubert Languet, who in a letter to Philip Sidney in 1574 dismissed the writer who 'repeatedly proclaims himself a Cambrian, not an Englishman' and his 'follies' as 'totally destitute of common sense'. The twenty-year-old Sidney agreed and they exchanged a joke about the ridiculous notions of 'our poor Cambro-Briton'.[29] This was not a view shared by Philip's father, Sir Henry Sidney, the lord president of the Council in the Marches, who in 1583 requested his chaplain, David Powel of Ruabon, to prepare for the press the manuscript in Sidney's possession of Lhuyd's translation of 'Brut y Tywysogion' (The Chronicle of the Princes). Powel's *Historie*, which contained this translation (as well as that of Sir John Price's 'Description of Cambria'), was dedicated by the ingenuous author to Sir Philip Sidney in the fond hope that he would emulate his father and 'beare countenance and favour to the countrie of Wales'.[30]

David Powel, as he explained in the preface to *The Historie of Cambria*, was concerned to counter the bad press which Welshmen had received in English histories. He printed by way of introduction Humphrey Lhuyd's 'A description of Cambria now called Wales', in which it is affirmed that Welsh 'is the same language which the Brytaines spake at the beginning'. For this reason Tudor humanists preferred to describe the language as 'the British tongue' rather than Welsh,[31] and Lhuyd voiced the common objection of the Welsh antiquaries to English designations: 'for the Welshmen themselves doo not understand what these words Wales and Welsh doo signifie, nor know anie other name of their countrie or themselves but *Cambry,* nor of their language but *Cambraec,* which is as much to saie as *Cambers* language or speech'.

The apologia for the British History was complemented by a revised interpretation of the history of Wales as a distinct polity in the age of the princes and, after the conquest of 1282, as a dependent territory under English rule. The account which Lhuyd and Powel presented of Wales in the fifteenth century differed in significant ways from the 'Tudor myth' in its contemporary English version as much as it did from the view of Anglo-Welsh relations reflected in the earlier prophetic poetry of that period. David Powel disapproved of Owain Glyndŵr as much as he deplored the civil interdict which the Lancastrian kings had imposed upon the Welsh in retaliation for his rebellion. Glyndŵr was a false

[29] W. A. Bradley (ed.), *The Correspondence of Philip Sidney and Hubert Languet* (London, 1912), 36–7.
[30] In addition to his defence of Geoffrey of Monmouth in *The Historie of Cambria, now called Wales* (London, 1584), Powel printed in 1585 a summarised version of the British History. He had been granted access to state records by Burghley, *DWB*.
[31] R. Brinley Jones, *The Old British Tongue: the vernacular in Wales 1540–1640* (Cardiff, 1970), *passim*.

deliverer, his title to the princely title was 'altogether frivolous', and he lived 'in a fool's paradise' in his deluded belief that the time had come 'wherein the Britaines through his meanes might recover againe the honour and liberties of their ancestors'.[32] The true Owain of the prophecy had been Henry Tudor's grandfather, Owain Tudur of Penmynydd, who far from being an upstart adventurer at the Lancastrian court is made out to have been of noble ancestry (he was Glyndŵr's kinsman). In Lhuyd's tract his disparagement of the Lancastrian kings led him to recognise the legitimacy of the Yorkists' claim to the throne as well as their descent through the Mortimer line from the Prince Llywelyn ab Iorwerth ('the Great'). This implied a recognition of the fact that Henry VIII's inherited title to the Principality was more convincingly traced through the lineage of his mother, Elizabeth of York, than in the Tudor line deriving from Ednyfed Fychan, seneschal to Llywelyn the Great.[33] Humphrey Lhuyd ended his transcription of 'Cronica Wallia' with the rebellion of Madog ap Llywelyn (1294) and the words: 'After this there was nothinge donne in Wales worthy memory, but that is to bee redde in the English Chronicle.'[34] Thus did Lhuyd, who insisted that a familiarity with the Welsh texts was essential for understanding the history of the 'British' people, reflect on the end of his country's separate history with the extinction of the native line of princes. The succession of the princes of Wales 'of the blood royall of England' is respectfully related in Powel's *Historie*, but both historians displayed a selective amnesia about the activities of the Welsh in the post-conquest period. The subtext is that the subsequent rise of the Tudors was sufficient recompense for the loss of independence.[35]

In his *Commentarioli* Lhuyd commended the way the Welsh had responded to the favours conferred on them by the Tudors: laying aside their old manners, they had been enriched 'and do imitate the Englishmen in diet & apparell'. For they were high minded, proud of the nobility of their ancestry, given to physical culture and apt to learn

---

[32] *The Historie of Cambria*, 286. The same attitude to Glyndŵr is recorded in the Welsh Chronicle of Elis Gruffydd, written in Calais c. 1548–1552: N[ational] L[ibrary of] W[ales], Peniarth MS 158, fo. 285v.; *HMC Report on Manuscripts in the Welsh Language: vol. 1, Mostyn Manuscripts*, ed. J. G. Evans (London, 1898), xii, 221. Glyndŵr's stock as a hero of resistance against English oppression was to rise again in later nationalist histories.

[33] The Mortimers were also the ancestors of Henry Fitzalan, earl of Arundel, Lluyd's patron. Ieuan M. Williams, 'Ysgolheictod hanesyddol yr unfed ganrif ar bymtheg', *Llên Cymru*, 2 (1952–3), 115–16, 210–11.

[34] *Ibid.*, 114. Lhuyd evidently did not know of Elis Gruffydd's MS Cronicl (see note 32 above).

[35] The account of the Welsh and English princes contained in *The Historie of Cambria* was to have a lasting influence on subsequent Welsh historiography.

courtly behaviour, and therefore preferred before the English for service with the nobility. With some exaggeration he claimed that there were few English nobles whose retinue did not consist mostly of Welshmen, who also predominated among the students of civil law. The Welsh had recently taken to dwelling in towns, to trade, tillage and crafts after the fashion of the English whom they surpassed in their assiduousness in placing their children in schools and the universities.[36] For Lhuyd the special significance of the 'Act of Union' lay in making the Welsh and English equal in all things, and he was concerned that the English should acknowledge this. He was moved to rehabilitate the historic reputation of his compatriots so that they would be accepted as honourable and equal members of the kingdom.[37]

Judging by the reactions of Philip Sidney it may be doubted that Lhuyd succeeded in this aim and, with the exception of Ortelius, he failed to impress the humanists of other countries. Languet's scepticism was shared by George Buchanan, for in defending the British heritage the intemperate Lhuyd, unlike Owen Lewis, parted company with the northern inhabitants of Britain. Whereas the Catholic Lewis was prepared to make overtures to the Scots, Lhuyd heaped abuse not only on Polydore Vergil for defaming the ancient Britons and obscuring the glory of the British name, but also on Hector Boethius who 'goeth about to rayse his Scots out of darknesse and obscuritie' and attributed whatever good the Romans or Britons had done in this island 'unto his Scots, like a foolish writer'. When in *Rerum Scoticarum Historia* (1582) Buchanan paid Lhuyd back in the same coin, it was plain that national pride was more powerful than a common protestant outlook in these historians' interpretation of the British inheritance.[38] Thus did the notion of Britishness take on different nuances as it was developed in

---

[36] He was not entirely uncritical: he castigated his compatriots for being somewhat 'impatient of labour', boasting of their own noble descent, and for neglecting handicrafts. Their contentious energies had been channelled into the pursuit of ruinous actions in the law courts (itself an index of the success of the Henrician settlement in curbing disorder). *The Breviary of Britayne*, trans. T. Twyne (1573), 59–60.

[37] I. M. Williams, 213. Modern nationalist commentators have argued that what moved these humanist historians to defend the dubious glories of the past with such intensity was the consciousness that Wales *per se* had no independent future. A. O. H. Jarman, *Sieffre o Fynwy: Geoffrey of Monmouth* (Cardiff, 1966).

[38] For a modern Scottish historian's appraisal of Lhuyd, Boece and Buchanan, see Roger A. Mason, 'Scotching the Brut: politics, history and national myth in sixteenth-century Britain', in Mason (ed.), *Scotland and England 1286–1815* (Edinburgh, 1987), 73–4. 'Buchanan may well have been a vain and deceitful old fraud [Trevor-Roper's judgement], but so also was Humphrey Lhuyd'. Cf. Hugh Trevor-Roper, 'George Buchanan and the ancient Scottish constitution', *English Historical Review*, Supplement 3 (1966), 28–9.

each of the component territories of Britain in the course of the reformations of the sixteenth century.

Lhuyd evidently received a more sympathetic hearing from Ortelius for his attack on the prejudices of those misled by Vergil and Boethius whose ignorance of 'the British tongue' prevented them from consulting authoritative sources.[39] 'Cambriae typus', Lhuyd's pioneer map of Wales, was sent to Ortelius in 1568 and printed in the supplement to the 1573 edition of the *Theatrum*. It continued to be reprinted until 1741, long after the British History had been exploded everywhere except in Wales, and to that extent Lhuyd's cartography was far more influential than his antiquarian writings in projecting his perceived image of the country. He explained to Ortelius the significance of the name *Mona*, the Latin name for Anglesey. 'Môn, mam Cymru', Anglesey, the mother of Wales, held a place of honour in Welsh history: it was the home of the druids and at Aberffraw the princes of Gwynedd had held their court. Moreover, though Lhuyd does not mention it, Penmynydd in Anglesey was the ancestral home of the founder of the Tudor family fortunes, Owain Tudur ap Maredydd.

While the bards continued to descant on the Tudor link with Anglesey, the Elizabethan historians' pride in the Welsh ancestry of the Tudors was not focused on any association with a particular house in the Principality. Owain Tudur's descendants in Wales had failed to capitalise on their kinship with the ruling dynasty, and by the end of the century the Tudors *alias* Theodores of Penmynydd had joined the ranks of the *déclassé* gentry. So obscure had the family become that when a privy councillor attempted to identify its representatives in 1603 he could scarcely credit their connection with the dynasty.[40]

The Cecils' kinsmen in the Welsh borders, unlike the Tudors of Anglesey, lost few opportunities to exploit their grand connections. In the case of William Cecil, if not his son Robert, the interest was reciprocated, and David Powel was commissioned to compile a pedigree

---

[39] His communication to Ortelius, 'De Mona druidum insula ... Epistola', dated 5 April 1568, was published as an appendix to the first edition of *Theatrum Orbis Terrarum* in 1570.

[40] One Owen Theodore or Tudor had become embroiled in the affairs of Arabella Stuart, but when Sir Thomas Egerton was requested by Robert Cecil to investigate his background, he drew a blank. He reported that of three brothers, 'all pretending to be of the house of the great Owen Tydder', the youngest, John Owen Tydder, 'followed the wars, and as I have heard, served with the enemy'. Egerton, despairing of making any sense of these connections, closed his letter of 3 Jan. 1603 to Cecil: 'and so I leave it to you to make you merry with a Welsh pedigree'; E. Owen, 'The decline of the Tudors of Penmynydd, Môn', *Transactions of the Anglesey Antiquarian Society* (1935), 83.

of the Welsh 'Seissyll'.[41] Burghley's family piety and his patronage of Welsh antiquarian studies contributed to the revival of Welsh national consciousness after the union and to the presentation of the reform programme in a British context. Even before the defence of the British History was publicised in the printed works of Price, Lhuyd and Powel, it seems to have found an uncritical follower in William Cecil, who at one stage turned to these traditions for materials to write an anti-papal tract. The surviving fragment 'England Triumphans' is undated but was probably drafted as a riposte to the papal bull excommunicating Queen Elizabeth. Addressed to the powers of continental Europe, it expounded 'in a historical form the power, pre-eminence and glory of Britain' and its independence of Rome in spiritual matters from the earliest times.[42] We can only speculate about the reasons for abandoning the project, but if Cecil had lost confidence in the relevance of the British History for the purposes of anti-papal propaganda, he was quite prepared to espouse another cause dear to Welsh humanists – the translation of the Scriptures into Welsh – and to use it as a political measure aimed against post-Tridentine Catholicism.[43]

Cecil's interest in Welsh antiquities was shared by Parker who was collecting materials for his own church history. The antiquarian studies fostered by the archbishop involved a close collaboration between those engaged in works of translation and church history in England and Wales. Bishop Richard Davies of St Davids contributed to the production of the Bishops' Bible (he translated the books of the Old Testament from Joshua to 2 Samuel) as well as the Welsh New Testament. Both Davies and Salesbury corresponded with Parker in 1565–6 on points of antiquarian research. Cases from the laws and records of

---

[41] A. L. Rowse, 'Alltyrynys and the Cecils', *English Historical Review* (1960), 54–76.

[42] Burghley's composition takes the form of a *prosopopeia* in which England apostrophises the rulers of Christendom, urging them to disregard the seditious calumnies lately spread to foment rebellion, and to expel the fugitives and traitors from their lands. God has blessed England with heavenly and earthly benefits surpassing all others, and yet envy and malice are directed against the queen, 'whome I maie call Elizabethe the great'. The people of Wales are acknowledged to be the descendants of the ancient Britons, and it is clear that the author subscribed to the traditions of the Trojan Brutus, the British mission of Joseph of Arimathea, and the Christian King Lucius. The Emperor Constantine, son of the British Queen Helena, was chosen by the Britons to be named 'the kyng of Great Brittany' as well as to wear the crown imperial. Cecil's draft elaborates upon the theme of papal presumption and usurped authority, and breaks off abruptly after a cursory relation of the summoning of general councils by the Christian emperors. PRO SP12/75/55, 58. The draft is wholly in Cecil's hand, and the fair copy in a clerk's hand bears many corrections and additions by him.

[43] At least retrospectively: his attitude to the passing of the act of 1563 is not recorded, but he later listed it among five measures held by the Catholics to be inimical to their cause. Roberts, 'The Welsh language', 62.

medieval Wales were cited by Salesbury as precedents for the marriage
of clergy in the reformed church. Thus the customs not only of the
Celtic church but of the Welsh church under the native princes were
invoked to justify aspects of the Reformation in the newly united
England and Wales.[44] In the same correspondence Parker also inquired
about Anglo-Saxon records at St David's. This curiosity about the
practices of the Saxon church signalled an active sponsorship of Anglo-
Saxon studies by Parker and his circle that was eventually to supersede
their interest in the Celtic and British traditions.

V

The Welsh connection of the Tudors and the authenticity of the British
History as expounded by the Welsh antiquarians were themes explored
by Dr John Dee in formulating his concepts of dynastic imperialism.
According to Dee, the Tudors had inherited a historic claim to the new-
found lands in the west, first through King Arthur and then through
Prince Madoc. It was Humphrey Lhuyd who, in his 'Cronica Walliae'
(c. 1559), first publicised the legend that the Welsh prince Madog ab
Owain Gwynedd (fl. 1170) had sailed across the Atlantic and discovered
America. Modern historians of Elizabethan sea-faring and navigation
have explained the way in which the Madoc legend circulated at this
time in terms of Dee's acquaintanceship with English antiquaries and
mariners.[45] But Dee conducted his own archival research and he
evidently had access to Lhuyd's tract before it was printed in David
Powel's *Historie* (1584),[46] where the story is embellished to enhance the

---

[44] In 1550 Salesbury had printed an extract out of the law of Hywel Dda (914) to prove
that 'priestes had lawfully married wives at that tyme', and in 1565 he produced for
Parker an excerpt to the same effect from the Red Book of St Asaph referring to an
agreement of 1261 between the bishop of Bangor and Prince Llywelyn ap Gruffydd.
John Bale also used this information obtained from Salesbury in his *Index Britanniae
Scriptorum*. Robin Flower, 'William Salesbury, Richard Davies and Archbishop Parker',
NLW Journal, 1 (1941–2), 7–14. No doubt these precedents for clerical marriage
helped to bolster Parker's courage in coping with the queen's disapproval of his married
status.

[45] Sir George Peckham wrote a pamphlet on the subject in 1583, a year before Powel
published Lhuyd's version. Peckham cites the authority of 'an ancient Welsh
Chronicle', and both of them name the chief source, the mariner David Ingram. Dee,
Ingram and Peckham knew one another at least as early as 1582: *The Private Diary of
John Dee*, ed. J. O. Halliwell, Camden Society, xix (1842), 17; cf. *The Voyages and
Colonising Enterprises of Sir Humphrey Gilbert*, ed. D. B. Quinn, Hakluyt Society (2 vols.,
1940), ii, 459.

[46] Dee marked a passage in a copy of Lhuyd's MS which came into his hands, adding the
comment: 'Madoc sonne to prince Owen sayled to the land west of Ireland which
afterwards about 400 yeres was judged to have byn first by the Spaniards (and others)
discovered.' BL Cotton MSS, Caligula Avi. In one of the surviving MSS of the Latin

historical reputation of the Welsh. Powel suggests that the land which Madoc found must have been Florida: 'Whereupon it is manifest, that the countrie was long before by *Britaynes* discovered, afore either *Columbus* or *Americus Vespatius* lead anie *Spaniardes* thither.'[47]

Dee's researches in the 'British' sources also involved a search for his own identity. His father, Rowland Dee from Radnorshire, gentleman server to Henry VIII, had settled in London and married an English-woman, but their son considered himself a Welshman. He drew up a pedigree purporting to trace his father's descent from Rhodri Fawr, prince of all Wales, and he claimed a distant connection with the queen.[48] Dee belonged to an 'Anglo-Welsh intelligentsia' based in London who cultivated an interest in Welsh antiquities and in publi-cations in the language.[49] His library at Mortlake contained some manuscripts and four printed books in Welsh. Though he employed his *protégé* Morys Kyffin as translator of the Welsh sources which he consulted, he himself had enough of a grasp of the language to find his way around the texts. Passages in other books in his possession relating to the British History or to the history of the Welsh are heavily annotated, and these Welsh studies were concentrated in the years 1576–80, when he was composing his *General and Rare Memorials* and his *Title Royal*.[50] In these works Dee sought to persuade Queen Elizabeth to make good her rightful claim to a 'British Empire' overseas which she had inherited from King Arthur and Prince Madoc.

It was Humphrey Lhuyd who first coined the phrase 'British Empire'

Life of Gruffydd ap Cynan, four lines from the celebratory poem by Meredydd ap Rhys (*fl.* 1450–85), beginning 'Madoc wyf maryedig wedd ...' are written in Dee's own hand. BL Cotton Vitellius Cix, fo. 143v. J. Roberts and A. G. Watson, *John Dee's Library Catalogue* (London, 1990), 39–40. The only reference to the legend in a Welsh source dating from the sixteenth century is to be found in a prose work of 13 March 1583, which represents Madoc ab Owain Gwynedd as an adventurous sailor who voyaged to foreign lands, though it does not mention America. E. D. Jones, 'The reputed discovery of America by Madoc ab Owain Gwynedd', *National Library of Wales Journal*, 14 (1965), 122–4.

[47] Powel, *The Historie of Cambria*, 227–8.

[48] He kept a journal of a journey to the Welsh borders in 1574, when he met Mr T. Powel of Oswestry and consulted his pedigrees of the princes of Wales; and he asked Burghley for a licence to search the records at Wigmore Castle. BL Harleian MS 473, fo. 10v. Cf. Dee's letter to his 'cosin', Nicholas ap Meredith, at Presteigne: NLW Peniarth MS 252, fo. 227.

[49] Gwyn A. Williams, *Welsh Wizard and British Empire: Dr John Dee and a Welsh Identity* (Cardiff, 1980), 21–5; R. J. Roberts, 'John Dee and the matter of Britain', *Transactions of the Honourable Society of Cymmrodorion* (1991), 143. Maurice Kyffin's *Deffiniad Ffydd Eglwys Loegr*, a Welsh translation of Jewel's *Apologia Ecclesiae Anglicanae*, was published in 1595.

[50] Roberts and Watson, *John Dee's Library Catalogue*, 39–40. The Welsh books are nos. 1644–1647 in the Catalogue.

in describing ancient British kingship,[51] but it was Dee who used the term for the first time in the context of overseas possessions. His vision was less exclusive and more all-embracing than Lhuyd's and 'he envisaged something into which he, as a "British gentleman" was inviting the English and perhaps the Scots'.[52] King Arthur had conquered territory circling the Arctic and had colonised these lands to form a Christian empire independent of Rome. Queen Elizabeth had not only a title to these lands as the heir of the British line of kings but a divinely ordained duty to expand the English state and church in the western world. Dee proposed the creation of a 'perpetual pety navy Royal' to recover and protect this lost inheritance. Even the navigations of the pacific King Edgar, 'being but a Saxon', were cited as a precedent for 'this Imperiall Brittishe monarchie'.[53] Dee's politico-religious programme gave a new twist to the Tudor ideology of empire. While the historical argument for the 'English' empire of the preamble to the act of appeals of 1533 had owed something to the traditions of British kingship,[54] Dee's notions derived directly from these materials and, as he claimed, from divine inspiration. For a brief period in the middle of the reign British legends and Welsh mythology were exploited to justify the claims made for England's destiny in the New World. The propaganda for the imperial ideal also contributed to the process of state-building in the sense of reinforcing the identification of the Welsh nation with the dynasty and with protestantism.

Dee had several audiences with the queen to explain his schemes between 1577 and 1580. Late in 1580 Elizabeth assured him that Burghley 'had greatly commended my doings for her title royall, which he had to examine', but he later expressed his doubts.[55] Though the

[51] B. W. Henry, 'John Dee, Humphrey Llwyd, and the name "British Empire"', *Huntington Library Quarterly* (1972), 189–90.

[52] *Dee's Library Catalogue*, 39.

[53] Dee's *British Monarchy* cited in Richard Hakluyt, *The Principall Navigations and Voiages and Discoveries of the English Nation, 1589*, ed. W. Raleigh (12 vols., Glasgow, 1903–5), i, 16; P. J. French, *John Dee: the World of an Elizabethan Magus* (London, 1972), 195–8.

[54] Among the research materials known as the 'Collectanea' which bolstered the theory of empire on this occasion there was an extract from a document compiled in King John's reign and 'drawing its inspiration and much of its information from Geoffrey of Monmouth' which contained 'an unambiguous statement of the imperial status of the English crown'. Graham Nicholson, 'The Act of Appeals and the English Reformation', in C. Cross et al. (eds.) *Law and Government under the Tudors*, 24.

[55] The 'title royall' is likely to be a reference to 'A brief Remembrance' (now redated 1580) which Dee drew up for presentation to Elizabeth. Graham Yewbrey, 'A redated manuscript of John Dee', *Bulletin of the Institute of Historical Research*, 50 (1977), 249–53. Burghley appears at first to have taken Dee's claims seriously: he noted that 'Arthur kyng of Britain was the conqueror of these contreys . . .' and made an epitome of Dee's book of pedigree of English monarchs descended from the ancient British kings. BL Lansdowne MS 94, art. 51, fo. 121.

queen and her minister continued to humour Dee, his sea-borne 'British Empire' remained in the realm of theory. It had become a lost cause even before his departure for Bohemia in 1584, though the Arthur and Madoc stories were repeated as precedents for English endeavour by Richard Hakluyt in his *Principal Navigations* in 1589. By that time the first edition of Camden's *Britannia* had appeared (1586), with its subtle challenge to the Trojan origins of the British, and except in poetry and pageantry the matter of Britain lost favour at court. In 1587 Thomas Churchyard lamented that 'King Arthur's reign (though true it weare)/ Is now of small account.'[56] At least the Welsh did not forget the wider reaches of the Atlantic archipelago in its British dimension as this had been retrieved for them by Dee. In Charles I's reign William Vaughan, 'Cambro-Britannus', of Golden Grove, inspired it seems by the Madoc legend, attempted to plant a Welsh colony called Cambriol in New-foundland which he claimed was divinely 'reserved ... for us Brit-aines'.[57]

There was a less positive side to the cultural impact of American exploration on the British consciousness of the Welsh Elizabethans. The physical image of a proto-Briton was a late entrant into the portrait gallery of the early inhabitants of the islands which illustrated anti-quarian works, but the depiction of the American Indians as naked savages led to the devising of a similar image for the ancient Britons. This begins to be noticeable in the illustrations to Lucas de Heere's *Description of Britain* (c. 1575),[58] and the contrast with the invariably armoured and elaborately dressed invaders, Roman, Saxon and Dane, was unmistakable. The juxtaposition of the relatively sophisticated later incomers to the island with the primitive aboriginal Briton may well reflect the more sceptical approach of English antiquaries to the claims of the British History. The association in this imagery of savagery with nobility did not carry with it any suggestion of disgrace, but so little did it correspond to the perception of the Britons as the Christian ancestors of the Welsh that it could not fail to strengthen the case of the

---

[56] *The Worthiness of Wales*, cited in T. D. Kendrick, *British Antiquity* (London, 1950), 43, 108–9.

[57] William Vaughan, *Cambrensium Caroleia Cambriola* (London, 1625). In one of the dedicatory verses to the author, John Guy likened him to Prince Madoc. In *The Golden Fleece* (London, 1626), Vaughan paused in the middle of an anti-Catholic tirade to describe Newfoundland as destined for a Welsh colony (sig. Aa3). For the subsequent history of the legend, see G. A. Williams, *Madoc: the making of a myth* (London, 1979).

[58] A figure of the half-naked and woad-stained Briton was prominently placed on the title page of John Speed's *Theatre of the Empire of Great Britain* (1611) and reproduced in the atlases of his successors, Janssen and Blaeu. Kendrick, *British Antiquity*, 123–5.

demythologisers.[59] Even so, Brutus continued to have his English champions: when in 1593 Richard Harvey brought out a tract in defence of the British History, he did so partly 'in respect of our owne Countreimen and neighbours'.[60]

VI

The circle of Welsh antiquarians based in London to whom Dee belonged has been described as 'the first Welsh intellectuals fully to enter an English language cultural universe through a British identity'.[61] They did so at a time when Welsh culture itself was at a crossroads. The tension between the values of humanism and traditional bardic culture was highlighted in the literary 'contest' or disputation on their relative merits which was conducted in Welsh verse between the churchman Edmund Prys and the bard Wiliam Cynwal in the years 1581–7.[62] The bard Edward ap Raff complained around 1600 that the world had gone all English ('Saesneg arbennig yw'r byd').[63] In the event Welsh poetry in the traditional metres was to survive the passing of the bardic order, which did not entail the immediate loss of the patronage of the gentry, and the language itself was revitalised by the scriptural translations which drew on bardic literature and lexicography as well as humanist scholarship.[64] The impact of the 'cultural bifurcation'[65] in Welsh society and literature should not be exaggerated, at least as a Tudor phenomenon, for the activities of the translators delayed the anglicisation that was latent in the legislation of union. The linguistic crisis feared by Salesbury and the other humanists did not materialise in their own generation, thanks in part to their own achievements. Not everyone considered the Welsh language to be vulnerable in relation to the privileged status of the dominant culture. In a letter of thanks for a complimentary copy of Dee's *General and Rare Memorials* his 'cousin', the Welsh civil lawyer William Aubrey, expressed his respect for the venerable 'British tongue', even going so far as to suggest that it was

---

[59] However, Speed in 1611 did mark out the 'more civil ancient Britons' from the rest; *ibid.*, 124–5.

[60] He followed Lhuyd in owning the seniority of the Welsh language and he 'considered the "Britons" superior to the other members of the growing British empire'. C. B. Millican, *Spenser and the Table Round* (Cambridge, Mass., 1932), 84–94.

[61] R. J. Roberts, 'John Dee and the matter of Britain', *Transactions of the Honourable Society of Cymmrodorion* (1991), 143.

[62] Gruffudd A. Williams, *Ymryson Edmwnd Prys a Wiliam Cynwal* (Cardiff, 1986).

[63] Cited in A. H. Dodd, *Studies in Stuart Wales* (Cardiff, 1952), 6.

[64] Roberts, 'The Union with England', 65–6.

[65] Williams, *Welsh Wizard and British Empire*, 21–5.

more flexible than English for rhetorical discourse.[66] Camden, like Dee, had acquired a smattering of Welsh in preparing his *Britannia*, but while he recognised the seniority of that language, in his *Remaines* he affirmed his belief in the incomparable copiousness of English.[67]

In two loyalist effusions in 1587, *The Worthiness of Wales* and *The Blessedness of Brytaine, or a Celebration of the Queenes Holyday*, Thomas Churchyard and Morys Kyffin respectively hastened to assure the queen of the steadfast devotion of Wales in the wake of the Babington Plot, in which two Welsh gentlemen were implicated. Kyffin implored

> Ye Bryttish Poets, Repeat in Royall Song,
> (With waightie words, used in King Arthurs daies)
> Th'Imperial Stock, from whence your Queene hath sprong;
> Enstall in verse your Princesse lasting prayes.[68]

The bards, particularly Sion Tudur, yeoman extraordinary of the chamber,[69] continued to pay their tributes to the Tudors, but there was no direct response to Kyffin's challenge. It was the English poets, notably Edmund Spenser, who now espoused the British and imperial theme which had become the staple of the English writings of the 'British' antiquarians. At the close of the Tudor period it would also be expounded by other men of letters who, as self-styled 'Cambro-Britons', made their careers in England and addressed an international audience.

A counterpoint to the protestant cult of the queen was sounded in the subversive 'Welsh libel' in verse which came to the attention of the

---

[66] Aubrey congratulated Dee on the substance and method of the discourse and on attaining such eloquence of exposition that 'I did nott beleve our tonge (I meane the Englyshe) to be capable of: Marie our Brittishe for the riches of the tonge in my affectionate opinion is more copiouse and more advawnageable to utter any thinge by a skillfull artificer'. A tribute may have been implied to the quality of the Scriptural translations printed in 1567, and an acknowledgement that the Welsh humanists had succeeded in their self-appointed task of rehabilitating the status of the language. Aubrey's letter, 28 July 1577, and Dee's copy of it: Bodleian Library, Ashmole MS 1789, fos. 33r–34v.

[67] Kendrick, *British Antiquity*, 120. Camden's motive in compiling *Britannia* was 'to bolster the idea of imperial England' in a quite different context from Dee's. The phrase is F. J. Levy's, see his 'The making of Camden's *Britannia*', *Bibliothèque d'Humanisme et Renaissance*, 26 (1964), 97.

[68] Maurice Kyffin, *The Blessedness of Brytaine, or a Celebration of the Queenes Holyday, 1587*. Cymmrodorion Society facsimile (London, 1885), sig. B4; Thomas Churchyard, *The Worthiness of Wales* (London, 1587).

[69] Like the translators and the antiquaries, Sion praised the progressive bounty to the Welsh of Henry VII, Henry VIII and Elizabeth. Though he retired from the court and London in disillusionment, his loyalty to the crown was undiminished. BL Royal MS 7 cxvi, fo. 93; *DWB*: E. P. Roberts, *Gwaith Sion Tudur* (2 vols., Cardiff, 1980), i, 378–81. Huw Machno also praised Elizabeth in verse for bestowing the honour of the Bible in Welsh on the nation. J. G. Jones, *Concepts of Order and Gentility in Wales, 1540–1640* (Llandysul, 1992), 187–8.

authorities on the eve of the last major crisis of the reign. This was an ode cast in fourteen stanzas in defence of the old faith which urged the Welsh to rise in rebellion against the heretical protestant English. William Morgan, bishop of Llandaff, was sufficiently alarmed by it to send a copy to Archbishop Whitgift on 26 January 1601. The poem struck an atavistic note in invoking the ancient hostility between the two nations to very different purpose from that in the protestant humanist version of early Celtic church history.

> Curwch a brethwch, Brython – waed Cymru:
> Mae g'lanas Iesu ar g'lonnau Saeson!
> [Strike them with sword you Welsh of British blood:
> The murder of Jesus lies in the hearts of the Saxons!]

Less than a fortnight after the bishop's letter the Essex Revolt took place; but the call to arms was not answered by the earl's followers in the country and the Catholics in Wales did not stir.[70] It would be rash to conclude from this that protestantism was firmly rooted in the country by this time, but it does appear that invocations of the British identity of the Welsh worked towards cementing Anglo-Welsh bonds in the new Tudor state formed in 1536, not towards undermining them.

The Welsh prophetic tradition had not survived the accession of Henry VII as a serious ideology of subversion. The threat of a recrudescence following Bishop Ferrar's allegedly incendiary sermon in 1551 had been exaggerated by his enemies.[71] On two occasions in the sixteenth century dangerous rumours surfaced which associated the Welsh with the Scots and the Irish respectively in anti-English prognostications, but these had no resonances that we know of in Wales. In the indictment of Rhys ap Gruffydd of Dinefwr for treason in 1531 it was alleged that he had contrived the king's death by entertaining a Welsh prophecy foretelling how 'king Jamys with the red hand and the ravens should conquere all England'. This was the pretext for executing an overmighty magnate who was brought down by court intrigue and Henry VIII's paranoia, for there is no independent evidence that this old

---

[70] PRO SP15/127/258–61v. It was incorrectly described as a Protestant poem and dated to Mary's reign in *Calendar of State Papers, Domestic, 1601–1603, with Addenda 1547–65*, ed. M. A. E. Green (London, 1870), 483. The poem is convincingly dated and the bard identified in R. G. Gruffydd, 'Awdl wrthryfelgar gan Edward Dafydd', *Llên Cymru*, 5 (1959), 155–63; 8 (1964), 65–9. I have tried to improve on the Victorian translation of T. W. Hancock printed in *Bye-gones Relating to Wales and the Border Counties*, 2nd ser. 6 (1899–1900), 50–3.

[71] See above pp. 18–19. One deponent did, however, testify to the commotion stirred in the congregation of St Peter's church, Carmarthen, 'now prophecyes is preachid yn pulpytes openlye' after they had been forbidden by the king's laws. One Welsh 'reader' had declared that he had buried a book of prophecies which if he still had it he would not give up for a 100 shillings. BL Harleian MS 420, fo. 122–22v.

prophecy was then current in Wales or that Rhys had ambitions to be another Owain Glyndŵr.[72] Glyndŵr's name crops up in connection with a prophecy circulating in Ireland in January 1599, when some Welsh soldiers were reported to have interpreted the name of the earl of Tyrone as 'Tir-Owen', the Welsh for 'Owen's land'. The canard was spread about that Tyrone was descended from Glyndŵr, 'who had interest both in Ireland and Wales' and had been proclaimed prince of Wales.[73]

The prophecies in which the Celtic countries are expected to make common cause against the English represented a deviation from the traditional *Brut* theme of the ultimate restoration of British unity which had been appropriated in early Tudor dynastic propaganda. At no time in the sixteenth century did any Welsh writer contribute to the literature of projects for the political unification of the island, but on one occasion old prophecies to this effect were cited in the debate on the succession question. In his unpublished 'Tract on the Succession to the Crown' (1602), Sir John Harington ventured to analyse the ambiguities of the Welsh prophetic verse which had helped Henry VII's cause, and he construed them as favourable to James VI's claim to succeed the Tudors. Fifteenth-century vaticinatory poetry foretelling the coming of 'the son of prophecy' who 'shall make the ile of Brutus whole and unparted' was thus given currency again, in a new context and in English translation. It remained as subversive and clandestine as it had ever been, for Elizabeth had forbidden any public discussion of the sensitive subject of the succession, and so the tract could circulate only in manuscript.[74]

The folk customs still observed in Snowdonia at the turn of the century, like the 'Welsh libel' of 1601, reveal an atavistic national ethos very different from that recorded by the antiquaries. The ordinary people would meet for recreation on the mountainsides on Sundays and holy days to listen to the harpers and minstrels singing the heroic deeds of their ancestors in the wars against the English. They would 'ripp up their pitigre at lenght, how eche of them is discended from those theire ould princes', and commemorate the lives of Taliesin, Merlin, Beuno, Cybi and other saints and prophets of the nation. All this is reported in a hostile report on the state of religion in north Wales which also deplores the persistence of pilgrimages to holy wells. These lingering customs are

---

[72] R. A. Griffiths, *Sir Rhys ap Thomas and his Family* (Cardiff, 1993), 100–11.

[73] *Calendar of State Papers, Ireland, 1598–99*, ed. E. G. Atkinson (London, 1895), 462.

[74] Harington cites extracts made by an unnamed friend, including some verse dating from Henry VIII's reign and purportedly addressed to the king himself, foretelling a ninth Henry. Howard Dobin, *Merlin's Disciples: prophecy, poetry and power in Renaissance England* (Stanford, Calif., 1990), 112–15.

indulged by the 'common sorte' of country gentlemen, who are given to boasting the prowess of 'the Dominion of Wales, preferringe the same to be more than the valor of the kingdome of Scotlande, and the abilities of the people of that province or part of this realme to be more able to mainteyne a regal estate than be the Scottes'.[75] This braggadocio sounds like the defensive reaction of the backwoods squires, many of whom were known recusants, to the prospect of a Stuart succession. All unauthorised assemblies were suspect in the eyes of the regime but it is unlikely that these provincial survivals posed a serious threat to its stability. They reveal another layer in the xenophobic character of popular patriotism and the absence of any Celtic fellow-feeling with other 'Britons'.[76]

VII

Protestant Welshmen, on the other hand, were reconciled to the advent of the presbyterian King of Scots to the English throne. On his accession writers were free to invoke the old prophecies as well as his Tudor ancestry in support of the Stuart title and a revamped concept of the 'British identity'. Elizabeth died before Hugh Holland could present her with his long poem, *Pancharis* (1603), celebrating the marriage of Owen Tudor and Queen Catherine, and the resourceful author dedicated it instead to King James, to whom he confidently expected that the subject would be of equal interest.[77] It was not the bards as in 1485, but Welsh writers of English and Latin prose and verse, 'Cambro-Britons' such as John Davies of Hereford and John Owen the epigrammatist, who celebrated James I's accession as a fulfilment of Merlin's prophecy in an even more complete sense than that of his forebear, Henry Tudor, had been. In addressing a readership wider than their own countrymen, these authors strained to compensate for the loss of a dynasty of Welsh extraction by engaging in the redefinition of 'Britishness' which was occasioned by the union of the crowns.

Owen pointed out that, with James's accession, the Welsh would now have to share the name of Briton with the English and Scots, for (as rendered in Thomas Harvey's translation of 1677):

---

[75] BL Lansdowne MS 11, fo. 10.
[76] A similar hostility to a Scottish succession was expressed by the Catholic exile Roger Smyth, who supported the Spanish claim on the grounds that English would not be displaced as the second language of Wales by the anglophone king of Scots. Roberts, 'The Welsh language', 69–70.
[77] *Pancharis: The First Booke. Containing the Preparation of the Love between Owen Tudyr and the Queene, Long Since Intended to her Maiden Majestie and now Dedicated to the Invincible James* (London, 1603).

The Golden Age is come, long since foretold,
When but one King should wear Brute's Crown of Gold.

In this vision of a pan-Celtic alliance, it was the turn of the English to be marginalised.[78] The triple empire of Britain was restored to the British blood through James's descent from Henry VII, who had united the red rose and the white, and his forebear, Owen Tudor from Ynys Môn, 'British Anglesey'.

> *auctorem Monadis tulit insula Mona Britannae;*
> *fortuna Monas filia, Mona parens.*

For Owen the birth-place of the founder of Tudor dynastic fortunes was the first island in the British archipelago.[79]

A similar note is struck in the defence of Geoffrey of Monmouth written c. 1610 by John Lewis, a London barrister and an associate of John Dee. This was to circulate in manuscript for over a hundred years before it was printed, by which time it had ceased to be of much interest to anyone outside Wales.[80] *The History of Great-Britain* (1729) includes a dedication to Prince Henry and a discourse on the isles belonging to the island of Great Britain which 'make as yt were a Microcosmus, or Little World', and James I is hailed by Lewis as king of these isles, the British archipelago.[81] In his *Microcosmos*, dedicated to James I in 1603, John Davies of Hereford (?1565–1618) affirmed the senior status of Wales among the British nations which were now reunited through the Stuarts' descent from Brutus, Arthur and the Tudors.[82]

---

[78] Modern commentators have noticed an anglophobia in the writings of Hugh Holland and in those of Davies and Howell 'a clear sense of superiority: the English are either ignored or patronized'; Raymond Garlick, *An Introduction to Anglo-Welsh Literature* (Cardiff, 1970), 28. Cf. Ronald Mathias, on *Pancharis*, 'probably the most anti-English poem of the century': *Anglo-Welsh Literature* (Bridgend, 1986), 25.

[79] *John Owen's Latin Epigrams*, englished by Thomas Harvey, London 1677, 2nd book, nos. 6, 37, 39; J. H. Jones, 'John Owen, *Cambro-Britannus*', *Transactions of the Honourable Society of Cymmrodorion* (1940), 130–43.

[80] Theophilus Evans, a clerical opponent of 'enthusiasm', gave the Galfridian version of the early history of Wales a new lease of life in what was to become a classic of modern Welsh prose, *Drych y Prif Oesoedd* (1716). By this time support for the British History was confined to the Anglican, royalist tradition of Welsh historiography, though aspects of it were to gain currency in the literature of the Romantic Revival to exert a further formative influence on perceptions of national identity.

[81] An early draft of the work survives as NLW Peniarth MS 252, fos. 265–374, with a dedicatory letter to James I, in whom 'the long expectacion of the auncient Brittyns [is] fulfilled & accomplished'. The book also contained an account of the early history of Scotland and Brittany; G. M. Griffiths, 'John Lewis of Llwynwene's defence of Geoffrey of Monmouth's "Historia"', *NLW Journal*, 7 (1951–2), 228–34. For the eclipse of the British History, see Kendrick, *British Antiquity*, 99–133.

[82] The book includes the poem 'Cambria', addressed to Henry, future prince of Wales, assuring him that in his principality he will find '*Brutes* venerable *Stocke*' who regard

The Stuart descent from Owen Tudor was also laid out in a Welsh translation of James's *Basilikon Doron*, prepared for the press by Robert Holland in 1604. Only a fragment of the book survives, the printing having been interrupted by an outbreak of the plague in London. A *Genealogy* of the king, intended to be published with it but in the event issued separately, traces his lineage through Owen Tudor to the Welsh princes and British kings. In the preface to the aborted publication, Holland declares that the 'Brytish, English, Scottish and Irish Nations are united' through James' descent 'by law of Nature and Consanguinity from all foure.' James is hailed as the heir to Cadwaladr, while the Welsh, remnants of the ancient Britons, had retained their language unpolluted for a millennium and were the first inhabitants of the island to espouse the true faith.[83]

The Welsh squire-antiquaries voiced similar revelations. George Owen, the historian of Pembrokeshire, proclaimed James to be the first king of the whole island of Britain since the death of Brutus, 'being now 2710 years sithence'.[84] Sir William Maurice of Clenennau was convinced that the king's accession was providentially ordained to fulfil the prophecy 'that out of the Bryttishe line shold desende one that sholde restore the kingdom of Brittaine to the pristine state'.[85] Maurice did not hesitate to introduce these pseudo-historical arguments into the discussions of the royal scheme for 'a more perfect union' of Scotland and England to complement the regal union. He was alleged to be the first to address James as 'king of Great Britain',[86] and it was the Welsh/British inheritance that Maurice had in mind when, as knight of the shire for Caernarfonshire, he went so far as to propose in the Commons in 1604 that the king should proclaim himself 'emperor of Great Britain'.

him 'as the *Creame* of their best *bloud*'. In seeking a bride Henry should follow his ancestor's example:

> Witnesse our *Owen Thewdor*, who could give
> True *demonstration* how to court a Queene.

The tribute earned Davies the reward of the post of writing-master to the Prince, on whose death he composed an elegy; John Davies, *Microcosmos* (Oxford, 1603), 29–38.

[83] In the dedication to the king, Holland acknowledges the support and encouragement of Sir James Perrot, John Philips and George Owen of Henllys, and the assistance of George Owen Harry in the translation. *Basilikon Doron by King James I: fragment of a Welsh translation by Robert Holland, 1604* (facsimile edn, Cardiff, 1931); cf. also William Harbert, *A Prophesie of Cadwallader, Last King of the Britaines* (London, 1604).

[84] George Owen, *The Description of Penbrokeshire*, ed. H. Owen (4 parts, London, 1902–36), part i, 263.

[85] An undated and mutilated draft letter to an unnamed cousin, who is commended for his diligence in collecting historical arguments to be set forth in parliament in an important cause, presumably by Maurice himself. T. Jones Pierce (ed.), *Clenennau Letters and Papers* (Aberystwyth, 1947), 134–5.

[86] Maurice's sister refers to this in a letter to him of 6 Feb. 1604: 'you are his Godfather and intiteled his highnes "Kinge of Great Britaine" . . .' *ibid.*, 61.

Maurice returned to the theme in parliamentary speeches or motions in 1606, 1607 and 1610, not always with royal sanction, it seems, and he succeeded only in alienating the sympathies of his fellow members.[87] Parliament would not countenance the suggestion that the name of England should be subsumed under that of Britain, and James was reduced to assuming the style 'king of Great Britain' by proclamation. As for the imperial title, though the antiquaries – Dee, Camden and Speed – proceeded to describe 'Great Britain' as an empire, the designation had no constitutional significance.

The loyal assurances which greeted James on his accession attest to the reformulated concept of 'British identity' entertained by the Welsh literati after the regal union.[88] The king was receptive to some of the notions of a destiny fulfilled, which were also propagated by Scottish pamphleteers, but in acknowledging them he made no more than symbolic gestures such as quartering the arms of Cadwaladr and Edward the Confessor on the great seal.[89] From the various expositions of his English and British inheritance which were brought to his attention, James selected what best suited his purposes. There are few indications that the writings addressed or dedicated to him by the Welsh publicists ever reached the king, let alone altered his preconceptions. He expressed little interest in the Welsh Tudors, and if he himself had a consistent vision of a 'British identity' it was a circumscribed one in which he could bracket the English and the Welsh together as 'our Subjects of South Britaine'. In his campaign for a more comprehensive union he was to cite the Henrician incorporation of Wales with England as a happy precedent, a point which had been rehearsed for him by the pamphleteers and antiquaries. When he formally revived the title of prince of Wales, first for Henry and then for Charles, he may have been influenced, indirectly, by the case made out for the constitutional status of the Principality by George Owen.[90] The creation of Henry as prince

---

[87] G. D. Owen, *Wales in the Reign of James I* (London, 1988), 46; B. Galloway points out that he did not always speak with the king's authority: *The Union of England and Scotland, 1603–1608* (Edinburgh, 1986), 21, 81, 94, 150.

[88] *Pace* Jenny Wormald, who argues that 'there was little enthusiasm for being "British" ... the Welsh can hardly he said to have bothered, or for that matter to have had their opinion particularly sought'; 'James VI, James I and the Identity of Britain', in B. Bradshaw and J. Morrill (eds.), *The British Problem, c. 1534–1707: state-formation in the Atlantic Archipelago* (London, 1996), 155.

[89] 'It is impossible to assess how much weight James gave to these messianic ideas', Galloway, *Union*, 48.

[90] George Owen may have had some formative, if indirect, influence in preparing the ground for the revival of the princely title in 1610. His tract arguing the case against the claim advanced by David Powel in *The Historie of Cambria* (1584), that the Principality had been subsumed in the crown with the Act of Union of 1536, is dated 1 March

of Wales had been anticipated by Robert Holland in 1604 when, in his Welsh translation of *Basilikon Doron*, he expressed the pious hope that the work would enable the heir apparent, 'whose presence amongst vs would wonderfully reioyce all' the Welsh, to learn their language.[91] In the event, the ceremonies of creation and investiture for each prince, held successively in London in 1610 and 1613, were honorific affairs signifying little more than celebrations of the pluralistic character of Jacobean monarchy. A survey of the crown estates in Wales conducted in preparation for Henry's principate had revealed the value of the principality lands to be disappointingly low. Although antiquaries were consulted about the traditional privileges of princes of Wales, the motive was to recover untapped sources of patronage for the court. In the event historical research yielded little to satisfy the avid curiosity of the officers of Prince Henry's household. Consequently there was no attempt to elevate the prince of Wales into a regional magnate, and the Council in the Marches continued to govern the country in the king's name.[92]

As with the historic Principality, so with the concepts of Britain and a 'British empire', the impact which their Welsh and Anglo-Welsh exponents made on policy-making was limited, in James' reign as in Elizabeth's. After 1603 their interpretation of the shift in the relationship of Wales with the reigning dynasty and with the other component nations of Britain, while it served to reorientate Welsh/British loyalties, was not perforce conducive to the preservation of the sense of a separate Welsh national identity. The island of Britain had been unified under a single ruler but the Principality of Wales was very much a junior member within the multiple kingdoms of the Stuarts. Though the Welsh persisted in their devotion to the British History, their claim to be the 'true' Britons could no longer go unchallenged, and the description of their native tongue as the 'British' language would have far less purchase in the political culture of the age than it had retained under the Tudors. The conservatism of Welsh society ensured that the country would

---

1608; Cardiff City Library MS 2.88, fos. 51–7. Owen's argument is repeated virtually verbatim, though without acknowledgements, in the treatise which Richard Connack presented to the king in July 1609; Trinity College, Cambridge, MS R5.25.

[91] Holland, 'The Epistle' to the king.

[92] The device for Prince Edward's principality ('a breviat of the effectes devised for Wales', c. 1540–1) survives among the papers collected by Sir Robert Cotton at this time, though there is no evidence that it was ever considered as a blueprint for the revised Stuart principality. P. R. Roberts, 'Wales and England after the Tudor "Union": Crown, Principality and parliament 1543–1624', in C. Cross et al. (eds.), *Law and Government under the Tudors*, 122–7; Francis Jones, *The Princes and Principality of Wales* (Cardiff, 1969), 132–40; R. W. Hoyle (ed.), *The Estates of the English Crown 1558–1640* (Cambridge, 1992), 421 and n. 10.

remain largely royalist in the Civil War, but one significant corollary of religious division and the crisis of loyalties was that a close identification with the ruling dynasty no longer featured among the cultural matrices which sustained for all the protestants of Wales the enduring consciousness of a distinct nationality.

2 The English Reformation and identity formation in Wales and Ireland

Brendan Bradshaw

Current revisionist interpretations of the history of the Reformation in England and Ireland provide an intriguing paradox. In England the received wisdom, as variously purveyed in the magisterial studies of A. G. Dickens and G. R. Elton, represents the reform movement as triumphing under the Tudors.[1] In latter years, however, the long-established consensus has been shattered by means of a revisionist enterprise, heralded in the work of localist historians such as Margaret Bowker but mainly recently under the aegis of Christopher Haigh. This has challenged the notion of a decadent late medieval church heading for extinction and, conversely, has demonstrated the widespread survival of the ritualistic, quasi-magical elements of late medieval religion throughout the sixteenth century, despite the general acquiescence in the 'religion by law established' – a thesis now massively corroborated in both respects by Eamon Duffy's authoritative study of the religious culture of the period.[2] The effect of the revisionist challenge, therefore, has been to throw serious doubt upon the impact of the Reformation on English religion in the sixteenth century whether from 'above' (Elton) or 'below' (Dickens). In contrast the conventional wisdom which held that the attempt to convert the Irish to the Reformation failed in the

[1] Indicative of his conception, A. G. Dickens' classic account closes with a chapter entitled 'The foundations of Elizabethan England' (ch. 14). This analyses the so-called Elizabethan Settlement of 1559–63; the final section outlines what Dickens sees as 'The Revolution of 1559'. After that there remain only 'The residual problems' (ch. 15), Dickens, The *English Reformation* (London, 1964), 339–77; Elton for his part maintains that 'by 1553 England was almost certainly nearer to being a Protestant country than to anything else', G. R. Elton, *Reform and Reformation* (London, 1977), 371.

[2] Haigh's most comprehensive statement of his position is contained in Christopher Haigh, *English Reformations* (London, 1993); the local study on which much of Haigh's later work has been built is his *Reformation and Resistance* (Cambridge, 1975). Perhaps the most seminal of the earlier local studies which challenged the notion of a decadent late medieval church is Margaret Bowker, *Henrician Reformation* (Cambridge, 1981). Duffy's recent magisterial account in the same vein, drawing copiously on East Anglian evidence, is *The Stripping of the Altars* (Yale and London, 1993). Duffy's thesis was to some extent anticipated in J. J. Scarisbrick, *The Reformation and the English People* (Oxford 1984).

sixteenth century has also been challenged. Nicholas Canny has boldly asserted that the conventional approach which takes the failure for granted and seeks simply to explain it is begging the real issue. It assumes what requires to be demonstrated, namely that the religious struggle between the Reformation and the Counter Reformation was fought to a conclusion in sixteenth-century Ireland. On the contrary, he asserts, the Counter Reformation scarcely made more headway there than the Reformation at this period. Historians have been deceived, he argues, by identifying the 'traditional religion' of the late middle ages – with its quasi-magical rituals and its admixture of Celtic paganism – with the reformed Catholicism of the Counter Reformation. It was the former that held the allegiance of the Irish generally throughout the sixteenth century and, indeed, continued to do so until it finally succumbed to the ultramontane 'devotional revolution' of the nineteenth century. It was not until then, therefore, that the religious struggle initiated in the sixteenth century was finally resolved, leaving the Church of Rome in triumph and the Church of Ireland 'as by law established' defeated.[3] Paradoxically, then, the discovery of the phenomenon of survivalism has prompted a revisionist challenge both to the notion of the triumph of the Reformation in England and of the Counter Reformation in Ireland.[4]

Interestingly, no such challenge to the accepted view has emerged in the case of the third of the Tudor dominions. The basis on which the consensus has been maintained in the case of Wales, I wish to suggest, provides a cautionary tale for the revisionists. More importantly, it also indicates the need to reappraise the impact of the confrontation between the Reformation and the Counter Reformation throughout the multi-national conglomerate governed by the English monarch in the sixteenth century.

The consensus view of the course of the Reformation in sixteenth-century Wales is conveniently summarised in Glanmor Williams' two chapters on the religious history of the period in his authoritative general survey contributed to the *Oxford History of Wales* multivolume series. There, assessing the progress of the Reformation campaign under the Tudors, he likens the situation at the end of the reign of Elizabeth to that obtaining in the 'dark corners of the land' in England. As in the more remote English regions, zealous reform-minded pastors and evangelists waxed indignant on the subject of the persistence of abomin-

---

[3] Nicholas Canny, 'Why the Reformation failed in Ireland', *Journal of Ecclesiastical History*, 30 (1979), 423–50.

[4] For the concept of survivalism see John Bossy, The *English Catholic Community* (London 1975), *passim*.

able idolatries': '"the sacrifice of bullocks to Bueno"; pilgrimage-going; open carrying of beads to church; calling on saints to help in all extremities; crossing themselves persistently when closing windows, leaving cattle in the field and burying the dead'.[5] Perhaps the most scandalous evidence of the general persistence of Welsh unregeneracy was the unreformed state of the lower clergy. In the last decade of Elizabeth's reign, Williams points out, as balanced and moderate a churchman as Hugh Lewys is found castigating his fellow clergy 'for still performing only a sacerdotal rather than an instructive role'.[6] In face of such evidence, therefore, Williams acknowledges that at the end of the sixteenth century 'the task of transforming the "collective Christians" of the Middle Ages into individual believers with a strong sense of personal responsibility had hardly begun'.[7] However the instructive feature of Williams' treatment for present purposes is that the evidence of widespread unregeneracy does not prevent him from ascribing success to the Reformation. He is not moved by such a spectacle to launch a revisionist challenge, arguing in the manner of Canny, as it might be, that the struggle between the Reformation and the Counter Reformation remained unresolved until the 'survivalist' religious culture of the Welsh succumbed to the Methodist 'devotional revolution' of the eighteenth century. On the contrary, he is satisfied that the issue was already decided by the end of the sixteenth century.

Perhaps the most significant achievement of the religious movement in that regard – and certainly the most remarkable one – was the identification of the *English* Reformation with a newly burgeoning Welsh patriotism. In this way the reformed religion, he points out, became 'increasingly associated [with] two kinds of loyalty; the one Tudor, the other Welsh'. The effect of the former association, as Williams explains was 'a growing attachment to a whole complex of institutions, including the crown and the dynasty, common law and parliament, and the Established Church and the Protestant settlement'.[8] The effect of the latter was complementary. It elicited 'the concept of the reformed religion as a return to that great fountain-head of Welsh religious life, the Celtic Church'.[9] On the other hand, the achievement of the Reformation campaign by inversion was to 'smear' Catholic dissent by associating it with 'disloyalty, subversion and conspiracy ... with the menace of internal disorder and foreign invasion and domination' so that 'it could be propagated only in secret and outside the law'.[10] Thus,

---

[5] Glanmor Williams, *Recovery, Reorientation and Reformation: Wales c. 1415–1642* (Oxford/Cardiff, 1987), 305–31, at 327.
[6] Williams, *Wales*, pp. 326–7.   [7] *Ibid.*, 327.   [8] *Ibid.*, 330–1.
[9] *Ibid.*   [10] Williams, *Wales*, 330.

in the words of Williams' conclusion: 'No matter what shortcomings may have defaced the Elizabethan Church, however much ignorance and superstition might have survived in its midst, it was, in the eyes of the social groups that mattered, a central and irreplaceable bulwark of continuing order and prosperity.'[11]

What this meant in practical terms is reflected in a survey of Welsh dioceses taken in 1603. This yielded a return of only 808 avowed recusants. Even making generous allowance for inefficiency and negligence on the part of the inquisitors, and building in an estimate in respect of 'church papists' and children, Williams calculates that the total number of Catholic dissenters can scarcely have exceeded 3,500 from a church-going population estimated at 212,450. As time would increasingly show, the circumstances in which the Counter Reformation might have secured a popular success no longer existed in Wales by the end of the sixteenth century while, conversely, the conditions for securing popular adherence to the religion by law established were now in place. In short, the Counter Reformation had effectively shot its bolt and the Reformation had triumphed.[12]

As the foregoing indicates, the recent historiography concerning the confrontation between the Reformation and the Counter Reformation in sixteenth-century Wales has recourse to a distinction – centrally, albeit tacitly – which has been overlooked elsewhere to the confusion of the issue. Thus, Williams' interpretation hinges on a difference of emphasis as between two modes in which the religious affiliation of a community may manifest itself in social terms. In one, the mode emphasised in recent revisionist historiography, religious commitment is assessed under the aspect of a 'discipline' – as the contemporary usage deploys the term. Here the criterion is established in 'practice': in the adherence of the community to a prescribed routine of ceremonial and ethical observances. The mode emphasised by Williams, however, relates to religion as a creed or confession, to use the contemporary terminology. Under that aspect religious affiliation manifests itself as a collective mentality, a world view or ideology that characterises the community's mode of self-identity; and commitment is gauged accordingly in terms of the socio-cultural values and attitudes which the community affirms as central to its common identity.[13] It was in that respect, in relation to the ideology of the Reformation, that the commit-

[11] *Ibid.*

[12] *Ibid.*, 328. For a more recent survey which generally corroborates Williams and provides additional evidence see J. Gwynfor Jones, *Early Modern Wales, c. 1525–1640* (London, 1994), ch. 4, especially 164–70.

[13] For this distinction I am particularly indebted to R. Po-Chia Hsia, *Social Discipline in the Reformation* (London, 1989), especially chs. 4, 6, 7, 8. See also Euan Cameron, *The*

ment of the Welsh community was secured in the course of the sixteenth century.

Viewed in the light of that distinction the revisionist challenge to the received orthodoxy for England and Ireland seems less secure than when viewed in isolation. Thus, if the religion 'by law established' made such progress in Wales by the end of the century, it seems reasonable to argue, as has been more recently argued by Diarmaid MacCulloch, that it is likely to have been no less successful even in the darkest corners of the land in England.[14] Viewed in the Irish context the distinction raises quite a different prospect. The possibility that arises here is of reinstating the received wisdom concerning the triumph of the Counter Reformation. That is the consideration to which this study addresses itself. The argument in that regard will be that what impresses by comparison in this other Celtic borderland dominion of the English monarch is the vehemence and confessional awareness with which the religion by law established came to be resisted in favour of the proscribed Catholicism of the Counter Reformation. Thus the effect of the analysis will be to highlight a paradox: the failure of Ireland to conform to the pattern that established itself elsewhere throughout Europe whereby the religion of the prince – the magistrate – sooner or later became the religion of the community. Further, it will emerge that confessional dissent characterised the response of both of the island's historic communities, the native Gaelic Irish who inhabited the westward boggy and upland regions, and the Old English, as the descendants of the medieval Anglo-Norman colonists now came to be called, who occupied the fertile lowland regions eastwards. Thus resistance to the Tudor Reformation marks the beginning of the process whereby the two historic communities, traditional enemies, began to undergo a transformation of identity from which they would emerge as a single community, the Catholic Irish. The remainder of the chapter will be concerned to explore the circumstances in each case that produced such contrasting responses to the onset of the Reformation from the English crown's two Celtic borderland dominions, a contrast, as will be seen, fraught with significance for the history of Britain and Ireland and for the history of the relationship between them into the modern period.

European Reformation (Oxford, 1991), ch. 20. However, the analytical application deployed here is my own.

[14] Diarmaid MacCulloch, *The Later Reformation in England, 1547–1603* (London, 1990) As with historians of the Reformation in Wales, McCulloch's analysis implicitly deploys the concept of confessionalism without utilising the term. The concept of confessionalism remains to be assimilated by British historiography generally.

I

To start then with the response from the Irish dominion, the point that must first be stressed is that the issue was by no means beyond doubt from the outset. In the case of the colonial community the initial response to Henry VIII's claim to a royal ecclesiastical supremacy, if not wildly enthusiastic, seemed to indicate at least a certain openness to the proposition on the part of a substantial section of the people who mattered. The relevant legislation was voted through without demur in the Irish Reformation parliament of 1536–7, apart from an attempted filibuster mounted by the proctors of the lower clergy.[15] Similarly, the two Henrician lord deputies, Lord Leonard Grey and Sir Anthony St Leger, reported little resistance in administering the accompanying oath within the colony – even in the remote colonial enclaves of Cork, Limerick and Galway on the western seaboard.[16] However, the so-called mid-Tudor crisis marked a shift in attitude. No doubt the promulgation in rapid succession of a protestant Reformation under Edward VI, and then of a Catholic restoration under Mary – the occasion of much jubilation in the colony – and, finally, of a virtual reversion to the Edwardian status quo ante in the form of the Elizabethan Settlement, brought home to the Old English community the implications in practical terms of the crown's claim to supreme ecclesiastical jurisdiction.[17] Thereafter, in any case, the story is one of mounting opposition. True, the Elizabethan Acts of Supremacy and Uniformity were duly enacted by an Irish parliament in 1560 in which the Old English still held a considerable majority. However, the inward history of that episode remains shrouded in mystery. All that can be said for certain is that the lord deputy, the earl of Sussex, was much exercised beforehand by the prospect of opposition and was casting about for a means to overcome it. This lends credibility to the allegations which began to circulate in the aftermath that the passage of the statutes was in fact, secured by a combination of sharp practice and intimidation on the part

---

[15] See my 'Opposition to the ecclesiastical legislation in the Irish Reformation parliament', *Irish Historical Studies*, 16 (1969).

[16] *State Papers Henry VIII*, iii, 55, 57, 169, 248. Also Bradshaw, *Irish Constitutional Revolution of the Sixteenth Century* (Cambridge, 1979), 158–9, 165–6, 245–51; Bradshaw, 'The Reformation in the cities', in John Bradley (ed.), *Settlement and Society in Medieval Ireland* (Kilkenny, 1988), 445–76 at 452–3.

[17] Bradshaw, 'Edwardian Reformation in Ireland', *Archivium Hibernicum*, 24 (1976–7), 83–99. Steven Ellis challenges my thesis by means of a revisionist reading of one of the main sources which attest to the hostility provoked by the Edwardian liturgical innovations in the colony in 'John Bale, bishop of Ossory, 1552–3', *Journal of the Butler Society*, 2 (1984). I do not find his interpretation, against the grain of the generally accepted reading, persuasive.

of the lord deputy.[18] Be that as it may what ultimately matters for present purposes is the incontrovertible fact that five years later the religion 'by law established' remained practically a dead letter in the colony by the contrivance of precisely that group whose representatives supposedly enacted the measures in parliament.

This was the situation that came to light when the recently appointed head of the commission for ecclesiastical causes in Ireland, Archbishop Adam Loftus, instituted an inquisition into the observance of the religious decrees in the four shires of the Pale, the area in the hinterland of Dublin which constituted the crown's most effective sphere of government. To Loftus's dismay enquiry showed that 'her majesty's most godly laws and proceedings' were everywhere disregarded, and that the local socio-political elite actively connived at this situation. First they failed as magistrates and justices of the peace to give effect to the laws' penal clauses. Worse still as Loftus' investigation revealed, so little disposed were they towards religious conformity that 'the most part of them, by their own confession, had continually since the last parliament, frequented the mass and other services and ceremonies inhibited by [her] majesty's laws and injunctions [while] very few of them ever received the Holy Communion or used such other kind of public prayer and service as is presently established by law'.[19]

Significantly, Loftus' first report as head of the ecclesiastical commission set the tone for a whole spate of such reports from agents of the Reformation in Ireland for the rest of the century. These chart a situation which, from the crown's point of view, was steadily deteriorating. For while the mass non-conformity encountered by Loftus in the 1560s might well be attributed to survivalism, the mere attachment of a conservative society to the rituals of traditional religion, by the 1580s non-conformity was increasingly assuming a more defiantly recusant aspect, more theologically informed and more ideologically orientated. Thus, in striking contrast to the experience of his Henrician predeces-

---

[18] Bradshaw, 'Beginnings of modern Ireland', in Brian Farrell (ed.), *The Irish Parliamentary Tradition* (Dublin, 1973), 67–87 at 80–1. Cf. R. D. Edwards, *Church and State in Tudor Ireland* (Dublin, 1935), 177–83. This interpretation is generally corroborated in S. G. Ellis, *Tudor Ireland* (London, 1985), 210–11. It is challenged in Jefferies, 'The Irish parliament of 1560', *Irish Historical Studies*, 26 (1988), 128–41. Jefferies' account scarcely carries conviction. He concedes that the contemporary evidence amply testifies to the government's fear of serious opposition and that care was taken in anticipation to make 'a strong party' in support of the crown in the Lower House. However, lacking any hard evidence of the actual proceedings of the parliament, he is prepared to dismiss contemporary and near contemporary allegations of intimidation and trickery as 'incredible', and to argue that while 'some opposition ... was clearly manifested ... it was so ineffective one can *only* (sic) assume that it was quite limited'.

[19] The report is reproduced in E. P. Shirley (ed.), *Original Letters and Papers of the Church in Ireland* (London, 1851), no. 70, 194–7 at 196.

sors, when Lord Deputy Perrot sought to have the Oath of Supremacy generally administered in 1584–5 the attempt failed at the first hurdle: the socio-political elite of the Pale could neither be prevailed upon to take the oath themselves nor to act as justices of the peace for the purpose of administering the oath in their localities.[20] Similarly, when the attempt was made at Perrot's parliament to update the ecclesiastical legislation by introducing a series of penal measures passed in England over the previous two decades, the assembly, in contrast to 1560, refused to be intimidated, and proceeded to reject practically the entire legislative programme of the government.[21]

Moving on a further decade, a lengthy report from Bishop Lyon of Cork in the mid 1590s provides an illuminating case study of religious attitudes within the Old English community at the end of the Tudor period. In that regard the first point to note is that on the criteria usually applied Lyon's report might seem to indicate that this remote outpost of English order and civility in the south west of Ireland had remained quite untouched by the attempt to win 'hearts and minds' on the part alike of Reformation and Counter Reformation evangelists. Speaking with the experience of an apostolate of twenty-five years' duration behind him, the bishop lamented – in unison, it might be said, with a veritable chorus of reforming evangelists of both churches and from all parts of Ireland – the 'ignorance' and 'superstition' that still prevailed within the diocese: 'a great part are no better than mere infidels, having but the bare name of Christians without any knowledge of Christ or light of His truth ... many of them being sixty years of age or upwards [are] not able to say the Lord's Prayer or the Articles of the Christian Faith, neither in English, Latin nor Irish'.[22] In that light, therefore, it might seem, bearing out Nicholas Canny's contention, that by the end of the sixteenth century in Cork, not only did the struggle for 'hearts and minds' remain unresolved: so far as the community itself was concerned it had not even started.

[20] W. M. Brady (ed.), *State Papers Concerning the Irish Church* (London, 1868), nos. LXIX, 88, LXXII, 100–2. For general corroboration of the situation depicted in Loftus' report and for the emergence of a self-conscious recusant stance among the lay elite of the Pale over the ensuing two decades see Helen Coburn Walshe, 'Enforcing the Elizabethan Settlement', *Irish Historical Studies*, 26 (1989), 352–76. For corroboration by means of a detailed case study of the Dublin patriciate see Colm Lennon, *The Lords of Dublin in the Age of Reformation* (Dublin, 1989), 128–65.

[21] Victor Treadwell, 'The Irish parliament of 1585–6', *Proceedings of the Royal Irish Academy*, 65, C (1966), no. 10, 259–308.

[22] *Cal. S.P. Ire, 1596–7*, 13–20 at 16. For a report from the bishop of Waterford, Marmaduke Middleton, in 1580, mirroring in detail the situation described by Lyon see Brady (ed.), *State Papers*, no. XXV, 39–41. For the situation which these particular instances illuminate in detail see Edwards, *Church and State*, 263–5 and Walshe, 'Enforcing'.

In fact such an impression is quite mistaken. For, as Lyon's report vividly conveys, the religious state of the people of Cork had been radically transformed in consequence of the struggle between the Reformation and the Counter Reformation. The key to what occurred is contained in the distinction postulated at the outset between religion considered as 'practice', as a code of behaviour – as 'discipline' or 'observance' – and religion considered as 'ideology', as 'creed' or 'confession', subscribed to as a form of socio-political identity, and affirmed by means of a set of socio-political attitudes and values. It was in the latter respect that a religious transformation was effected in Cork in the course of the sixteenth century.

How this came about is readily explicable. To begin with, as Lyon's report shows, the confessional divide impinged upon the community as a matter of daily experience. It manifested itself, in the first instance, as a facet of the material environment and of the social routines of the city. Thus, one aspect of confessionalism was presented by the parish churches: stripped of images and shrines, occupied by reformed, increasingly English clergy, providing worship according to the legally prescribed Prayer Book. At the same time, the other face of confessionalism was presented in a new environmental feature, less conspicuous to the eye but no less visible on the social horizon. This was the clandestine 'massing house' where the Tridentine liturgy was celebrated by 'the pope's legates, friars, priests and seminaries', as Lyon distinguished them, noting to his chagrin, 'ten seminary and seducing priests resident within the city'.[23]

Reinforcing its environmental manifestation, confessionalism impinged on the consciousness of the Cork community more importantly in the form of a choice between alternative modes of corporate worship: on the one hand, the Prayer Book liturgy, austere, word-centred, vernacular; on the other hand, the Holy Sacrifice, offered according to the Roman rite, in Latin, with all its priestly panoply. Here, then, the first gauge of the struggle for 'hearts and minds' presents itself: in the form of a choice which confessionalism imposed as between two modes of corporate worship. In that regard the significant point is that Lyon's report reveals a situation in Cork as little to his satisfaction as that encountered by Loftus in Dublin and its adjacent shires.

Emboldened by the crisis of the 'Ulster' rebellion, the bishop believed, the people had abandoned their parish churches. His own sermons could now scarcely attract an audience of 5, whereas formerly, he claimed, there might have been 1,000; and attendance at parish

[23] *Cal. S.P. Ire., 1596–7*, 14.

Eucharists had dwindled from as many as 500 to as few as ˥ ⸱⸱⸱⸱-municants. This recalcitrance, he complained, affected all kinds and conditions: women – 'not one woman either at Divine Service or Communion'; children, 'no more than the older sort' – they played truant from school when the master was instructed to bring them to divine service; 'not so much as the country churls' could now be got to go to church. And the same dismal story was to be told with regard to the parish church's other special function, the administration of baptism. Parents refused to bring their children; and even when, by exception, they contrived to do so they found that sponsors (gossips) were not forthcoming.[24] Finally, again corresponding with Loftus' account, Lyon traced the source of the problem of absenteeism to the social elite whose failure to impose the statutory fines enabled the local community, themselves included, to flout the law with impunity: they refused to take on the office of churchwarden because these had responsibility to levy the fines for absenteeism in the first place; and even when they agreed to fill the office they neglected their penal function.[25] Complementing that picture and clinching the issue so far as the corporate worship of the community is concerned, Lyon depicted in exasperated detail the way in which the people, having forsaken their parish churches, were streaming to the services of the massing houses. All 'follow their seducers the priests' who 'say mass, baptise, minister the sacraments and other their popish and heretical ceremonies in their private houses'. And in that regard also, echoing Loftus, Lyon singled out the social elite as the principal culprits. For it was 'the Aldermen and merchants of the city' who 'kept and maintained' the priests; it was they who 'conveyed them forth of the town when they go to say mass in the country abroad'; and it was 'the young merchants among them' who stood guard 'with their daggers and pistols ready prepared' while the priests performed their ministrations.[26]

As is now perhaps becoming clear, one of the interests of Lyon's vivid pen-picture is the glimpse it provides of an early stage of formation of that Catholic counter-culture which was to become a defining characteristic of the Old English community until its dissolution at the end of the seventeenth century. So far as the significance of that development for the question in hand is concerned, not the least valuable aspect of the bishop's account is the sense it conveys of the counter-culture's ethos. Apropos of this, two features of Cork non-conformity to which the report directs attention are especially relevant. One is the repudiation by the community of the ideological assertion at the heart of the English

---

[24] *Ibid.*, 18.   [25] *Ibid.*, 15–16.   [26] *Ibid.*, 13.

Reformation, the claim to a royal ecclesiastical supremacy. Here Lyon discovered, as had Loftus already in Dublin, that the time when the claim might have been generally conceded – in a fit of absent-mindedness almost, as seems to have been the case in the 1530s – had now passed. On the contrary, the claim had become a burning question of conscience by reason of the fact that the pope's claim to a universal *potestas jurisdictionis* had come to be perceived as *de fide Catholica* – a fundamental dogma of the Catholic religion. Thus while, as Lyon complained, the Counter Reformation clergy went about 'swearing the people to the pope', the oath to the royal supremacy was everywhere evaded. When required to swear as a condition of entering public office – as mayor, alderman, justice of the peace or bailiff – the social elite either neglected the statutory obligation or declined to serve or, in the last resort, if pushed that far, 'utterly refused' to swear against their conscience.[27] Meanwhile, the bishop was outraged to discover the local schoolmasters engaged on a campaign of active subversion: the page displaying the queen's style and title had been systematically excised from the grammars used in schools throughout the diocese; and two of the teachers responsible when called to account proved so intractable as to be ready to endure imprisonment rather than 'acknowledge Her Majesty's said title'.[28]

The second feature of Cork non-conformity which reflected the ethos of the emergent counter-culture trenched on an issue of no less fierce confessional controversy. This was the church's worship and sacramental system and, as a necessary corollary, the *potestas ordinis*, the spiritual 'power of order' in virtue of which the central act of christian worship, the Eucharist, is celebrated and its sacraments administered. Set in the context of that debate it emerges that more was involved in the liturgical non-conformity of the Cork community than the unreflecting attachment of a conservative society to the rituals of 'traditional religion'. Rather, it reflected a stance on the confessional debate in line with that purveyed by Counter Reformation polemic and iconography, a stance diametrically opposed, needless to say, to the view of the matter purveyed in Lyon's own apocalyptic rhetoric. Thus, on the one hand, the citizens of Cork branded the Prayer Book liturgy 'the Devil's worship' and its ministers 'Devils': encountering the reformed ministers in the streets the people hurried past, 'blessing themselves in the popish manner' for protection.[29] On the other hand, the Counter Reformation missionaries found themselves elevated to a status never

---

[27] *Ibid.*, 14. For a similar development in the Pale see Brady, *State Papers.*
[28] *Cal. S.P. Ire., 1596–7*, 17.   [29] *Ibid.*, 15.

accorded the medieval lower clergy: fraternising as social equals with the patricians of the city; 'so well entreated and so much made of among the people', indeed, that the incumbents of country parishes 'forsake their benefices to become massing priests'.[30]

To summarise, therefore, the reports of Loftus and Lyon indicate that the failure of the Old English to conform to the religion 'by law established' in the Elizabethan period cannot be explained away as mere survivalism, as the unreflecting adherence of a conservative society to the rituals of 'traditional religion'. On the contrary, they illustrate the way the non-conformity of the Old English was informed at every social level by perceptions and values which were simply unavailable before the sixteenth-century fissure of Western christendom gave rise to the confessional distinction between Catholic and protestant. More precisely, they testify to the fact that already by the late Elizabethan period the non-conformity of the Old English had taken the mould of a counter-culture which affirmed the confessional ideology of Counter Reformation Catholicism. That is to say, drawing on the implication for the question at issue, by the late Elizabethan period, so far as the Old English community is concerned, the religion of the Counter Reformation had been assimilated as central to the community's collective identity while the Reformation had come to be regarded as an alien innovation.

II

Such being the case within the area of the medieval colony, the traditional 'land of obedience', it might seem *prima facie* – as the traditional wisdom has it – that such is all the more likely to be the case in the Gaelic and gaelicised lordships, traditionally the 'land of disobedience', which continued to retain more or less jurisdictional autonomy until, with the surrender of the Ulster rebels in 1603, the Tudor conquest was at last completed. Looked at in another light, however, the extension of the Reformation to the Gaelic and gaelicised lordships has seemed to provide the Canny thesis with a particularly strong *prima facie* claim to consideration. The argument is that, granted, as is supposed, the cultural backwardness of the 'Celtic fringe', the failure of the inhabitants of the 'land of disobedience' to conform to the religion 'by law established' must represent nothing more than a continuing adherence to 'traditional religion', replete in this instance, with a sub-stratum of Celtic paganism. That line of thought has received wide currency in

[30] *Ibid.*, 15. For general corroboration of this point see Colm Lennon, *Sixteenth-Century Ireland* (Dublin, 1994), 320–2.

the form of an ingenious revisionist thesis concerning the impact of the religious struggle on relations between the island's two historic communities. Contrary to the conventional wisdom it claims that the effect of introducing the Reformation to Ireland was not to erode racial animosities and to conduce to the fusion of the two communities by reason of their common experience as persecuted Catholics. The effect was rather to deepen the cultural chasm between them. This was because the old colonial community took the impress of the Counter Reformation whereas the Gaelic natives remained hidebound by religious traditionalism. That circumstance serves to explain, so the argument runs, why the medieval colonists came to adopt the designation Old English in the opening decades of the seventeenth century: it signified their Christian civility over against the unregenerate barbarity of the Irish.[31] *Prima facie* it must be agreed that such an argument seems no less plausible than the account purveyed by the received orthodoxy. Suffice it to comment at this introductory stage, therefore, that it behoves the post-revisionist historian to pay special attention to Canny's admonition against taking for granted what requires to be demonstrated.

That having been said, the brunt of the exposition that follows is to indicate nevertheless that the documentary evidence traces a pattern with regard to the Gaelic community not dissimilar to that already observed in examining the response to the competing claims of the Reformation and the Counter Reformation within the colony. Thus, initially the auguries for the religion 'by law established' seemed relatively auspicious. Representatives of the crown were able to secure acquiescence on those occasions when they sought formal acknowledgement of the royal ecclesiastical supremacy from territorial lords and native bishops in the course of the last decade of the reign of Henry VIII.[32] Furthermore, the initial response to the mission of the Counter Reformation seemed, in contrast, decidedly inauspicious. The two Jesuits sent to assess the situation in 1542 were dismayed by the religious state of the people and, even more, by the cool reception they were accorded by the Ulster lords whose territories they visited, most especially by the aloofness of the two greatest Ulster magnates, Conn O'Neill and Manus O'Donnell. They abandoned the mission within five weeks of arrival, convinced that Ireland was a lost cause in the church's struggle against the Reformation.[33] Here, again, however, the mid-

[31] Aidan Clarke, 'Colonial identity', in T. W. Moody (ed.), *Nationality and National Consciousness* (Belfast, 1982), 57–72.
[32] Bradshaw, *Constitutional Revolution*, 158–9, 245–51.
[33] F. R. Jones, 'The Counter-Reformation', in P. Corish (ed.), *A History of Irish Catholicism*, iii, fasc. 3 (Dublin, 1967), 5. Bradshaw, *Constitutional Revolution*, 247–8.

Tudor crisis seems to mark something of a turning point. At all events, coinciding with the militant stance of Pius V, 1565–72, and more especially with the excommunication of Elizabeth I in 1570, the Counter Reformation mission within the lordships can be seen to gain added momentum.

One manifestation of this to which agents of the crown in touch with the situation 'on the ground' drew repeated attention was a vibrant resurgence among the mendicant orders. In December 1572, for instance, Lord Deputy Sidney, commenting to Burghley on a report from Connacht remarked that it was 'no new thing to have friars gad up and down in Ireland'. The report conveyed news of information he had received from Connacht concerning a general council of friars held the previous autumn in Galway, of bands of friars from Ulster ranging through the countryside conducting missions, and of the recent return of the Dominican provincial from Rome with a papal indulgence which he published at Sligo.[34] In 1573 the friars were reported to have repossessed the abbey of Adare, the Fitzgerald stronghold some 10 miles west of Limerick city.[35] Then, the following year, a disturbing survey estimated the number of mendicant communities operating in Mayo as twenty-one, with eleven in Sligo, some twenty in Galway, at least four in Roscommon and one in Clare.[36] By 1583 the Franciscans were reported to have penetrated as far as their ancient site at Multy-farnham in Co. Westmeath, inside the borders of the Pale, where they had resumed secret occupation and 'begun their superstition afresh'.[37] This mendicant revival constitutes, therefore, a central feature of the Counter Reformation mission in Gaelic and gaelicised Ireland. The contribution of the friars was to supply the function provided by the Jesuits elsewhere as the spiral shock-troops of the movement.

A complementary feature of no less importance resulted from the adoption by the papacy of a policy of appointing to all vacancies in the Irish episcopate – whether as bishops or as vicars apostolic – and of providing also to parochial benfices wherever feasible. This policy, pursued systematically from 1567 onwards, had two important consequences. The first was the remarkable phenomenon of an alternative diocesan system functioning under papal jurisdiction over against that of the church 'by law established'. The second was to leaven the papally appointed local diocesan clergy with a steady succession of continentally

---

[34] The report is reproduced in Myles Ronan, *The Reformation under Elizabeth* (London, 1930), pp. 420–1. The mission of the friars is generally surveyed in Patrick Corish, *The Irish Catholic Experience* (Dublin, 1985), 74–6.
[35] Edwards, *Church and State*, 243.   [36] *Ibid.*
[37] *Cal. State Papers, Ire.*, ii, 469 (78).

trained, zealous Counter Reformation activists.[38] Among the latter are listed, to single out a handful of special eminence by way of example: David Wolf, the Limerick Jesuit, appointed papal nuncio as early as 1560 with eleven years experience of the continental mission behind him;[39] his fellow citizen, Richard Creagh, a former merchant who trained for the priesthood at Louvain and, having attracted the favourable attention of Ignatius Loyola, returned to his native city in the reign of Mary to promote the Counter Reformation there before being appointed to the primatial see of Armagh in 1564;[40] the Cistercian abbot, Maurice MacGibbon, described as the prototype of the militant Irish Counter Reformation cleric – contriving to advance the cause with the catechism in one hand and the sword in the other – who was appointed metropolitan of Cashel in 1567;[41] Edmund Tanner, by contrast with Mac-Gibbon, in the Borromean mould of the *pastor bonus* – imprisoned by the Reformation bishop of Waterford he preceeded to reconvert him to Catholicism – who returned to Ireland as bishop of Cork and Cloyne in 1572 after a lengthy continental sojourn;[42] Dermot O'Hurley, in the same mould, one of the earliest and saintliest of the Irish martyrs, who succeeded MacGibbon as metropolitan of Cashel in 1581;[43] finally, two militant crusaders of the 1590s, Edmund MacGauran who succeeded to Armagh in 1590 and proceeded to organise the confederacy which initiated the Nine Years War against the crown from 1593 onwards;[44] and the Old English Jesuit, James Archer, who acted as personal adviser to the arch-conspirator, Hugh O'Neill, over the same period.[45]

[38] The point is elaborated in Jones, 'Counter-Reformation', 4–5, 10–11, 18, 36, 38–41; see also Jones, 'The Irish Mission', *Irish Theological Quarterly*, 20 (1953), 152–71. Edwards, *Church and State*, 101–9.

[39] The most detailed account of Wolfe's career is contained in John Begley, *Diocese of Limerick* (London, 1927), ii, passim. A useful vignette is provided in Herbert, *Worthies of Thomond*, 3rd ser., 54–6. Also *DNB*, q.v. and Jones, 'Counter-Reformation', 8–13. Cf. Bradshaw, 'Fr Wolfe's description of Limerick', *North Munster Antiquarian Journal*, 17 (1975), 47–53.

[40] *DNB*, q.v. and Bradshaw, 'Reformation in the cities', in Bradley (ed.), *Settlement and Society*, 445–76 at 468–71.

[41] Jones, 'Counter-Reformation', 13–16, 18, 20–1. A detailed account of MacGibbon's mission to Philip II seeking military assistance for rebellion in Ireland is provided in D. A. Binchy, 'An Irish ambassador at the court of Philip II', *Studies*, 10 (1921), 353–74, 573–84, 11 (1922), 199–214, 12 (1923), 83–105, 461–80, 13 (1924), 115–28, 14 (1925), 102–15.

[42] On Tanner see Ronan, *Reformation under Elizabeth*, 540–7.

[43] On O'Hurley see Edwards, *Church and State*, pp. 268–70. Colm Lennon, 'The Counter Reformation in Ireland', in C. Brady and H. Gillespie (eds.), *Natives and Newcomers*, 85–6.

[44] Jones, 'Counter-Reformation', 41–5; J. J. Silke, 'The Irish appeal of 1593 to Spain', *Irish Ecclesiastical Record*, 5th ser., 12 (1959), 279–90, 326–71.

[45] Archer remains a shadowy figure but see Jones, 'Counter-Reformation', 18, 38, 47, 50.

Even a cursory review of the evidence such as the foregoing, therefore, serves to convey something of the sustained dynamism with which the Counter Reformation mission was pursued within the Gaelic and gaelicised lordships throughout the greater part of the reign of Elizabeth. However, the relevant issue so far as present considerations are concerned is not the mission as such, of course, but the response it elicited. Here, first, it must be acknowledged, on the testimony of the missionaries themselves, that in pastoral terms their ministrations seem to have enjoyed no greater success – perhaps even less – than the efforts of protestant evangelists to advance the Reformation in the colony. In that regard a survey compiled by Edmund Tanner in 1571 – from exile but drawing on information received from 'grave men' with first-hand knowledge – may serve by way of illustration. This strikes a note of gloom which was to resound in similar surveys by Counter Reformation missionaries for the rest of the century and which was anticipated, in fact, in what constitutes the prototype of the *genre* drawn up a decade earlier in 1560; a note it should be added, significantly in tune with the lamentations of protestant evangelists concerning the state of religion in the colonial territory.[46] Briefly, Tanner's survey may be summarised in terms of two categories of problems. One concerned the laity, in particular the ignorance and superstition that characterised their practice of religion. Few, he complained, were capable of reciting the Lord's Prayer, the Creed or the Ten Commandments, and fewer still showed any understanding of them. The frequentation of the sacraments was similarly marked by ignorance and superstition: people did not seem to have any clear idea whether these were the work of God or the invention of men. Underlying this lamentable situation was the abysmal quality of the parish clergy. Lacking pastoral zeal, they seldom preached and neglected the administration of the sacraments, leaving their flocks uninstructed and unregenerate. In view of such testimony it has proved all too easy for revisionists to confuse themselves and the historiography by dismissing the impact of the Counter Reformation mission out of the mouths of its very protagonists. The source of their confusion, to return to a central thesis of this study, lies in the failure to distinguish between religion as 'practice', as discipline or observance, and religion as 'ideology', as creed or confession. It may well be the case, so far as the reform of ingrained habits and social customs is concerned, that the Counter Reformation missionaries achieved as little in the lordships as protestant evangelists in the colony. Be that as it may, what cannot be

---

[46] Tanner's report is fully calendared in *Cal. S.P. Rome*, i, 467 ff. For the earlier report of 1560 see Jones, 'Counter-Reformation', 35–6.

doubted is that in confessional terms the religious struggle elicited a response no less decisive from the one community as from the other.

Turning briefly to review the evidence, an instructive starting point is provided by Edmund Tanner's survey. It takes the form of a reassurance offered by his 'grave informants' to the effect that despite the abounding ignorance and superstition not a hundred heretical Irishmen were to be found throughout the island.[47] Such heartening optimism is illuminating insofar as it draws attention to a distinctive feature of Counter Reformation surveys of the Elizabethan period generally. These are found to share the same confidence, in significant contrast, on the one hand, to the despairing conclusion of the Jesuit missionaries who visited Ireland in the 1540s, and, on the other, to the general despondency of protestant evangelists who – incidentally endorsing the assessment of their antagonists – perceived themselves as contending with a people immersed in popery. The question that arises, then, is the implications of these contrasting perceptions of the response to the Reformation within the lordships. The answer, it seems reasonable to suggest, is that they point to a shift in attitude on the part of the inhabitants whereby, following an initial period of openness or prevarication, they came to identify themselves as adherents of the pope, and of the Catholic Church over which he presided as supreme pastor, over against the Church of the Reformation and its royal ecclesiastical governor.

This reading is confirmed by reference to evidence which reflects attitudes within the lordships more directly. An instance is provided by the response of the dynastic lords to the fundamental ideological tenet of the English Reformation, the royal supremacy. In line with the response of the Old English socio-political elite, as we have seen, no difficulty apparently was encountered in securing formal acknowledgement of the royal title in indentures concluded with the dynastic rulers in the course of the Henrician Reformation. In the Elizabethan period, however, the relevant clause was tacitly omitted in negotiating such formal agreements. Most strikingly, crown representatives forbore to press the matter in negotiating terms of submission with rebellious lords in the concluding stages of the Nine Years War, 1594–1603, when the débâcle of Kinsale had supposedly left the rebels prostrate; instead all that was demanded was a vague and ambiguous acknowledgement of the queen as 'only sovereign under God' to the exclusion of 'any other power or potentate'.[48] Here again, therefore, the evidence presents a contrast which points towards an underlying shift in attitude within the lordships. It suggests, in short, that the claim to a royal ecclesiastical

[47] *Cal. S.P. Rome*, i, 468.   [48] Edwards, *Church and State*, p. 291.

supremacy came to constitute as sensitive an issue for the Gaelic and gaelicised dynastic lords in the reign of Elizabeth I as for the socio-political elite within the colony.

Further testimony to the same effect is provided by literary evidence which, complementing the evidence already considered, serve   ill-minate the changing religious ethos of the lordships   This is presented by the corpus of bardic poetry. In i   .d it sh... first of all be acknowledged that puzzlingly, or so it   seemed, the religious struggle has left relatively little discernible impact on the sixteenth-century bardic corpus. So little for the reign of Henry VIII, indeed, that research so far has turned up only one reference, and that in a poem which is, in any case, unusual. Here the anonymou poet, departing from the conventional eulogistic mode, castigates a whole catena of dynastic lords for collaborating with the conciliatory programme of 'surrender and regrant' inaugurated by Lord Deputy Sir Anthony St Leger: the relevant reference occurs by way of a peroration which reproaches the collaborators for having 'forsaken the son of Mary'.[49] Such paucity of evidence need cause little puzzlement, in fact, bearing in mind the special character of the bardic *genre*. Professional, functional, conventional, rigidly formal, bardic poetry was not in the least accommodating to changing circumstances or sensibilities. In that light the contrast provided by the Elizabethan corpus emerges. This hinges on the content rather than the quantity of the evidence. As against the perfunctory reference surviving from the Henrician period a cluster of poems dating from the late 1560s onwards are found to register a response to the Elizabethan Settlement in quite specific and ideologically informed terms. New motifs now make their appearance which were to become staples of the seventeenth-century *genre*: the mass is affirmed as well as the cults of the Blessed Virgin and the saints; the Catholic priesthood is extolled together with the religious orders; conversely the 'battalions of Luther and Calvin' are excoriated, and, corresponding with Lyon's mortifying experience in Cork, the rites of the Prayer Book and its ministers are demonised.[50] Here, then, is

---

[49] For text and commentary see Brian Ó Cuív (ed.), 'A sixteenth century political poem', *Éigse*, 15 (1973–4), 261–76.

[50] I am indebted here to Marc Caball's D.Phil., 'A study of intellectual reaction and continuity in Irish bardic poetry composed during the reigns of Elizabeth I and James I' (Oxford, 1991). Our analyses of the implications of the corpus as evidence for a 'mental shift' differ in emphasis but not, I believe, in substance. Caball's thesis is succinctly reformulated below, pp. 112–13, see also Brian Ó Cuív, 'The Irish language in the early modern period', in T. W. Moody *et al.* (eds.), *New History of Ireland*, iii (Oxford, 1976), 509–45, esp. 520–8. A contrary interpretation is presented in two recent studies which argue that the poets failed to perceive the radical transformation of their world until the medieval Gaelic order had been virtually destroyed with the

brought into view the initial stages of a process of literary innovation that was to culminate in the Baroque renaissance – if it may be so called – of the native literature in the seventeenth century. Here, also, by the same token – which is the relevant consideration for present purposes – is brought into view a confessional consciousness in process of formation within the lordships. And that ethos, in turn, provides the context in which the sensitivity of the dynastic lords to the central ideological assertion to the English Reformation assumes its full significance, apropos of which, it should be added to complete the contrast with the Henrician evidence and to highlight its implications, the reproach of the dynastic lords for religious apostasy fails to recur in the Elizabeth poetry – the implication being that such apostasy now rarely occurred. Instead poetic obloquy is directed against those few native clerics who, as it is perceived, betrayed the faith for the sake of ecclesiastical preferment.

III

The final evidence to be cited in support of the thesis argued here in respect of both the colonial and the native communities derives from the history of rebellion over the period. Here again a shift in attitude may be discerned as between the rebellions of the earlier and later sixteenth century. The contrast emerges in the first instance in relation to considerations of scale and frequency. It is, of course, the case that one of the most devastating conflagrations of the century dates from the reign of Henry VIII, coinciding, indeed, with the onset of the Henrician Reformation. This was the Kildare Rebellion, which convulsed the heartland of the colony, the Pale and adjacent districts in 1534–5. Nevertheless, the fact remains that the Kildare Rebellion stands as the solitary example of violent disruption on a large scale throughout the first six decades of the century – reckoning the débâcle of the Geraldine-Gaelic League, 1539–40, as its final whimper.[51] By contrast, the mid-

completion of the conquest in the mid seventeenth century. Tom Dunne, 'The Gaelic response to conquest and colonisation: the evidence of the poetry', *Studia Hibernica*, 20 (1980), 7–30. Michelle O'Riordan, *The Gaelic Mind and the Collapse of the Gaelic Order* (Cork, 1990). The argument of the latter has been subjected to penetrating criticism and seriously undermined in Breandán Ó Buachalla, 'Poetry and politics in early modern Ireland', *Eighteenth Century Ireland*, 7 (1992), 149–75 and Marc Caball, '*The Gaelic Mind and the Collapse of the Gaelic Order*: an appraisal', *Cambridge Medieval Celtic Studies*, 25 (1993), 87–96. Cf. Bradshaw, 'The bardic response to conquest and colonisation', *Bullán: an Irish Studies Journal*, 1 (1994), 119–22. For further discussion of the evidence see Bradshaw below pp. 105–9 and Caball below, pp. 112–39 *passim*.

[51] For recent and varying interpretations of the Kildare Rebellion see Bradshaw, 'Reform and the Kildare Rebellion', *Transactions of the Royal Historical Society*, 5th ser., 27 (1977), 69–93; Steven Ellis, 'The Kildare Rebellion and early Henrician reform', *Historical Journal*, 19 (1976); Ellis, 'Henry VIII, rebellion and the rule of law', *Historical*

Tudor crisis, inverting the pattern elsewhere in the Tudor dominions, led on in Ireland to a period of ever intensifying and protracted militant protest. And, once more, the *terminus a quo* is found to date from the late 1560s. The phase was ushered in by the episode in 1569–70 which brought the swashbuckling scion of the Munster branch of the Fitzgeralds, James Fitzmaurice Fitzgerald, to prominence in the arena of national politics: the spate of interconnected dynastic rebellions which swept through the south and west, from the Butler territories in south Leinster, through the extensive area of Munster under Fitzgerald hegemony, to the lordship of the fully gaelicised Clanrickard Burkes in Lower Connacht.[52] Worse was to follow. Ten years later the return of Fitzmaurice from continental exile at the head of a small force of mercenaries provided the spark for a rebellion led by the Fitzgerald earl himself which convulsed the entire south west. Rebellion smouldered on in Munster until the assassination of Earl Gerald in 1584 by which time the crown's scorched-earth strategy of suppression had reduced the province to a state of utter devastation and famine.[53] Meanwhile rebellion had ramified into the O'Byrne territories in Leinster, and into the Pale itself under the leadership of the idealistic Viscount Baltinglass.[54] Finally, mounting tension in Ulster erupted in the last decade of the century in what was to become the Nine Years War, 1594–1603, which engulfed the whole of the island and, as it turned out, provided the final ghastly episode of the Tudor Conquest.[55]

The relevance for present concerns of the contrast this provides with the history of rebellion elsewhere in the Tudor dominions lies not in the escalation of rebellion as such but in the transformation of religious

---

Journal, 24 (1981); Lawrence McCorrisdine, *The Revolt of Silken Thomas* (Dublin, 1987), passim.

[52] Nicholas Canny, *The Elizabethan Conquest of Ireland* (Hassocks, 1976), 137–53; Edwards, 'Butler revolt', *Irish Historical Studies*, 28 (1993), 228–55. For general surveys see Ellis, *Tudor Ireland*, 256–70, and Lennon, *Sixteenth-Century Ireland*, 210–16.

[53] The background and course of the Munster Rebellion and the revolts in Leinster are surveyed in Ellis, *Tudor Ireland* (London, 1992), 270–4, 278–84, and Lennon, *Sixteenth-Century Ireland*, 216–28. Both accounts are deeply indebted to Ciaran Brady, 'Faction and the origins of the Desmond Rebellion in 1579', *Irish Historical Studies*, 22 (1981).

[54] Ellis, *Tudor Ireland*, provides a succinct summary of earlier more detailed accounts of this phase of the Rebellion on pp. 281–2. See also Bradshaw, 'Native reaction to the Westward Enterprise', in K. R. Andrews *et al.* (eds.), *The Westward Enterprise* (Liverpool, 1978) and Bradshaw, *Irish Constitutional Revolution*, 285–8.

[55] The background and origins of this, the greatest and most prolonged challenge in arms offered to the Tudor regime anywhere in its dominions, have attracted the monograph they deserve in Hiram Morgan, *Tyrone's Rebellion: the outbreak of the Nine Years War in Tudor Ulster* (London and Dublin, 1993). The episode is surveyed, availing of Morgan's close research and insights, in Lennon, *Sixteenth-Century Ireland*, ch. 10; Ellis's earlier survey remains useful, *Tudor Ireland*, 297–312.

perceptions and values which it illuminates. The significant feature in
that regard is the way rebellion came to take the impress of the
continental Wars of Religion. For purposes of demonstration the
Kildare Rebellion again provides an instructive starting point in that by
seeming to challenge the thesis, it serves to prove it. The claim made for
the revolt led by the Kildare heir, Silken Thomas, in 1534–5, to
constitute the 'first of the Wars of Religion in Ireland' is not altogether
without foundation. Its leader, under the tutelage of his chaplain, Dr
John Travers, and with an eye to continental support, asserted that
loyalty to the pope against the 'heretical pretensions' of Henry VIII was
a principal motivation of the rebellion.[56] In similar vein, Manus
O'Donnell, seeking to rekindle the flame in 1537 by means of the
Geraldine-Gaelic League is found, in a letter to Pope Paul III, protesting
his abhorrence that 'the king had taken on him the whole power of the
pope'.[57] Nevertheless, as even historians in the Catholic nationalist
tradition agree, the Reformation was not central to the concerns of the
rebels at this stage.[58] Their perception of the conflict was dominated by
the exigencies of late medieval dynastic politics. The issue as it impinged
upon their consciousness was the breach of good lordship involved in
the transference of crown government in Ireland, and with it crown
patronage, from the Kildare earl and his clientship network to a lobby of
Cromwellian political reformers; a breach made all the harder to suffer
by the affront to the colonists' chauvinistic susceptibilities it entailed, in
that the beneficiaries included a substantial element of New English
intruders.[59] On the crown's side, no doubt, the perception was novel
and 'modern' – disastrously so for the 'overmighty' Kildare magnate
and his dynastic faction. Yet here also the political element remained
dominant. The issue was the high notion of sovereignty implied by the
recent assertion of the crown's claim to an 'imperial monarchy', in
virtue of which subjects of whatever rank were required to yield
unconditional obedience.[60] As to the episode of the Geraldine-Gaelic
League, suffice it to point out that it was the fomenters of the alliance,
the resourceful Manus O'Donnell and Conn O'Neill, whose aloofness
so discomfited the Jesuit missionaries in 1542: the erstwhile rebels were
by then deeply immersed in negotiating terms of 'surrender and regrant'

[56] Edwards, *Church and State*, 3–5; Lennon, *Sixteenth-Century Ireland*, 107–8, 150–1.
[57] *Letters and Papers, Henry VIII*, xvi, no. 339; Bradshaw, *The Dissolution of the Religious
Orders in Ireland* (Cambridge, 1974), 210–11.
[58] E.g. Patrick Corish 'Origins of Catholic nationalism' in Corish (ed.), *A History of Irish
Catholicism*, iii, fasc. 4 (Dublin, 1968), 6.
[59] Bradshaw, 'Cromwellian reform and the origins of the Kildare Rebellion', *Transactions
of the Royal Historical Society*, 5th ser., 27 (1977).
[60] See also below, pp. 87–8.

with Sir Anthony St Leger, earning by their *volte face* a prominent place in the catena of dynastic lords castigated by the anonymous Gaelic poet for having 'forsaken the son of Mary'.[61]

Turning to review the history of rebellion in the reign of Elizabeth, the shift in the stance adopted by both communities is striking. The difference is that for the Gaelic natives and medieval colonist alike, whatever the political issues involved, rebellion now became suffused with the perceptions, the values and the rhetoric of the European Wars of Religion. To begin at the beginning, with the spate of dynastic revolts in 1569–70, the shift is well illustrated in a letter by James Fitzmaurice Fitzgerald to the citizens of Cork. The novel feature, in line with the contrast noted in the poetry, is the range of confessionally resonant language to which Fitzmaurice has recourse by comparison with the perfunctory allusions of Silken Thomas and Manus O'Donnell. Thus, he demanded the expulsion of all protestants, 'especially them that be Hugenots', from the city, and, by way of justification, urged the loyal citizens to consider how the queen, 'not satisfied with our worldly goods, bellies and lives' sought also 'to council us to forsake the Catholic faith by God unto His Church given, and by the See of Rome hitherto prescribed to all Christian men'.[62] The same militant Catholicism finds more developed expression in a letter written by Archbishop Mac-Gibbon to Philip II on behalf of the rebel leaders. Here, perhaps for the first time, the theme of 'faith and fatherland' is deployed in an elaborated form as the ideology of rebellion in Ireland. The letter begins by explaining how 'the nobles and people of this realm one and all wish to follow in their fathers' footsteps ... in the faith and unity of the Catholic Church as also to persevere even to their last breath in their immemorial obedience to the Roman Pontiffs and the Apostolic See'. Then, proceeding to demonstrate their fidelity by reference to recent history, MacGibbon adumbrates a complementary notion that was to feature henceforth as a major trope of the ideology: the steadfastness of the Irish in the faith in contrast to 'the errors and fickleness of the English who, during the recent schism under King Henry VIII and King Edward VI, robbed and plundered the churches and monasteries [and] proscribed and persecuted the bishops and religious'.[63] Finally, on that basis, MacGibbon solicited aid for the rebels. Here also his letter is seen

---

[61] Bradshaw, *Irish Constitutional Revolution*, 220–1, 245–57; Edwards, *Church and State*, 117–18; Ó Cuív, 'Irish language'.

[62] See e.g. *Cal. Carew MSS* i, no. 267 ('Declaration of James Fitzmaurice Fitzgerald'). For examples of letters written by Fitzmaurice at this time which articulate an incipient 'faith and fatherland' patriotism see Caball, below, pp. 133–4.

[63] The relevant section of the letter is reproduced in translation in Jones, 'Counter Reformation', 15–16.

to be ideologically innovative in that it formulates an aspiration that was to engage – and elude – successive generations of rebels in Ireland down to the eighteenth century: the aspiration, as it has been succinctly expressed, to 'a national confederation ... bound together by loyalty to the faith ... in the approval and encouragement of the Pope, and lastly in military assistance from the Catholic powers on the continent'.[64] In short, as these letters illustrate, and as the historiography generally agrees, the episode of 1569–70 provides the first example of rebellion in Ireland taking the mould of a struggle in arms on behalf of Roman Catholicism.[65] The implication to be drawn from such a development, should be emphasised, is not that religion now constituted the *fons et origo* of rebellion, or even, indeed, that it provided its sole ideological dynamic. Rather the suggestion is that the rhetoric of Fitzmaurice and MacGibbon reflects the emergence of a confessional consciousness within the lordships generally, not just among a small elite of rebel leaders. The argument is that the deployment of confessional rhetoric by the rebel leaders points towards the concurrent development of a collective confessional mentality without which it would lack emotive resonance.

That such a mentality was, in fact, taking increasing hold within both the colonial and native lordships becomes abundantly clear from a consideration of the two remaining conflagrations of the century. In the case of the first, vivid testimony is provided by the response from the side of government to the crisis. The significant feature here is the conviction borne in upon royal agents in a good position to judge that the spate of uprisings sparked off by the return of Fitzmaurice with his motley force of papal mercenaries in 1579 represented a radical departure from the traditional pattern of rebellion in Ireland. The case is graphically presented in a report on the situation sent to the earl of Leicester in August 1580. The author, Sir Nicholas Malby, a military captain and member of the Irish Council with long experience of conditions in Munster and Connacht, was concerned to show that the 'quarrel upon religion' was fast threatening to 'dismember' the realm.[66] His point was that religion worked to divide the kingdom against itself, by lending cohesion to the forces of opposition. In particular its

---

[64] *Ibid.*, 17.

[65] The sincerity of Fitzmaurice's religious commitment is not doubted whatever other considerations may be held to have motivated his actions, Ellis, *Tudor Ireland*, 259–60, Lennon, *Sixteenth-Century Ireland*, 213–14. For a study that sets the activity of Fitzmaurice in the context of factional politics see C. Brady, 'Faction and the origins of the Desmond Rebellion of 1579', *Irish Historical Studies*, 22 (1981), 289–312.

[66] *Cal. Car. MSS*, ii, no. 476. For general surveys of the episode see Ellis, *Tudor Ireland*, 278–84 and Lennon, *Sixteenth-Century Ireland*, 221–8.

influence in that respect was to transform the very character and menace of rebellion. Its transforming impact was twofold. First it operated to alter the structure of such militant protest. In keeping with the political culture of dynasticism the traditional pattern had been kin-based and localised, 'risen upon private quarrels'. Now, however, such disjointed dynastic uprisings were being subsumed under the frame of a general war of religion, 'they having converted all their private quarrels to a general matter of religion'. The second development provided a corollary to the first. It concerned the attitude of those normally well-disposed members of the Gaelic and gaelicised socio-political elite on whom the crown traditionally relied to contain recalcitrance within the lordships. These, here again mirroring the situation in the colonial territory, were now withholding cooperation in all that pertained to the religious issue, thereby severely circumscribing the capacity of the government to deal with rebellion conducted in the name of Catholicism: 'the best', Malby declared, 'cannot be made to do anything against the rebellious papists'. As the metaphor of modern revolution theory would have it, religious solidarity provided a 'pool' for the rebels to 'swim in'. Malby then went on finally to point up the urgency of the crisis by drawing Leicester's attention to a series of incidents which in his interpretation took on a deeply sinister significance. Malcontented members of the Butler kindred had gone off with their followers to swell the rebel forces of Lord Baltinglass in the Pale while others had 'gone on their keeping' in the mountains of Lower Connacht where they had made contact with disaffected kinsmen of the earl of Clanrickard. Meanwhile the problem of 'enemies within the gates' had manifested itself in the form of wholesale desertion from the forces of the crown to the rebels: Garret Jones who had been 'entertained for the defence of the Pale and to serve Her Majesty with 50 shot' had 'gone over to the said traitor [Baltinglass]', and, to add salt to the wound, 'he and his company did most to annoy us on the day of the encounter'; indeed 'most of the Fowlers in the English Pale, being men trained amongst us [were] now with the rebels'.[67]

This interpretation of the crisis, as subsequent reports to London show, reflects a perception of the interplay between religious dissent and the politics of violence that was soon to establish itself within government circles generally. Later reports, however, sometimes add a modification which needs to be noted for the purposes of the present discussion. This may be illustrated by reference to a joint report to Walsingham fifteen months later by the acting heads of the administra-

---

[67] *Cal. Carew MSS*, ii, no. 476.

tion, Archbishop Loftus, now lord chancellor, and the vice-treasurer, Sir Henry Wallop. Following the lines of Malby's communiqué these described how religion had served to give cohesion to a series of disparate dynastic uprisings: 'we conceive the same first took beginning from part of the nobility in Connaught and Munster ... than brake out Baltinglass into action in July who drew after him Feagh McHugh, the O'Birnes and O'Toole ... and so the stirs grew and since continued'.[68] The added modification reflects their concern to forestall reproof from London for recklessly provoking the crisis by immoderate enforcement of the religious policy. They insisted accordingly that at the time of the outbreak of rebellion 'neither Desmond nor Clanrickard, nor any other in Ulster, Munster or Cannaught [were] restrained in any Religion, but had free use of all papistry and maintenance of the friars and friars' houses'. Rather, a variety of grievances, stemming from the encroachment of the crown's policy of political reform on material interests had provided the spark for rebellion in each case: in Munster and Connacht the appointment of provincial presidents and, in particular, restraint on the maintenance of 'idle men' by coin and livery; in the case of Desmond, personal ambition and the investigation of the liberties of Kerry; in the Pale, the reimposition of cess – a military subvention – by 'composition'. Religion, therefore, they insisted, provided no more than the 'colour' for rebellion: a cover under which, in Malby's words, 'private quarrels' could be 'converted' into a 'general matter', and which provided a justification for violent protest well calculated to win sympathy.[69] This Machiavellian, not to say proto-Marxian, gloss on Malby's analysis needs to be borne in mind, therefore, in reaching a conclusion concerning the implications of the rebellions of the 1580s for the question of the development of confessionalism in the Elizabethan period. In that connection the point made earlier concerning the significance of the rhetoric deployed by the rebels of 1569–70 bears repetition. That is to say, the relevant consideration relates not to the origins but to the ideology of rebellion. The point is that the possibility of subsuming local dynastic quarrels under the frame of a Catholic religious crusade presupposes the existence in the lordships of a collective mental environment attuned to the perceptions and values of the Counter Reformation.

The case is clinched by reference to the final rebellion of the Tudor period. That cataclysmic turning point in the course of Irish history is, of course, variously interpreted: by romantic nationalists as a struggle for national liberation; by liberals in the Whig tradition as the death

---

[68] Brady (ed.), *State Papers Concerning the Irish Church*, no. LXIII.   [69] *Ibid.*

spasm of a barbaric Celtic civilisation succumbing to modernity in the form of the Renaissance and Reformation; by hard-nosed revisionists as a power struggle between a consolidating sovereign monarchy and quasi-autonomous local dynasts.[70] Whatever the value of any or all of these interpretative models, to deny that from start to last the rebellion assumed the aspect of a war of religion would be to fly in the face of the evidence. Thus it can rightly be claimed that the architect of the rebellion was neither one of the disaffected Northern dynasts, O'Rourke, Maguire or O'Donnell, nor all three in combination, nor, for that matter, the *politique* Hugh O'Neill, manipulating the hot-heads. It was rather the militant Counter Reformation churchman Edmund MacGauran. It was he who in 1592, as primate and archbishop of Armagh, after a two-year mission to Spain seeking assistance for a war on behalf of religion in Ireland, convened the council of bishops in Ulster which led to the commitment of the disaffected northern dynasts to a 'struggle for the defence of the Catholic faith'.[71] Thus, also, from the outset, the rebel leaders and their clerical promoters sought to win support for their cause, at home and abroad, by appeal to the ideology of 'faith and fatherland': their platform was neatly summarised by Peter Lombard for the benefit of Pope Clement VIII as 'the vindication of the Catholic religion, the glory of God, the liberty of their country and their own security.[72] Then, in turn, the confessional ideology espoused by the rebels found practical expression in the form of a demand for 'liberty of conscience' which featured at the head of their agenda when, from 1596 onwards, they entered negotiations with the crown with a view to exploring the terms of a settlement.[73] Finally, as the rebellion continued, it came increasingly to be acknowledged by the Catholic protagonists of the European religious struggle as a crusade on behalf of the *fides Catholica*. In that regard a major breakthrough on the diplomatic front was the appointment early in 1600 of Lombard – the well respected Old English theologian and Louvain professor – as a 'virtual Irish

---

[70] For the romantic nationalist version see John Mitchel, *The Life and Times of Aodh O'Neill* (Dublin, 1845), passim; for the Whig clash of civilisation version, David Mathew, *The Celtic Peoples and Renaissance Europe* (London, 1933). The thrust of Ellis's account is quietly but firmly revisionist, *Tudor Ireland*, 297–312.

[71] J. J. Silke, 'The Irish Appeal of 1593 to Spain: some light on the genesis of the Nine Years War', *Irish Ecclesiastical Record*, 5th ser., 22 (1959), 278–90, 362–71. Cf. Jones, 'Counter-Reformation', 41–5 and Hiram Morgan, *Tyrone's Rebellion*, 139–43.

[72] Quoted in Jones, 'Counter-Reformation', 48. For a path-breaking post-revisionist interpretation along these lines see Hiram Morgan, 'Hugh O'Neill and the Nine Years War in Tudor Ireland', *Historical Journal*, 37 (1993), 21–37.

[73] Morgan, 'Hugh O'Neill', 24.

ambassador' on the rebels' behalf at the Vatican.[74] The immediate fruit was a papal bull issued the following April in which Clement VIII, against the grain of his own 'peaceful co-existence' diplomacy, formally and publicly acknowledged the rebellion as part of an ongoing war waged by the Catholics of Ireland, first under James Fitzmaurice, then under his cousin, John Fitzgerald, 'to throw off the yoke of slavery imposed on you by the English, deserters from the Holy Roman Church'. Accordingly he granted the crusading indulgence to all who now continued the battle 'under our beloved son, Hugh O'Neale ... captain general of the Catholic army in Ireland'.[75] By that time also five years of intensive diplomatic activity between the rebels and the sword-arm of the Counter Reformation himself, Philip II, was about to culminate – disastrously in the event – in the dispatch of a substantial Spanish force to Ireland, thus establishing the island, in the manner of France and the Netherlands, as a major theatre of the international power struggle waged between Catholic Spain and protestant England.

In drawing out the implications of all of this for the question at issue, the pertinent consideration, to insist yet again, is not whether religion served, solely or in combination, to generate the conflict. It is rather that whatever considerations of rational self-interest may have provided the spark, the Nine Years War was fuelled ideologically from first to last by appeal to the values and perceptions of Counter Reformation Catholicism. And the significance of that consideration is that it illuminates in turn the confessional susceptibilities of the inhabitants of the lordships generally. For without the existence of a collective religious mentality the ideology of faith and fatherland to which the rebels appealed would have failed to provide the catalyst necessary to transform localised, dynastic disaffection into a coherent nationwide movement.

Finally, some corroborating testimony from an inverted perspective may be cited. It concerns the episode when, as the rebellion neared its climax, O'Neill, on campaign in the south, sought to draw the few dynasts loyal to the regime in Munster to the side of the rebels. Seeking the support of Lord Barry in West Cork, he urged him to bear in mind that the rebel confederacy was pledged to 'the maintenance of the Catholic religion ... as also [to] the expelling of our enemies from their continued treachery used towards this poor country'. Demurring, Lord Barry professed to be able to reconcile compliance and conscience in

---

[74] Jones, 'Counter-Reformation', 48. One consequence of Lombard's appointment was his elaboration of the first full-scale antiquarian treatise on Ireland written from a faith and fatherland perspective by way of briefing the pope and the curia, *De regno Hiberniae, sanctorum insula, commentarius*. It is succinctly summarised and analysed in Morgan, 'Hugh O'Neill', 30–1.

[75] *Cal. Carew MSS*, iii, 523 (*Cal. S.P. Ire.*, ix, 83).

virtue of the practical toleration accorded by crown government. Avowing the same confessional commitment as the rebels, he maintained, nevertheless, that the queen had never restrained him in matters of religion and he had never hesitated to succour poor Catholics, in the knowledge of her majesty's clemency and indifference in that regard.[76] Barry's response holds a double significance in the context of the concerns of this study. In relation to the immediate point at issue, it illustrates once more the pervasiveness of the collective confessional mentality by appeal to which the rebels justified and claimed nationwide support for their resistance to crown government. Implicitly, however, Barry's demurral also brings to attention the central aspiration of an alternative, *constitutional*, version of the 'faith and fatherland' ideology, one that was to engage – and elude – successive generations of constitutionalists in Ireland into the nineteenth century: the aspiration to secure by non-violent political action a constitutional arrangement whereby, on the one hand, all due obedience could be yielded to the *Ecclesia Catholica* and to its supreme pastor, *iure divino*, while, on the other hand, submitting in all things necessary to a civil regime which acknowledged the sovereignty, 'next under God', of a protestant monarch. Such for instance, to bring this section of the discussion full circle, was the attitude reflected in the 'revolt' of the towns of the south when, on news of the death of Elizabeth in 1603 the townspeople extruded the state clergy from their churches and reinstalled the outlawed Catholic clergy.[77]

IV

To sum up, then, the cumulative force of the evidence relating to the response to the Reformation within the Gaelic and colonial territories is irresistible. In both areas the mid-Tudor crisis marks a transition to a period in which the community came increasingly to resist the claims of the religion 'by law established' and to identify itself with the proscribed religion of popery. One significant feature here is the contrast between the new note of confidence struck by agents of the Counter Reformation in the Elizabethan period concerning the failure of the heretical Reformation creed to take root and the despairing tone of their antagonists. This assessment is corroborated by evidence which reflects attitudes more directly. Thus, the reluctance of *politique* crown governors in the reign of Elizabeth to implement the recusancy laws within the colony or

---

[76] *Cal. Carew MSS*, iii, nos. 345–9. For this exchange see Morgan, 'Hugh O'Neill', 33–4.
[77] This episode is described in detail in a series of reports to London extensively calendared in *Cal. S.P. Ire., 1603–6*, 32–57.

to press for formal acknowledgement of the royal ecclesiastical supremacy in concluding indentures of peace with the dynastic lords indicates a new sensitivity on the part of the political elites of the two communities to the central ideological tenet of the English Reformation. Further evidence of a new religious sensibility is provided in the corpus of native literature. From the late 1560s onwards a *genre* of baroque religious verse began to make its appearance – cultivated by native literati and Old English littérateurs alike – characterised by a range of polemical motifs, on the one hand proclaiming loyalty to the pope, to the Catholic clergy and to the liturgy and the devotional cults of Counter Reformation Catholicism, while on the other hand excoriating the heresiarchs Luther and Calvin, and demonising the liturgy of the Prayer Book and its ministers.

The clinching evidence relates to the history of rebellion over the period. First, mirroring the growing alienation from the regime of the political elites of the island's two historic communities, the incidence of rebellion dramatically increased in Ireland as the century progressed whereas the reverse holds for the rest of the Tudor dominions. Second, beginning with the spate of revolts in the south and west in 1569–70 which brought James Fitzmaurice Fitzgerald to prominence, the character of rebellion in Ireland underwent a significance mutation. The traditional, localised and sporadic, protests in arms of disaffected dynastic kindreds were transformed not only in frequency, in scale and duration but most significantly in the range of issues to which the fomenters of rebellion appealed to justify and win support for them. Increasingly, by means of an appeal to the shared values of 'faith and fatherland', rebellion came to transcend the customary boundaries of locality, kin-alliance and ethnic identity, to assume the aspect of a national war of religion. Increasingly, in consequence, Ireland came to be regarded as another theatre of the struggle-in-arms being waged in France and the Netherlands between the forces of the Reformation and the Counter Reformation. The interest of this transformation for the subject in hand, as emphasised earlier, lies not in the knotty question of the function of religion as a motivating force for rebellion. It lies rather in the function of religion as an ideological catalyst, serving to provide a common cause, capable of transforming localised resistance into a movement of national dimensions. In short, the history of rebellion, taken in conjunction with the other evidence of resistance to the Reformation, testifies to an intellectual mutation within the two historic communities under the impact of the Counter Reformation mission whereby a cultural ethos was moulded highly responsive to the perceptions and values of the new patriotism now burgeoning throughout

Europe, and of Tridentine Catholicism. And the implication of that consideration, in turn, is that the revisionist characterisation of the religion of Ireland in this period as survivalism, as the mere persistence of traditional forms and modes within a deeply conservative, not to say hidebound, cultural *milieu*, is profoundly mistaken. On the contrary, the evidence indicates that, as in the Old English colony, so in the Gaelic and gaelicised lordships, whatever the state of religious observance, a religious consciousness had now taken hold within both communities that pivoted upon the confessional ideology of the Counter Reformation, as the religion of their *patria* and, as such, an essential dimension of their collective self-identity.

V

The effect of the foregoing analysis has been to reinstate the received orthodoxy, albeit in post-revisionist form, concerning the outcome of the confrontation between the Reformation and the Counter Reformation in sixteenth-century Ireland. Having done so, it is now possible to resume discussion of the struggle in its British context embarked on at the outset. For the effect of restoring the received orthodoxy is to restore to the agenda of sixteenth-century British history what constitutes probably its most problematic item, as well as the one most fraught with long-term significance, the triumph of the Counter Reformation over the Reformation in Ireland. The problematical aspect of such an outcome is highlighted by reference to the resolution of the conflict between the Reformation and the Counter Reformation in Europe generally. The effect was to produce a configuration of confessional states in accordance with the formula devised at the Treaty of Augsburg, *cuius regio eius religio*. True, in Ireland also, with the submission of the rebellious dynasts in 1603, the 'struggle in arms' was resolved in favour of the religion of the king, the English monarch and self-proclaimed supreme governor of the church throughout the English crown's dominions. However, at the same time, as we have seen, the 'struggle for hearts and minds' was resolved in favour of the proscribed religion of Roman Catholicism. Thus, set in the context of the confessional map of post-Reformation Europe, the kingdom of Ireland represents an anomalous paradox: a polity in which, in defiance of the contemporary norm – one faith, one law, one king – the vast majority of the subjects refused to conform to the faith of their king as by law established.[78]

However, the interpretative challenge here brings the shortcomings of

[78] Cameron, *European Reformation*. In the Dutch Netherlands and Scotland the community extruded Catholic sovereigns; in France Henry of Nevarre was obliged to conform

the received orthodoxy to attention in turn. Conventionally the challenge has been missed or too easily dismissed by appeal to Ireland's geographical location. The island's status as medieval Europe's *Ultima Thule* has been wielded as a kind of master key to explain, on the one hand, the resistance of the inhabitants to the state-sponsored religion and, on the other, the failure of government to secure religious conformity. Thus, ingrained conservatism, a traditionalist culture and insulation against innovatory forces operating elsewhere, all stemming from the island's remote location, supposedly account for the failure of the reformed religion to strike a responsive chord with either of the two historic Irish communities. Likewise the problem of control at such a remove from the centre of government is held to have rendered the law a blunt instrument of enforcement.[79] In exposing the superficiality of such an approach the British perspective provides an illuminating vantage point.

As noted in the introductory discussion, Welsh historians are agreed that by the end of the reign of Elizabeth – the protests of puritan evangelists concerning the persistence of superstitious observances notwithstanding – the English Reformation had secured widespread acceptance from the Welsh community and conversely the Counter Reformation had been discredited by association with traitors and the threat of foreign invasion.[80] The question arises therefore why if, in extending the 'religion by law established' to that Celtic borderland of the Tudor dominions, the difficulties imposed by the remoteness of the location, the conservative dispositions of the inhabitants, and the limitations of crown government on the periphery, did not present an insurmountable obstacle, they should have done so in the case of Ireland? Even allowing that such difficulties were magnified in the case of Ireland in virtue of its further remoteness and the sea in between, the consequential difficulties might have been expected merely to slow the progress of reform not to reverse the process altogether.[81] To pose the question in that form is to suggest the possibility of a solution. The answer, it suggests, may lie in a comparative analysis designed to highlight the circumstances that ensured the success of the state-sponsored religion in Wales as a means of identifying the circumstances which explain its failure in Ireland.

Proceeding accordingly, the first task is to identify the set of con-

to Catholicism to ensure recognition of his title to the throne; in Bohemia the Habsburg monarch succeeded in overturning the already established Protestant religion.
[79] E.g., Edwards, *Church and State*, pp. xl–xliii, 244–5.   [80] Above 45–6.
[81] Steven Ellis makes the same point in relation to the similar economic problems of the church in Wales and Ireland, 'Economic problems of the church: why the Reformation failed in Ireland', *Journal of Ecclesiastical History*, 41 (1990).

tingent circumstances that converged to condition the reception of the state-sponsored Reformation in Wales on its introduction. Here conventional assumptions regarding the pre-conditions of the Reformation stand in need of correction. Conventionally, and, no doubt correctly, the historiography draws attention to the absence in Wales of those religious dynamisms 'from below' which have been adduced to explain the success of the ecclesiastical revolution 'from above' in England. It is indeed the case that the Welsh evidence reveals little trace of the late medieval traditions of anti-clericalism and Lollard heresy which are represented as presaging the Reformation in England. Nor does it seem that the corrosive critique of traditional religion which came into vogue in English humanist circles in the opening decades of the sixteenth century made much impression on the Welsh elite – at least before the onset of the Reformation there in the mid 1530s. Finally, there is no evidence to suggest that the radical currents of protestant heterodoxy which began to infiltrate England from the early 1520s had penetrated Wales to any appreciable extent by the mid 1530s.[82] Nevertheless, the conclusion to which these considerations might seem to lead, that Wales, in virtue of its intellectual isolation and its conservative, traditionalist cultural environment, constituted unpropitious soil in which to implant the English Reformation, can be seen to be profoundly mistaken. On the contrary, it is clear that historical forces emanating from nearer to home than the continental mainland operated to dispose the Welsh favourably towards the Reformation on its introduction.

Odd though it may appear, the crucial factor in conditioning the initial reception of the Reformation in Wales was precisely its 'magisterial' provenance; its introduction as the ecclesiastical corollary of the so-called Tudor revolution in government. First, in that context the significance of the ideological climate of Wales at this time comes to attention. The combination of patriotism and euphoria generated by the accession of the Welsh Tudors to the throne of England, a development construed in Wales as the revival of the ancient British monarchy, was such as to render the community highly receptive to the fundamental tenet of the English Reformation, the royal ecclesiastical supremacy.[83] In a more immediate way also the inauguration of the Reformation as

[82] Williams, *Wales c. 1415–1642*, pp. 179–80. Cf. Williams, *The Welsh Church from Conquest to Reformation* (Cardiff, 1976), ch. 14, and Jones, *Early Modern Wales*, 128–34.

[83] I have developed this point more fully in 'The origins of the British Problem' in Bradshaw and John Morrill (eds.), *The British Problem* (London, 1996), 51–2. See also Williams, *Wales c. 1415–1642*, 219–50. In this respect an early path-breaking article was Peter Roberts, 'The Union with England and the identity of "Anglican" Wales', *Transactions of the Royal Historical Society*, 22 (1972).

the ecclesiastical corollary of the Tudor revolution in government served to enhance the prospects for a favourable response from the local community. This was because the association of the revolution in the church with a revolution in the state, which the Welsh for very palpable reasons perceived as a liberation, lent all the more credibility to the propaganda of royalist apologists who sought to portray the reform movement not as a heterodox innovation but as the repudiation of the 'usurped authority of the bishop of Rome' and, thereby, the liberation of the church from papal greed and corruption – a perception to which the Welsh were peculiarly susceptible as redounding to the glory of a native son, the British monarch, Henry Tudor.[84] In short, the effect of analysing the initial reception of the Reformation in Wales in the context of the circumstances that conditioned the local response to the inauguration of the Tudor revolution in government is to indicate that the former, as the ecclesiastical corollary of the latter, found its moment.

Turning now to the complementary aspect of the task, concerned with identifying the circumstances that converged to condition the Welsh community's response to the Reformation as experienced in practice, the contextual approach adopted here continues to pay rich interpretative dividends. For a start the implementation of the Reformation programme like the implementation of the programme implementing the union involved a patronage bonanza for the elite of the localities. Crucially, in that regard, the Welsh gentry became the overwhelming beneficiaries of the redistribution of landed wealth that followed upon the confiscation of the monastic properties. 'Sooner or later', as Glanmor Williams explains, 'nearly all the gains accrued to the native landowners.'[85] No less crucially for the course taken by the Reformation in Wales, the local elite became the beneficiaries also of a redistribution of ecclesiastical benefices. The royal supreme governor, reversing medieval practice – whether by choice or necessity – consistently favoured local candidates in promotions to the episcopal bench and to other plum benefices: thirteen of the sixteen promotions to the four Welsh bishoprics in the reign of Elizabeth were in favour of local churchmen.[86] The significance of this feature in conditioning the Welsh response to the Reformation needs to be emphasised. Its importance hinges on three main considerations.

The first is that it ensured the continuing support of the local elite for the ecclesiastical revolution. The other two considerations relate to the administrative implications of the combined patronage bonanzas, and incidentally draw attention to the way in which the Welsh elite, in the

---

[84] Bradshaw, and Morrill, *British Problem*.
[85] Williams, *Wales, c. 1415–1642*, 290–2.   [86] *Ibid.*, 307.

ecclesiastical as in the civil sphere, were enabled to have their pudding and eat it.

The consequence of the crown's largesse was to constitute the local elite the agents of the revolution in church and state since it was upon them as governors for the crown of the Welsh shires and dioceses that the programme of 'reform by statute' depended.[87] This proved crucial to the outcome of the Reformation in Wales under the Tudors. Its significance is twofold. Immediately it serves to explain how a vigorous Reformation campaign came to be mounted there at all given the problem of supervision posed to the crown by the remoteness of the region from the administrative centre and the sparsity of protestant evangelists to undertake the task of preaching and instruction. These needs were supplied by the local elite who as beneficiaries of the revolution were willing to promote the programme of religious reform by 'sword and word' in accordance with the classical magisterial strategy. The related consideration, in contrast, brings to light in the ecclesiastical domain the self-subverting dimension of the revolution also observable in relation to the revolution in government. For in constituting the Welsh elite the local governors of Wales on behalf of the crown the effect of the patronage bonanza was, of course, to constitute them the arbiters of crown policy in the region also. Thus it was that the Welsh elite as the local agents of the Tudor revolution in church and state contrived to implement it in accordance with their own conservative and patriotic predilections. The consequences, as already observed, were momentous not only for the outcome of the Reformation in Wales but for the course of Welsh history more generally. First, wielding the sword as officers of the shires and of the dioceses, the local elite strove determinedly from the outset to root out sources of active opposition. The oath to the royal supremacy was everywhere extracted in the course of the Henrician Reformation and, as early as the mid 1530s, the Observant Franciscans who turned up in Cardiff to foment opposition were promptly taken into custody and sent off to London.[88] In the same way the vigilance of the local elite largely explains why the resentment provoked by the protestant innovations under Edward VI

---

[87] To that extent, as Williams claims, the paradoxical effect of the Union was to grant the Welsh virtual 'self-government in the sixteenth century sense of the term', *Wales, c. 1415-1642*, 274. For a succinct discussion of the outcome of the Tudor Revolution which develops this point see Jones, *Early Modern Wales*, 85-90. Cf. Peter Roberts, 'Wales and England after the Tudor "union": crown, Principality and parliament 1543-1624', in C. Cross *et al.* (eds.), *Law and Government under the Tudors* (Cambridge, 1988), 111-38.

[88] For a survey which draws together a swathe of detailed case studies see Glanmor Williams in *Wales, c. 1415-1642*, chs. 12, 13; for this incident see *ibid.*, 281-3.

failed to erupt into violent protest as it did in the 'dark corners of the land' in England.[89] And again in the 'dangerous year of 1569', as Williams describes it, when the Catholic Queen Mary fled south from Scotland, and a conservative revolt convulsed the north of England, no sign of disloyalty ruffled Wales, for the same reason.[90] Finally, in the 1580s and 1590s, when the Counter Reformation mission at last launched a determined assault it was repulsed by an intensive campaign of legal attrition mounted jointly by the local civil and ecclesiastical authorities.[91]

Conversely it is clear that the determination of the local elite to resist active subversion of the religion 'by law established' went hand in hand with a generally indulgent attitude, in line with their own conservative predilections, towards those 'survivalist' accretions – incantations, pilgrimages, saints' cults, and the like – which persisted to scandalise Puritan evangelists at the end of the century. No doubt in that regard the outraged recrimination of the latter against the slackness of local policing was well directed.[92]

In the matter of outward conformity, therefore, the response of the local elite to their role as wielders of the sword goes far towards explaining the widespread persistence of survivalism within Wales throughout the sixteenth century. At the same time, however, it also explains why, the proclivities of the community towards Catholic 'superstitions' notwithstanding, Wales was preserved safe for the English Reformation. With regard to the more positive aspect of the magisterial strategy, the evangelising campaign designed to foster inner commitment, it is no less apparent that the outcome was crucially determined by the response of the Welsh elite to their function as local agents. The vital consideration in this connection is their insistence, in keeping with their patriotic predilections, on inculturation – to use the modern term – as a necessary condition of a successful strategy of evangelisation.

Inculturation as essayed by the elite had two main aspects. One related to a central plank of the Reformation programme, vernacularisation. Here the elite insisted, by appeal to the pastoral needs of a largely monoglot Welsh population, that the mother tongue, not English, must

[89] Ibid., 295–6, 300–1.   [90] Ibid., 316.

[91] Ibid., 312–13. Bishop Nicholas Robinson of Bangor nicely captures the attitude in his account of his activities in his diocese: 'I am termed by my countrymen beyond the seas a persecutor for that of long time I have laid wait for their massing priests and such as bear them, and do make in question twice every year through every parish for that purpose whereby though sometime they were many that did withdraw themselves from the Church now in my whole diocese there be but six', quoted in J. Gwynfor Jones, Wales and the Tudor State (Cardiff, 1989), 103.

[92] Williams, Wales, c. 1415–1642, 312–13. For general corroboration of this point in a survey that extends down to 1642 see Jones, Early Modern Wales, 121–34.

constitute the medium of evangelisation and of worship – all due lip-service being paid to the ideal of anglicisation as the goal for a remote future. Accordingly, from an early stage of the campaign Welsh evangelists and humanists began to initiate measures designed to ensure that the reformed religion could be 'understanded of the people'.[93] As early as 1542 Bishop Bulkeley of Bangor is found directing the clergy, school-masters and heads of households in his diocese to provide religious instruction in the Welsh language.[94] The following year the task of providing essential texts for the purpose got underway with the appearance of manuscript translations of parts of Tyndale's New Testament and of Cranmer's recently promulgated Litany and Order of the Communion.[95] Then in 1546–7 the new technology began to be exploited for the purpose. One of the first two printed books in Welsh to appear was a religious primer containing translations of the Creed, the Lord's Prayer and the Ten Commandments. Setting a trend, it was produced and published at his own expense by Sir John Price, significantly a member of the Cromwellian reforming circle.[96] A further advance is recorded some four years later when William Salesbury, like Price, a lay reformer devoted to humanist scholarship, produced translations of the scriptural lessons and the Articles of Religion used in the reformed Edwardian liturgy.[97] Salesbury's translations represent the first substantial gesture towards realising the major aspiration of the vernacularists – formulated already in the preamble to Price's primer – for a translation of the complete texts of the scriptures and of the liturgy. That aspiration was brought a stage nearer realisation in 1563, when, in response to the initiatives of influential Welsh reformers, the notion was endorsed by parliamentary statute.[98] The year 1567 saw the most substantial contribution to the project so far in the form – after years of sometimes testy collaboration between William Salesbury, Bishop Richard Davies of St David's, and the dean of the latter's cathedral, Thomas Huet – of a Welsh translation of the Prayer Book and the complete New Testament.[99] Finally, in 1588 the goal was gloriously attained with the

---

[93] Quoted in Roberts, 'Identity of Anglican Wales', 63. Roberts' article provides general corroboration of this analysis of the 'vernacularisation' programme of Welsh religious reformers. The campaign is studied in detail in G. Williams, 'Religion and Welsh literature in the age of the Reformation', *Proceedings of the British Academy*, 69 (1983). For a survey that emphasises the problems of those humanists who sought to produce and disseminate a Welsh Reformation literature see Jones, *Early Modern Wales*, 153–61.
[94] Williams, *Wales, c. 1415–1642*, 295.   [95] *Ibid.*
[96] *Ibid.*, and Roberts, 'Identity of Anglican Wales', 63.
[97] Williams, *Wales, c. 1415–1642*, 298.
[98] Roberts, 'Identity of Anglican Wales', 63–5. Jones, *Wales and the Tudor State*, Williams, *Wales, c. 1415–1642*, 314.
[99] Williams, *Wales, c. 1415–1642*, 315.

publication – to general acclaim then and ever since – of Bishop William Morgan's Bible: a landmark not only in the religious history of Wales but in its cultural history also in that it provided for Welsh what Luther's translation of the Bible provided for German, an exemplar of the best contemporary usage in matters of style, syntax and grammar of suffi-cient authority to set the standard for a modernised literary language.[100]

The enthusiastic reception accorded Morgan's bible reflects a mood that served to generate a veritable shoal of contributions to the corpus of vernacular reform literature in the closing decades of the century. Catechetical and devotional works in prose added to the substantial body of contributions to that *genre* which had accumulated since the appearance of Price's primer. Increasingly in this period also, a *genre* of reform-inspired religious verse was cultivated, marking a significant 'toneshift' by contrast with the howl of protest elicited from the bards by the Edwardian innovations forty years earlier.[101] Finally, a number of polemical forays added to the steady spate of apologetical writings that had appeared from the earliest stages, many of them in the form of introductions to publications of texts or anthologies, as for instance that by Bishop William Davies to the 1567 New Testament. The translation of John Jewlel's classic *Apology* which appeared in 1595 was the most important addition at this period.[102]

With good reason, therefore, Glanmor Williams claims the work of the vernacularists to represent the 'supreme achievement of the Welsh church in the sixteenth century'.[103] At the same time, however, it is necessary to stress the ambiguity of the achievement. For the contri-bution of the vernacularists could hardly be bettered as an example of the way in which the Welsh elite, as the local agents of the crown's ecclesiastical revolution, both ensured its successful extension to Wales and at the same time subverted the imperialistic designs of its architects. The point is that the outcome of the activity generated by the vernacu-larists, most especially their contributions to modernising the literary language, was to launch a Welsh cultural renaissance.[104] Thus, ironi-cally, in ensuring the success of the English Reformation in Wales, the vernacularists at the same time undermined a central design of its imperialistic perpetrators by unseating English as the privileged lan-guage of the new dispensation.

The complementary aspect of inculturation involved 'naturalising' the

[100] G. Williams, 'Bishop William Morgan and the first Welsh Bible', in *The Welsh and their Religion: Historical Essays* (Cardiff, 1991); 173–229; Roberts, 'Identity of Anglican Wales', 64–5. Jones, *Wales in the Tudor State*, 107–12.

[101] Williams, *Wales, c. 1415–1642*, 300, 323–4.   [102] *Ibid.*, 323.

[103] *Ibid.*, 335–6, 449–50.   [104] *Ibid.*; Roberts, 'Identity of Anglican Wales', 66, 69.

ecclesiastical revolution, to use the apt phrase of Peter Roberts, by rooting it in Welsh tradition. This was achieved by three main means. One, stemming from the vernacularist movement, was by identifying commitment to religious reform with commitment to the Welsh cultural heritage. Partly in consequence of personal predilection, and partly in pursuit of the goal of a religion 'understanded by the people', humanist reformers such as Price, William Salesbury, Bishop Davies and Bishop William Morgan came to involve themselves closely in promoting the cultivation of Welsh as a literary language. Salesbury, for instance, collected and put into print an anthology of Welsh proverbs, *Oll Synnwyr Penn*, while Bishop Davies made his residence at Abergwili near Carmarthen 'a prime centre of cultural activity where professional bards were granted hospitality'. For their part the bards responded to such gestures with eulogies in the traditional manner extolling the reformers, and with free-metre verse designed to inculcate the reformed doctrine.[105] These were the circumstances in which the religious movement became associated with the launching of a Welsh cultural renaissance. In time the association was intensified as the bardic order declined and the church assumed the mantle of custodian of the native cultural heritage.[106] A second area in which the enthusiasms of humanist reformers happily combined to 'naturalise' the ecclesiastical revolution was that of antiquarianism. The outcome here was a project designed to provide the religious movement with a Welsh spiritual lineage by identifying it with the religious tradition of the early medieval Celtic church and, thereby, with the religion to which Joseph of Arimathea converted the British in the first century as the legend had it. In that regard Bishop Davies of St David's emerges once more to special prominence as the chief exponent of the thesis. His contribution here may well be compared with that of the English martyrologist, John Foxe, who contrived to naturalise the protestant Reformation in England by inserting it within the frame of a reworked British history.[107]

The final feature of the Reformation campaign which contributed to the 'naturalisation' of the English Reformation in Wales capitalised on the other two. This was the rhetorical strategy cultivated by Welsh reformers. The ploy here was to seek commitment to the values of the reformed religion by locating the appeal in Welsh patriotic sentiment, exploiting for that purpose the ideological implications of vernacularisation and of the Reformation's alleged British lineage. An early example of the ploy is provided by the introduction to William Salesbury's book

---

[105] Roberts, 'Identity of Anglican Wales', 66–9.   [106] *Ibid.*, 63–5, 67–9.
[107] *Ibid.*, 69; Jones, *Early Modern Wales*, 153–4.

of proverbs. Here the patriotic implications of vernacularisation are reinforced by appeal to the Reformation's British lineage:

If you do not wish to become worse than animals ... obtain learning in your language: if you do not wish to become more unnatural than any other nation under the sun, love your language and he who cherishes it. Unless you wish utterly to depart from the faith of Christ, unless you wish to have nothing at all to do with him, unless you wish utterly to forget his will, obtain the holy scriptures in your tongue as your fortunate ancestors, the ancient British.[108]

Another example of the technique is provided by Bishop Davies's introduction to the New Testament of 1567. In this he exploits not only the patriotic implications of vernacularisation and of the British lineage but also tacitly invokes the closely related theme of the Welsh cult of the Tudors:

O Welshman thou dost not participate in anything of the good fortune of the great light which has spread over the face of the world because no one has written nor printed anything in thy language. Behold I have shown thee thy pre-eminence and thy privilege of old and thy humiliation and thy deprivation afterwards. Therefore, by proper meditation and recognition of thine own self thou shouldst be glad and frequent thy thanksgiving to God, to her grace the Queen, to the Lords and Commons of the Kingdom who are renewing thy privilege and honour. For by their authority and their command thy bishops ... are bringing to thee in Welsh and in print the Holy Scriptures .... [109]

In these various ways, therefore, through its association with the Welsh cultural renaissance, through its alleged links with an ancient British spiritual tradition, through the suffusion of the rhetoric of the reformers with Welsh patriotic sentiment, the English Reformation came to be identified with the Welsh nation and its heritage. It is scarcely necessary to stress the contribution of that achievement towards eliciting commitment from the community for the religion 'by law established'. This above all surely explains how the Welsh came to yield loyalty to the English Reformation as a patriotic duty – its Saxon provenance notwithstanding – and how conversely the Counter Reformation came to assume for the Welsh connotations of disloyalty and subversion.

However, what needs to be stressed, in conclusion, is the ambiguity of this achievement viewed within the frame of the design of the revolution in church and state as conceived by the regime in England. In this respect inculturation provides another notable example of the self-subverting dimension of the programme of the revolution in Wales as implemented in practice. The way in which it operated to that end may be illustrated by reference to the introduction to the greatest and the

---

[108] Quoted in Jones, *Wales in the Tudor State*, 237–9 and 238.
[109] Quoted in *ibid.*, 242.

most influential of all the contributions to the vernacular corpus of Welsh Reformation literature, Bishop Morgan's Bible. In his introduction Morgan essayed to resist the proposition that the reformed religion ought to be disseminated in Wales through the medium of English. His case rests partly on pastoral exigency: the upshot, he argued, would be to leave the people to wallow in blind superstition and sinfulness during the unconscionable period required to teach them English. More importantly for present purposes, he brought his case to rest finally on a philosophical or, more accurately, an ideological argument. This revolved upon the issue of how the English and the Welsh, now constitutionally united, could achieve common accord and a common identity as a single integrated community. Circumventing the idea of anglicisation propounded in the preamble to the 'act of union' Morgan held up the alternative ideal of two ethnic groups, diverse in language and culture, united inwardly, however, by a common religious profession, their mutual commitment to the faith of the ancient British:

For, although it is much to be desired that the inhabitants of the same island should be of the same speech and language, it must equally be borne in mind, that to effect this end, so much time and trouble is required, that to be willing, much less to suffer God's people to perish in the meantime from hunger of His Word, were both barbarous and cruel. Moreover there can be no doubt that unity is more effectually promoted by similarity and agreement in religion than in speech.[110]

It may be useful by way of closure to draw together the conclusions of this investigation of the success of the English Reformation in Wales despite the obstacles placed in its way by the territory's intellectual isolation, its conservative traditionalist cultural environment and the problem of effective jurisdiction posed by its remoteness from the administrative centre of government in London. The explanation emerges in terms of a conjuncture between two sets of historically contingent developments that conditioned the local response to the religious movement. One set operated to mould a benign perception of it on its introduction. Here the ideological climate, with its burgeoning patriotism focused on the revival of the British monarchy and the cult of the native royal dynasty, the Tudors, as well as the transformation of the socio-political elite from a power-obsessed feudal nobility to an acquisitive modernising gentry, disposed the Welsh to perceive the state-sponsored Reformation in line with official propaganda, not as a heterodox innovation imposed from England but as the repudiation of a usurped papal authority by the British monarch and the liberation of the

---

[110] Quoted in Peter Roberts, 'The Welsh language, English law and Tudor legislation', *Transactions of the Honourable Society of Cymmrodorion* (1989) at 71.

church thereby from long centuries of papal greed and corruption. In accounting for the precise outcome, however, it is no less essential to ponder the implications of the set of historical contingencies that operated to condition the Welsh experience of the Reformation as implemented in practice. The significance of that consideration is threefold. First, the crown's programme of religious reform, reciprocally with the reform of the polity, turned out to provide a patronage bonanza for the local elite, thereby vindicating the Welsh elite's benign perception of the ecclesiastical revolution and ensuring their continuing support for it. Second, the combined effect of disposing of key ecclesiastical benefices to local churchmen, and, at the same time, of relying on the local gentry to administer the newly established Welsh shires, was to devolve crown government in Wales in church and state upon the elite of the localities. It follows that the effect was to constitute them both the agents and the arbiters in Wales of the Tudor revolution. The response of the elite in that role, as has just been seen, ultimately serves to explain the outcome of the Reformation in Wales under the Tudors. On the one hand, it explains how the Reformation succeeded in securing confessional commitment from the Welsh despite the obstacles arising from the region's status as a Celtic borderland. It did so, as has been seen, because of the willingness of the Welsh elite as the beneficiaries and local agents of the revolution in church and state to implement its programme. On the other hand, it also explains the ambiguity of the achievement. That is to say that the consequence of constituting the Welsh elite the local agents of the state-sponsored Reformation was to enable them to implement it in accordance with their own conservative and patriotic predilections. Thus, the priorities which the local elite brought to bear in executing the magisterial strategy of 'sword and word' finally explain the twofold ambiguity of its triumph: the existence, side by side with confessional allegiance to the reformed religion, of widespread indifference to it as a discipline or observance; and the failure of institutional incorporation in the *Ecclesia Anglicana* to pave the way for cultural anglicisation as envisaged by the imperial architects of the revolution.

It remains to bring to bear the insights gleaned in accounting for the success of the English Reformation in the Welsh Celtic borderland, in explaining the paradox of its failure in Ireland.

VI

In the light of the outcome of the extension of the state-sponsored Reformation to Wales the problem posed by the outcome of the attempt to extend it to Ireland may be formulated more precisely as follows: if the obstacles presented to the enterprise in the former case by reason of Wales' Celtic borderland state – intellectual isolation, cultural traditionalism and remoteness from the centre of government – could be successfully overcome, why could they not be overcome in the case of Ireland? To formulate the question in those terms is also to point the way towards a solution. The answer may lie in a comparative analysis designed to identify the variables that conditioned the extension of the crown programme to its two Celtic borderland dominions.

Proceeding therefore to the analysis, the first variable highlighted by the comparison relates to the feature on which the entire explanation for the outcome in the Welsh case pivots: the composition of the sociopolitical elite as it had evolved in the prelude to the revolutionary changes of the 1530s. In Wales, the effect of a process of attrition that set in in the aftermath of the Glyndŵr Rebellion was to undermine the magnate power structure and the culture of the marcher lordships and plantation boroughs, thereby ensconcing the gentry as the residual legatees of the leadership role in the localities.[111] The concomitant process in late medieval Ireland provides a striking contrast. There the effect of trends that gained increasing momentum in the aftermath of a no less disastrous native rebellion a century earlier – the Bruce adventure in the second decade of the fourteenth century – was to entrench a power structure and a political culture in both the native and colonial territories of the island that brought the dynastic lords a degree of dominance in their localities unparalleled elsewhere in the Tudor dominions.[112] Thus, whereas in Wales the Tudor revolution and Reformation encountered a situation in which the historical process had obligingly removed the 'overmighty subject' as the dominant feature of the political landscape and brought an acquisitive gentry to the fore as local leaders, the trend of developments in Ireland was in the inverse direction: towards ensconcing dynastic magnates as local warlords and regional satraps, elevating them as such to a degree of power and status unparalleled elsewhere in the Tudor dominions. Therefore, following this lead, the enquiry now comes to focus on the implications of the differences between the composition of the two local elites for the outcome of the Tudor reform of church and state in the two Celtic borderlands.

In Wales, it will be recalled, the revolution was favoured by its moment. There two sets of circumstances coincided to persuade the

---

[111] Bradshaw, 'Origins of the British Problem', 49 and references there cited.
[112] For a fuller exposition of what follows together with supporting footnote references see *ibid.*, 55–7.

elite to look upon the union as a benign, indeed a providential, consummation. One set related to the practical benefits it promised as these affected the mundane concerns of an emergent and aspiring gentry. The prime consideration here was the release which the union offered from the legal and political constraints with which the gentry found themselves shackled by reason of Wales' medieval constitution as enshrined in the provisions devised for the government of 'the land of Wales' in the aftermath of the Edwardian conquest.[113] By fortunate coincidence, as was also noted earlier, a second process set in motion by an unexpected turn in English dynastic politics in the late fifteenth century greatly facilitated such a perception. This was the burgeoning in Wales of a British patriotism triggered by the accession of Henry Tudor to the throne of England. Seizing upon his tenuous Welsh lineage, the native literati were emboldened to hail Henry VII as *rex Britanicus redivivus* and to project upon the Tudor dynasty in consequence their hopes for the fulfilment of ancient prophecies concerning the restoration of the British monarchy and with it the deliverance of the Welsh as the remnant of the original British nation from Saxon thraldom. Thus the Welsh gentry were enabled to combine self-interest and patriotism in choosing to perceive the incorporation of their country within the English Kingdom not as an imperialistic annexation but as a liberation.[114]

Turning to identify in that light the combination of historically contingent developments that combined to condition the perception of the Tudor revolution by the elite in Ireland it becomes clear that historical forces there conspired to provide no such favourable moment. On the contrary, the effect first of all was to pre-empt the possibility that the extension of the programme to Ireland could hold out the prospect of the kind of cornucopia of liberties and privileges that so palpably disposed the Welsh gentry towards the union. This was because Ireland as a Lordship appended to the English crown boasted in like manner to the English kingdom an 'ancient constitution', and came to be governed accordingly as a self-subsistent polity by means of a set of political instruments which duplicated those of the kingdom.[115] Second, the moment of the revolution was still less fortunate in the ideological climate it encountered. True, the colonial community's historical experience as the defenders of a receding enclave served to instil in them a keen awareness of their ethnic origins and, as a corollary, served to mould an ideological posture of loyalism through which they defined

---

[113] *Ibid.*, 50–1. W. R. B. Robinson, 'The Tudor Revolution in Welsh Government', *English Historical Review*, 103 (1989), 1–20.
[114] Bradshaw, 'Origins of the British Problem', 51–2.   [115] *Ibid.*, 58.

themselves over against the 'disobedient Irishry' as 'English by blood' and as such the king of England's faithful and obedient subjects. At the same time, however, their experience as the self-perceived victims of centuries of metropolitan political bullying, economic fleecing, cultural *hauteur* and, in time of need, indifference and dereliction, served to instil a countervailing, anti-metropolitan sensibility and with it the consciousness of a distinct colonial identity predicated upon Ireland as the community's historic *patria*.[116] And the effect of the emergence of a colonial patriotism predicated upon Ireland as the community's *patria*, their native land, was to pre-empt the development of a British consciousness also, the burgeoning of which in Wales so effectively camouflaged the imperialist designs of the union from the chauvi elite of the territory. Meanwhile, the entrenchment of bastard feudalism as the pivot of colonial politics and local government in contrast to the withering away of the phenomenon in Wales had the effect of corroding the community's sense of the duty of devotion and obedience owing to their monarch in two ways: first, by interposing the colonial magnates between king and subject as the focus of their 'worship' and more importantly, as shall be seen, by bringing the duty of 'good lordship' (protection and patronage) into play as the reciprocal condition upon which the subjects' 'service' was to be rendered.

The inherently unstable relationship thus created between the crown and the ruling elite of the Lordship was further unbalanced by the revival of monarchical government with the readeption of Edward IV in 1471. As the revival impinged on the colonial elite it took the form mainly of a succession of reformist missions from London – at least one every decade from the 1460s – sent thither to restore the effectiveness of monarchical government in the Lordship.[117] The missions invariably got underway with a purge of the Dublin administration involving the removal of the local Fitzgerald magnate as lord deputy in favour of the head of the commission, and the intrusion of a bevy of English officials to the jeopardy of Kildare's clients ensconced in the plum offices of the administration. Invariably as a corollary the missions entailed an assault upon bastard feudalism in the localities – thus jeopardising the structure on which the political hegemony of the magnates rested – by the deployment of bonds and recognisances *ad terrorem* in accordance with the strategy adopted to such telling effect in England. While the series of reforming initiatives inaugurated by the 'new monarchy' in the Lordship did little to ameliorate what, so far as the colonial community was concerned, constituted the crown's most urgent problem of government,

[116] *Ibid.*, 58–9.   [117] *Ibid.*, 59–62.

the need to curb the debilitating encroachments of the 'disobedient Irishry' on the colony, they seemed designed to undermine the local elite's monopoly of power and patronage. Their effect in sum was to conflate in the consciousness of the colonists' self-interested resentment with a high-minded defence of the Lordship's constitutional autonomy; concomitantly, in doing so to re-energise the ideologically inspired sensibilities associated with the colonial community's most cherished political heritage, its ancient constitution, bringing these to bear now upon the reviving monarchy's reforming initiatives; third, then, the effect was to suffuse reciprocally the colonists' self-interested hostility to the reforming initiatives with this patriotically fuelled separatist sentiment; and finally the outcome of the fusion was to appropriate colonial separatism as an explosive ingredient of a newly burgeoning ideology of opposition to 'reform from the centre'. A concomitant consequence is brought to light by the consideration that the chain of rebellions that marked the advent of the crown's reformative commissions to the Lordship represented in organisation and strategic conception the conventional expedient of bastard feudal politics for bringing the grievances of a magnate vassal to the attention of his liege lord: defiance in arms, offered by means of a 'rising out' at his bidding of the magnate's kindred and 'well-willers'. The point is that the apparent effectiveness of this traditional mode of bastard feudal political protest under Edward IV and Henry VII disposed the aggrieved colonists to assume that its ideological corollary, the conditional bond of the bastard feudal code of honour – 'good lordship' as the due reward of 'service' – also continued to provide the norm by which their relationship with the English crown was to be regulated in the era of the monarchical revival. In that light in turn the catalystic function of rebellion as a mode of resistance to the reforming initiatives of the reviving monarchy emerges. The effect of the fusion thus engendered was to appropriate the conditional bond of the code of honour for the colonial elite's burgeoning ideology of opposition to 'reform from the centre' as a norm of political conduct that served to elevate defiance in arms to the level not merely of a chivalric obligation of honour but of a patriotic duty imposed by the call to defend once more the 'liberties and privileges' justly due to the traditional custodians of the Lordship of Ireland in the age old struggle against metropolitan overbearance and exploitation.

In surveying the contribution of the earlier phase of the monarchical revival towards predisposing the local elite to resist reform from the centre one more feature calls for attention. This is its *sine qua non*, the accession of the Tudors. Ironically, that auspicious turn in the fortunes of the monarchy, marking the resolution of the war of succession that so devastated royal power and authority during the faction struggles around the throne misnamed the Wars of the Roses, marking also, as noted earlier, an upward turn in relations between the crown and its borderland dominion of Wales – a turn highly auspicious, for the reception there of the state-sponsored revolution – nevertheless resulted in compounding the problem presented to the crowns by its Irish patrimony. This had to do not simply with the failure, already observed, of the Tudors' British lineage to strike the same patriotic resonance with the socio-political elite of the colony as with the atavistically 'British' Welsh gentry – having been pre-empted in that regard by a burgeoning sense of colonial identity predicated upon Ireland as the community's historic *patria*. It had to do also and more ominously with the effect of the installation of the Tudor dynasty in positively vitiating relations between the monarchy and the colonial cohort that dominated both government and politics in the Lordship, the Kildare Fitzgeralds and their allies. The source of the problem was twofold.[118] First it was a matter of power politics. On the one hand, the Tudors not only resented the monopolisation of crown government and patronage by the Fitzgeralds but mistrusted them as manifestly unrepentant Yorkists. On the other hand, the Geraldines were determined, their Yorkist affiliations notwithstanding, to retain their status as virtual rulers of the Lordship and with it their monopoly of crown patronage, arrogantly confident of their capacity to do so as, in effect, the Lordship's power-brokers. The second source of tension related to a transmutation of the ideological ambience at the centre. This resulted from the achievement of a coterie of royalist legists and rhetoricians in appropriating the exalted concepts and values of the Justinian civil code as associated with princely rule by court humanists in Italy for the purpose of inflating the status and accordingly the pretensions of England's reviving feudal monarchy. The resultant imperial consciousness constitutes the ideological concomitant of the ambition to reassert royal power and authority that fired the first two Tudors. In a word, the nexus is constituted by the attribute of sovereignty (*imperium*) which, according to the civil code of Justinian, inheres in the emperor as lawgiver, in so far as it elevates the ruler above all other *loci* of power and authority. Imperialism then was the ideology that was to inform the revolution in church and state launched under the auspices of the king's erastian chief minister, Thomas Cromwell, in the 1530s.

The precise consequences of this volatile political environment for the reception of the Reformation in Ireland remain to be considered.

[118] *Ibid.* at 62–4.

However, before doing so a religious dimension must be added to the context. No doubt the religious situation encountered by the Reformation in Ireland presents in most respects the same dismal aspect as it does in Wales: that of a deeply traditionalist not to say hidebound cultural ethos; the laity in thrall to quasi-magical ritualism; parish cures everywhere served by simple massing priests who neglected to preach or to provide religious instruction; the monastic orders in steep decline, with lax observance the norm and downright immorality by no means rare while vocations dwindled.[119] Nevertheless, the comparison draws attention to a beacon of light in the Irish case, one moreover that assumes heightened significance when viewed in the context of the struggle between the Reformation and the Counter Reformation as will later appear. Its source was a vigorous movement of reform among the mendicant orders known as Observantism.

Whereas in Wales the Observant reform does not seem to have taken hold at all, and even in England numbered only seven foundations among its adherents – all of them Franciscan – it flourished in Ireland. Introduced from the continent to the Gaelic territories in the west in the mid fifteenth century, it expanded steadily throughout the Gaelic area.[120] By the turn of the century it had established itself in the colonial lordships and the port towns and was gaining ground within the Pale itself. Three decades later, when the Tudor revolution burst upon the Lordship, Observantism claimed forty Franciscan convents – two-thirds of the entire complement of this the largest and most dynamic of the mendicant orders in Ireland. By then also eight of the twenty-two Augustinian communities were Observant, and elsewhere among the conventuals it had individual adherents: the prior of the conventual community in Dublin in the 1530s who was also their provincial superior, Richard Nangle, was an Observant. Again in the case of the Dominicans the impact of the movement was clearly greater than the bare statistic of eight foundations from a total of twenty-two might seem to indicate. When the Order of Preachers established a separate Irish province in 1484 its first provincial superior was an Observant, and six of the conventual communities went over to the reform in the course of the following twenty years, no small testimony to the vigour of the movement in the new province. The Carmelites alone seem to have been generally

---

[119] For the conventional pessimistic picture, Ellis, *Tudor Ireland*, 183–93; Lennon's survey is more hopeful, *Sixteenth-Century Ireland*, 113–34. Revisionist historians who argue for the vigour of the pre-Reformation Church in England acknowledge its manifest flaws and failings. For a study of the Irish Church in the same vein in a localist context, J. Murray, 'The Reformation in Dublin', Ph.D. dissertation, Trinity College, Dublin 1997.

[120] The Observant reform movement is treated more fully in Bradshaw, *The Dissolution of the Religious Orders* (Cambridge, 1975), 8–16, 35–6.

unresponsive, though a stained-glass window in one of the houses honouring Blessed John Sareth, the Carmelite superior general from 1452 to 1471 and a zealous promoter of the regular observance, may indicate sympathy at least with the ideal of which he was so ardent an advocate. The significance of the Observant reform for the response to the Reformation in Ireland hinges on three related considerations. One is that it provided the late medieval Irish church with a clerical elite, numerous and widely dispersed both throughout the colony and the native lordships. Second, the Observants' manner of life and their strong pastoral orientation ensured them a voice that commanded a special moral authority among the laity.[121] Thus an early-sixteenth-century commonwealth treatise, for all its lamentation of the state of Ireland generally, singles out the 'poor friars beggars' for commendation in alone attending to the pastoral function of preaching the word of God to the people. Complementing that testimony a dispatch of the imperial ambassador in London in 1534, coinciding with the inauguration of the state-sponsored Reformation in the Lordship, informed the emperor in a tone of obvious astonishment that, according to reports the Cordeliers [Observants] were held in such veneration among the 'wild Irish' that they were feared, obeyed and almost adored such that even their lords submitted to chastisement from them with a stick.[122] Third, in consequence of the Observants' pastoral involvement they took to exploiting the vernacular as a medium of evangelisation. In the process they became associated with those professional families whose task it was to preserve and cultivate the native cultural heritage: as witness, Pilib Bocht Ó hUiginn, scion of the distinguished bardic family of that name and an accomplished practitioner of the family profession. The point is that he was also an Observant Franciscan who devoted his art to propagating the cause of Observantism and in doing so established himself as the major exponent of religious verse in the classical bardic mode in the fifteenth century.[123] What emerges from all of this then is that the ambience into which the Tudor revolution in church and state was introduced in Ireland differed significantly from that of the crown's other Celtic borderland dominion not only politically but also in religious terms. Unlike Wales or indeed England, Ireland uniquely possessed in the orders of friars a spiritual elite – the fruits of the Observant reform movement – numerous, widely dispersed, pastorally dynamic, respected by the laity of all social degrees, and well attuned to the vernacular as a mode of evangelisation.

---

[121] *Ibid.*, 11.   [122] *Ibid.*, 11–12.

[123] What is known or can be reliably surmised concerning Pilib Bocht is summarised in the introduction to the scholarly edition of his poems, Lambert McKenna (ed.), *Pilib Bocht Ó hUiginn* (Dublin, 1931), pp. ix–xiv.

VII

Such then were the bleak auguries under which the Henrician Reformation was introduced in Ireland. Nevertheless, it would be wrong to assume, as the received wisdom had done, that the cause was lost from the outset. As noted earlier the response to Henry VIII's claim to a royal ecclesiastical supremacy was ambiguous. No doubt it encountered stiff opposition among the clergy. No doubt also its promulgation coincided with a rebellion unprecedented in scale since the Bruce Rebellion in the second decade of the fourteenth century. Further again, no doubt, the Irish Reformation parliament, 1536–7, witnessed protracted opposition to the crown's legislative programme. Yet close examination reveals that, the clergy apart, the issue was not the king's ecclesiastical pretensions but the threat the crown's reform policy presented to the political and economic interests of the socio-political elite of the colony.[124] The latter seem to have been ready enough to acknowledge the royal supremacy when required to do so, by assenting to the relevant statutes in parliament, for example, and by swearing the oaths there prescribed when formally tendered. Indeed, to stress a point made in passing earlier, the prospects of the state-sponsored Reformation began to look positively bright for a brief interlude in the 1540s in the benign atmosphere generated by the conciliatory initiative launched by Lord Deputy Sir Anthony St Leger under the tutelage of a group of colonial commonwealth reformers led by Sir Thomas Cusack. Thus, the first Jesuit mission on behalf of the Counter Reformation in 1542 found such little support in the Gaelic heartland that it was abandoned within a few weeks, the would-be evangelists having come to the conclusion that the cause was lost in Ireland.[125] Therefore, however central the place to be accorded the preconditions in accounting for the outcome of the struggle between the Reformation and the Counter Reformation in sixteenth-century Ireland these do not constitute a sufficient explanation. Ultimately the issue was decided in the course of the struggle itself and, it would seem, at some point subsequent to the reign of Henry VIII: whether in reaction to the full-blown protestantism introduced under the boy-king Edward VI, 1547–53; or in consequence of the steadying effect of the reversal of the crown's ecclesiastical policy under the Catholic Queen Mary, 1553–8; or, perhaps most plausibly, as a cumulative process with the advent of a more self-confident and confessionally aware younger generation in the reign of the religiously

[124] Bradshaw, 'The opposition to the ecclesiastical legislation in the Irish Reformation parliament', *Irish Historical Studies*, 16 (1969), passim.
[125] Edwards, *Church and State*, 127–8; Jones, 'Counter-Reformation', 5.

enigmatic Elizabeth I who gave Anglicanism its distinctive identity by providing the moderately protestant doctrine and ritual she prescribed with a Catholic tincture derived from medieval Catholicism, most notably an episcopalian institutional structure under the jurisdiction of the monarch as supreme governor.[126]

The purpose of this concluding section is not so much to establish the precise juncture at which the tide may be said to have turned ineluctably against the state-sponsored Reformation. Rather, it is intended to bring to light, against the background of the historical circumstances that preconditioned the reception of the Reformation, the dynamics that operated in the course of the struggle itself to clinch the issue. In doing so it is proposed to adhere to the comparative method of analysis that has proved so rich in insights hitherto. Sure enough, the effect will be to identify certain variables in the manner in which the crown sought to implement its programme of reform, in the two Celtic borderlands, that assume major significance in the context of the outcome of the struggle between the Reformation and the Counter Reformation. Ironically, it will be seen, the source of these, for the most part, is found in a feature that the Reformation in both places shared in common, its magisterial provenance, its extension to the borderlands as the ecclesiastical corollary of the Tudor revolution in government. For the effect of the political revolution in Ireland, in contrast to the benign experience it provided in Wales, was to confirm the previous experience of the local elite of reform from the centre as an encroachment upon their material and political interests, a violation of a cherished heritage of liberties, and an affront to their separatist sensibilities.

The analysis proceeds therefore by way of an examination from this comparative perspective of the revolution in government as extended to the Irish Lordship in the 1530s under the aegis of its so-called architect, Thomas Cromwell. Already at that point a stark contrast emerges between the response elicited by the crown's programme of reform in the two Celtic borderlands. Whereas the annexation of Wales as a 'very member and joint' of the English Kingdom in accordance with the statute of 1536 provoked scarcely a murmur of protest so far as can be traced, the effect of the apparently less radical programme applied in Ireland – where no such union was proposed – was to precipitate a major crisis. And, as already indicated, as the history of reform began in the two Celtic borderlands so it continued. By the reign of Elizabeth, Welsh humanists had taken to celebrating the union as the culmination

---

[126] Dickens, *English Reformation.*

of a process of liberation, and to eulogising the first two Tudors accordingly as *reges Britanici redivivi*. On the other hand, in Ireland, although the Kildare rebellion was ruthlessly stamped out, and the opposition in parliament assuaged by compromise, the crisis of the 1530s, inverting the pattern in mainland Britain, marked the onset of a sequence that spiralled in scale and intensity throughout the century culminating in the addled parliament of Lord Deputy Perott in 1584–5 and the Nine Years War that raged from 1594 to the death of Elizabeth in 1603. In the 1530s, then, it may be, lies in germ the explanation for the contrasting outcome of Tudor reform in the two Celtic borderlands. Sure enough the effect of the comparative exercise will be to trace the origins of the Irish problem to the strategy adopted to inaugurate the revolution in the 1530s. They lie, as will be seen, in certain new departures then made in the system whereby the Lordship was governed which, given the volatility of relations between the regime and the local elite at the time, could hardly have been better calculated to ignite the powder. The point is that these innovations came to be adopted in the aftermath of the conciliatory interlude of the 1540s as central aspects of the strategy by which the Tudors sought to pacify and reform the Irish polity. Thus, ironically, the effect of the strategy instead was to institutionalise the innovations as flashpoints which permanently destabilised Anglo-Irish relations not only under the Tudors but so long as, and to the extent that, Ireland has retained its British connection.[127]

This Tudor *hereditas damnosa* stemmed in specific terms from the new-found determination of Henry VIII, steeled to it by his chief minister, Thomas Cromwell, to face down Irish-style bastard feudalism. Its effect first of all was to terminate the late medieval system of devolved government whereby a powerful colonial magnate was deputed to head the administration as lord deputy and given *carte blanche* in filling virtually all other offices of government. Thus, the earl of Kildare, the mighties of the king's overmighty subjects in Ireland, was now displaced as lord deputy and with him the coterie of clients he had installed in the plum offices of government. They were replaced by an upstart English professional soldier – 'the gunner' Skeffington – as lord deputy and by a bevy of officials sent from London to reform the administration. The same procedure had been tried before of course in reforming forays from England.[128] The difference now was that the Cromwellian new

---

[127] See above, pp. 70–2.

[128] Bradshaw, 'Cromwellian reform and the origins of the Kildare rebellion', *Transactions of the Royal Historical Society*, 5th ser., 27 (1977); Ellis, 'The Kildare rebellion and the early Henrician Reformation', *Historical Journal*, 19 (1976); Ellis, 'Thomas Cromwell and Ireland', *Historical Journal*, 23 (1980).

departure set the pattern that was to be adhered to henceforward. A colonial magnate was never again to be deputed to act as chief governor by the Tudors. So also the appointment of English officials to office in Ireland continued apace throughout the century, the period of the conciliatory interlude in the 1540s alone excepted. Moreover, it should be added, the Tudor pattern became set in marble thereafter: the single variation down to the establishment of the Free State in the 1920s was the favour – well recompensed – shown by the Caroline Stuarts to the first duke of Ormond in the mid-seventeenth century. The potency of this Tudor new departure in destabilising the Irish polity, it is important to bear in mind, derived not only from the resentment of the local elite at the loss of power and patronage entailed. Equally, if not in greater measure, it derived from the threat posed in consequence to the established socio-political structure. For as English administrators and soldiers availed of the opportunity of a tour of duty in Ireland to advance their careers and fortunes by exploiting contacts with well-placed patrons in England they transformed themselves in increasing numbers from transitory carpet-baggers on the make to settlers greedy for estates on which to set themselves up as dynastic patriarchs. The result was to set a transformation of the socio-political structure in motion whereby over the next century or so these New English, as they came to be called, first challenged the dominance of the existing elites – colonial (Old English) and native (Gaelic) alike – and then ousted them altogether. The anglicisation of crown government in Ireland then and the challenge it presented to the old order constitutes the first of the flashpoints engendered in Anglo-Irish relations by the Tudor revolution.[129]

The second was engendered as a corollary of the first. Its source was the means devised to remedy the security problem posed by the termination of the medieval system of devolved government. Hitherto the crown had relied for the purpose on a local feudal host, mobilised as occasion required – mainly to curb marauding native borderers – by the colonial magnate favoured at the time with the office of lord deputy. The Cromwellian alternative was a small garrison force, some 300 troops in all recruited from the army sent from England to quell the Kildare Rebellion.[130] Once again the Cromwellian new departure came to be adopted by succeeding Tudor regimes as an essential feature of the strategy whereby they sought to pacify and reform the Irish polity. Further, in the aftermath of the conciliatory interlude the garrison

---

[129] Bradshaw, *Constitutional Revolution*, 258–63; cf. Canny, *Elizabethan Conquest of Ireland*, 36–8; Lennon, *Sixteenth Century Ireland*, 164–6.
[130] Bradshaw, *Constitutional Revolution*, 121–3.

increased and multiplied its presence throughout the island in tandem
with the scale of the security problem presented by the combined effects
of recurring domestic political crises and the increasing vulnerability of
Ireland strategically in consequence of England's embroilment in a
power struggle with Spain, these two powers now constituting the sword
arms respectively of the Reformation and Counter Reformation. In
consequence the function of the garrison underwent a significant
mutation. From an instrument of pacification and reform it became in
effect an army of occupation engaged upon a piecemeal, unplanned
and, so far as the Tudor regime itself was concerned, reluctant conquest.[131] As such, needless to say, it was heartily resented by the
inhabitants of the quasi-autonomous native and nativised lordships.
However, it was also heartily resented by the civil population. First, they
resented the economic burden that fell upon them, mainly of maintaining the army whether by way of billeting, under-cost purveyance of
goods, or cess – an extra-parliamentary tax levied in lieu of provisioning
and billeting. Second, the soldiers behaved no better than any early
modern undisciplined and underpaid army; living off the country by
scavenging and extortion, and generally seriously disrupting the civil
order. The English garrison therefore constitutes the second of those
flashpoints that resulted from the innovations introduced under the
Cromwellian reform programme of the 1530s. It should be added that
this Tudor new departure, like the anglicisation of the administration,
became set in marble thereafter as central to the system by which the
Irish polity was governed down to the establishment of the Free State in
the twentieth century.[132] The combined effect of these two Tudor
innovations therefore was to constitute the system of crown government
in Ireland an exception, much resented, to the system whereby the
British conglomerate generally was governed. As such they go far
towards explaining the continuing instability of the Irish polity within
the British state-system: the garrison in particular came to represent an
emblem of subjection to the increasingly politically aware and increasingly disadvantaged Irish. Meanwhile, to return to the matter in hand,
the more immediate effect of the two was to fuel the mounting tension

---

[131] *Ibid.*, 268–75, especially 262, n. 13; Ellis, *Tudor Ireland*, 176–80; Lennon, *Sixteenth-Century Ireland*, 164–75.

[132] Bradshaw, *Constitutional Revolution*, 166–7; Ellis, *Tudor Ireland*; C. Brady, 'Conservative subversives', in P. J. Corish (ed.) *Radicals, Rebels and Establishments*', Historical
Studies, 15 (Belfast, 1985), 11–32. For an authoritative account of cess and its
significance for the developing crisis in Anglo-Irish relations see C. Brady, *The Chief
Governors: the rise and fall of reform government in Tudor Ireland, 1536–88* (Cambridge,
1994), 216–40. On the unique military character of the Irish government see
'Introduction', above, pp. 6–7 and n. 12.

between the crown and the local elite in the sixteenth century and to further entrench the perception of the latter of reform from the centre as not only inimical to their interests but a violation of long-cherished liberties and an affront to their separatist sensibilities.

The third innovation may be seen partly as a function of the other two, partly also as a response to pressures driven by the new enterprise culture emerging in England. First, as the number of English officials and soldiers settling in Ireland multiplied, a plantation policy gained increasing favour within reforming circles in government. The theory was that strategically placed settlements of civil English subjects would serve both as bastions of loyalty and as a leavening influence whether among the barbarous native or the degenerate old colonial inhabitants. Reciprocally, the success of enterprising English officials and soldiers in transforming themselves into substantially endowed settlers drew the attention of adventurous fortune-seekers generally in England to Ireland as a more accessible land of opportunity to colonise than the newly discovered, remote, overseas territories. Gradually then plantation projects were put in train with a view to advancing the Tudor programme of reform and pacification: by means of state-sponsored projects in the midlands (Laois–Offaly) in the 1550s and in Munster (Cork, Kerry and Limerick) in the 1580s; by means of government-authorised private ventures in the Ards Peninsula on the Antrim coast and in West Cork in the 1570s. The snag, in so far as pacification and reform is concerned, was that such projects added a new dimension to the challenge posed to the existing pattern of land distribution in Ireland by the increasing tendency of New English officials and soldiers to remain on as settlers. For the plantations necessarily encroached upon the patrimonies claimed by the old elites as theirs by ancient inheritance.[133] The sensitivity of these to the implications for their possessions and status was ominously foreshadowed in the 1530s. It was precisely apprehensions of that kind that lay at the root of the dogged filibustering by the old colonial elite of the crown's legislative programme at the Reformation parliament. The fear was that the gainers from the vast transfer of land to the crown proposed in the act for the dissolution of the monasteries would be New English interlopers. Ominously in the event the fear proved well founded. Even under the compromise secured by stalling, the greater share of the spoils went to endow unwelcome newcomers.[134] Meanwhile the sensi-

---

[133] Lennon, *Sixteenth-Century Ireland*, 164-6, 229–36, 274–83; M. MacCarthy-Morrogh, *The Munster Plantation* (Oxford, 1986), passim; Canny, *Elizabethan Conquest of Ireland*, ch. 4.

[134] Bradshaw, 'The opposition in the Irish Reformation parliament', *Irish Historical Studies*, 16 (1969); Bradshaw, *Dissolution of the Religious Orders*, 198–203.

tivity of the native elite – then totally unrepresented in parliament – was manifested still more ominously. The effect of the ruthless suppression of the Kildare protest in arms, the subsequent attempt by the crown to exterminate the dynasty by a process of judicial execution, the appropriation of the Kildare lands by attainder, and, to cap it all, the ferocious mopping-up operation conducted among the Fitzgeralds' allies in the native lordships, was to revive the spectre of a resumption of the long-suspended English conquest and of the extrusion of the ruling septs altogether from their ancestral patrimonies. The upshot was the Gaelic League which unleashed an invasion of the Pale in 1539–40. Significantly the League was the first quasi-national alliance to take up arms against the crown since the Bruce Rebellion more than 220 years earlier.[135] Fatefully it was not to be the last such rebel alliance that century despite its collapse after the rout of Bellahoe where the forces of the crown caught the invaders napping. For in the aftermath of the conciliatory interlude of the 1540s the Tudor regime turned increasingly to military methods to assert its authority in Ireland. By these means – mainly by the extension of a network of garrisoned forts throughout the island and by the establishment of militarised regional presidencies – it sought increasingly to impose order on the quasi-autonomous lordships.[136] When then concurrently the plantation projects began to trespass increasingly on the patrimonies of the old elite the effect was to endow the shadowy spectre of conquest and dispossession with a very palpable presence and to undermine the credibility of the crown's Irish version of the 'kicks and ha'pence' strategy – coercion and conciliation – so successful in Wales. Ultimately the effect was to spark a chain of rebellions of increasing scale and intensity, as the ruling kindreds became increasingly persuaded of the need to combine under a common banner to defend their patrimonies. The consummation was reached in the Nine Years War, waged in the name of 'faith and fatherland' that convulsed the polity in the final years of the Tudor era. With the submission of the Ulster rebels in 1603 and their flight to continental exile in 1607 the Tudor Conquest was brought to completion: in fits and starts and by way of a succession of stop-gap military solutions to recurring crises rather than as a well-deliberated, concerted strategy. The process of plantation remained to be completed by James I (Ulster, 1610–14), Cromwell (virtually all the land still unplanted east of the Shannon in the 1650s), and by William and his Hanoverian successors (more or less everything else saving a few isolated pockets in the 1690s and succeeding decades). Already,

---

[135] Bradshaw, *Constitutional Revolution*, 172–85.
[136] Canny, *Elizabethan Conquest of Ireland*, chs. 2, 3; Ellis, *Tudor Ireland*, 177–80 and ch. 8; Lennon, *Sixteenth-Century Ireland*, 164–75.

however, in the second half of the sixteenth century, as noted, plantation had established itself as the third Tudor innovation through which Ireland became a glaring exception to the norm politically and socially that obtained in the English crown's multinational conglomerate. As such it represents the third of the flashpoints stemming from the new departures of the 1530s and institutionalised in the second half of the century that comprised the Tudor *hereditas damnosa* to the embryonic British state that developed with the succession of the Scottish Stuarts to the throne of England.

These three increasingly charged flashpoints – the anglicisation of the personnel of government, the militarisation of the system of government itself, and plantation pursued as a key instrument of pacification and reform – steadily exacerbated the tensions between the local elites and the regime at the centre as the campaign on behalf of the English Reformation proceeded. As such they go far towards explaining the chequered history of the campaign and its anomalous outcome. As the prejudices of the elites against reform from the centre were increasingly confirmed by bitter experience so their attitude towards the crown's ecclesiastical innovations hardened from initial ambiguity in the reign of Henry VIII to tacit and finally forthright resistance in the reign of Elizabeth. In Ireland as in Wales however the cooperation of the local elite was crucial to the implementation of the reform programme. No doubt the Old English were increasingly disregarded in the staffing of the central administration. Nevertheless they and the native elite continued to rule the roost in the localities into the Stuart period. Hence the crown remained dependent on both as the instruments of local government whether to operate the shire system in the colonial territory or to act as officers in the rudimentary system of local government that began to be set in place as the conquest gained ground in the native and nativised lordships.[137] It was upon the local elite, therefore, as in Wales, that the crown perforce devolved responsibility for securing conformity with the religion of their prince as by law established. Unlike the Welsh elite, however, their counterparts in Ireland led the way in dissenting from the officially promulgated religion. As noted in the survey of the course of the Reformation campaign earlier they increasingly evaded and eventually outrightly refused to swear to the supremacy or to participate in the rites prescribed in the Elizabethan Prayer Book. They failed to impose the recusancy fines as churchwardens and magistrates. In parliament they blocked the Draconian recusancy laws, even in

---

[137] Bradshaw, *Dissolution of the Religious Orders*, 202–3; Ellis, *Tudor Ireland*, 166–70; Brady, *Chief Governors*, chs. 5, 6, 7, passim.

modified form, enacted in England in the 1570s and 1580s.[138] Conversely as their attitude towards the Reformation hardened so their attitude to the Counter Reformation became more open. Thus, under Henry VIII they turned a blind eye to clerical resistance of the king's claim to a royal ecclesiastical supremacy. In the reign of Mary they took the initiative in reintroducing the rites of the old religion, anticipating official authorisation. In the early years of the reign of Elizabeth they allowed the missionaries of the Counter Reformation to gad up and down throughout their territories and to reoccupy the religious houses from which they had been extruded. In the succeeding decades they proceeded increasingly to promote the mission, according its clergy a social status quite above anything shown them in the medieval period. Further, they ensured that their children were soundly instructed in matters of religion, sending them to school to masters of a reliably Catholic persuasion, and for higher studies to Counter Reformation centres on the continent in preference to the now tainted Oxford and Cambridge. In consequence, a new generation of leaders of the two historic communities was moulded deeply committed to Roman Catholicism and to its propagation in their territories. Meanwhile, their siblings similarly schooled but lacking an inheritance provided ready recruits for the armies engaged on the Catholic side in the European Wars of Religion or for the Counter Reformation mission in Ireland. Needless to add that where the local elite led the people followed in a social environment highly attuned to deference.[139]

    That much said, the credit for ensuring the triumph of Roman Catholicism as the confession of the broad mass of the Irish people must go ultimately to the missionaries themselves. Their achievement was to avail of the opportunity thus offered to inculturate their creed within the living tradition while at the same time undermining the credibility of the state-sponsored Reformation as an alien, heretical innovation. Here the contribution of the fifteenth-century movement of Observantism assumes major significance in preconditioning the environment in which the religious struggle was engaged. First its effect was that the crown's programme of ecclesiastical reform encountered stiff clerical resistance from the outset and that the movement of opposition immediately sought to establish links with the incipient Counter Reformation movement on the continent. Thus already in the 1530s the friars were singled out, the Observants to the fore, as the mainspring of clerical resistance to Henry VIII's assumption of a royal ecclesiastical supremacy in Ireland. In that respect, it might be noted in parenthesis, they differed

[138] Bradshaw, 'The beginnings of modern Ireland'.
[139] Lennon, *Sixteenth-Century Ireland*, 315–24.

from their continental brethren who provided a valuable source of
evangelists for the Reformation – Luther, after all, was an Augustinian
friar, indeed an Observant. As early as 1534, two years before the
Henrician Reformation was promulgated by statute in Ireland, and four
years before the campaign on its behalf was launched there, the superior
general of the Franciscan Observants, passing through London on his
way to visit the Irish communities, felt able to assure the imperial
ambassador that his Irish brethren could be relied on to withstand
Henry VIII's ecclesiastical pretensions.[140] His confidence was fully
vindicated in the event. When in 1539–40 the Geraldine League
descended upon the Pale the friars, under the aegis of the Observants,
were found to be mounting a propaganda campaign on its behalf,
preaching it up as a religious crusade and promising eternal reward to
those who should lose their lives while engaged on it. This was the news
brought back by a Galway merchant in the early summer of 1539 from a
trading expedition into O'Donnell's country (Donegal) in Ulster.[141]
Meanwhile a prominent member of the Dublin administration, John
Alen, warned Cromwell in London that should the forces of the League
invade the Pale, the supposedly loyal colonists could not be relied on to
resist 'much the rather, I doubt nothing, by the enticement and conduct
of our friars obstinates [Observants] and other our religious persons'.[142]
Similar testimony is provided by the policy of the papacy at this time in
favouring the friars as nominees for ecclesiastical promotion: six of the
ten papal provisions to Irish bishoprics between 1539 and 1540 were
made in their favour.[143] Finally and most significantly as an augury of
later developments, the Observants took the initiative from the outset in
establishing links between the movement of resistance in Ireland and the
incipient Counter Reformation movement burgeoning on the continent.
Thus in 1540 the vicar-provincial of the Irish Franciscan Observants
embarked on a continental mission to solicit the support of the pope and
the emperor for the resistance campaign while a separate delegation was
dispatched to the recently formed (Counter Reformation inspired)
branch of the Franciscans, the Capuchins, to appeal for the introduction
of the fraternity to Ireland.[144] What emerges from all of this then is that
the religious situation encountered by the Reformation in Ireland
differed significantly from that prevailing at the same time in Wales or
indeed in this respect in England. Unlike these latter, Ireland possessed

---

[140] Bradshaw, *Dissolution of Religious Orders*, 208.
[141] *Ibid.*, 210–11.   [142] *S.P. Henry VIII*, iii, 145, 223.
[143] Bradshaw, *Dissolution of Religious Orders*, 209; Cf. Jones, *Counter-Reformation*, 3–4.
[144] F. X. Martin, 'The Observant movement in Ireland', *Irish Catholic Historical Committee
Proc.* (1960), 14–15; Bradshaw, *Dissolution of Religious Orders*, 208.

in the orders of friars a dynamic, numerous, widely dispersed and highly respected spiritual elite – the fruits of the Observant movement of reform – who directed their formidable resources to subverting the state-sponsored religious innovations from the outset and linked the resistance with the Counter Reformation just then burgeoning on the continent.

Second, the high repute gained for the friars in pre-Reformation Ireland by the Observant renewal ensured that the voice of dissent carried special moral authority among the laity. Such is the disconsolate message contained in the dispatch of Thomas Agarde, a reform-minded New English official in 1538 who lamented that:

The false and crafty bloodsuckers, the Observants, as they will be called most holiest, so that there remains more virtue in one of their coats and knotted girdles than ever was in Christ's passion. It is hard for any poor man to speak against their abusions here, for here is none from the highest to the lowliest may abide the hearing of it spiritual ... nor temporal. And in especial they that rule all, that be the temporal lawyers which have the king's fee.[145]

Agarde's testimony is especially valuable for directing attention to the attitude of the professional elite of the colony, the lawyers, in contrast to their Welsh counterparts. The attitude of the lawyers there is exemplified in the incident noted in surveying the Reformation campaign there, in which the Observants who attempted to mount a campaign of resistance to the Reformation in Cardiff were pounced upon by the local magistracy and sent packing under arrest to London.[146] As will have been gathered from the earlier survey of the mission the reputation of the friars remained undiminished into the Elizabethan period. It is attested in Holinshed's *Chronicles* no less at the beginning of the 1570s. There Richard Stanyhurst, that idiosyncratic chronicler of contemporary Ireland, reported, in rather the same astonished tones as the imperial ambassador in 1534, that the native Irish, despite their state of general unregeneracy, 'honour devout friars ... suffer them to pass quietly, spare them and their mansions whatever outrage they show the country besides'.[147] Contemplating Stanyhurst's comment the personal testimony of a native bard three decades later may be cited. Here Lochlainn Ó Dálaigh elegises the recently dissolved Franciscan foundation at Multyfarnham – razed by the forces of the crown in 1601 – in a poem which testifies from personal experience to what the friars' presence meant to the inhabitants of the lordships.[148] He laments the

---

[145] Quoted in Bradshaw, *Dissolution of Religious Orders*, 11.
[146] Above, p. 76 and n. 88.   [147] Quoted, Bradshaw, *Dissolution of Religious Orders*, 11.
[148] The poem is reproduced in C. Mhág Craith, OFM (ed.), *Dán na mBráthar Mionúr* (Dublin, 1967), no. 21. Caball, 'Intellectual reaction and continuity', 142–3.

loss of Multyfarnham – and in doing so incidentally celebrates it – as a place of worship and of divine reconciliation for the people, as a haven of charity for the poor, as a convivial meeting-place for the nobility, as a treasure-store of learning and of books for the literati, and finally, as an edification to all by the holy lives of its community. Writing hard upon the Kinsale débâcle in 1601 and the subsequent collapse of the rebellion with the submission of the Ulster earls in 1603, Ó Dálaigh no doubt conceived his poem as an epitaph for a world now past. History was to prove him wrong. Even as he mourned, the friars were regrouping, adapting to the new world established by the Tudor Conquest and entering upon yet another phase of vigorous expansion. Their place in the esteem and affection of the historical communities of the island was to remain secure through the dark era of religious persecutions on which Ireland was now entering. So far as the immediate matter in hand is concerned, however, the point is that the effect of the fifteenth-century reform among the friars was not only to ensure that the Reformation was resisted in Ireland from the outset by a spiritual elite that was numerous and widely dispersed, one moreover that proceeded to establish links with the Counter Reformation movement on the continent, but its further effect was to endow the voice of dissent with special moral authority among the lay community.

The final consideration building on the other two concerns the contribution of Observantism towards the actual process itself by which the Counter Reformation missionaries succeeded in inculturating Tridentine Roman Catholicism as the religion of 'faith and fatherland' in Ireland. In that regard it is as well to begin by noting that in one important respect the promoters of the Reformation stole a march on the mission. This was in the translation and publication of texts. The first evidence that the mission had taken the matter in hand dates as late as the last decade of the century. True, this brings the friars to the fore once more. It concerns the Franciscan expatriate community at St Anthony's, Louvain, soon to emerge as the pivot of the Franciscan missionary effort in Ireland. Here in 1597, Flaithrí Ó Maoilchonaire (Florence Conry), scion of a family of native historiographers, took the initiative in translating a catechism from Spanish into Irish and in dispatching it to the mission.[149] The first printed text in Irish, again a catechism compiled by another member of the community, the erstwhile bard, Giolla Brighde Ó hEodhusa, did not appear until 1611.[150] A spate

---

[149] Brian Ó Cuív, 'The Irish language in the early modern period', in T. W. Moody, F. X. Martin and F. J. Byrne (eds.), *New History of Ireland*, iii (Oxford, 1976), 509–45 at 532–3.

[150] *Ibid.*, 511–12.

of other printed texts followed in the course of the decade: a devotional
work by Ó Maoilchonaire in 1616; a book on the sacrament of penance
by Aodh Mac Aingil in 1618; and a summary of the Franciscan rule
again attributed to Ó Maoilchonaire, which is dated to between 1610
and 1614.[151] Although the friars emerge here also in the vanguard of the
Counter Reformation mission, nonetheless it must be acknowledged
that in this sphere they lagged behind the promoters of the Reformation.
As early as 1564, Elizabeth I herself, perhaps alerted by the agitation on
behalf of vernacularisation in Wales, indicated her support for a similar
approach to the campaign in Ireland by recommending a candidate for
the see of Kildare on the grounds that 'he is well able as we heare saye,
to preache in the Irish tongue'. More to the point in the mid 1560s she
funded a scheme for the translation and printing of the New Testament,
and chivied the Dublin administration, where the project, as so many
others relating to the campaign, seems to have been buried. Her nagging
notwithstanding it did not come to fruition until 1603 – still anticipating
by eight years the first of the Louvain publications. Meanwhile, moreover, as early as 1571 the first Reformation catechism in Irish appeared
in print, sponsored by William Ussher, grandfather of the famous
protestant archbishop of Armagh, and patriarch of one of the few
Dublin patrician families that conformed permanently to the religion by
law established. Then, in the 1580s, the Munster planter, William
Herbert, significantly a Welshman, arranged for the dissemination of the
Our Father, Creed and Ten Commandments in Irish among his
tenants.[152] All to no avail as time would show. By 1603, as outlined
earlier, the religion of the Counter Reformation had come to be
perceived as the ancient faith of the Irish and the reformed Church of
Ireland had been repudiated as an heretical alien innovation.

A number of factors combined to negate the apparent advantage
gained by the state-sponsored Reformation in the translation and
publication of texts. In the first place, the various initiatives noted above
were neither sustained nor coordinated. By far the greater number of
Reformation evangelists in Ireland, unlike Wales, remained wedded to
the imperialist doctrine classically expounded in Edmund Spenser's *A
View of the present state of Ireland*.[153] This held that the necessary
precondition of a successful campaign of evangelisation was a process of
anglicisation which was itself the precondition, so the imperialist logic

[151] *Ibid.*
[152] *Ibid.*
[153] Bradshaw, 'Robe and sword in the conquest of Ireland, in C. Cross, D. Loades and
    J. J. Scarisbrick (eds.), *Law and Government under the Tudors: essays presented to Sir
    Geoffrey Elton on his retirement* (Cambridge, 1988), 139–62.

ran, of civilising the Irish.[154] Thus at best the few enthusiasts for vernacularisation were left to their own devices when not actively discouraged and thwarted.[155] The problem was compounded by an absence of the necessary political will to drive the project forward. The administrators whether in Dublin or in London either shared the imperialist mentality of Spenser or, as *politiques*, accorded priority to the more immediately impinging political situation.[156] Further, in any case the translation and printing of texts could only be turned to advantage by evangelists linguistically equipped to utilise them for worship and for the instruction of an overwhelmingly monoglot, Irish speaking population: even in the old colonial territory the vast majority of the inhabitants were monoglot Irish speakers. In that light it can be seen that, as in Wales, the response of the local elite was crucial for only from its ranks could such evangelists be recruited. However, in contrast to Wales, as noted earlier, the elites of the two historic communities of the island were to the fore in resisting the religion 'by law established'. Inversely it was from these that the missionaries who conducted the campaign on behalf of the Counter Reformation were recruited. So it transpired in Ireland that the Counter Reformation mission not the Reformation campaign was conducted in the language 'understanded of the people'. Even the missionaries recruited from the old colonial elite, despite their ingrained cultural prejudices regarding the 'wild Irish', sooner or later came to realise the importance of Irish as a medium through which to propagate their message.[157] So it transpired in turn, despite the head-start of the Reformation in the matter of translation and publication of texts, Counter Reformation Catholicism became entrenched in Ireland as the religion of faith and fatherland.

The processes through which this remarkable feat was achieved in defiance of the 'will of the prince' and the resources of the state, provide a mirror image of the processes through which the English Reformation acquired similar status in the case of Wales. First, the fact that the

---

[154] *Ibid.*

[155] Bradshaw, 'Sword, word and strategy in the Reformation in Ireland, *Historical Journal,* 21 (1978), 475–502.

[156] Ellis, *Tudor Ireland,* ch. 7 passim.

[157] The case of Richard Creagh, the first Counter Reformation archbishop of Armagh, may be cited as an early example of the change of heart. Although his background as a member of a prominent merchant family in Limerick endowed him with all the cultural prejudices of the Old English, he composed an Irish grammar clearly intended to assist in equipping Old English missionaries to evangelise in Irish, Bradshaw, 'The Reformation in the cities'. Creagh's response may be taken to reflect an early stage of the mental shift whereby the literati of the two communities would soon begin to articulate a patriotic affirmation of their common identity as the Catholic Irish, see Caball below, pp. 112–39 *passim.*

mission was conducted almost solely by activists recruited from the elites of the two historic communities lent credibility to its message among the people generally. Second, a central feature of the missionaries' evangelising strategy was to suffuse their preaching with patriotic sentiment. In particular, Tridentine Roman Catholicism was preached up as the religion of the ancient Celtic church, the cherished heritage handed on through the centuries since the conversion of the Irish by St Patrick in the fifth century; conversely, the state-sponsored Reformation was denounced not merely as heretical but as an alien innovation.[158] Third, by propagating that message through the medium of Irish, the language in which the Patrician heritage was enshrined and handed on, the missionaries not only ensured its intelligibility but enhanced its credibility among the people. Fourth, the credibility of the message was further reinforced by the exploitation, as an instrument of evangelisation, of the various cultural modes, literary, historical etc., in which native values, aspiration and collective consciousness generally found expression. All the more was this the case because an incidental consequence as in similar circumstances in Wales was to generate a native cultural revival which flowered in due time in a baroque Renaissance in the seventeenth century.[159] Finally, the association of the Counter Reformation with native culture was clinched when in response to the strategy outlined above, the mission began to attract evangelists from the professional families of bards, historiographers, genealogists, scribes etc. whose task it was to preserve, cultivate and transmit the native cultural heritage.[160] By these means then Counter Reformation Catholicism came to be identified with that same heritage, and the state-reformed Church of Ireland rejected as alien and heretical – an Eaglais Gallda' [The Foreign Church/The English Church].

Assessing the significance of Observantism for this achievement it can be said that the missionaries, led by the friars, harvested where the

---

[158] See above pp. 98–102.

[159] The coinage 'baroque Renaissance' is my own. However the notion of a renewal of native learning in the seventeenth century has been increasingly canvassed by intellectual historians in recent years e.g. Breandán Ó Buachalla, 'Na Stiobhartaigh agus an tAos Léinn: Cing Seamas', Proceedings of the Royal Irish Academy, 83, C (1983), 81–134. 'Annála Ríoghachta Éireann is Foras Feasa ar Éirinn: an Comthéacs Comhaimseartha', Studia Hibernica, 22–3 (1985), 59–105. 'James our true king: the ideology of Irish royalism in the seventeenth century', in D. G. Boyce et al. (eds.), Political Thought in Ireland Since the Seventeenth Century (London, 1993), 7–35; Marc Caball, 'Intellectual reaction and continuity'; Bradshaw, 'Geoffrey Keating's Forus Feasa: an apologia for Irish Ireland' in B. Bradshaw, W. Maley and A. Hadfield (eds.), Representing Ireland. Literature and the Origins of Conflict, 1534–1660 (Cambridge, 1993), 172. The material is generally surveyed, though not within such an interpretative frame, in Brian Ó Cuiv, above n. 53.

[160] See Ó Buachalla, 'Na stiobhartaigh', and Aisling Ghéar (Dublin, 1997).

fifteenth-century reformers ploughed and harrowed. As the career of the zealous Observant and master of bardic religious verse, Pilib Bocht Ó hUiginn, serves to illustrate they simply developed a strategy pioneered earlier by the Observants in exploiting the resources of the vernacular. These also had recourse to the modes of native culture.[161] In consequence they also became associated with the professional families dedicated to the cultivation of the lore in which the heritage was transmitted. No accident then that the Counter Reformation friars as the heirs of the Observant tradition led the way in inculturating Roman Catholicism in the native tradition. In that connection the contribution of the Franciscan community of St Anthony's, Louvain, to which Breandán Ó Buachalla has drawn attention, deserves special emphasis.[162] These above all deserve credit for mediating and developing the Observant tradition of evangelisation. Their contribution in the translation and publication of texts, in generating original works in literature – in poetry and prose as well as in the staple fare of catechisms, devotional reading and polemic – and in scholarship, most especially of an antiquarian nature, assuredly constitutes St Anthony's a veritable powerhouse in driving the process of inculturation and in launching the seventeenth-century native baroque Renaissance.[163] Further, it was by no means incidental to the achievement that St Anthony's established itself at the same time as an intellectual centre of international status through its contribution to the Counter Reformation's often neglected Augustinian revival.[164]

Finally, it may serve to round off the discussion to illustrate the process of inculturation in practice by observing the development of a Counter Reformation mentality in Irish poetry in its early stages. The work of three priest-poets of the decades straddling the sixteenth and seventeenth centuries provides apt illustrative material. One, Giolla Brighde Ó hEodhusa, already encountered as the compiler of the first catechism in Irish to appear in print, was among the earliest of the bardic poets who gave up their careers to join the mission – in his case as a Franciscan friar. The poem he composed to mark the transition illustrates the shift in values now taking place within the profession under the impact of the Counter Reformation. Giolla Brighde's poem constitutes an apologia as well as a valedictory.[165] He insists that his abandonment of his career implies no slight on the profession. Nor was

---

[161] Above, p. 90.   [162] Ó Buachalla, 'Na Stiobhartaigh'.   [163] *Ibid.*

[164] For instance, St Anthony's produced the Counter Reformation edition of St Augustine's *Opera Omnia*. It was also closely associated with the work of Petrus Jansenius who lived next door.

[165] The edited text is in Mhág Craith *Dán na mBráthar Mionúr*, no. 5. For a translation see *ibid.*, ii, 11.

it motivated by disillusionment in response to the reduced prospects offered the poet in the new Ireland now emerging in the aftermath of the conquest. Rather, he protests, his departure grieved him sorely. However, he accepted the sacrifice as the cost of attaining to a knowledge more precious even than that preserved in bardic lore, the knowledge of God acquired through the study of sacred theology. The second priest-poet is not known to have practised bardic poetry before opting for a priestly vocation. Yet he might be said literally to personify the continuity of the tradition dating back to Observantism whereby members of the bardic families offered themselves for service in the priesthood. This is Maolmhuire Ó hUiginn, no less distinguished in his day, as metropolitan archbishop of Tuam, than his brother Taghd Dall, dean of sixteenth-century bardic poetry: they hailed from the same family of professional bards that gave Pilib Bocht to the Observants.[166] Whatever Maolmhuire's earlier formation he took to the practice of the family profession as a priest-missionary. Two poems he composed in the service of the mission provide a special insight into the mind of a native *literatus*, schooled in the values of the Counter Reformation, as he reflects on the fate that had overtaken his native country.[167] The tone of the poems is sombre, depicting the *Gaeil* languishing under an oppressive civil regime and a draconian code of penal religious legislation. Seeking the meaning of their misfortune within the scheme of God's providence – a characteristic preoccupation of religious commentators throughout Europe at the time – he finds it by reference to an Old Testament parallel, the Chosen People in bondage in Egypt. The plight of the *Gaeil* therefore, Maolmhuire urges, is to be regarded as a trial sent by God to chastise a people who had proven wantonly unfaithful. Yet it should be noted – all the more so since the *motif* was to become a characteristic trope of seventeenth-century religious verse in Irish – that the lesson he draws is not one of passive resignation. *Pace* recent revisionist commentators the lesson rather is the need for moral regeneration with a view to liberation. Restored to God's favour, Maolmhuire urges, the *Gaeil* will be enabled to throw off the yoke now laid upon them, just as were the Israelites of old having undergone their forty years' desert purgation.[168]

The interest of the third case study lies partly in the fact that the priest-poet concerned, Eoghan Ó Dubhthaigh, is not linked by kinship

---

[166] Caball, 'Intellectual reaction and continuity', 139–40.

[167] *Ibid.*, 140–1. For a third poem by Maolmhuire which articulates the new Renaissance patriotism now being assimilated within the bardic corpus see Caball, below, pp. 117–18.

[168] Bradshaw, 'The bardic response'; Caball 'The Gaelic Mind'; O Buachalla, 'Poetry and politics'.

to a bardic family. For despite the lack, Ó Dubhthaigh displays 'a clerical mind rooted in the Gaelic tradition' as Marc Caball aptly phrases it.[169] From the point of view the lengthy poem now to be considered is instructive not only in terms of its content but also for its formal structure.[170] Formally it combines the traditional *genres* of eulogy and satire in a poem that constitutes at one and the same time an edificatory paean to the Virgin Mary and a polemic against the false teachings of the Protestants. In substance then it extols the sinless Mother of God held up as the model of all Christian virtue. As polemic it satirises three native priests who conformed to the religion by law established for the sake, Ó Dubhthaigh alleges, of securing ecclesiastical preferment. The two themes are combined by elaborating a contrast – *ad nauseam* it might be felt – between Mary the model Christian and the three priest-apostates, most especially the notorious Miler McGrath – Giolla Brighde plays on the irony that his name proclaims him to be a servant of Mary – who, wallowing in ill-gotten luxury, personify the vices of the unregenerate. Deploying the contrast emblematically Ó Dubhthaigh proceeds to endow it with a wider polemical reference in the context of the religious struggle for hearts and minds in Ireland. In that struggle Mary becomes the 'type' of the Catholic Church of the Counter Reformation which continues to honour her and the saints in accordance with the traditional faith handed on to the *Gaeil* from the time of Patrick and the Golden Age of Celtic Christianity. On the other side, the turncoat clerics represent the so-called Church of Ireland established by Henry VIII which seeks to entice the people to betray their heritage by submitting to the new heresies of Luther and Calvin and which accordingly reviles Mary and the saints, and lures souls to perdition as manifested in the lifestyles of the apostates now esconced in Church of Ireland bishoprics.

Two points must be made before concluding concerning the value of the foregoing examples as illustrations of the confessional ethos which, it has been argued here, took hold in Ireland in the second half of the sixteenth century. First, a caveat; the suggestion is not that the small cluster of confessional verse that survives from the period played a central part in transforming the native mind-set. Then as now after all bardic poetry was an elite taste. Rather, it is suggested, the case studies reflect the content of the popular preaching of the Counter Reformation missionaries who, with the connivance of the elite, were gadding up and

---

[169] Caball, 'Intellectual reaction and continuity', 136.
[170] Mhág Craith (ed.), *Dán na mBráthar Mionúr*, i no. 27 (trans. *ibid.*, ii, 58–71). For another exposition of Ó Dubhthaigh's oeuvre in the same vein see Caball, below, p. 119.

down the country since the 1570s at the latest. Second, that suggestion seems all the more persuasive in the light of the correspondence that appears between the attitudes and values affirmed in the verse and those manifested by the two communities as revealed in the evidence reviewed earlier. Particularly telling in that connection is the correspondence between the attitudes and values these Gaelic poems affirm and the confessional stance of the people of Cork and its environs, that bastion of Old English loyalism in the south west, as described in detail in the disconsolate report of the reformer Lyon, its Church of Ireland bishop.[171]

Finally, to return to the significance of Observantism as a variable between the factors conditioning the religious struggle in the English crown's two Celtic borderland dominions. In the light of the foregoing it seems reasonable to claim not only that the fifteenth-century reform movement among the friars ensured that the Reformation was resisted from the outset by a dynamic, numerous and widely dispersed clerical elite who initiated contact with the incipient Counter Reformation movement on the continent; not only further that the voice of dissent commanded special moral authority among the historic inhabitants of the island. Additionally and crucially now the Observants may be credited with pioneering the evangelical strategy developed by the Counter Reformation missionaries which secured the identification of Tridentine Roman Catholicism with the religion to which the Irish were converted by St Patrick in the fifth century and thereby with the religion handed down from the ancient Celtic church as the heritage of the nation. The Observant reform in short played no small part in ensuring that by the end of the sixteenth century Tridentine Roman Catholicism had come to be adopted as the religious confession of the two historic communities of Ireland, and the English Reformation rejected, the will of their prince notwithstanding, as a heretical foreign innovation. For that reason therefore the movement earns a special place in the story of an identity shift that affected the entire course of modern Irish history. By the end of the sixteenth century the process was well under way by which the Gaelic natives and the Old English were to find a common identity as the Catholic Irish.

Two reflections may be permitted in retrospect by way of epilogue. One concerns an issue raised early on but set aside: the precise juncture at which the forces identified here coalesced to give the Counter Reformation an irreversible momentum. That historic turning point remains elusive. Nevertheless a suggestion may now be ventured. If, as

---

[171] Above, pp. 50–4.

is argued, the state-sponsored Reformation campaign was virtually pre-empted by a counter-campaign of resistance to Henry VIII's ecclesiastical pretensions, mounted by a much respected local clerical elite who sought to forge links with the incipient Counter Reformation on the continent; and if, as is argued further, the response of the lay elite to the state-sponsored campaign was increasingly soured from the earliest stages by the Reformation's magisterial provenance as the ecclesiastical corollary of the Tudor revolution in government, and if, as is finally argued, the cooperation of the elite was essential for the implementation of the crown's ecclesiastical programme, then it seems reasonable to suggest that by the time the battle for hearts and minds was fully joined by the two movements in the 1570s the circumstances were such as to render the outcome well nigh a foregone conclusion.

The second reflection addresses the subject proposed in the title and maintained at the centre of the analysis thereafter: the implications of the religious struggle for identity formation in Wales and Ireland. In that connection it appears that the state-sponsored Reformation campaign as the ecclesiastical corollary of the Tudor revolution in government served as a catalyst in both Celtic borderlands. For the Welsh the Tudor revolution in church and state served to confirm their euphoric expectations from the Tudors as British monarchs thus facilitating the painless assimilation of the community within the English imperial kingdom, the modern multinational British state in embryo. However, contrary to the imperialistic designs of its architects, the effect of the union was to enhance the awareness on the part of the Welsh of their national identity now subsumed under a new – or if preferred a newly recovered – sense of Britishness. To that end the revolutions in church and state worked symbiotically, as tailored in each case to suit the predilections of a patriotic and conservatively minded local elite to whom the Tudor regime chose to entrust the implementation of both revolutionary programmes.

It was quite to the contrary in Ireland. The implementation of the two revolutionary programmes operated symbiotically to bring to fruition a long-germinating sense of alienation from the English metropolis while at the same time precipitating a process whereby the two ethnic communities, traditionally mutual enemies, forged a new racial identity as the Catholic Irish. Thus the political programme, with its three-pronged strategy of anglicisation, militarisation and plantation, transformed the separatist sensibilities of the old colonial elite into a form of Anglo-Irish patriotism which affirmed Ireland as the communities' native *patria*. Concurrently the effect on the inhabitants of the Gaelic and gaelicised lordships was to cause them to subsume their sept-focused, socio-political horizons under a new – or, if preferred, newly intensified – awareness of the island as the common heritage of the native Irish. The process by which these by no means complementary collective consciousness were fused into the common identity of the Catholic Irish was further facilitated by the emergence, as a function of the crown's reform strategy, of a new colonial elite to undermine the existing socio-political order. The appearance of the protestant New English to challenge the hegemony of the two established elites provided the latter with a common enemy, an alien 'other', over against whom the old elites could identify themselves as the joint custodians of a common faith and fatherland. The process was further facilitated by a constitutional transformation effected in conjunction with the Anglo-Welsh union. This resulted incidentally, but nonetheless with incontrovertible legal validity, from the enactment in 1541–2 of the crown's absolute and sovereign title over its Irish dominion. The effect was to elevate the status of the island reciprocally from that of a medieval Lordship to that of a kingdom – appended to the English crown but autonomous from the English kingdom, so the Irish were to maintain thereafter.[172] However the force that proactively operated to forge these bonding sensibilities into a common identity based on a common faith and a common fatherland originated mainly in the evangelising strategy of the Counter Reformation missionaries. It was the achievement of the missionaries in rooting Tridentine Roman Catholicism in the cultural heritage of the two communities that led both to perceive themselves as together forming the historic Irish. In sum, the cataclysm of the Tudor revolution in church and state in Ireland marks paradoxically the moment at which the island's assimilation within the multinational conglomerate of the modern United Kingdom was preempted.[173]

---

[172] For an elaboration of this thesis by reference to the corpus of contemporary Gaelic poetry see Caball, 'Intellectual reaction, and continuity.

[173] Bradshaw, *Constitutional Revolution*, ch. 9, especially 263–7. Cf. Smyth, below, pp. 301–20.

3   Faith, culture and sovereignty: Irish nationality and its development, 1558–1625

Marc Caball

This chapter is intended to outline and explore aspects of the evolution of Irish nationality and consciousness during the reigns of Elizabeth I and James I. It concludes with a consideration of why the implications of such a development pre-empted the possibility of an easy incorporation of the Irish within an overarching British identity, as successfully undertaken in Wales where the English crown's reforming initiatives over the same period encountered conditions in a Celtic fringe territory in many ways similar to those in the neighbouring island. It spans a period encompassing a process of critical political and social change in Ireland. In a country dominated by regional and localised potentates, and thus lacking an indigenous centralised political structure, it is tempting to infer a corresponding absence of a common political culture, ideology and mode of discourse. Paradoxically, however, the diffused nature of political organisation was counterbalanced by the homogeneity of elite Gaelic culture. The island, with the effective exception of the Pale area in and around the city of Dublin, was characterised by the centuries old and highly refined modes of Gaelic civilisation. Indeed, this Gaelic cultural ambience was not simply an insular phenomenon but extended from the Scottish Hebrides to the southern extremities of Ireland. When the Tudor monarchs began an ultimately cumulative drive to assert hegemony over the quasi-autonomous neighbouring island, they confronted an ancient and sophisticated culture which bound together the decentralised power bases of Ireland. Gaelic cultural dominance was highlighted by the effective acculturation of the descendants of the twelfth-century Anglo-Norman settlers, particularly those beyond the Pale. It will be seen here how the prolonged English conquest and its religious ancillary, the protestant reform movement, were significant factors in propelling, by way of reaction, the development of a revised and dynamic Irish identity in the late sixteenth and early seventeenth centuries.[1] This emergent sense of Irish nationality was predicated upon

---

[1] A contrary interpretation of early modern Gaelic literature stressing its supposed limited political understanding and provincialism has been advanced at length by Michelle O

three factors: insular territorial sovereignty, Gaelic cultural hegemony and allegiance to Roman Catholicism. A common historical consciousness and its corollary, a shared cultural *mentalité*, were the operative influences on the evolution of an early modern Irish sense of nationality.[2] The common institutional and professional characteristics of medieval Gaelic scholarship ensured that it was particularly well placed to sustain an innovative and resourceful reordering of cultural priorities in the period 1558–1625, despite the apparent handicap of a decentralised political structure.

Before going on to examine the manifestation and implications of early modern Irish nationality some discussion of the nature of the Gaelic source material may be useful at this introductory stage. Historians of Gaelic society have no corpus of public records to call upon in their researches. However, the survival of a relatively extensive bank of Gaelic literature from the period offers an alternative resource for the study of Gaelic cultural and political history. Literary activity at this point may be said to have been largely dominated by the work of an hereditary caste of bardic poets (*fileadha*) whose functions were as much political as literary. They operated within a professional structure which had taken shape as early as the thirteenth century, composing poetry according to common bardic referential and metrical paradigms and functioning in a pan-Gaelic social context. Employment of the standardised and conventional literary medium known as classical Irish further facilitated ideological projection against a national communal background. The primary outlet for bardic activity centred on a network of elite Gaelic and gaelicised households located throughout the island. In return for material patronage, bardic poets undertook an essentially political function for the seigneurial class. Drawing on a common and established stock of literary motifs and conventions, poets validated the dynastic status or aspirations of a poem's addressee. Bardic practice was communal in application and thus possessed public political

Riordan, *The Gaelic Mind and the Collapse of the Gaelic World* (Cork, 1990). O Riordan's thesis has been heavily criticised in Breandán Ó Buachalla, 'Poetry and politics in early modern Ireland', *Eighteenth-Century Ireland*, 7 (1992), 149–75; Marc Caball, '*The Gaelic Mind and the Collapse of the Gaelic World*: an appraisal', *Cambridge Medieval Celtic Studies*, 25 (1993), 87–96; Brendan Bradshaw, 'The bardic response to conquest and colonisation', *Bullán: An Irish Studies Journal*, 1: 1 (1994), 119–22. O Riordan's argument is basically an elaboration of a reading first proposed by T. J. Dunne, 'The Gaelic response to conquest and colonisation: the evidence of the poetry', *Studia Hibernica*, 20 (1980), 7–30.

[2] Regarding the importance of senses of the past in early modern political cultures, see Orest Ranum (ed.), *National Consciousness, History, and Political Culture in Early-Modern Europe* (Baltimore and London, 1975), 5.

implications. The political role of the poets is particularly evident in panegyrics composed for ruling lords. In these poems the standardised traits of lordliness, such as bravery, righteousness and generosity, are lauded in an act of overt legitimation. The poets located their subjects within a coded referential framework of validation and in doing so set an ideological seal of endorsement on their patrons' aspirations. A bardic ideological grammar placed poets in an influential social position, and they enjoyed easy access to the seigneurial class and consequently they wielded indirect political power. The poet/patron nexus not only explains the bardic class's intellectual importance, but assigns their poetry special importance in the canon of Gaelic source material.[3] In addition to bardic poetry which is the most extensive of extant Gaelic sources, historians have at their disposal a variety of genres in Irish, including law texts, miscellaneous poetry, annals and narrative prose texts.[4] In this study, bardic testimony is drawn upon for the most part, with occasional references to prose texts.

The appearance of Brendan Bradshaw's study of poems composed for members of the O'Byrne family of Gabhal Raghnuill in Wicklow during the period 1550 to 1630 marked the beginning of an ongoing debate about what the poetry reveals of contemporary *mentalités*. Bradshaw's reading of the O'Byrne poems stressed what he saw as an emerging dynamic outlook and increasing ideological relevance to contemporary political conditions. He argued that a portion, admittedly small, of the material was unambiguous in its illustration of national consciousness in the face of English military expansion.[5] Subsequent work in this area produced a contrary interpretation arguing for an apparently anachronistic backward-directed outlook on the part of the literati which precluded the development of a politicised national consciousness. The most elaborate presentation of this antiquarian reading of bardic poetry has been made by Michelle O Riordan. She argues for an essential ideological continuity in the bardic corpus in the late medieval and early modern periods, and she has drawn a picture of a static political culture

---

[3] Detailed introductions to bardic poetry and poets are to be had in J. E. Caerwyn Williams, 'The court poet in medieval Ireland', *Proceedings of the British Academy*, 57 (1971), 85–135; and Pádraig A. Breatnach, 'The chief's poet', *Proceedings of the Royal Irish Academy*, 83: C:3 (1983), 34–79. More generally on the poetry as an historical source see Marc Caball, 'Bardic poetry and the analysis of Gaelic mentalities', *History Ireland*, 2:2 (1994), 46–50.

[4] For recent work on prose material see Caoimhin Breatnach, *Patronage, Politics and Prose* (Maynooth, 1996).

[5] Brendan Bradshaw, 'Native reaction to the westward enterprise: a case-study in Gaelic ideology', in K. R. Andrews *et al.* (eds.), *The Westward Enterprise: English activities in Ireland, the Atlantic and America, 1480–1650* (Liverpool, 1978), 65–80.

characterised by acceptance of the *fait accompli*.[6] The extent to which the antiquarian reading of the material has been unquestioningly enshrined in current Irish historiography is typified by an extract from an essay by Roy Foster on Anglo-Irish relations:[7]

The evidence of the literature, notably that of bardic poetry, implies a culture where praise-poems were produced for English settler patrons almost as easily as for Gaelic lords, and where bonds were perceived along lines of caste solidarity or client relationships rather than territorially, much less nationally. Borders existed more obviously within the island.

Contrary to the notion of early modern Ireland as constituting a patchwork of provincial and politically limited family allegiances, this essay posits a more complex scenario of local seigneurial elites inter-linked by a shared political culture which was coloured by a common view of the past and which culminated in the development of an inclusive politicised sense of nationality during the reigns of Elizabeth and James.[8] While various and different issues have been raised in the historiographical debate regarding the assessment of Gaelic responses to conquest and colonisation, the primary focus here is on perceptions and expressions of national consciousness. In the absence of an evolving nation-state in early modern Ireland, the consolidation of which in several European countries served as a focus for burgeoning notions of nationality, delineation of a specifically Irish awareness is occasionally opaque. Orest Ranum has observed that places, missionaries, saints, martial heroes, miraculous events, peoples and lands all went to make up the catholic range of elements providing varieties of consciousness in the medieval period.[9] In sixteenth-century Ireland these and similar factors continued to contribute to the sum total of ethnic identity. It is possible that they might have continued as the sole determinants of identity were it not for the intrusion of an external force which sought to impose alternative administrative, social and linguistic structures thereby challenging the medieval assumptions of the Gaelic elite and demanding that they re-evaluate and reinvigorate notions of collective

[6] See note 1 above.

[7] R. F. Foster, *Paddy and Mr Punch: connections in Irish and English history* (Harmondsworth, 1993), 87. Foster cites no authority in support of his comprehensive verdict on the Gaelic source material. In the same interpretative vein see also Joep Leerssen, 'Wildness, wilderness, and Ireland: medieval and early modern patterns in the demarcation of civility', *Journal of the History of Ideas*, 56:1 (1995), 25–39, 36.

[8] For a discussion of nationality in early medieval Ireland see Donnchadh Ó Corráin, 'Nationality and kingship in pre-Norman Ireland', in T. W. Moody (ed.), *Nationality and the Pursuit of National Independence*, Historical Studies, XI (Belfast, 1978), 1–35. See also Proinsias Mac Cana, 'Early Irish ideology and the concept of unity', in Richard Kearney (ed.), *The Irish Mind: exploring intellectual traditions* (Dublin, 1985), 56–78.

[9] Ranum, *National Consciousness*, 2–3.

identity and self-depiction.[10] Working from a conceptual triad of sovereignty, culture and religion, Gaelic and gaelicised Anglo-Norman literati enunciated an Irish national consciousness which was both dynamic and inclusive.

I

The motif of female personification of political and territorial sovereignty is long-attested in the Gaelic literary tradition. In the eleventh-century text *Baile in Scáil* the sovereignty figure is depicted dispensing the drink of sovereignty to a succession of Irish kings, both prehistoric and historical.[11] A sovereignty figure could, as the occasion demanded, represent the island of Ireland or a local territorial unit. Marriage between a sovereignty figure and the lord of a territory symbolised legitimate consummation of political power. Literary representations of marital harmony or in effect actual possession of political hegemony included agricultural fecundity as well as peace and stability within a lord's lands. The marital theme of goddess and king occurs quite early in the bardic corpus. In a poem composed by Giolla Brighde Mac Con Midhe (d. c. 1272) sometime after 1262 for Domhnall Óg O'Donnell (d. 1281), he styled his subject spouse of Ireland and he noted that ten of Domhnall's line had preceded him in similar marital union.[12] The motif remains current in bardic poetry down to the seventeenth century, and beyond in popular verse. In a poem of anonymous authorship composed for Philip O'Reilly (d. 1596), a minor nobleman who briefly held the lordship of east Bréifne, the topos is invoked to bolster his seigneurial aspirations. The motif was approached from a national angle with the poet declaring that Ireland awaited union with Philip.[13] It goes without saying that O'Reilly enjoyed no realistic chance of assuming a dominant political position in Ireland. Yet a literal reading of this reference oversimplifies and decontextualises its significance. The poet was not so much concerned with highlighting a possible political scenario as with seeking to validate his subject's ambitions within an ideological context. Employing a traditional mode of validation of both

---

[10] See Brendan Bradshaw, 'Nationalism and historical scholarship in modern Ireland', *Irish Historical Studies*, 26:104 (1989), 329–51, 345.

[11] Kuno Meyer (ed.), 'Mitteilungen aus irischen Handschriften: Baile in Scáil', *Zeitschrift für Celtische Philologie*, 3 (1901), 457–66. For a recent treatment of the sovereignty goddess see Máire Herbert, 'Goddess and king: the sacred marriage in early Ireland', in L. O. Fradenburg (ed.), *Women and Sovereignty* (Edinburgh, 1992), 264–75.

[12] See N. J. A. Williams (ed.), *The Poems of Giolla Brighde Mac Con Midhe*, Irish Texts Society (London, 1980), no. 8, 86, quatrain 17.

[13] James Carney (ed.), *Poems on the O'Reillys* (Dublin, 1950), no. 1, 7, l. 156.

aspiring and established authority, the poet aimed to sanction O'Reilly's actions publicly and to focus attention not only on his aspirations but also on his genealogical and other supposed credentials. While the practical effect of numerous such allusions in the bardic corpus was simply to locate and validate an individual's local position, the overall significance of the personification of Ireland is relevant to this study. The prevalence of the sovereignty motif in medieval and early modern literature establishes that the theory, if not the actuality, of Ireland's insular territorial integrity was commonly accepted by the Gaelic literati. The fact that the contractual focus of bardic political eulogy was invariably local in scope does not mean that the poets' ideological grammar was inherently provincial. On the contrary, despite the regional and local requirements of their professional activity, the poets operated within a pan-insular ideological context where the ultimate theoretical source of validation centred on the personification of the sovereignty of Ireland. In short, early modern bardic poets inherited a political vocabulary equipped to express political consciousness in an all-island setting. If there was no development in Ireland of the nation-state apparatus then emerging in parts of Europe, this should not be taken to deny all traces of early modern Irish national consciousness. It is argued here that bardic and other poets were able to draw on traditional notions of Ireland's territorial integrity to articulate a political response to conquest and colonisation along the lines of a national paradigm.

The idea of Ireland's geographical integrity is clearly evinced in poems composed during the reigns of Elizabeth I and James I. While the idea of insular sovereignty was already present in the Gaelic tradition, a significant flow of military, religious and commercial exchange between Ireland and the European continent in the late sixteenth and early seventeenth centuries served further to develop indigenous intellectual perceptions of territorial integrity.[14] For instance, the Renaissance notion of *patria* seems to be reflected in a series of poems composed either in exile or on the point of departure from Ireland.[15] Maolmhuire Ó hUiginn (d. c. 1591), sometime archbishop of Tuam and brother of the famous bardic poet Tadhg Dall, composed one such exile poem

---

[14] For the Irish abroad see, for example, Gráinne Henry, *The Irish Military Community in Spanish Flanders, 1586–1621* (Dublin, 1992).

[15] Regarding the concept of *patria* see J. H. Elliott, 'Revolution and continuity in early modern Europe', *Past & Present*, 42 (1969), 35–56, 47–50; Brendan Bradshaw, *The Irish Constitutional Revolution of the Sixteenth Century* (Cambridge, 1979), 276–7. See also Mícheál Mac Craith, 'Gaelic Ireland and the renaissance', in Glanmor Williams and Robert Owen Jones (eds.), *The Celts and the Renaissance: tradition and innovation* (Cardiff, 1990), 57–89, at 68.

apparently in Rome on the occasion of a return of a friend to Ireland. Favourable opening references to Rome, Italy, Spain and France frame discussion of Ireland in a European context. Indeed, Ó hUiginn contends that the western island not only deserves to be included in this company but also exceeds all other countries in comparison.[16] The addressee is reminded that the island's beauty justifies the difficulty of travelling there. On sight of Ireland the poem's subject will be relieved of depression and sadness. The poet lovingly chronicles the attractions of the country and he couches his description in terms redolent of biblical paradise. Ireland is depicted as an 'angelic land' and a 'fortress of Paradise'.[17] Indeed, Irish residence and devotion to God are explicitly linked when Ó hUiginn expresses confidence that should his subject stay in Ireland, which he defines as the 'fatherland' (*athardha*), he will remain loyal both to the Almighty and to native culture.[18] Two poems by William Nugent, Oxford-educated son of Richard Nugent (d. 1559), eighth baron of Delvin, are also indicative of a new type of Renaissance patriotism inclusive of the entire island. The poem beginning *Diombáidh triall ó thulchaibh Fáil* (It is sorrowful to leave the hills of Ireland) suggests a date of composition sometime around Nugent's departure for Oxford where in 1571 he was recorded as a student at Hart Hall.[19] Like Ó hUiginn he paints an idyllic picture of the island and declares that he loves no country other than Ireland.[20] A dichotomy is drawn between England and Ireland when he notes that were God to allow him return to his native land, he would not be concerned to visit England's noble families.[21] Given the eulogy of the island's physical qualities and the virtues of its people, this dichotomy unquestionably presents Ireland in the more positive light. The contrasting duality is further developed in Nugent's second poem of exile. On this occasion experience of life in England enables the author to mention aspects of culture and religion specific to Ireland.[22] Significantly, in view of the author's Anglo-Norman ancestry, he refers to the island as the land of both the Gaelic Irish (*Gaoidhil*) and the Anglo-Normans (*Gaill*).[23] The ethnic rapprochement

---

[16] For this poem see Thomas F. O'Rahilly (ed.), *Measgra dánta: miscellaneous Irish poems* (2 vols., Dublin and Cork, 1927), ii, no. 52 (*A fhir théid go Fiadh bhFuinidh*), 139–43. Ireland is described as a land without comparison to other countries ('iath nách samhail d'iath oile': l. 11).

[17] O'Rahilly, *Measgra*, ii, 140–1, ll. 38, 55 ('tír ainglidhe'), l. 64 ('port Pardhais').

[18] *Ibid.*, 141, ll. 57–60.

[19] Gerard Murphy (ed.), 'Poems of exile by Uilliam Nuinseann mac barúin Dealbhna', *Éigse: A Journal of Irish Studies*, 6 (1948–52), 8–15. Cf. Bradshaw, *The Irish Constitutional Revolution*, 285–8.

[20] Murphy, 'Poems', 11, quatrain 2 ('ní char fód oile acht Éirinn').

[21] *Ibid.*, 12, quatrain 5.

[22] *Ibid.*, poem II (*Fada i n-éagmais inse Fáil*).   [23] *Ibid.*, 15, quatrain 7.

between Ireland's historic communities is discussed later in this chapter but for the moment it is instructive to draw attention to an Anglo-Norman mind-set which encompassed inclusive ethnicity in the context of a consciousness of territorial integrity. Contact with a foreign culture and removal from Ireland also prompted heightened awareness in a poem composed by Fearghal Óg Mac an Bhaird, a prominent bardic poet in the northern part of the country in the late sixteenth and early seventeenth centuries. While he is primarily concerned with what he interprets as the adverse effects of the Reformation in Scotland, he also posits a dichotomy similar to that articulated by Nugent. In this instance a binary distinction is drawn between protestant Scotland and an Ireland loyal to the traditional faith. Probably composing in the early fifteen eighties Mac an Bhaird regrets that the quest for patronage has drawn him to Scotland, and fearing that he should die there he implores Jesus to allow him return home.[24] Here again, the evidence suggests a finely etched conception of Ireland's distinct territorial separateness. Likewise, the Franciscan and non-professional poet Eoghan Ó Dubhthaigh (d. 1590) in addressing the issue of religious conflict utilises the image of Catholic Ireland pitted against aggressive and heretical outsiders.[25] Apostrophising the island, he warns of the danger facing it, noting the predatory designs of Scots and Englishmen. Crucially, Ó Dubhthaigh urges Ireland not to become a 'little England' and comments on the country's distinguished status abroad.[26]

Not surprisingly, the notion of Ireland's geographical integrity retains its validity in the Jacobean period when English administrative hegemony was firmly established and the country's social and cultural landscape was in the process of significant change. If anything, external stimulus further encouraged oppositional notions of an insular territorial identity. Continuity in the exile genre is evident in a poem composed by a Roman Catholic clergyman, Brian Mac Giolla Phádraig (d. c. 1652), in 1614/15 prior to his departure for the continent.[27] Addressing

---

[24] Lambert McKenna (ed.), *Aithdioghluim dána: a miscellany of Irish bardic poetry* (2 vols., Dublin, 1939–40), i, no. 53 (*Dursan mh'eachtra go hAlbuin*), 204–7. In 1581 Mac an Bhaird was paid £100 for bardic poetry he had composed for James VI. See John Bannerman, 'The Scots language and the kin-based society', in Derick S. Thomson (ed.), *Gaelic and Scots in Harmony* (Glasgow, 1990), 1–19, at 10.

[25] Cuthbert Mhág Craith (ed.), *Dán na mbráthar mionúr* (2 vols., Dublin, 1967–80), i, no. 28 (*A Bhanbha is truagh do chor!*), 151–3; Mhág Craith, *Dán na mbráthar mionúr*, ii, 186–7.

[26] Mhág Craith, *Dán*, i, 152, quatrain 3 ('Narab tusa Saxa óg, a Bhanbha mhór, is fearr ainm!'). In *Mo thruaighe mar táid Gaoidhil!*, composed in the aftermath of the Ulster plantation, Fear Flatha Ó Gnimh warned of 'a new England called Ireland' ('Saxa nua dan hainm Éire'): O'Rahilly, *Measgra*, ii, no. 54, 147, l. 90.

[27] Cuthbert Mhág Craith (ed.), 'Brian Mac Giolla Phádraig', *Celtica*, 4 (1958), (*Truagh t'fhágbháil, a Inis Chuind*), no. VII, 103–205, at 115–20. For Mac Giolla Phádraig see

Ireland directly the poet speaks of his sorrow at the prospect of leaving so beautiful a country as his native land. However, on this occasion he was leaving not out of love for another country but simply because he wished to undertake further studies abroad. A marked feature of this composition centres on its author's dual-faceted approach. While the poem is initially directed to and concerned with the island of Ireland the poet also addresses the subject of its inhabitants, for his imminent removal from them as much as his departure from Ireland itself is a cause of regret.[28] He names families of both Gaelic and Anglo-Norman provenance in a list of those he holds dear. This dual perception is another example of the cumulative process in Gaelic literature pointing to an interethnic rapprochement at this period.

The conceit of Ireland personified as sovereignty's embodiment was also manipulated in a decidedly political fashion. This ideological refocusing of a conventional bardic theme is an example of how an innovative and dynamic resonance could be imparted to an apparently antiquated literary device.[29] The immediate implication of the invocation of the motif was to highlight the island's theoretical unity thus lending credence to the notion of immemorial insular integrity. The theme's appearance in the ideological context of early modern upheaval is indicative of a refinement or development of a political convention. In a bardic poem of Jacobean provenance entitled *Iomdha éagnach ag Éirinn* (Ireland has many sorrows), the island is presented in conventional female guise. However, on this occasion the poet presents a figure abandoned and defiled.[30] An insensate and disgraced Ireland lies at the service of the unworthy while those concerned for her are denied the opportunity to lament her fall.[31] Incoming foreigners treat her like a harlot while she herself accommodates all newcomers.[32] The poet speaks of covetous approaches made to her by various groups, including the English, Welsh and Scots. Confronted with the depredations of competing foreigners Ireland lies acquiescent.[33] Interestingly he suggests that

---

William Carrigan, *The History and Antiquities of the Diocese of Ossory* (4 vols., Dublin, 1905), i, 113–14.

[28] 117, quatrain 14.

[29] Breandán Ó Buachalla, 'Na Stíobhartaigh agus an t-aos léinn: cing Séamas', *Proceedings of the Royal Irish Academy*, 83, C, 4 (1983), 81–134, at 86.

[30] Lambert McKenna (ed.), *Dánta do chum Aonghus Fionn Ó Dálaigh* (Dublin, 1919), no. 53, 73–5. The earliest extant copy of *Iomdha éagnach ag Éirinn*, preserved in Dublin, Royal Irish Academy, MS 23. F. 16 (156), is attributed to Flann Mac Craith (fl. c. 1614). For this poet see James Carney (ed.), *Poems on the Butlers* (Dublin, 1945), xvii.

[31] 'Gach éin-fhear dá héignioghadh' ('Every man violating her'); 'bean gach aon-duine Éire' ('Ireland is at the disposal of all men'): *ibid.*, 73, quatrains 4, 5.

[32] *Ibid.*, 73, quatrain 6.

[33] *Ibid.*, 73–4, quatrains 7, 10 ('Danair ag éad 'r oile / ag milleadh mná Laoghaire').

Ireland has passively accepted her degraded status, if not actually
yielding voluntarily to marauding foreigners. Though the reputation of
her children remains unsullied, Ireland herself has participated in her
own debasement.[34] To add to her pitiful state, she now has to bear also
the imposition of unjust laws and new customs.[35] Indeed, Irish noblemen
wed foreigners while aristocratic Irish women marry lowborn Englishmen. In sum, Ireland is a widow distressingly reduced in circumstance while carrying the burden of a partially orphaned family.[36] The
author may be using the theme of Ireland as harlot to draw attention to a
deficiency in the native response to contemporary political developments. The notion of an Ireland abandoned and widowed suggests a
political scenario in need of overt direction. Whatever the author's
precise intention may have been, the poem's central and dominant
metaphor is of obvious relevance to this chapter. Its interpretative framework bears no trace of regional allegiance or particularity. Its focus is
coherently pan-Hibernian. The poet articulates a unitary definition of
Ireland facing an external threat presented by racially divergent newcomers, a group portrayed in binary opposition to the island's native
population. If this poem is a plea for a coherent Irish political programme, it also advances a perception of territorial and ethnic cohesiveness central to the formulation of elements of national consciousness.

The same political manipulation of the sovereignty theme is explicit in
the lament composed by Fearghal Óg Mac an Bhaird on the death of
Hugh Roe O'Donnell (d. 1602) in Spain. O'Donnell had travelled there
with the intention of persuading Philip III to provide military aid to the
Irish. He died apparently of natural causes, not by poisoning as the
legend alleges, in Simancas, his objective unrealised.[37] The poet's main
premise centres on his representation of O'Donnell's passing as the
metaphorical demise of Ireland: *Teasda Éire san Easbáinn* (Ireland has
perished in Spain).[38] Ironically, while the author of *Iomdha éagnach ag
Éirinn* appears to regret the absence of a leader capable of steering
Ireland effectively in a time of crisis, Mac an Bhaird laments a hero
whom he considers to have been just such a national figure. The honour
of the five historic Irish provinces has perished along with O'Donnell
and the vitality of Ireland and her people has been prematurely cut

---

[34] *Ibid.*, 74, quatrain 8.   [35] *Ibid.*, 74, quatrain 13.

[36] *Ibid.*, 74–5, quatrains 17, 19 ('baintreabhach bhocht ar neimhni ... clann gan athair
aici-se').

[37] C. P. Meehan, *The Fate and Fortunes of Hugh O'Neill, Earl of Tyrone, and Rory O'Donel,
Earl of Tyrconnel* (Dublin, 1868), 2.

[38] Pádraig A. Breatnach (ed.), 'Marbhna Aodha Ruaidh Uí Dhomhnaill', *Éigse: A Journal
of Irish Studies*, 15 (1973), 31–50.

short.[39] In a typical bardic legitimatory parallel the poet notes that his subject was not the first great Irish hero to die abroad. Three earlier renowned heroes of the Gaelic tradition, Niall of the Nine Hostages, Da Thí and Donnchadh, son of Brian Boru, had perished overseas.[40] Although their deaths were an occasion of torment for the country, Hugh's demise is the most bitter of all.[41] Ireland is not the same after Hugh, and the country has been gradually overrun by foreigners.[42] Consequently, the Irish had been deprived of their prosperity and their country was akin to a rudderless vessel.[43] Mac an Bhaird depicts his subject as having been devoted to the service of the entire island. He invokes the fertility conceit associated with the legitimate espousal of sovereignty to her partner to describe nature's decline while the elements mourn him in all their savage splendour.[44] Hugh's death is not elegised in terms of a grievous loss to his own family and region, as might be expected, but more particularly his fate is tied to that of the whole country. O'Donnell has taken his native land's soul with him to the grave; her body remains a lifeless image.[45] The poet speaks of his subject as not having been spared to assume the 'sovereignty of Ireland'. Rather he was among those who had given his life in defence of the island.[46] Such is Mac an Bhaird's manifest concern with loss of sovereignty in this poem that it is tempting to suggest that he exploited the opportunity presented by a formal medium to articulate wider ideological implications. He did so in explicitly national terms and his reference to 'Ireland's sovereignty' indicates his conception of potential political unity centred on the island's territorial integrity. His imagery bears no trace of a regional allegiance predicated at the expense of a broader political unity. Mac an Bhaird's vividly expressed national consciousness is paralleled in a poem in which he depicts a bereaved Nuala O'Donnell mourning in solitude before the tomb in Rome of her kinsmen. Mac an Bhaird who accompanied the northern earls into exile in 1607 probably composed this piece circa 1608–9 while on the

[39] *Ibid.*, 35, quatrains 4, 5.
[40] *Ibid.*, 35–6, quatrains 7–11. Regarding Niall of the Nine Hostages see Francis John Byrne, *Irish Kings and High-kings* (London, 1973), 70–86; for Donnchadh (d. 1065) see Aubrey Gwynn, 'Ireland and the continent in the eleventh century', *Irish Historical Studies*, 8:31 (1953), 193–216, 196.
[41] Breatnach, 'Marbhna', 36, quatrain 11.
[42] *Ibid.*, 36, quatrain 12 ('Ní hionand is Éire iar nAodh / danair indte in gach éntaobh').
[43] *Ibid.*, 37, quatrains 13, 14 ('Arthrach gan sdiúir Banbha Breagh').
[44] *Ibid.*, 38–9, quatrains 18–25.
[45] *Ibid.*, 41, quatrains 35, 37 ('Íomháigh gan anam Éire').
[46] *Ibid.*, 42, 45, quatrains 38 ('flaitheas Éirionn'), 56 ('A dtug a mbeatha 's a mbás / ar dhíon Éiriond ar uathbhás ... do ba díobh Aodh oirnidhe').

continent.[47] He is primarily concerned here to argue that had Nuala's kinsmen died at home she would not have been forced to bear the burden of their passing alone. In spite of the Ulster origins of the deceased, Mac an Bhaird successfully locates his outlook within a pan-insular context; when for instance he proclaims that had they been buried in their native place they would certainly have been keened throughout the island.[48] Likewise he presents his subjects not as local warlords but as leaders who had played their part in the defence of Ireland.[49] Their passing presaged an unhappy future for Ireland.[50] As in the elegy on Hugh Roe O'Donnell, Mac an Bhaird on this occasion also utilises a formal bardic medium to define his perception of a fundamental political concept: Ireland as a distinct national entity.

Expressions of sovereignty are found too in the work of non-professional *littérateurs* who, with the institutional decline of the bardic tradition, came increasingly to dominate literary composition in Irish from the latter part of James's reign. Geoffrey Keating (c. 1570–c. 1644) is a prominent example of the type of gentleman amateur who, combining old and new elements, reinvigorated Gaelic literature and scholarship in the early seventeenth century. Famed for his prose history of Ireland, *Foras Feasa ar Éirinn*, in which he sought to provide an historiographical basis for the historic achievements of the Irish nation, Keating is a towering presence in the literary and historical landscape of seventeenth-century Ireland.[51] In addition to his historical work, Keating, a Roman Catholic priest of Anglo-Norman origin who had studied theology in France, produced a significant corpus of devotional literature in Irish and this material enjoyed wide circulation in manuscript form.[52] Given his Gaelic sympathies and allegiance to Counter Reformation doctrine it is not surprising to find that much of his oeuvre

---

[47] Eleanor Knott (ed.), 'Mac an Bhaird's elegy on the Ulster lords', *Celtica*, 5 (1960), 161–71 (*A bhean fuair faill ar an bhfeart*). He depicts Nuala mourning her brothers Rory (d. 1608) and Cathbharr O'Donnell (d. 1608) and her nephew Hugh O'Neill (d. 1609), son of the earl of Tyrone, at their burial place in Rome. See Standish Hayes O'Grady, *Catalogue of Irish Manuscripts in the British Library* (2 vols., reprint Dublin, 1992), i, 371–2; Paul Walsh, *The Will and Family of Hugh O Neill, Earl of Tyrone* (Dublin, 1930), 30. Regarding Mac an Bhaird's continental exile see Micheline Kerney Walsh, *'Destruction by Peace': Hugh O Neill after Kinsale* (Armagh, 1986), 124, 185.

[48] Knott, 'Mac an Bhaird's elegy', 162, quatrains 5–7.

[49] *Ibid.*, 166, quatrain 17 ('ag cosnamh Críche Féilim').

[50] *Ibid.*, 168, quatrain 30; cf. 170, quatrain 39.

[51] For an introduction to Keating's historical outlook see Breandán Ó Buachalla, *Foreword to 1987 Reprint of Foras Feasa ar Éirinn*, Irish Texts Society (London, 1987); and Brendan Bradshaw, 'Geoffrey Keating: apologist of Irish Ireland', in Andrew Hadfield et al. (eds.), *Representing Ireland: literature and the origins of conflict, 1534–1660* (Cambridge, 1994), 166–90.

[52] See, for instance, Osborn Bergin's edition of Keating's *Trí bior-ghaoithe an bháis: the three shafts of death* (reprint Dublin, 1992).

is political in tone. A poem he composed possibly around 1642 provides an excellent example of how contemporary *littérateurs* perceived the island as a national entity whose sovereignty has been violated.[53] In the conventional mode he portrays Ireland as a tragic female figure who has been forced to exchange happiness for sadness in consequence of foreign oppression. Ireland has been widowed, and until her offspring have been restored, she has no chance of finding a suitable mate.[54] Ireland's sovereignty (*flaitheas*) rested with the native Irish, and now that they had been dispossessed, the country resembled a debased harlot.[55] Keating, along with the poets already mentioned, presents the stock motif of the female embodiment of sovereignty in a context relevant to the contemporary political situation. While precise referential details vary from poem to poem, an underlying premise of Ireland's territorial integrity is constant in the poetry analysed here. Notions of an insular entity were well established in the medieval Gaelic tradition. However, in this period it seems clear that the concept acquired a resonance relevant to its immediate political context. The classical female representation of sovereignty was manipulated to express a perceived ideological hiatus in the Irish polity. In particular, violation of Ireland's territorial integrity was articulated through reference to the ravished embodiment of sovereignty. The image of the island defiled and abused by foreigners, and its implicit corollary, an Ireland whose sovereignty lay in native hands, are central to the articulation of national consciousness in early modern Ireland.

II

The concept of Gaelic ethnicity and culture is well refined in the medieval canon, thanks in particular to the racial scheme elaborated in the magisterial late-eleventh-century summation of Gaelic origins and history, the *Lebor Gabála Érenn* (Book of Invasions). This *vade mecum* of Gaelic civilisation, detailing Ireland's legendary history from the world's creation to the point of compilation, was a major determinant of Gaelic attitudes to ethnicity, literature and history down to the early modern period.[56] In that light it may be argued that the Gaelic literati, while placing a premium on Gaelic cultural integrity, re-evaluated received formulations of ethnicity in favour of an inclusive assessment of nation-

[53] Brian Ó Cuív (ed.), 'Mo thruaighe mar tá Éire', *Éigse: A Journal of Irish Studies*, 8 (1956–7), 302–8.
[54] *Ibid.*, 303–4, quatrains 1, 4, 5, 8.
[55] *Ibid.*, 305–6, quatrains 12, 13, 17 ('Meirdreach gan iocht gan onóir').
[56] John Carey, *A New Introduction to Lebor Gabála Érenn*, Irish Texts Society (London, 1993).

ality predicated more often on loyalty to a Gaelic cultural vision than criteria of a strictly racial character. The literature of both classical bardic poets and their non-professional successors provides widespread evidence of Anglo-Norman assimilation to Gaelic cultural norms and, in turn, their incorporation on the part of Gaelic coevals into an ideological nexus of language and culture. Furthermore, the momentum towards ethnic rapprochement in the early modern period was powered not only by an internal intellectual imperative but also externally by the negative impact of English colonial attitudes which increasingly viewed the island's entire population through a distinctly uncomplimentary lens.[57] The expansion of English authority in Ireland, motivated in part by supposed racial superiority, combined with religious dissension, high- lighted ethnic differences and tensions. English denigration of the Gaelic Irish and their relegation to alleged barbarity, accompanied by the assertion of the degeneration of the medieval colonial community to a like state, contributed to the conception of an influential and age-old English/Irish dichotomy.[58] By James's reign one English commentator could write of the Irish as 'more uncivil, more uncleanly, more barbarous, and more brutish in their customs and demeanures then in any other part of the world that is knowne'.[59] Confronted with the self- justifying ideology of a colonising elite the Gaelic Irish and gaelicised Anglo-Normans responded with a forceful assertion of an inclusive Irish identity taking native culture and Roman Catholicism as constituent elements. The fact that these features were common to both groups facilitated the emergence of a self-conscious awareness of shared for- tunes and the articulation of a joint identity.

Tadhg Dall Ó hUiginn's (d. 1591) poem entitled *Fearann cloidhimh*

---

[57] Nicholas P. Canny, *The Formation of the Old English Elite in Ireland* (Dublin, 1975), 27.

[58] English perception of Gaelic 'primitiveness' finds expression, for example, in the antics of Elizabeth's courtiers who, on one occasion, apparently dressed in the costumes of American Indians and Gaelic Irish to celebrate the anniversary of her accession to the throne. Ronald Hutton, *The Rise and Fall of Merry England* (Oxford, 1994), 148. See also Nicholas Canny, 'Identity formation in Ireland: the emergence of the Anglo-Irish', in Canny and Anthony Pagden (eds.), *Colonial Identity in the Atlantic World, 1500–1800* (Princeton, 1987), 159–212, at 162; Nicholas Canny, *Kingdom and Colony: Ireland in the Atlantic World, 1560–1800* (Baltimore and London, 1988), ch. 2; Brendan Bradshaw, 'Robe and sword in the conquest of Ireland', in Claire Cross, David Loades and J. J. Scarisbrick (eds.), *Law and Government under the Tudors* (Cambridge, 1988), 139–62, at 156.

[59] Barnabe Rych, *A Short Survey of Ireland* (London, 1609), 1–2; Charles Vallancey (ed.), 'A chorographical description of the county of West-Meath. Written A.D. 1682 by Sir Henry Piers', *Collectanea de rebus Hibernicis* (Dublin, 1770), i, 104–5. For a brilliant account of how one English settler mediated notions of supposed Gaelic barbarity see Richard A. McCabe, 'Edmund Spenser, poet of exile', *Proceedings of the British Academy*, 80 (1991), 73–103. More generally regarding colonialist legitimatory premises see Edward W. Said, *Culture and Imperialism* (London, 1993).

críoch Bhanbha (Ireland is a swordland) is significant in its advocacy of
what may be termed a conceptual rapprochement in Gaelic/Anglo-
Norman relations. Composing around 1579 he sought to provide an
extended theoretical justification for the status of Seán, the Lower
MacWilliam (d. 1580).[60] His thesis is simple but convincingly logical
from an Anglo-Norman standpoint. While bardic poets were traditionally not beyond endorsing the immediate aspirations of Anglo-Norman
patrons, the manipulation of such themes in this poem must not be
divorced from its Elizabethan context.[61] He argues that land title in
Ireland is based effectively on force of arms. Drawing on the pattern of
successive ethnic occupational phases outlined in the *Lebor Gabála*, Ó
hUiginn points out that various peoples have been displaced by mili-
tarily stronger groups. Crucially, the *Gaoidhil* had no more entitlement
to Ireland than that of conquest.[62] The same basic principle under-
scored Anglo-Norman settlement in Ireland.[63] All the island's inhabitants whether of Gaelic or Anglo-Norman provenance were simply
transitory occupiers of Ireland and the status of both communities was
equally provisional.[64] The importance of Ó hUiginn's reinterpretation
of conventional historical lore should not be underestimated. He
manipulated a traditional precept of Gaelic supremacy to legitimate the
Anglo-Norman presence. He did not deny the ideological validity of the
Gaelic presence, rather he established Gaelic and Anglo-Norman tenure
on an equal footing. If some traditional bardic assessments of Anglo-
Norman authority were inimical to Gaelic status, Ó hUiginn's refocusing of the paradigm left each community's honour intact. Ironically, it might be argued, though Ó hUiginn does not do so, that the
New English were concurrently taking his interpretative schema a stage
further on exactly the same basis of superior force.

Another poem ascribed to Ó hUiginn provides more evidence of
Gaelic accommodation of the inculturation of Anglo-Norman families.
The piece beginning *T'aire riot, a Riocaird Óig* (Heed thyself, Richard
Óg), probably composed for Richard Óg Burke (d. 1586) of the Lower
MacWilliam family, is a forceful defence of the indigenous socio-

---

[60] Eleanor Knott (ed.), *The Bardic Poems of Tadhg Dall Ó Huiginn (1550–1591)* (2 vols.,
    London, 1922–6), ii, no. 17, 254–9.
[61] Regarding bardic political 'adaptability' see Eleanor Knott, *Irish Classical Poetry* (Cork,
    1978 edn), 67.
[62] Knott (ed.), *The Bardic Poems of Tadhg Dall Ó Huiginn*, i, no. 17, 120–31, at 120,
    quatrain 4.
[63] *Ibid.*, 121, quatrains 8–11.
[64] *Ibid.*, 122, quatrains 17, 18 ('cia san ghurt bhraonnuaidhe bhinn / nách lucht aonuaire
    d'Éirinn?').

political apparatus.[65] It appears that Burke had been offered a new title and confirmation of his inheritance by the authorities in exchange for the implicit or explicit rejection, the poem is unclear in this regard, of the Gaelic-style appellation 'Richard, son of MacWilliam'.[66] While it seems that the subject had occasioned bad blood between author and addressee, the poem none the less presents a full statement of why a traditional title was deemed to be superior to an externally sourced designation. It is argued that Richard's possession of an ancient title had created and underwritten his social standing. The poet urges Burke not to reject his inherited designation in favour of a possibly short-lived title and the system underpinning it and he urges him to reject a new title lest his patrimony be endangered.[67] Prior to his acceptance of English favour Richard had been seen as an important figure in Ireland. The loss of such status, the author urges, would hardly be compensated for by his proposed elevation.[68] The traditional assignation is implicitly identified with continuity, legitimacy and prosperity, while their opposites are evoked in references to the status conferred by the alien title. Drawing on a customary bardic device to emphasise a point under discussion the author recounts an exemplum in which the son of a French knight saves an aspiring monarch from the folly of his myopic ambition. The young man had received a precious stone from his father on setting out to tour the world with the injunction that his son should present the stone to the most foolish person he encountered on his travels. In due course the youth happened upon a city which replaced its king annually, condemning each monarch in turn to a perpetual and solitary island exile. Coming face to face with the latest heir-apparent he presented him with the precious stone and explained his father's counsel. Realising the stupidity of exchanging future happiness for the immediate gain of a one year reign the heir-apparent renounced the kingship.[69] Burke is admonished that he too is in danger of behaving recklessly in exchanging an ancient title for one foreign in origin.[70] Notwithstanding that the socio-

[65] In addition to Ó hUiginn, this poem has also been attributed to Brian Ó Domhnalláin (d. 1582). See Knott, *ibid.*, ii, 263.

[66] *Ibid.*, i, no. 22a, 160–8, at 163, quatrain 23 ('lá an athanma dhaoibh do dháil, do thaoibh h'athardha d'fhagháil'). The latter reference may suggest that the poem was composed to the background of the 1585 land settlement known as the Composition of Connacht. If this were the case, the poem's attribution to Ó hUiginn would appear fairly reliable.

[67] *Ibid.*, 161, quatrains 9, 12.   [68] *Ibid.*, 162–3, quatrains 19, 21.

[69] *Ibid.*, 163–6, quatrains 23–46; cf. Stith Thompson, *Motif-index of Folk-literature* (6 vols., Bloomington and London, n.d.), iv, p. 55, J711.3.

[70] Knott, *Bardic Poems*, 167, quatrain 48 ('ainm síor ar ainm n-iasachta ... dob aimhghlic dhuit a dhéineamh'). The Anglo-Norman tendency to take Gaelic-style designations is raised in Anon., *The Present State of Ireland* (London, 1673), 14.

logical assumptions of the author's thought merit their own analysis the relevant consideration here lies in his unselfconscious incorporation of an Anglo-Norman nobleman within a Gaelic social structure. An example of successful inculturation, the poem assumes automatic loyalty on the part of its subject to Gaelic norms, presenting his possible acceptance of a political alternative as a freakish aberration. Certainly the MacWilliam Burkes had long been gaelicised culturally and linguistically by the time of this poem's composition but it serves to highlight perceptions of a cultural and social patrimony shared by *Gaoidhil* and *Gaill* alike.

Bardic poetry is not the only extant guide to the phenomenon of the Gaelic/Anglo-Norman socio-religious nexus being forged at this period. In the previous section William Nugent's poems were discussed as evidence for the self-conscious perception of an insular territorial integrity. A poem in the same individualistic vein ascribed to Richard Weston, a Dundalk merchant and confidant of Hugh O'Neill, is indicative of the extent to which Anglo-Norman inculturation might also have been motivated by personal loyalties and sympathies. Apparently composed in Louvain during the earl of Tyrone's sojourn there in 1607–8, the studied and idiosyncratic use of Irish exhibited in Weston's poem and its open identification with O'Neill and Roman Catholicism invest *Beir mo beanocht go Dún Dalck* (Convey my farewell to Dundalk) with peculiar significance.[71] The author displays an ambivalent mixture of guilt for having left his wife and son in Ireland with pride in his relationship with the exiled Tyrone. However, the latter emotion triumphs, for Weston would have his audience believe that his loyalty to O'Neill was stronger than any attachment to his spouse.[72] However seriously this declaration is to be taken it is clear from the poem that his devotion to O'Neill stemmed from a combination of personal and religious factors. Aside from shared friendship Weston makes it clear that he has found a welcome change of religious authority in Louvain. Able to attend Mass at will in the company of O'Neill, the author rejoices in the absence of what he perceives as an overbearing Established Church in Ireland.[73] He no longer has to endure the prying attentions of the reformed clergy seeking out Catholic priests or alternatively demanding that Weston acknowledge the king's religious authority.[74] The religious sentiments expressed by Weston will be

---

[71] For the poem's text and a discussion of Weston's background see Tomás Ó Fiaich (ed.), 'Richard Weston agus "Beir mo bheannacht go Dundalk"', *Seanchas Ard Mhacha Journal of the Armagh Diocesan Historical Society*, 5:2 (1970), 269–88.

[72] *Ibid.*, 283, quatrain iv.   [73] *Ibid.*, 284, quatrain x.

[74] *Ibid.*, 284, quatrain xi.

returned to more fully in a later section. Meanwhile it should be noted that his remarks illustrate two of the factors determining a nascent early modern Irish identity: religion and culture. His manipulative though coherent distortion of standard grammatical usage implies that Weston knew Irish quite well, and justifies the conclusion that he had immersed himself in Gaelic culture. The poem's cultural subtleties also highlight the dangers of presenting the ethnic communities in late-sixteenth and early-seventeenth-century Ireland as comprising hermetically sealed and incompatible blocks of linguistic and cultural particularism. The degree of cultural exchange between *Gaoidhil* and *Sean-Ghaill* exemplifies a high degree of mutual enrichment and cross-fertilisation.[75]

For example, a bardic poem composed early in James's reign for the Anglo-Irish judge, Sir Nicholas Walsh (d. 1615), illustrates a two-way process of cultural enfranchisement. In *Labhram ar iongnadh Éireann* (Let us speak about the wonder of Ireland), Tuileagna Ó Maolchonaire (fl. 1603) utilises conventional panegyric structures to assimilate the traits of a sedentary chief justice of common pleas within the heroic warrior-centred Gaelic framework. While Walsh is presented through the medium of a traditional literary form, the traits for which he is praised do not conform to the paradigm within which the traditional praise-poem was given expression. First, Walsh was not a local warrior-potentate exacting swift retribution from disruptive and criminal elements. On the contrary, he is presented as a legal grandee, impervious to sectional interests and dedicated to the notion of justice for all people.[76] Whereas the sword was the usual weapon of the Gaelic hero, Walsh's weapons are his clerks' pens writing out his judgments.[77] Ó Maolchonaire stresses that the judge is incorruptible, unyielding to

---

[75] It would be inaccurate to imply that Gaelic/Anglo-Norman cultural interchange was exclusively early modern in date. For the work of earlier Anglo-Norman poets writing in Irish see the examples of Gerald, third earl of Desmond (d. 1398) and Richard Butler in the fifteenth century: Robin Flower, 'Ireland and medieval Europe', *Proceedings of the British Academy*, 13 (1927), 271–303, at 291–2; and see also Flower's introduction to T. F. O'Rahilly (ed.), *Dánta grádha: an anthology of Irish love poetry (A.D. 1350–1750)* (Cork, 1976 edn), xii–xiii; and Alan Bliss, 'Language and literature', in James Lydon (ed.), *The English in Medieval Ireland* (Dublin, 1984), 27–45.

[76] An extract from this poem has been published in Tomás Ó Raghallaigh (ed.), *Fili agus filidheacht Chonnacht* (Dublin, 1938), no. 18a, 264–9, 268, quatrain xxix. Regarding Ó Maolchonaire see T. F. O'Rahilly, 'Irish poets, historians, and judges in English documents, 1538–1615', *Proceedings of the Royal Irish Academy*, 36, C, 6 (1922), 86–120, at 88–9. Details of Walsh's career are given in C. Litton Falkiner, *Essays Relating to Ireland* (London, 1909), 231–2. For a portrait of Walsh as constitutional Anglo-Irish nationalist see Brendan Bradshaw, 'The beginnings of modern Ireland', in Brian Farrell (ed.), *The Irish Parliamentary Tradition* (Dublin, 1973), 68–87, 85–7.

[77] Ó Raghallaigh, *Fili agus filidheacht*, 265, quatrains ix, x.

bribery and determined to eliminate injustice.[78] As judge he will rid Ireland of all malefactors especially the outlaws of Munster and Leinster who now face a stark choice, submission or flight. Meanwhile, employing the power of his intellect, Walsh had persuaded many criminals and reivers to submit to the king's authority.[79] While a lack of evidence precludes consideration of the precise contractual implications of this composition its general significance is substantial in tracing the course of Anglo-Norman accommodation to Gaelic mores. Like classical bardic eulogy this poem remains concerned with professional validation of the addressee. Yet the modalities of endorsement differ in quality and objective. In this case, the addressee is legitimated within an administrative framework as opposed to the warrior context in which eulogy is usually given expression. If the presentation is different, the conceptualisation retains a distinctly Gaelic and heroic timbre. Adapting to Walsh's status as a government functionary he is praised accordingly for his impeccable incorruptibility and devotion to the achievement of justice. In its adept filtering of potentially conflicting elements it is an excellent reminder of the subtle accommodation of Gaelic/Anglo-Norman experiences and the richness of the resulting palimpsest.[80]

Two poems by Geoffrey Keating evidence a mature stage of Anglo-Norman accommodation to Gaelic social norms. In these compositions the author aligns himself religiously, politically and culturally with Ireland and its people, be they of Gaelic or Anglo-Norman background. He takes the rapprochement between the two communities to its ultimate conclusion with his advocacy of an inclusive Irish national identity, no longer *Gaoidheal* (Gaelic) or *Gall* (Anglo-Irish) but *Éireannach* (Irish). In his poem entitled *Mo thruaighe mar tá Éire* (Woeful is Ireland's state), Keating, perhaps composing around the year 1642, presents an assessment of the contemporary political situation in which

---

[78] *Ibid.*, 266, quatrains xiv–xvii.

[79] *Ibid.*, 268, quatrains xxiv–xxvi. In a letter to the earl of Salisbury, Walsh gives a first-hand account of the peremptory justice dealt out to 'rebels' and various criminals in west Munster in 1606: C. Litton Falkiner (ed.), *Illustrations of Irish History and Topography, Mainly of the Seventeenth Century* (London, 1904), 141–2.

[80] The poem addressed to Nicholas Walsh may be compared in terms of cultural perception with that composed for another Anglo-Norman magnate, Sir Theobald Dillon (d. 1624). In *Beag mhaireas dár ndeaghdaoinibh* ('Few of our noble stock remain'), Cormac Ó hUiginn praises Dillon who had remained loyal to the crown during the Nine Years War for his devotion to Gaelic style notions of hospitality. The poem is preserved in Dublin, Trinity College Library, MS 1356, 101. Regarding Dillon see Bernadette Cunningham, 'Theobald Dillon, a newcomer in sixteenth-century Mayo', *Cathair na Mart Journal of the Westport Historical Society*, 6, 1 (1986), 24–32. For a seventeenth-century attempt to supply the Dillons with a Gaelic pedigree see Brian Ó Cuív, 'Bunús mhuintir Dhiolún', *Éigse: A Journal of Irish Studies*, 11 (1964–6), 65–6.

both historic Irish communities endure the yoke of foreign oppression.[81] He invokes the traditional motif of Ireland as the deserted and abused harlot to heighten the impact of his political reportage. He accords the *Gaoidhil* political primacy, apparently by reason of the fact that they had preceded the medieval colonists.[82] More generally he attributes the predicament of the Irish to their internal dissensions, and he suggests that until the exiled *Gaoidhil* return Ireland can expect no amelioration of her distress.[83] In *Mór antrom inse Banbha* (Great is Ireland's oppression), composed around 1642, Keating also concerns himself with the island's contemporary political climate which he unambiguously qualifies in terms of conquest and subjugation.[84] His portrayal of a racial triad, comprising Gaelic Irish, Anglo-Norman and New English is of particular significance. While alluding to the colonial origins of the Anglo-Norman community, termed *Sean-Ghoill* (Old English) to distinguish them from newer and less welcome arrivals, Keating is insistent that they had formed a community of interest with the *Gaoidhil*. Specifically, he notes that marriage ties, familial links and a shared religious allegiance had bound both groups together.[85] Crucially both now faced the threat of New English (*Nua-Ghoill*) aggression, and already many of Gaelic and Old English origin had perished in defence of their native country.[86] Keating's treatment affords an overview of the racial symbiosis peculiar to the late sixteenth and early seventeenth century in Ireland, a development visible in contemporary literature. Two particular elements facilitated this accommodation: a widespread common loyalty to the Counter Reformation Church and Anglo-Norman access to and participation in the rituals of Gaelic cultural expression. The dynamic responsible for a certain elision of ethnic sensibilities may be ascribed to a congruence of political, cultural and religious factors. Yet it should also be stressed that the Gaelic literati played a crucial part in this highly important process.

III

Roman Catholicism was the third element in the amalgam constituting the early modern nascent Irish sense of nationality. Shared confessional loyalties along with common cultural concerns bound the *Gaoidhil* and gaelicised Anglo-Normans ever closer. The dichotomy emerging from

[81] Brian Ó Cuív (ed.), 'Mo thruaighe mar tá Éire', *Éigse: A Journal of Irish Studies*, 8 (1956–7), 302–8; see 308, n. 18 for the poem's possible date of composition.

[82] *Ibid.*, 305, quatrain 12.   [83] *Ibid.*, 304, quatrains 8, 10.

[84] Eoin C. Mac Giolla Eáin (ed.), *Dánta amhráin is caointe Sheathrúin Céitinn* (Dublin, 1900), no. xiv, 62–7, 62, quatrain v ('Ar feadh Banbha an conncas').

[85] *Ibid.*, 63, quatrains vii, viii.   [86] *Ibid.*, 63, quatrain xii.

the oppositional implications of divergent religio-political allegiances between the two historic communities on the one side, and the New English on the other, further determined the character of the new national consciousness. Whether perceived or actual, popular association of the Anglican Church in Ireland with a new colonial elite actively shaped indigenous reactions to the religious Reformation. Indeed it may be argued that this type of negative perception of protestantism undermined its various manifestations in Ireland down to the modern period. The corollary of apparent colonial links was the emergence of an ideological connection between the Roman faith and Gaelic culture where no conscious linkage had previously been articulated or required. The literary evidence illustrates a deliberate project to align a degree of Irish political and cultural autonomy with adherence to Catholicism while equating the established church with varieties of English expansionism. A number of vernacular sources suggest that the linkage between Catholicism and Gaelic culture gained currency in the fifteen seventies, although the attitudes encompassed in the phrase 'faith and fatherland' appear to find a considerably earlier echo in a poem probably composed around 1542-3.[87] The anonymous author of *Fúbún fúibh, a shluagh Gaoidheal* in the course of a poem castigating various Gaelic lords for their emollient attitude to the English, notes that the Irish have brought discredit upon themselves by their acquiescence in 'the denial of Mary's son'.[88] This apparent allusion to Gaelic acceptance of Henry VIII's ecclesiastical policies, even though fleeting, is important in that it demonstrates at an early date the political implications of sectarian conflict.[89] Later references document an unambiguous Irish perception of faith and fatherland in the context of English expansionism. For instance Corc Óg Ó Cadhla, a doctor and scribe, has left an intriguing mini-political commentary in a manuscript he was transcribing in 1578. In this marginal note to a medical text he observes that Ireland had never been so completely under English control.[90] While seeming to acknowledge Elizabeth's sovereignty in Ireland, he denies English claims

---

[87] For the politicisation of religion see Patrick J. Corish, *The Catholic Community in the Seventeenth and Eighteenth Centuries* (Dublin, 1981); Hiram Morgan, 'Faith and fatherland or queen and country?', *Dúiche Néill Journal of the O Neill Country Historical Society,* 9 (1994), 9–65. For a discussion that surveys much of the same ground examined in what follows but from a rather different perspective see Bradshaw, above, pp. 61–70, 91–111, esp. 102–9.

[88] This poem ('Shameful is your course of action, men of the *Gaoidhil*') has been edited and supplied with an historical commentary by Brian Ó Cuiv (ed.), 'A sixteenth-century political poem', *Éigse: A Journal of Irish Studies,* 15 (1973–4), 261–76. On this and what follows see also Bradshaw, above, pp. 55–6, 63–4.

[89] *Ibid.*, 273, quatrain 9.

[90] Paul Walsh (ed.), *Gleanings from Irish manuscripts* (2nd edn, Dublin, 1933), 158.

to supreme authority in matters of faith. On the contrary, Ó Cadhla holds that only the pope can be head of the 'holy Catholic church'.[91] Insofar as it came under her control the queen presided over a corrupt church. He complains that under the new ecclesiastical regime traditional feast days and church holidays had been abandoned while holy sites were dishonoured. As for the English, he claims that in all Europe they are the most given to pride and murder.[92] In fact Ó Cadhla expresses surprise that God should have tolerated their ascendancy for so long. However he consoles himself with the thought that they would suffer long and hard in due course. Significantly, in suggesting that the Irish had themselves incurred divine wrath he uses the racially inclusive term *Éireannach* to describe the island's inhabitants.[93]

Three letters in Irish penned by James FitzMaurice (d. 1579) also reveal the emergence of a distinction between 'Catholic' Irishmen and 'heretical' Englishmen intent on usurping the land of Ireland. These, dating from 1579, may be survivals from a whole series of letters sent by FitzMaurice to various sept leaders in search of support for his military challenge to English authority in Ireland. His thinking was influenced by Counter Reformation attitudes and it is clear from his correspondence that he linked political self-determination and loyalty with adherence to the Roman Catholic Church. As might be expected from an Anglo-Norman nobleman, FitzMaurice's expression of an insular identity is racially inclusive. In two letters to the mercenary leader Austin Mac-Donnell he is explicit in predicating his call for military action upon two key premises. According to FitzMaurice, the forces raised would seek to defend the Roman faith from 'heretical' onslaught and they would also proceed in defence of Ireland against foreign domination.[94] In sum, the Irish were fighting for their faith and homeland ('sinne ag cosnamh ár g-creidimh agus ár ndúthaighe') while the English sought to subvert that very faith and to deprive the Irish of their patrimonies ('agus iad san ag cur an chreidimh ar gcúl, agur ar tí ár nduthuidhe féin do bhuain dínne').[95] The Irish cause was synonymous with truth, justice and loyalty to Catholicism, while that of the English was equated with

---

[91] *Ibid.*, 158.
[92] *Ibid.*, 159. As far back as 1554 a scribe called Flann Mac Cairbre, also writing in a marginal note, welcomed Mary's accession and her reversal of Henrician and Edwardian ecclesiastical reforms. He complained of the banishment of religious orders and of liturgical innovations. Charles Plummer, *Irish Litanies* (London, 1925), xi, n. 3.
[93] Walsh, *Gleanings*, 159.
[94] John O'Donovan (ed.), 'The Irish correspondence of James Fitz Maurice of Desmond', *The Journal of the Kilkenny and South-East of Ireland Archaeological Society*, 2, 2 (1858–9), 354–69.
[95] *Ibid.*, 363.

falsehood, injustice and heresy. Such was his confidence in the legitimacy of the cause he so actively promoted that FitzMaurice declared those following the banner of faith and fatherland were guaranteed their reward in heaven.[96] The sentiments articulated in the letters provide an important marker of the evolution of a politicised Catholicism linking itself to Irish national consciousness in the context of the officially promulgated protestant reform movement in Ireland.

Two compositions attributed to the Franciscan priest Eoghan Ó Dubhthaigh (d. 1590) are particularly vivid in their depiction of Irish protestantism as an essentially anglocentric cultural phenomenon. He composed *Léig dod chomhmórtas dúinn* (Cease from your comparisons) as a paean to the Virgin Mary while also launching a brilliantly caustic attack on three Irishmen elevated to episcopal status in the established church. He castigates Mathew Seaine, bishop of Cork (1572–82/3), Uilliam Ó Cathasaigh, bishop of Limerick (1571–91) and the infamous Miler Magrath, archbishop of Cashel (1571–1622) for turning their backs on Catholicism and for indifference to the Marian cult. Furthermore, the poet was evidently infuriated by Magrath's marriage to Áine Ní Mheadhra, who suffers her own share of vituperation in the poem. For good measure he also accuses several bardic poets of displaying an excessively worldly outlook in their poetry.[97] Of immediate interest in this intriguing and multilayered poem is the portrayal of protestantism as an English colonial imposition. For example, Ó Dubhthaigh speaks of the Anglican clergy as having come across from England and, unusually for Gaelic poetry of this period, he employs English terminology to berate immigrant divines.[98] Moreover the Protestant bishops and their clergy are characterised by their 'seduction' and 'corruption' of justice.[99] The author accuses Anglican priests of both English and Irish birth of having brought misfortune on Ireland.[100] He is certain in his identification of the Elizabethan administration as the presiding influence of the religious reform movement. Satirically, he declares that the Virgin would be given short shrift were she to present herself in person at the seat of the English administration, Dublin Castle. In contrast he observes sourly that the wives of the Church of Ireland bishops enjoy every deference at the Castle.[101] Uilliam Ó Cathasaigh is singled out for his special fraternity with the English, most graphically when he is accused of being more familiar with the English than with God.[102] All in all, this coruscating *tour de force* is a vivid testament to the bitter passions generated by religious and political conflict. In his shorter poem, *A*

---

[96] *Ibid.*, 362–3.   [97] Mhág Craith (ed.), *Dán na mbráthar mionúr*, i, no. 27, 127–51.
[98] *Ibid.*, 133, quatrain 25.   [99] *Ibid.*, 138, quatrain 42.   [100] *Ibid.*, 144, quatrain 67.
[101] *Ibid.*, 134, quatrains 26, 27.   [102] *Ibid.*, 150, quatrain 89c.

Bhanbha, is truagh do chor! (Pitiful is your plight, Ireland!), Ó Dubhthaigh elaborates on his portrayal of the established church as a creature of the Dublin administration in a distinctly political attack on the English presence and the claims of Anglicanism.[103] Ireland's fate is lamented and he prays to Jesus to come to the aid of an island subject to the designs of the English and Scots such that the country risked becoming a junior offshoot of England.[104] He calls on Ireland to resist Calvinist and Lutheran blandishments, and instead to follow her own St Patrick.[105] In this instance also, the author aligns protestantism with a foreign power while Catholicism is implicitly presented as the legitimate religious confession long indigenous to Ireland. Significantly, Ó Dubhthaigh was not a professional bardic poet and his membership of the Franciscan order highlights the emergence of clerical writers in Irish who both manipulated and extended the Gaelic literary tradition according to the dictates of a Counter Reformation agenda. While the established church made fitful and sporadic attempts to evangelise through the medium of Irish, such initiatives did little either to dilute its overwhelmingly anglocentric quality or to render its cultural timbre less alien to a majority of Irish people.[106]

A crucial development in the process of Gaelic/Roman symbiosis was the establishment of the Irish Franciscan College of St Anthony at Louvain in 1607. The publication of Giolla Brighde Ó hEódhusa's Gaelic catechism in 1611 launched a systematic Franciscan effort to provide printed vernacular devotional material containing a Counter Reformation message. Other important works appeared in 1616 and 1618 thanks to the labours of Flaithrí Ó Maolchonaire and Aodh Mac Aingil respectively. Significantly, Ó Maolchonaire (d. 1629) was an active opponent of English government in Ireland. He had accompanied the Spanish force to Kinsale in 1601, subsequently leaving the country for good with Hugh Roe O'Donnell. Nominated to the archbishopric of Tuam in 1609, he was involved as late as 1627 in a proposed invasion of Ireland to overthrow English authority. Mac Aingil, a renowned theo-

---

[103] *Ibid.*, no. 28, 151–3.   [104] *Ibid.*, 151–2, quatrains 1–3.
[105] *Ibid.*, 152, quatrains 5–6 ('Pádruig do ghénerál féin'). The Established Church also claimed spiritual descent from St Patrick's mission in Ireland. See Alan Ford, ' "Standing one's ground": religion, polemic and Irish history since the reformation', in James McGuire *et al.* (eds.), *As by Law Established: the church of Ireland since the reformation* (Dublin, 1995), 1–14, 2.
[106] See Alan Ford, 'The Protestant reformation in Ireland', in Ciaran Brady and Raymond Gillespie (eds.), *Natives and Newcomers: the making of Irish colonial society 1534–1641* (Dublin, 1986), 50–74. The official character of early Irish Anglicanism is evident in the obsequious 'epistle dedicatorie' to Lord Deputy Chichester in Uilliam Ó Domhnuill's translation of the *Book of Common Prayer*. See Ó Domhnuill (trans.), *Leabhar na nUrnaightheadh gComhchoidchiond* (Dublin, 1608).

logian, had served as tutor to O'Neill's sons before entering the Franciscan order around 1603.[107] Although all three were obviously concerned to curb the growth of protestantism in Ireland, it is evident also that a sense of patriotism motivated their work. For instance, Mac Aingil was conscious of a deficiency in the Irish contribution to the Counter Reformation effort and it pained his sense of national pride to note that 'every other Catholic nation' possessed appropriate material for doing so in their vernacular languages. He argued that the persecution of Catholicism in Ireland resulted in a particular need for such works in his own 'nation' ('atáid do riachdanas ar an náision dá bhfuilmídne go spesialta').[108] While the movement to publish devotional tracts in Louvain was partly inspired by the example of contemporary continental Catholicism and was supposedly purely religious in character the end results were to prove as much political as religious. It is difficult to quantify the impact of such printed works in Ireland due to a dearth of evidence. Yet their popularity in manuscript form, especially Ó hEódhusa's catechism, attests to their wide circulation.[109] Given the established church's more or less persistent antipathy to the use of Irish for evangelisation at this stage it is hardly surprising that the manuscript circulation and oral delivery of vernacular Counter Reformation material helped promulgate a popular association of Gaelic culture with the Roman faith.[110] The political implications of such a pattern in the development of Irish national consciousness are self-evident in the context of protestant English colonial consolidation. The potency of the identification of Catholicism and Irish nationality was such that Geoffrey Keating, in the introduction to his history of Ireland, *Foras*

[107] Ó Buachalla, 'Na Stíobhartaigh'; Marc Caball, 'A study of intellectual reaction and continuity in Irish bardic poetry composed during the reigns of Elizabeth I and James I' (unpublished D.Phil. thesis, University of Oxford, 1991), 250–6.

[108] Aodh Mac Aingil, *Scáthán shacramuinte na haithridhe* (Dublin, 1952 edn), edited by Cainneach Ó Maonaigh, 4–5. When Roibeard Mhac Artúir (d. 1636) entered the Franciscan order in Louvain in 1610, he directed that his wealth be used for the provision of an Irish typeface which he hoped would increase the honour of God and extend the fame of his 'nation': Colm Ó Lochlainn (ed.), *Tobar fíorghlan Gaedhilge 1450–1850* (Dublin, 1939), 97.

[109] Bonabhentura Ó hEodhasa, *An Teagasg críosdaidhe* (Dublin, 1976 edn), (ed.), Fearghal Mac Raghnaill, xi. Religious books and images were smuggled into Ireland from the Continent, as is clear from a shipment seized off the Cork coast in 1617: A. B. Grosart (ed.), *The Lismore Papers*, 2nd ser. (5 vols., London, 1887–8), ii, 116. Cf. Henry Jones, *A Remonstrance of Divers Remarkeable Passages Concerning the Church and Kingdome of Ireland* (London, 1642), 23.

[110] Later in the seventeenth century, Jeremy Taylor accused the Roman Catholic clergy of using all means at their disposal to keep their flock 'to the use of the Irish tongue, least if they learn English, they might be supplied with persons fitter to instruct them'. Taylor, *A Dissuasive from Popery to the People of Ireland* (Dublin, 1664), unpaginated preface.

Feasa ar Éirinn, written between 1633 and 1636, argued that the Irish could bear favourable comparison with any other nation in Europe in three respects, their bravery, their learning and their firm commitment to the Catholic faith.[111] The wheel had come full circle: the *Gaoidhil* and *Sean-Ghaill* now stood together as an Irish nation characterised by commitment to what was perceived as a common Gaelic historical and cultural heritage, the sovereignty of the island and Roman Catholicism.

IV

In sum then, the reigns of Elizabeth and James witness the emergence of a new formulation of Irish identity which was predicated upon this threefold commitment. The intellectual momentum powering the process of reassessment came from the Irish-speaking literati, including bardic and gentlemen poets, as well as Catholic clerics. Their combined efforts resulted in an influential articulation of identity in the context of English political expansion and religious reform. Drawing on established precepts of territorial integrity and a phased historical interpretative schema the literati re-evaluated traditional exclusivist ethnic criteria to legitimate Ireland's two historic communities in the face of external threat. A process of communal rapprochement was facilitated by shared socio-cultural and religious experiences. The collective project of re-assessment was advantaged by the use of the standard literary medium of classical Irish which allowed for easy articulation of ideological concerns throughout a defined cultural sphere. The homogeneity of elite Gaelic cultural expression may be said to have compensated for the obstacles posed by the absence of centralised political structures and the practical communicative constraints imposed by a scribal and non-print culture.[112] If, because of adverse social and political conditions, print culture made no extended impact on early modern Gaelic society, the oral mode of Gaelic literary activity may well have guaranteed a wider audience than printed books could ever have hoped to reach. This factor suggests that appreciation of the implications of politicised nationality extended beyond the elite to exercise a wider influence.[113] The absence

---

[111] David Comyn and Patrick S. Dinneen (eds.), *The History of Ireland by Geoffrey Keating, D.D.* (4 vols., London, 1902–14), i, 78–9.

[112] For the importance of print in the development of national identity see Elizabeth L. Eisenstein, *The Printing Revolution in Early Modern Europe* (Cambridge, 1993 edn), 154–5, 165.

[113] Regarding the oral aspect of bardic practice see Edgar M. Slotkin, 'Folkloristics and medieval Celtic philology: a theoretical model', in Patrick K. Ford (ed.), *Celtic Folklore and Christianity* (Los Angeles, 1983), 213–25, at 214–15. The historical case for a total and unified cultural experience is made by Bob Scribner, 'Is a history of popular culture possible?', *History of European Ideas*, 10:2 (1989), 175–91.

of centralised indigenous political structures accounts to some extent for the variety of Gaelic political strategies to mediate conquest and colonisation, ranging from the posited emergence of a messianic leader to liberate the Irish from their bondage to the manipulation of the Stuarts' Gaelic links to the advantage of Irish interests.[114] The immediate focus of such strategies should not be allowed to obscure their significance as vehicles of an emerging Irish national consciousness. Moreover, the central role played by the literati in this process surely demonstrates that their reaction to contemporary political challenges was considerably more resourceful and cogent than some historians and literary scholars are prepared to admit.

The articulation of Irish nationality during the reigns of Elizabeth and James was of signal importance in its extended implications both with regard to native self-perception and to the assimilation of the British consciousness that evolved in other territories contemporaneously subject to the English crown. The development of an Irish identity which was a focus for dissidence in response to the Anglo-Saxon protestant hegemony implicit in the crown's programme of reform and reformation contrasts with the cultivation in Wales of an indigenous reformed consciousness amenable to projection along the lines of a British paradigm. Unlike Ireland, however, in Wales a combination of facilitative circumstances, particularly the local provenance of the Tudors and the accommodation of the church to a specifically Welsh context, resulted in a relatively painless unitary merger.[115] However in Ireland the Tudors enjoyed no such sentimental advantage and the Anglican Church, in addition to facing serious structural obstacles, did little to create an ecclesiastical environment congenial to the Gaelic and gaelicised Anglo-Norman communities. Moreover Elizabeth's reign witnessed the development of a politicised Irish Catholic national consciousness in direct ideological opposition to the aspirations of the protestant British political ascendancy in Ireland. Even the accession of

---

[114] The unpublished bardic poem 'Mór do mhill aoibhneas Éireann' ('Ireland's beauty has ruined many' by Fearghal Óg Mac an Bhaird) is particularly important for its presentation of Hugh O'Neill in the guise of a messianic Irish liberator: Marc Caball, 'Providence and exile in early seventeenth-century Ireland', *Irish Historical Studies*, 29:114 (1994), 174–88, p. 181. For the Gaelic literati and the Stuarts see Breandán Ó Buachalla, 'James our true king: the ideology of Irish royalism in the seventeenth century', in D. George Boyce *et al.* (eds.), *Political Thought in Ireland Since the Seventeenth Century* (London, 1993), ch. 1.

[115] Bradshaw, above, pp. 73–83; Roberts, pp. 8–20. Cf. P. R. Roberts, 'The union with England and the identity of "Anglican" Wales', *Transactions of the Royal Historical Society*, 5th ser., 22 (1972), 49–70; Roberts, 'The Welsh language, English law and Tudor legislation', *Transactions of the Honourable Society of Cymmrodorion* (1989), 19–75.

a Stuart king with Gaelic ancestry to the English crown in 1603 was too little and too late to alter significantly the potential for conflict inherent in the implications of two national identities embodying mutually exclusive world views. In fact, the articulation of Irish national identity at this critical juncture ensured that the country's presence within a dominantly Anglo-British jurisdictional structure would generally prove ideologically unsatisfactory and politically problematic for both the Irish and British nations.

4   From English to British literature: John Lyly's *Euphues* and Edmund Spenser's *The Faerie Queene*

Andrew Hadfield

In sixteenth-century England writers of literature were frequently unsure exactly how to employ the flexible national category at their disposal. Often authors found themselves caught between two related but opposed desires. On the one hand, they sought to elevate the status of English literature so that it could rival the achievements of the classical world and those European nations which had imitated that heritage rather more successfully – Italy, France and, less often, Spain. On the other hand, they used 'literature' as either an adjunct or supplement to political representation, arguing the need for a critical public sphere where national problems could be debated. The consequence was that a celebratory nationalism was pitted against a specifically critical nationalism. In trying to perform the impossible balancing act this involved, authors often solved the problem by imagining two or more different – often overlapping – communities representing the nation at specific points within their narratives, collections of lyrics, dramas, etc. Even to writers immediately concerned with the need to bring the category of the nation into sharp focus, it remained a shadowy, barely visible wraith, all too often realised in the gaps, fissures and contradictions which constitute the margins of the texts.[1]

The most frequently cited literary case of this problem of overlapping, conflicting and indeterminate national boundaries is the outburst by the Irish Captain Macmorris, serving in Henry V's army in France in Shakespeare's play of that name. In the scene before the battle of Harfleur, the four representatives of the British nations, Macmorris, Jamy, Llewellyn and Gower are left alone on stage, awaiting the start of battle. Llewellyn asks Macmorris to consider 'the disciplines of war', by

---

[1] Homi K. Bhabha, 'Introduction: narrating the nation', in Homi K. Bhabha (ed.), *Nation and Narration* (London: Routledge, 1990), 1. More generally see Richard Helgerson, *Forms of Nationhood: the Elizabethan writing of England* (Chicago,1992); Andrew Hadfield, *Literature, Politics and National Identity: Reformation to Renaissance* (Cambridge, 1994).

way of 'friendly argument' and 'communication'.[2] Macmorris responds
that it is no time to talk of war when 'there is throats to be cut'. Jamy
echoes Macmorris's call for action but adds 'I would full fain hear some
question 'tween you twae.' At this point Llewellyn takes offence:

LLEWELLYN: Captain Macmorris, I think, look you, under your correction,
    there is not many of your nation –
MACMORRIS: Of my nation? What ish my nation? Ish a villain, and a bastard,
    and a knave, and a rascal. What ish my nation? Who talks of my nation?

                                                        (III, iii, ll. 59–63)

Llewellyn objects further that Macmorris has taken 'the matter other
wise than is meant' and protests that he is as good a man as his Irish
counterpart who threatens to cut off his head before the English Gower
intervenes to calm the situation by suggesting that both are at fault:
'Gentlemen both, you will mistake each other.'

Macmorris' lines have been variously interpreted by commentators.[3]
It is indeed likely that Macmorris is a 'degenerate' Anglo-Irishman, his
name being a gaelicised form of the Anglo-Norman Fitzmaurice, so that
he could be said to belong to four distinct communities with importantly
different identities – English, Irish, Anglo-Irish and British – some of
which overlap and some of which are opposed.[4] Various conclusions can
be drawn from this encounter relevant to my purposes in this chapter.
First, it is unclear what either Macmorris or Llewellyn is referring to
when they use the term 'nation'. Does it correspond to 'race', and, if so,
does it label Macmorris as Irish or Anglo-Irish? Or does it correspond to
a territory, and, if so, is that territory Ireland or Britain? Or are these
questions simply missing the point in demanding a specific answer
because Llewellyn is suggesting no more than an anglicised allegiance of
factions in Henry's army? The incident seems designed to provoke
rather than answer such speculations, especially given the chorus's
apparently confident prediction of the earl of Essex's *English* conquest of
Ireland as the prelude to Act V, as well as the enigmatic style of the
exchange which stresses a series of communication gaps. Second, it is
noticeable that the possibility of conflict is prevented by the intervention

[2] William Shakespeare, *King Henry V*, ed. Andrew Gurr (Cambridge, 1992), III, iii, ll.
    39–40. All subsequent references to this edition.
[3] See Philip Edwards, *Threshold of a Nation: a study in English and Irish drama* (Cambridge,
    1979), 74–6; Willy Maley, review of Cairns and Richards, *Writing Ireland*, *Textual
    Practice*, 3 (1989), 291–6, at 293–6; David J. Baker, '"Wildehirissheman": colonial
    representation in Shakespeare's *Henry V*', *English Literary Renaissance*, 22 (1992),
    37–61, at 43–50; Michael Neill, 'Broken English and broken Irish: nation, language,
    and the optic power in Shakespeare's Histories', *Shakespeare Quarterly*, 45 (1994), 1–32,
    at 19–20.
[4] Neill, 'Broken English and broken Irish', at 19.

of the relatively taciturn Englishman, Gower (who has earlier in the scene praised Macmorris as 'a very valiant gentleman' (11–12)), implying that whichever way the peoples present in the army are separated, the English are the natural rulers. Third, one might suggest that the scene connotes both unity and disunity. The soldiers fight together to obtain a famous *English* victory – as Henry is never anything other than an English king – but their separate identities, mutual antagonisms and different interpretations are left unresolved to be carried into the space beyond the play which has subsequently been variously read as an unproblematical celebration of an English identity and a harsh indictment of a usurping dynasty leading the nation astray.[5]

In this chapter I want to suggest that English notions of national identity became more complex and problematic as Elizabeth's reign continued, a phenomenon recognised in the literature which often sought to help construct that sense of identity. Perhaps three related factors can be singled out: the development of colonialism, particularly in the Americas; the increasing importance of Ireland in English political and social calculations after the 1580s; and the desire for a united Britain fuelled by the succession crisis and speculation that James VI of Scotland would become king.[6] The change can be illustrated by means of two massively influential literary texts both of which sought to define a national literary style and influence the creation of a national literary identity, John Lyly's *Euphues* (1578) and its sequel, *Euphues and his England* (1580), and Edmund Spenser's *The Faerie Queene*, which appeared in a first edition of three books in 1590, to be followed by an edition containing a further three in 1596.

I

John Lyly's work is not without its contradictions, references to overlapping and competing conceptions of the nation, but these are confined within an English context rather than that of the British Isles and beyond. His two prose romances were among the best-selling works in Renaissance England. G. K. Hunter has remarked 'Every aspiring author in the period must have read *Euphues*' and Lyly's distinctive style

---

[5] See Shakespeare, *Henry V*, ed. Gurr, 'Introduction'; Michael Quinn (ed.), *Shakespeare: Henry V* (London, 1969); Jonathan Dollimore and Alan Sinfield, 'History and ideology: the case of *Henry V*', in John Drakakis (ed.) *Alternative Shakespeares* (London, 1985), 206–27.

[6] See Angus Calder, *Revolutionary Empire: the rise of the English-speaking empires from the fifteenth century to the 1780s* (London, 1981); Steven G. Ellis, *Tudor Ireland: crown, community and the conflict of cultures, 1470–1603* (Harlow, 1985); Marie Axton, *The Queen's Two Bodies: drama and the Elizabethan succession* (London, 1977).

– later labelled 'Euphuism' – came to define a dominant form of literary English.[7] As late as 1632, Edmund Blount, editor of Lyly's plays, commented 'our nation are [sic] in his debt for a *new English* which hee taught them' [my emphasis].[8] Lyly's characteristic style, consisting predominately of balanced shorter clauses and antitheses, made the 'Petrarchan paradox into the capstone of a whole view of life'. Lucilla when infatuated with Euphues, for example, endures 'termes and contraries', her heart caught 'betwixt faith and fancie ... hope and fear ... conscience and concupiscence'.[9] It is perhaps not too far-fetched to describe this style as a means of vernacularising Latin and of successfully finding a 'structural principle in English which would enable the language to deal adequately and in an ordered fashion with complex material, and thus do the work formerly done by the inflected endings of Latin'.[10] It also became the courtly style *par excellence*.[11] So dominant did Euphuism becomes that any author of prose seeking to thrust himself forward as the literary spokesman of Englishness had either to copy Lyly's writing or define his own in opposition to it. This is exactly what Sidney felt obliged to do in *An Apologie for Poetrie*, as he pitted the periphrasis he employed as a structural principle in the *Arcadia* against Lyly's balanced antitheses.[12]

As one of the earlier Elizabethan writers Lyly was in many ways writing in a vacuum and the experimental nature of his work must be taken into account.[13] Just as his style has precursors – William Pettie, John Rainolds' Latin[14] – but is clearly not simply derivative, so the form and generic identity of *Euphues: The Anatomy of Wit* and *Euphues and his England* have models – courtesy books of varying modes like Stefano Guazzo's *The Civil Conversation* (1574, translated into English by William Pettie in 1581 after the publication of Lyly's two books) and Sir Thomas Elyot's *The Boke Named the Governour* (1531), Roger Ascham's *The Scholemaster* (1570), and, in the corpus of classical and Renaissance literature, the Greek romances of Heliodorus (c. third century AD),

[7] G. K. Hunter, *John Lyly: the humanist as courtier* (London, 1962), 259.

[8] R. W. Bond (ed.), *The Works of John Lyly* (3 vols., Oxford, 1902), iii, 3; William Ringler, 'The immediate source of euphuism', *PMLA*, 53 (1938), 678–86, at 679.

[9] Bond, *Works of Lyly*, i, 205. All subsequent references to this edition in parentheses.

[10] Jonas A. Barish, 'The prose style of John Lyly', *ELH*, 23 (1956), 14–35, at 24, 27; Hunter, *John Lyly*, 264; Catherine Bates, *The Rhetoric of Courtship in Elizabethan Language and Literature* (Cambridge, 1992), 97–8.

[11] Bates, *Rhetoric of Courtship*, 97.

[12] Sir Philip Sidney, *An Apologie for Poetrie*, ed. Geoffrey Shepherd (Manchester, 1973, rpt. of 1965), 139; Hunter, *John Lyly*, 286–7.

[13] Walter N. King, 'John Lyly and Elizabethan rhetoric', *Studies in Philology*, 52 (1955), 149–61, at 161.

[14] J. Swart, 'Lyly and Pettie', *English Studies*, 23 (1941), 9–18; Ringler, 'The immediate source of euphuism'.

Boccaccio's *Decameron* (mid fourteenth century), as well as contemporary Italian prose romances – without actually resembling any individual one.[15]

Symptomatic of this mixed, experimental mode of writing is the fact that Lyly's conception of his project in his two prose works seems to have changed between the writing of the one and the other.[16] *Euphues: The Anatomy of Wit* tells the straightforward story of a witty but arrogant and morally suspect young Athenian who chooses to reside in Naples, where he betrays his friend, Philautus, in love, is himself then betrayed by the young woman, Lucilla, who dies in suitably miserable circumstances later, becomes reconciled to Philautus, realises that he has not behaved very well so far and returns to Athens to study moral philosophy, and proceeds to lecture all and sundry on the ins and outs of moral behaviour. Appended to the third edition of *Euphues: The Anatomy of Wit* is a letter to the gentlemen scholars of Oxford. Here, Lyly acknowledges that his work has been read allegorically and that criticisms he had made of the University in Athens (Athens is represented as effectively one giant university) had been read as criticisms of Oxford (I, p. 324). The text itself ends with Euphues crossing the sea to England where he expects to 'see a courte both braver in shewe and better in substance, more gallaunt courtiers, more godlye consciences, as faire Ladyes and fairer conditions' (I, p. 323). In the letter Lyly imputes these criticisms to 'the envious ... the curious by wit ... [and] the guiltie by their own galled consciences'; he promises that 'Euphues at his arrival I am assured will view Oxforde, where he will either recant his sayinges, or renew his complaintes' (pp. 324–5).

Such comments – and the title – probably lead the reader to expect a survey of the realm which only actually occurs at the end of *Euphues and his England* in passages which owe a great deal to William Harrison's well-known *Description of England* (1577), included in Holinshed's *Chronicles*.[17] The bulk of the story casts Philautus as the principal actor who suffers in love and courtship until he eventually woos and wins the chaste and beautiful Camilla. Euphues, alongside various other moral guides whom they meet during their stay, serves as a moral instructor,

[15] Hunter, *John Lyly*, 53–4; John Leon Livesay, *Stefano Guazzo and the English Renaissance, 1575–1675* (Chapel Hill, Calif., 1961), 78–83; Samuel Lee Wolff, 'A source of *Euphues: The Anatomy of Wit*', *Modern Philology*, 7 (1910), 577–85. This variety of sources accounts for the problems critics have had classifying the works: see Theodore L. Steinberg, 'The anatomy of *Euphues*', *Studies in English Literature, 1500–1900*, 17 (1977), 27–38.

[16] Hunter, *John Lyly*, 65.

[17] Euphues arrives in England armed only with Caesar's *De Bello Gallico* and experience shows him that more up-to-date accounts are required; Richard Helgerson, *The Elizabethan Prodigals* (Berkeley, Calif., 1976), 76.

returning to Athens before the end of the book where he pens his 'Glasse for Europe', a description of England and the English for the edification of 'the Ladyes and Gentlewomen of Italy': 'I am come out of Englande with a glasse, wherein you shall behold the things which you never sawe, and marvel at the sightes when you have seene. Not a Glasse to make you blush, yet not at your vices, but others vertues' (II, p. 189). All of which implies that the relationship between the two texts and questions of national identity is both undeniable and undeniably problematic. *Euphues and his England* has been taken at face value and read as a celebration of England and Englishness.[18] However, its inherently mixed generic nature would seem to preclude such a naive empiricist reading and use of evidence beyond context, as would the question of its readership. The 'Glass' is addressed to Italian ladies but within a work which is prefaced by two letters, one 'To the Ladies and Gentlewomen of *England*' [my emphasis] and one 'To the Gentlemen Readers'; *Euphues: The Anatomy of Wit*, in contrast, is addressed to a singularly male audience. Whilst the former promises to correct the misogyny of the previous volume and, most importantly, advertises itself as a work for female consumption – '*Euphues* had rather lye shut in a Ladyes casket, then open in a Schollers studie' (II, p. 9) – the latter is explicitly clubbish, using comparisons to denigrate women and bind a male audience together in recognising such tropes as means of sexual exclusion. Euphues is described 'as long in viewing of London, as he was in comming to it, not farre differing from Gentlewomen, who are longer a dressing their heads then their whole bodyes' (II, p. 11). Lyly draws attention to the complexities of reader response in this openly diacritical act of splitting up his audience into two separate groups.[19] What does connect these two groups is their Englishness, so that when a section is addressed to Italian ladies within a fiction which openly acknowledged that it had been interpreted allegorically, the English reader must surely entertain the probability that things are not what they seem. Not only is Euphues' 'Glass for Europe' really a glass for England to read itself, but when the fictional author specifically protests that the text is designed to make the reader blush 'not at your vices, but others vertues', it should be apparent that the vices and the virtues are both English. When, towards the end of the treatise, Euphues informs his audience that '*we can see our faults only in the English Glass*' [emphasised in the text] (II,

---

[18] E. D. Marcu, *Sixteenth Century Nationalism* (New York, Abaris, 1976), 79–81.

[19] For some reflections on the sexualising of national identity see Andrew Parker *et al.* (eds.), *Nationalisms and Sexualities* (London, 1992); Partha Chaterjee, *The Nation and its Fragments: colonial and postcolonial histories* (Princeton, 1993), chs. 6–7.

p. 202), the mirror is clearly self-reflexive. England is forced to take a hard look at itself isolated from the rest of Europe.

However, the precise relationship between 'Euphues' Glass for Europe', the rest of the text and the world outside that text has to be puzzled out by the reader and there is not necessarily one right answer or right way of reading. Ostensibly, the 'Glass' reads as a long eulogy to the virtues of England. However, careful inspection reveals much that demands closer scrutiny. For example, early on Euphues attacks English attitudes to attire as 'the greatest enormity that I coulde see in England' and comments, 'there is nothing in England more constant, than the inconstancie of attire, nowe using the French fashion, nowe the Spanish, then the Morisco gownes, then one thing, then another' (p. 194). Strangely enough, the last description we have of Euphues before his departure for Athens is that he was 'commonlye in the court to learne fashions' (p. 185), a seeming discrepancy which is not explained. Is Euphues merely learning about fashions? Does the word 'fashions' refer to something other than clothes despite the verbal echo? Is Euphues' leaving after this comment merely a coincidence? Or does the attack on the vagaries of English fashion refer to something more serious?

A similarly troubling passage occurs two pages later and needs to be quoted at greater length:

> Their Aire is very wholesome and pleasant, their civilitie not inferior to those that deserve best, their wittes very sharpe and quicke, although I have heard that the *Italian* and the *French*-man have accompted them but grose and dull pated, which I think came not to passe by the proofe they made of their wits, but by the Englishmans reporte.
>
> For this is straunge (and yet how true it is there is none that every travailed thether but can reporte) that it is always incident to an English-man, to thinke worst of his owne nation, eyther in learning, experience, common reason, or wit, prefereing alwaies a straunger rather for the name, then the wisdome. I for mine owne parte thinke, that in all *Europe* there are not Lawyers more learned, Divines more profound, Phisitions more expert, then are in *England*. (II, p. 196)

This also seems to read fairly straightforwardly as extravagant self-praise for an internal audience under the guise of correcting an undue modesty for the benefit of other nations (in some ways that is obviously the witty joke). Nevertheless, certain things do not appear to add up. Euphues provides no answer to his initial question as to whether the English are witty or not. He first gives an explanation for the poor reputation of the English – foreigners believe their bad accounts of themselves. He comments on the English lack of self-confidence. Finally he side-steps the issue by praising learned lawyers, profound divines and expert physicians. The question of the wit of the English is not solved.

My reading might seem a pedantic exercise in splitting hairs. However, it needs to be remembered that the first volume's full title is *Euphues: The Anatomy of Wit* and is in essence the story of a young man who abuses his natural wit at court where, incidentally, he has just come from in *Euphues and his England* and is the place in which he is really interested in the 'Glass'. Wit is nothing if not an ambiguous quality as represented in the text. Near the start of *Euphues: The Anatomy of Wit*, Euphues is observed by a wise old Neapolitan gentleman who respects his potential but fears for his future:

an old Gentleman in *England* seeinge his pregnant wiytte, his Eloquent tongue somewhat tauntinge, yet wyth delight, his myrthe wythout measure, yet not wythout wytte, hys sayinges vaineglorious, yet pythie, beganne to bewayle hys nurture; and to muse at his Nature, beeinge incensed agayunste the one as moste pernicious, and enflamed wyth the other as moste precious: for hee well knewe that so rare a wytte woulde in tyme eyther breede an intollerable trouble, or bringe an incomparable Treasure to the common weale: at the one hee greatly pittied, at the other he rejoysed. (I, p. 186)

Euphues stands poised between two extremes here: his story will either be that of national glory – for if Athens was read as Oxford, Naples was read as a representation of the English court[20] – or waste and shame. Unfortunately he uses his wit to bad purposes,[21] abusing the elderly gentleman with a series of clever logical reversals, going on to betray his friend before his deserved come-uppance, retreat into scholarship and the study of general ethics.

It would be false, I suggest, to read a simple dichotomy of good English court against bad Neapolitan court as represented in the behaviour of the sexually loose Euphues and Lucilla. Instead the question of English wit is quite deliberately left open and the reader forced to weigh up the advantages and disadvantages of witty conduct – whether it will bring 'intollerable trouble' or 'incomparable Treasure' to the nation – in the light of the story of Euphues' conduct.

In a sense what Lyly is arguing for, I believe, is that his work be read as a conduct book on a national level. In 'Euphues' Glass', the fictional author heaps praise upon the 'grave and wise Counsellors':

whose foresight in peace warranteth saftie in warre, whose provision in plentie, maketh sufficient in dearth, whose care in health is as it were a preparative against sicknesse, how great their wisdome hath been in all things, the twentie two yeares peace doth both shew and prove. For what subtilty hath thir bin wrought so closely, what privy attempts so craftily, what rebellions stirred up so disorderly, but they have by policie bewrayed, prevented by wisdome, repressed

---

[20] Hunter, *John Lyly*, 59; Helgerson, *Elizabethan Prodigals*, 75.
[21] King, 'Lyly and Elizabethan rhetoric'.

by justice? What conspiracies abroad, what confederacies at home, what injuries in anye place hath there beene contrived, the which they have not eyther fore-seene before they could kindle, or quenched before they could flame? (II, pp. 196–7)

This description becomes more disturbing as it continues. We move from the depiction of an ordered and happily stable nation, to being presented with an almost nightmare vision of a paranoid panoptican state with threats from both within and without the realm. The sug-gestion is of a nation which needs to be vigilant against the wiles of its enemies, exactly what one might expect given the fear surrounding the proposed marriage between Queen Elizabeth and the duke of Alençon, negotiations for which were taking place at the time that Lyly was writing his sequel.[22] Protestants – like Lyly – were particularly worried about two interrelated potential developments: a loss of English sover-eign integrity and the Catholic corruption of the English reformed church.[23]

This fear goes some way towards explaining the drastic and confusing generic change between *Euphues: The Anatomy of Wit* and *Euphues and his England*. 'Euphues' Glass for Europe' – possibly the germ of an original plan for the sequel – presents a hopeful but fragile ideal of an independent England, one which current events threatened to shatter in various ways. Lyly uses the survey not as an unqualified jingoistic celebration of England and its institutions but as a stick with which to beat it and spur it into action. In effect, Lyly, an aspiring courtier, is pushing himself forward as a sage counsellor whose literary offering is more valuable than the empty wit of court.[24] It is surely an obvious irony that Euphues' wisdom emerges only when he has returned to the university world of Athens and left the court, exactly the opposite journey to the one Lyly himself was hoping to make.[25] Symbolically, the wisdom of the ancients is being ignored, as is contemporary counsel.[26] Like Euphues's wit at the start of his tale, England has the potential for disaster or spectacular success and a careful look into the 'Glass' will reveal, if not the answers, then at least the right sort of questions to ask.

Both prose romances clearly demand to be read in terms of the

[22] See J. E. Neale, *Queen Elizabeth* (London, 1934), ch. 15; John Guy, *Tudor England* (Oxford, 1988), 282–5. More generally, see Philippa Berry, *Of Chastity and Power: Elizabethan literature and the unmarried queen* (London, 1989), chs 3–6; Axton, *Queen's Two Bodies*.

[23] Bond, *Works of John Lyly*, I, 74; Geoffrey Elton, *England under the Tudors* (London, 1965, rpt. of 1955), 324–5.

[24] Helgerson, *Elizabethan Prodigals*, 6–7, 77.   [25] Bates, *Rhetoric of Courtship*, 102–3.

[26] In a letter Euphues explicitly warns Philautus to 'avoyde solitariness, that breedes melancholy' (i, 256) an ironic reflection on his own status.

national form they attempt to produce and circumscribe. Their author would appear to be caught between conflicting desires and discourses, as, indeed, the idiosyncratic development of his hybrid prose works illustrates. At one level form and content appear to be out of sympathy: whilst Lyly develops a sophisticated courtly style to rival other European literatures, the logic of the text requires the ability to decode narratives in a more straightforward, allegorical manner. Rhetoric confronts logic and Lyly appears both to enjoy the copiousness of his style and simultaneously to be suspicious of it (as the praise of the counsellors who can see through the masks of conspiracies perhaps illustrates). One celebrates the achievements of an increasingly sophisticated court display while the other impulse values a more obvious moral truthfulness and fear of the present. Court confronts university, to say nothing of the suspicion that at the court of a queen there is a feeling that excessive politesse and flowery language are feminine values and therefore cannot represent the whole of the nation. As the two prefatory letters to *Euphues and his England* recognise, a fractured text will have a fractured audience and the nation cannot be united but will consist of different groups who will read the texts in different ways.[27] Such an awareness conflicts dramatically with the desire of the author to serve as a spokesman for the nation and advise the monarch at court. *Euphues* like so many sixteenth-century English literary texts, attempts to circumscribe and fix a national identity and, inevitably, becomes entangled in the logic of that slippery problem. In this sense, the text is both *about* the national question and *defined* by it. What is crucial to note, is that the nation in question is never anything other than an English entity.

II

Lyly's anglocentric preoccupation and confidence in the existence of an English nation, however that nation might be threatened by foreign invasion or infiltration, became much more difficult to sustain later in Elizabeth's reign. *The Faerie Queene*, a product of these later years, although the circumstances of its composition remain obscure in the absence of manuscript evidence, is often thought by critics to become more critical of Elizabeth's policies as its narrative progresses.[28] In this

---

[27] Helgerson, *Elizabethan Prodigals*, 68.
[28] On the composition of the poem see Josephine Waters Bennett, *The Evolution of The Faerie Queene* (Chicago, 1942); on Spenser's alleged increasing disillusion, see, for example, John D. Bernard, *Ceremonies of Innocence: pastoralism in the poetry of Edmund Spenser* (Cambridge, 1989).

chapter I propose t argue that from the start of his major poem
Spenser's poetry was critical of the queen, insisting on regarding
political problems in a British rather than an English context and urging
her to take a similar view.

After his encounter with the grisly Despair in *The Faerie Queene*, I, ix,
the Redcross knight is taken to the House of Holiness where he is
restored to physical and spiritual health ready to rescue the parents of
his betrothed, Una, from the dragon who hold them captive. Finally, he
is brought to Contemplation, an old hermit who leads him to the top of
a mountain and reveals his destiny and explains his past. The Redcross
knight is not a fairy, as he thinks himself to be, but an English changeling
deliberately switched by a fairy, whose destiny is to become Saint
George, the patron saint of England.[29] This leads the way for the last
two books to be read as a historical and spiritual allegory of mankind's
salvation from the forces of darkness and England's liberation from
Catholicism.[30]

Although there is evidence that contemporaries did read the poem in
this manner, there are numerous suggestions within the narrative that all
is not quite as it seems.[31] When questioning Contemplation as to his
role in life the Redcross knight asks if he will have to follow traditional
romance pursuits in his new incantation: 'But deeds of armes must I at
last be faine,/ And Ladies love to leave so dearely bought?' / Contemplation replies rather irritably, 'What need of armes, where peace doth ay
remaine,/ (Said he) and battailes none are to be fought? / As for loose
loves are vaine, and vanish into nought' (I, ix, 62). Contemplation has
shown the knight a vision of the New Jerusalem, so it needs to be
pointed out that he is referring to life after death in heaven: but this does
not square with Contemplation's assertion that the city of the Faerie
Queene, Cleopolis, imitates the New Jerusalem:

> Yet is *Cleopolis* for earthly frame,
> The fairest peece, that eye beholden can:
> And well beseemes all knights of noble name,
> That covet in th'immortall booke of fame
> To be eternized, that same to haunt,

---

[29] On Spenser's use of Saint George see Harold L. Weatherby, *Mirrors of Celestial Grace:
patristic theology in Spenser's Allegory* (Toronto, 1994), ch. 2.

[30] See, for example, Michael O'Connell, *Mirror and Veil: the historical dimension of
Spenser's* Faerie Queene (Chapel Hill, 1979), ch. 2.

[31] John Dixon, *The First Commentary on the 'Faerie Queene'* [1597], ed. Graham Hough
(privately printed, 1964); Alistair Fowler, 'Oxford and London marginalia to the *Faerie
Queene*', *Notes and Queries*, 206 (1961), 416–19; John Manning, 'Notes and marginalia
in Bishop Percy's copy of Spenser's *Works* (1611)', *Notes and Queries*, 230 (1984),
225–7.

And doen their service to that soveraigne Dame,
That glorie does to them for guerdon graunt:
For she is heavenly borne, and heaven may justly vaunt.   (I, x, 59)

The most obvious discrepancy is that the Redcross knight's immediate tasks, killing the dragon and marrying Una, do actually involve the sort of old style romance values which Contemplation claims are not part of his new role, thus setting the fallen world at odds with the ideal of heaven.[32] There is a pun on peece/peace in line two of the stanza which is later echoed in V, xii when Artegall, the knight of Justice, has to rescue Irena from the tyrant, Grantorto. In neither incident is the end result peace. The Redcross knight leaves the realme to fight the enemies of the Faerie Queene. Artegall is recalled to the Court of Cleopolis before he has managed to introduce true justice into Ireland (V, xii, 26–7).[33] The abrupt ending of the book itself is a further warning that England is a far from ideal realm, safe and secure from its enemies:

Her joyous presence and sweet company
In full content he there did long enjoy,
Ne wicked envie, ne vile gealousy
His deare delights were able to annoy:
Yet swimming in that sea of blissful joy,
He nought forgot, how he whilome had sworne,
In case he could that monstrous beast destroy,
Unto his Faire Queene backe to returne:
The which he shortly did, and *Una* left to mourne.   (I, xii, 41)

The last line strikes a bathetic note which would appear to undermine the married bliss of the lovers whose union is left unconsummated by the knight's need to keep his vow to serve his queen for six years against the 'proud Paynim king' (I, xii, 18–19), an interlude glossed as the reign of Mary by John Dixon, the poem's first known reader.[34] Indeed, the Redcross knight later appears as one of the knights in Malecasta's Castle Joyeous alongside her champions, which may well indicate that all is not as it should be (III, i, 63–6). The Redcross knight is clearly represented in the first edition of the poem as a traditional romance hero, ending the book bearing a passing resemblance to Chretian's Yvain. The allegorical narrative would seem to imply that England and its representative hero

---

[32] Weatherby claims that Spenser was attempting to displace the old image of Saint George derived from *The Golden Legend* with a truer image based on patristic writings; *Mirrors of Celestial Grace*, ch. 2. It is arguable that the Redcross knight/St George is less perfect than Weatherby claims and that an ideal is balanced against a less worthy figure.

[33] See Richard McCabe, 'The fate of Irena: Spenser and political violence', in Patricia Coughlan (ed.), *Spenser and Ireland: an interdisciplinary perspective* (Cork, 1989), 109–25.

[34] Dixon, *First Commentary*, 10.

fall short of the perfect state of peace and stability desired, a question of the reality failing to live up to the ideal, as in Lyly's romances.

However, it is not just a question of an ideal *English* polity being found wanting, as is the case in both *Euphues* texts. Rather, the very notion of Englishness as an ideal is called into question from the start of the poem. Contemplation calls the Redcross knight, 'Saint *George* of mery England' (I, x, 61), but his genealogy betrays a less harmonious state of affairs:

> For well I wote, thou springst from ancient race
> Of *Saxon* kings, that have with mightie hand
> And many bloudie battailes fought in place
> High reard their royall throne in *Britaine* land,
> And vanquisht them, unable to withstand[.]   (I, x, 65)

The Redcross knight's future is supposed to lead to peace but his origins are bloody. In fact, being a conquering Saxon sets him against the ostensible hero of the whole narrative, Prince Arthur. In the previous canto, Arthur has explained 'his name and nation' (I, ix, 2) to Una and the knight and, although also ignorant of his origins, he describes his education by Merlin and Timon beside the River Dee, significantly, the boundary between England and Wales. Arthur's status as the greatest king of the Britons was too well known to escape even the most ignorant Elizabethan reader so that Arthur's Britishness places him in opposition to that of the knight he has just saved.[35] As in the scene before Harfleur in *Henry V,* this implies both a potential union of the disparate peoples of Britain in a new peace, and harks back to older conflicts. It is for the readers of the poem to decide themselves how to conceive matters or which path to pursue.

Arthur's origins are never actually described although they play a crucial part in the development of the plot, not just in terms of the relationship between his own character and a real or imagined history outside the text, but also in terms of an authentication of both Britomart and Artegall who turn out to be Briton changelings – Britomart being the daughter of a Welsh king, Ryence (III, ii, 17–18, III, iii, 26).[36]

[35] See Hugh MacLachlan, 'Arthur, legend of' and Gordon Teskey, 'Arthur in *The Faerie Queene'*, in A. C. Hamilton (ed.), *The Spenser Encyclopedia* (London and Toronto, 1990), 64–6, 69–72; Charles Bowie Millican, *Spenser and the Table Round: a study in the contemporaneous background for Spenser's use of the Arthurian legend* (Cambridge, Mass., 1932); Anthea Hume, 'Britons and elves', in *Edmund Spenser: protestant poet* (Cambridge, 1984), ch. 7.

[36] The name of Britomart's father probably derives from the north Welsh king in Malory (as noted in Edmund Spenser, *The Faerie Queene* (ed.), A. C. Hamilton (London, 1977), 320), ed., who is an enemy of Arthur's ally, Lodegraunce, Guinevere's father, and whom Arthur hates; *The Works of Sir Thomas Malory*, ed., Eugene Vinaver (Oxford,

Merlin prophesises that Artegall will be slain, 'in words that recall the treachery of Mordred', who betrays and kills Arthur (III, iii, 27–8).[37] In Book III, the last book of the first edition of *The Faerie Queene*, dynastic history and the tracing of a genealogy becomes more important and occupies a large part of the first and last cantos of the Book as Britomart, the knight of Chastity, first discovers who she is and then what the future holds in store for her (Guyon, an elf by birth (II, i, 6), does not have the same focus placed upon his origins). Put another way, the book is framed by a consideration of Britomart's role in terms of her Britishness, a sense of identity which mirrors and develops that unfolded to the English Redcross knight in a much briefer narrative. The wider focus of the narrative moves from a sense of *Englishness* to a sense of *Britishness*. When Arthur reads the 'auncient booke, hight *Briton moniments*' (II, x, 59), left in an old chamber in Alma's House of Temperance, he is able to survey a line of British kings from the establishment of Britain by the eponymous Brutus, who drives out the savage giants to the accession of Uther Pendragon, Arthur's father, at which point the book breaks off abruptly. Arthur, unlike the Redcross knight, does not discover his own origins but the reader can clearly make the connection. The canto opens with a direct address to Elizabeth from the narrator, which helps to make sense of this very deliberate dramatic irony:

> Thy name O soveraine Queene, thy realme and race,
> From this renowmed Prince derived arre,
> Who mightily upheld that royall mace,
> Which now thou bear'st, to thee descended farre
> From mightie kings and conquerours in warre,
> Thy fathers and great Grandfathers of old[.]   (II, x, 4)

Elizabeth is represented as a Briton queen herself and it is up to her to discover her identity through reading the poem. Both she and Arthur are in the dark at this point and so will have to make sense of the developing moral allegory of the poem which demands a response to the direct historical/mythical references contained throughout the narrative in order to find out who they are and what they must do.[38] The two have already been directly linked through Arthur's bemusing erotic dream of the Faerie Queene (I, ix, 13–16), who, as the letter to Raleigh informs readers, was 'the most excellent and glorious person of our soveraine the

1947), 39–41. If such an allusion has been made, the unity of the British isles is further disrupted.

[37] Teskey, 'Arthur in *The Faerie Queene*', 70.

[38] See Paul Alpers, 'How to read *The Faerie Queene*', *Essays in Criticism*, 18 (1968), 429–43, for a comparable analysis of ways in which the poem positions its readers.

Queene'.[39] The time scale of the relationship is therefore double: Elizabeth is linked to Arthur as both future bride and descendant: literally, typologically and in terms of a moral allegory.[40]

This episode also details the battles of Briton kings against would-be invaders, principally the Romans but, more importantly, the Saxons. Spenser is relying on material taken from Geoffrey of Monmouth's *The History of the Kings of Britain*, the principal source of the British legends for the Tudors.[41] Spenser's adaptation of the narrative truncates a series of reigns and incidents so that there is only a gap of a stanza between the final defeat of Hengist and Horsa, the first two Saxon invaders of Britain, invited in to help Vortigern fight his civil wars, and the accession of Uther Pendragon, paving the way for Arthur. The effect is to highlight a contrast between ruinous civil war leading to invasion and the dawn of a glorious age, the implication being that Elizabeth has the power to establish the latter if she assumes the mantle of her descendant Britomart, the martial Briton warrior queen, a dichotomy which is to assume more importance as the narrative progresses.[42]

In III, ii–iii, Merlin shows Britomart her future, Briton husband, Artegall, and revels to her the 'Renowmed kings, and sacred Emperours, / Thy fruitfull Ofspring, shall from thee descend' (III, iii, 23), reviving a dynasty 'out of auncient *Troian* blood' (22). The subsequent prophetic visions establish Artegall as Arthur's half-brother, as he is the son of Igraine, Arthur's mother, wife to Gorlois, king of Cornwall. The two will return to Britain and 'withstand / The powre of forrein Paynims, which invade thy [Britomart's] land' (III, iii, 27). Then, the following narrative tells of the struggle between Britons and Saxons for the rule of Britain. Thus it reverses the earlier perspective of the Redcross knight (27–42), which ends with the seeming triumph of the Saxons and the expulsion of the Britons, following Geoffrey: 'The *Britons*, for their sinnes dew punishment, / And to the *Saxons* over-give their government' (41). However, not only do the Saxons start to fight amongst themselves as the ruling Britons had before them (46), but the chronicle is carried up to date with the reclaiming of the crown under the Tudors as a British dynasty, the assumption of peace and prosperity as a 'royall

[39] See Angus Fletcher, *The Prophetic Moment: an essay on Spenser* (Chicago, 1971), 86–8.
[40] For a fuller treatment of Spenser's levels of allegory, see Isabel G. MacCaffrey, *Spenser's Allegory: the anatomy of imagination* (Princeton, 1976), part 1.
[41] Geoffrey of Monmouth, *The History of the Kings of Britain*, trans. Lewis Thorpe (Harmondsworth, 1966); T. P. Kendrick, *British Antiquity* (London, 1950); Carrie Anna Harper, *The Sources of The British Chronicle History in Spenser's* The Faerie Queene (Philadelphia, 1910).
[42] See O'Connell, *Mirror and Veil*, ch. 3; Simon Shepherd, *Amazons and Warrior Women: varieties of feminism in seventeenth-century drama* (Brighton, 1981), ch. 2.

virgin' reigns, at which point the prophecy breaks off with Merlin overcome by what he has seen, refusing to disclose it to Britomart or her nurse, Glauce. Inspired by the hope of setting such events in process through augmenting her quest, Britomart sets off dressed in the armour of Angela, a great Saxon virgin, the most recent of a line of famous martial maids (53–8). Angela was often represented as the eponymous founder of England.[43]

Britomart's symbolic wearing of Angela's armour serves to unite Britons and Saxons, going beyond the earlier conflicts. The Redcross knight's Englishness now appears somewhat sectarian. But the abrupt ending of the chronicle reminds us that all may not turn out as harmoniously as the description of peace in Elizabeth's time suggests:

> But yet the end is not. There *Merlin* stayd,
> As overcomen of the spirites powre,
> Or other ghastly spectacle dismayd,
> That secretly he saw, yet note discoure:
> Which suddein fit, and halfe extatick stoure
> When the two fearefull women saw, they grew
> Greatly confused in behavioure;
> At last the fury past, to former hew
> Hee turnd againe, and chearefull looks (as earst) did shew.   (III, iii, 50)

The poem has moved into the present time and the future is unpredictable and uncertain. Britain may well become united as the prophetic visions suggest, or all may turn out to be a fantastic chimera. The last detail given in the chronicle is the supposed intervention in the Netherlands with Elizabeth stretching 'her white rod over the *Belgicke* shore' (49), a commitment Elizabeth was reluctant to make despite the pressure put on her by protestant factions at court, and which did not really happen.[44]

Towards the end of Book III, Britomart and the fickle, lustful knight Paridell tell stories of their ancestries. Paridell is descended from Paris, whose ravishment of Helen led to the destruction of Troy, and, therefore, indirectly, the establishment of Britain via Aeneas and Brutus. Paridell's celebration of his lineage suggests a myopic reading of history as his ancestor's action leads to the destruction of Troy. Paridell shows that he has learnt nothing from the burden of the past when he seduces Hellenore, his host Malbecco's wife, causing misery and disaster. Britomart is angered by Paridell's reaction as she shares an affinity with

---

[43] See Harper, *Sources of the British Chronicle History*, 65–8. Spenser has embellished the story considerably unless there is a lost source.
[44] For the history of Elizabethan responses to the revolt see Charles Wilson, *Queen Elizabeth and the Revolt of the Netherlands* (London, 1970).

the Trojans rather than the Greeks (III, ix, 38) and she forces him to tell the story of the founding of Britain and its cities (45–51). The point to be made here is that history can be read in various ways according to one's perspective. It can be used to build up a dynasty in a fruitful way, so that the nation prospers, or it can be used as a form of pointless seduction (the reason why Paridell tells his stories) and become merely self-aggrandising and, ultimately, self-destructive. Elizabeth, it is implied, has to choose which path she will follow, that of uniting Britain or of trapping it within a cycle of violence.[45] Or, maybe, seeing that Elizabeth was already past childbearing age in 1590 when the poem was published, it was all too late anyway and the die had been cast.

A year after the publication of the first edition of *The Faerie Queene*, Spenser published his collection of *Complaints* which included the autobiographical *Colin Clouts Come Home Againe*, a fictionalised account of Spenser's recent voyage to England in the previous year to oversee the publication of *The Faerie Queene* and probably to attempt to promote the poem at court.[46] Spenser now seems keen to cast himself as an English exile in Ireland or as an Anglo-Irishman. He prefaces the poem with a letter to Sir Walter Raleigh noting that the poem was written 'From my house of Kilcolman', the estate he purchased in the Munster Plantation in the late 1580s, having his fictionalised persona refer to Ireland as 'that land our mother' (line 226) in contrast to '*Cynthias* land' (289) over the sea.[47] This could be taken to signal a very deliberate change from the integrationist, British identity articulated in the first edition of *The Faerie Queene* and a promotion of a more colonialist outlook founded in an expatriate 'New' English community in Ireland.[48] In the second edition of *The Faerie Queene*, the question of the mismanagement of its colonial government by ignorant English authorities becomes a central issue, especially in Books V–VI.[49] The failure to spread justice to Ireland results in the destruction of any attempt to unify Britain. It is possible that this reflects the increasing pessimism of the author, who lost faith in Elizabeth's vacillating policies, as some

---

[45] See Hadfield, *Literature, Politics and National Identity*, 198–200; O'Connell, *Mirror and Veil*, 84–9.

[46] For details of Spenser's movements see Willy Maley, *A Spenser Chronology* (Basingstoke, 1994), 52–7.

[47] On the Munster Plantation and Spenser's involvement in its history see Michael MacCarthy-Morrogh, *The Munster Plantation: English migration to southern Ireland, 1583–1641* (Oxford, 1986).

[48] See Nicholas Canny, 'Edmund Spenser and the development of an Anglo-Irish identity', *The Yearbook of English Studies*, 13 (1983), 1–19.

[49] See Coughlan, *Spenser and Ireland*; Andrew Hadfield, 'The course of justice: Spenser, Ireland and political discourse', *Studia Neophilologica*, 65 (1993), 187–96.

have argued.[50] However, we do not know how the poem was composed and some sections of the later books could well be of a relatively early date, especially those which praise Spenser's patron of the early 1580s, Arthur Lord Grey De Wilton.[51]

III

The point to be made is that, from the start of *The Faerie Queene*, there could be no straightforward discussion of England as a self-enclosed political entity outside a British context, as there was in *Euphues* and *Euphues and his England*, whatever the anxieties betrayed in those texts. Spenser's poem deliberately replaces an English with a British context and becomes increasingly focused upon Ireland, specifically in the representation of Anglo-Irish political relations in Book V, the depiction of savages and the role of the Blatant Beast in Book VI, and, perhaps, most scandalously of all, in the depiction of Ireland as a mythical land of primeval chaos in the extant fragment of Book VII, abandoned by the myopic queen who cannot see that her hopes of a unified kingdom will not survive without its conquest.[52] *The Faerie Queene* also aroused the ire of the Scottish – soon to be British – king for its portrayal of his mother, Mary Queen of Scots as Duessa, specifically in the trial scene at Mercilla's court in V, ix.[53] Had Spenser survived Elizabeth's reign he would probably have found James's authoritarian British regime even less hospitable than that of Elizabeth.

What Lyly's work takes as its object, Englishness, is no more than a starting point for Spenser who cannot read Englishness apart from a Britishness which looks across to contemporary Ireland as well as back to the Arthurian heritage of the matter of Britain, both elements confronting each other in the poetic landscape of Faerieland. For Lyly the question is how to protect an identity in danger from foreign interference. For Spenser, that stage has not yet been reached as Britain is by no stretch of the imagination united. Whether putative versions of the published *The Faerie Queene* were more anglocentric we shall probably never know. But after its publication both the influence of the work on generations of protestant writers and the more integrated

---

[50] See, for example, Thomas H. Cain, *Praise in* The Faerie Queene (The University of Nebraska Press, 1978).

[51] For speculation on the composition of *The Faerie Queene*, see Bennett, *The Evolution of* The Faerie Queene.

[52] These themes are explored more fully in Hadfield, *'Wilde Fruit and Salvage Soyle': Spenser's Irish experience* (Oxford, 1997).

[53] On this last point see Richard A. McCabe, 'The masks of Duessa: Spenser, Mary Queen of Scots and James VI', *English Literary Renaissance*, 17 (1987), 224–42.

political geography of the British Isles as an 'English Empire' meant that such insularity became more problematic.[54]

[54] See William B. Hunter, Jr (ed.), *The English Spenserians: the poetry of Giles Fletcher, George Wither, Michael Drayton, Phineas Fletcher and Henry More* (Salt Lake City, Utah, 1977); Joan Grundy, *The Spenserian Poets* (New York, 1969); David Norbrook, *Poetry and Politics in the English Renaissance* (London, 1984), chs. 8–9; Hugh Kearney, 'The making of an English empire', in *The British Isles: a history of four nations* (Cambridge, 1989), ch. 7.

5   The British problem in three tracts on Ireland by Spenser, Bacon and Milton

Willy Maley

While the advent of a new genre, such as the new British history, invites the study of new texts, it also encourages us to look for new angles on old ones. In recent years there has been an increasing interest among historians in the 'British problem'.[1] This development has been unusual insofar as no significant concomitant development has occurred in literary studies. One can speculate as to why this should be the case. Some of the presently dominant, theoretically informed approaches to literature, such as post-structuralism and deconstruction, appear to play down questions of context in favour of close reading and an assiduous attention to language that can at times come down to cavilling on the ninth part of a hair. Others which do declare themselves to be historically grounded, such as new historicism and cultural materialism, have always acknowledged Ireland as a special case, an exemplary site of colonial activity, but have preferred to set it against some monolithic Englishness or Britishness – and often the terms are interchangeable – rather than to see it as part of a complex process of state formation. In this chapter I want to focus on a genre which has long been read as concerned almost exclusively with Irish history. I shall suggest that the three texts here chosen as representative of it can usefully be considered in terms of the 'British problem'. I should perhaps say at the outset that my interest in the so-called British problem in the early modern period is as a crisis of identity or crises of identities in Renaissance culture, and that I am particularly interested in the way in which Scotland disappears in terms like 'Anglo-Irish'. I shall argue that key texts in the English

[1] See Brendan Bradshaw and John Morrill (eds.), *The British Problem* (London, 1996); Jane E. Dawson, 'Two kingdoms or three?: Ireland in Anglo-Scottish relations in the middle of the sixteenth century', in Roy Mason (ed.), *Scotland and England, 1286–1815* (Edinburgh, 1987), 113–38; Steven G. Ellis and Sarah Barber (eds.), *Conquest and Union: fashioning a British state, 1485–1725* (London, 1995); Conrad Russell, *The Fall of the British Monarchies, 1637–1642* (Oxford, 1991), 'The British background to the Irish Rebellion of 1641', *Historical Research*, 61:145 (1988), 166–82; 'The British problem and the English Civil War', *History*, 72:236 (1987), 385–415; David Stevenson, *Scottish Covenanters and Irish Confederates: Scottish and Irish relations in the mid-seventeenth century*, (Belfast, 1981).

discourse on Ireland can productively be seen to be engaged in the construction of British consciousness, and to be quite specifically concerned with the formation of the British state.

The three texts singled out here provide exemplary cases from crucial historical junctures within the period under investigation – Edmund Spenser's *A View of the Present State of Ireland* (1596), Francis Bacon's *Certain Considerations Touching the Plantation in Ireland* (1609) and John Milton's *Observations upon the Articles of Peace made with the Irish Rebels* (1649).[2] Traditionally these three marginal texts by major canonical authors have been read specifically in relation to Ireland, with some attention to England.[3] I shall here endeavour to reveal a Scottish context which complicates the Anglo-Irish one conventionally adumbrated, and to suggest a broader 'British' perspective than has been acknowledged generally hitherto. The texts I have chosen are anomalous within the respective corpuses of their authors, and in their own ways quite untimely, perhaps even anachronistic. Those by Spenser and Bacon remained in manuscript for forty years, delaying their impact. Milton's text, on the other hand, was published within months of its composition. Each text deals with impending crisis points in British state-formation and can be read, as I wish to argue, in relation to more explicitly British projects within their respective canons.[4]

If Britain was an invention, it was arguably one that was patented chiefly in Scotland and Wales. On the other hand, it is in Ireland that we

---

[2] All references to the *View* are given by page numbers in the text and are to the first published edition, Edmund Spenser, *A View of the State of Ireland* in *Two Histories of Ireland*, ed. James Ware (Dublin, 1633). All references to Bacon are by volume and page number from James Spedding, Robert Leslie Ellis and Douglas Denon Heath (eds.), *The Works of Francis Bacon* (15 vols., London, 1857–74), and Spedding (ed.), *The Life and Letters of Francis Bacon* (7 vols., London, 1861–74). All references to Milton are to Don Wolfe (gen. ed.), *John Milton: complete prose works*, i, iii, iv (New Haven, 1960, 1962, 1966).

[3] Brendan Bradshaw is one of the few readers of the *View* to link it with Spenser's poetry explicitly in terms of a displacement of a radical protestant anxiety with the slow progress of the Reformation in England: 'The important consideration here is the function of the *Faerie Queene* as a historical epic celebrating the imperial destiny of England, and identifying that destiny with the success of the protestant Reformation in England. In that light it would be reasonable to assume that Book V, like the rest of the poem, is intended, in the first instance, to advance the cause of reformation in England' (Brendan Bradshaw, 'Edmund Spenser on justice and mercy', in Tom Dunne (ed.), *The Writer as Witness: literature as historical evidence*, Historical Studies, 16 (1987), 86).

[4] One thinks here of Bacon's *The Beginning of the History of Great Britain*, Milton's *The History of Britain*, and of course Spenser's *The Faerie Queene*. See Edwin A. Greenlaw, 'Spenser and British imperialism', *Modern Philology*, 9 (1912), 535–61. On the contemporary context of Milton's British history, see Gary D. Hamilton, '*The History of Britain* and its Restoration audience', in David Loewenstein and James Grantham Turner (eds.), *Politics, Poetics, and Hermeneutics in Milton's Prose* (Cambridge, 1990), 241–55.

find arguably the most fraught relationship with Britishness. 'Anglo-Irish' history is also, culturally and politically, 'British' history, the history of the British state, and as such it must necessarily include Scotland. Neither early modern nor modern Irish history can be understood or explained solely by reference to *English* colonialism, no matter how fractured that Englishness is shown to be. For instance, critics have persisted in reading Spenser's prose dialogue as exclusively a text on Ireland, often in conjunction with Book V of *The Faerie Queene*.[5] Yet neither the Legend of Justice nor the *View* can be regarded as 'all about Ireland' in any simple sense.[6] Another strand of Spenser scholarship has been concerned with aspects of Britishness but rarely in relation to the *View*.[7] There has been a tendency, both in literary or cultural studies, and in the historiography of the early modern period, to overlook this 'British' context – with all of its tensions and complexities – in favour of a pronounced anglocentrism.[8] The seventeenth century has been described by one Scottish historian as the 'Century of the Three Kingdoms', and one can indeed see why this century should be singled out for special attention.[9] It is the period in which the great revisionist process of the last few years has concentrated. The so-called, for so long, '*English* Civil War' is now recognised as a British – or perhaps more accurately, an Anglo-Celtic – conflict, a series of cross-border disputes within a multiple kingdom. Predictably enough the chief focus of this new historiography has been on the period between the Scottish

---

[5] On the *View* see Brendan Bradshaw, 'Robe and sword in the conquest of Ireland', in C. Cross, D. Loades and J. J. Scarisbrick (eds.), *Law and Government under the Tudors: essays presented to Sir Geoffrey Elton on his retirement* (Cambridge, 1988), 139–62; Ciarán Brady, 'Spenser's Irish crisis: humanism and experience in the 1590s', *Past & Present*, 111 (1986), 17–49; 'Spenser's Irish crisis: reply to Canny', *Past & Present*, 120 (1988), 210–15; Nicholas P. Canny, 'Edmund Spenser and the development of an Anglo-Irish identity', *The Yearbook of English Studies: Colonial and Imperial Themes*, 13 (1983), 1–19; '"Spenser's Irish crisis": a comment', *Past & Present*, 120 (1988), 201–9.

[6] For the argument that 'Ireland is not only in book 5 of *The Faerie Queene*; it pervades the poem', see Stephen Greenblatt, 'To fashion a gentleman: Spenser and the destruction of the Bower of Bliss', in *Renaissance Self-Fashioning: from More to Shakespeare* (Chicago, 1980), 186.

[7] See Andrew Hadfield 'Briton and Scythian: Tudor representations of Irish origins', *Irish Historical Studies*, 28:112 (1993), 390–408.

[8] For an article that takes issue with the incorporation of Ireland into the new British history, see Nicholas Canny, 'The attempted Anglicisation of Ireland in the seventeenth century: an exemplar of "British history"', in Ronald G. Asch (ed.), *Three Nations – A Common History: England, Scotland, Ireland and British History, c. 1600–1920* (Bochum, 1993), 49–82. For another view, see Steven G. Ellis, '"Not mere English": the British perspective, 1400–1650', *History Today*, 38:12 (1988), 41–8.

[9] See David Stevenson, 'The century of the three kingdoms', in Jenny Wormald (ed.), *Scotland Revisited* (London, 1991), 107–18. For an incisive treatment of an earlier period, see Dawson, 'Two kingdoms or three?', 113–38.

invasion of England in 1638, through the Ulster Rising of 1641, to the 'English Revolution', as it was once known, and, beyond, to the Restoration of 1660.

I

That is the story so far. However, the first question I want to address is the place of Spenser in all of this, and in particular the place of *A View of the Present State of Ireland*. The *View* is a prose dialogue that sits uncomfortably next to Spenser's achievements as a poet. It has always been regarded as his Achilles' heel insofar as it reveals a darker side of the 'gentle poet' than his admirers would wish to acknowledge. As a pre-Union text written in 1596, ten years before the invention of the Union Jack, it offers a fascinating insight into the British problem. Despite being treated primarily as an Elizabethan text on Ireland – which no doubt it was and is – it was not published until 1633 and is also importantly for that reason a document whose moment of impact was not Elizabethan but Caroline and ultimately Cromwellian.[10]

Renaissance means rebirth, and the early modern period is one in which old cultural forms were revived and presented as new. If period-isation is a problem in terms of publication and literary influence, then ethnicity and national identity are similarly subject to change through time. The early modern period in Ireland witnessed a struggle for supremacy between *varieties of Englishness*, as the Old English, Catholic descendants of the twelfth-century settlement gave way to the New English, post-Reformation protestant planters like Spenser.[11] The modern period has seen a preoccupation with *varieties of Irishness* with

---

[10] I have charted the post-publication reception of the *View* in 'How Milton and some contemporaries read Spenser's *View*', in Brendan Bradshaw, Andrew Hadfield and Willy Maley (eds.), *Representing Ireland: literature and the origins of conflict, 1534–1660* (Cambridge, 1993), 191–208.

[11] On 'Anglo-Irish', 'Old-English' and 'New English', and the interminable problem of terminology, see Toby Barnard, 'Planters and policies in Cromwellian Ireland', *Past & Present*, 61 (1973), n. 10; Karl Bottigheimer, 'Kingdom and colony: Ireland in the Westward Enterprise, 1536–1660', in K. R. Andrews, N. P. Canny and P. E. Hair (eds.), *The Westward Enterprise: English activities in Ireland, the Atlantic and America, 1480–1650* (Liverpool, 1978), 64; Brady, 'Spenser's Irish crisis', n. 21; 'Spenser's Irish crisis: reply to Canny', 212; Nicholas Canny, 'The formation of the Old English elite in Ireland', *18th O'Donnell Lecture* (Dublin, 1975), 2; 'Protestants, planters and apartheid in early modern Ireland', *Irish Historical Studies*, 25:98 (1986), 115; '"Spenser's Irish Crisis": a comment', *Past & Present*, 120 (1988), n. 9; Joseph Leerssen, *Mere Irish and Fíor-Ghael: studies in the idea of Irish nationality, its development and literary expression prior to the nineteenth century* (Amsterdam and Philadelphia, 1986), ns. 11, 12; Colm Lennon, 'Richard Stanyhurst (1547–1618) and Old English identity', *Irish Historical Studies*, 21 (1978), 121–43.

revisionist historians such as Roy Foster challenging the idea of a monolithic Irish nation.[12] Between times, in the space of a hyphen, it might be appropriate to speak of *varieties of Scottishness*. But posting something through that narrow letterbox between 'Anglo' and 'Irish' is not easy.

'Spenser and Scotland' is not, I shall maintain, as perverse a conjunction as it might first appear. An Englishman who settled in Ireland and never, as far as we know, ventured to Scotland, Spenser was none the less astute enough to recognise and address at some length the existence of a Scottish dimension in Anglo-Irish politics. In fact, his national epic *The Faerie Queene*, written in Ireland, was banned in Scotland when James VI took exception to Spenser's representation of his mother, Mary Queen of Scots, in Canto 9 of Book V which was published in 1596, the likely year of the *View*'s composition.[13] The objections of James VI to the poem, and his request to Elizabeth that it be seized and destroyed and the poet punished, may have had some bearing on the apparent suppression of the *View* in 1598.[14] Spenserians have long been aware of the means by which Scotland, or Scottish interests, impinged upon Spenser. They have been less aware, or less eager to note, that in the *View* Spenser cites the Scottish humanist George Buchanan, a radical Protestant with links to the Leicester–Sidney circle, as his principal intellectual influence.[15] The former tutor of King James was of course, as a proto-republican, no friend to either James or Elizabeth. Spenser's praise and use of Buchanan in the *View* may be another reason for its apparent suppression.

[12] See Roy Foster, 'Varieties of Irishness', in *Modern Ireland, 1600–1972* (Harmondsworth, 1988), 3–14.

[13] On this episode see Richard McCabe, 'The Masks of Duessa: Spenser, Mary Queen of Scots, and James VI', *English Literary Review*, 17:2 (1987), 224–42; Donald V. Stump, 'The two deaths of Mary Stuart: historical allegory in Spenser's Book of Justice', *Spenser Studies*, 9 (1988), 81–105.

[14] On the arguments surrounding the alleged suppression of the *View* see David J. Baker, '"Some quirk, some subtle evasion": legal subversion in Spenser's *A View of the Present State of Ireland*', *Spenser Studies*, 6 (1986), 147–63; Jean Brink, 'Constructing the *View of the Present State of Ireland*', *Spenser Studies*, 11 (1992), 203–28; Andrew Hadfield, 'Was Spenser's *View of the Present State of Ireland* censored? A review of the evidence', *Notes and Queries*, 240:4 (1994), 459–63; Christopher Highley, 'Spenser's *View of Ireland*: authorship, censorship, and publication', paper presented on the occasion of the conference 'Spenser at Kalamazoo' in 1994. I am grateful to the author for providing me with a typescript of this article.

[15] Having described his own historical method, Irenius pays his dues to his sources, ending with the most important: '*Buchanan*, for that hee himselfe being an *Irish* Scot or Pict by nation, and being very excellently learned and industrious to seeke out the truth of all things concerning the originall of his own people, hath both set downe the testimony of the auncients truely, and his owne opinion together withall very reasonably, though in some things he doth somewhat flatter' (p. 29).

To switch from Ireland to Scotland is not to take the heat off Spenser and Ireland but to leap out of the frying pan and into the fire. Here, I want to focus upon two passages in the *View*, one on origins and one on policy, both of which are informed by a consideration of a crucial Scottish component. That this Scottish aspect arises in the administrative and strategic section of the text as well as in the antiquarian disquisition on identity formation is revealing. The initial exchange between Spenser's two interlocutors, Irenius and Eudoxus, occurs during a discussion of the early history of Ireland. Eudoxus asks Irenius what he thinks of the current Irish claims to Spanish descent. Irenius first relates these claims to the present position of Spain as a European and world power, then dismisses them as mythological, together with all other origin stories, including, significantly, the English tale of Brutus. Irenius, having dispensed with the Irish claim to Spanish provenance, comments: 'But the *Irish* doe herein no otherwise, then our vaine *Englishemen* doe in the Tale of *Brutus*, whom they devise to have first conquered and inhabited this Land, it being as impossible to proove, that there was ever any such *Brutus* of *England*, as it is, that there was any such *Gathelus* of *Spaine*' (27).

Judith Anderson points to the anomalous undermining of the Brutus myth in the *View*: 'Nowhere in Spenser's writings is the split between two different versions of truth more obvious than in his treatment of the Brutus legend, first in poetry and then in history. Nowhere else does he so thoroughly debunk popular myths of origin – indeed, popular antiquities – as in the *View*.'[16] Hugh MacLachlan is equally vexed by Spenser's apparently contradictory position on this origin-myth:

It is uncertain how seriously Spenser regarded the story of Britain's Trojan ancestry. In one manuscript of the *Vewe of Ireland*, Irenius remarks of 'the Tale of *Brutus*' that it is 'as impossible to proove, that there was ever any such Brutus of England, as it is, that there was any such Gathelus of Spaine' ... Yet in telling the story of the chronicle history read by Arthur (II x 9–13), in Merlin's prophetic chronicle of Britomart (III iii 22), and in Paridell's account of his Trojan ancestors (III ix 3–51), he made it central to the dynastic and imperial themes of *The Faerie Queene*. Fittingly, then, when Arthur finishes reading *Briton moniments*, upon learning about 'The royall Ofspring of his native land' he exclaims: 'How brutish is it not to understand'.[17]

MacLachlan does not tell us that this passage appears in the published text by Ware. It seems not to trouble MacLachlan, or any other critic,

[16] Judith H. Anderson, 'The antiquities of Fairyland and Ireland', *JEGP* 86:2 (1987), 202–3.
[17] Hugh MacLachlan, 'Britain, Britons', in A. C. Hamilton (ed.), *The Spenser Encyclopedia* (London and Toronto, 1990), 113.

that Spenser's anxiety about Brutus appears in the first published edition of the *View*, or that this edition is unique in being produced by an Irishman in Dublin, dedicated to Wentworth, and one in which the editor wishes to credit a Scottish monarch, James VI, with the founding of the British state, as James I, rather than with any ancient British claim staked out by any vain Englishman such as Spenser or those whom he apparently discounts in this passage. John Breen provides a cautionary note: 'In the *View* Irenius appears to cast doubt upon the authenticity of the story concerning Britain's mythic origins ... However, it would be rash to suggest that, based on Irenius' comment, Spenser did not believe in the Brutus myth's romantic and nationalistic import.'[18]

Irenius, having dispensed with Gathelus and Brutus, proceeds to deconstruct meticulously the ethnic make-up of the inhabitants of Ireland. This is where Scotland, or the Scots, make their most note-worthy appearance. Irenius says that 'Scythians', hearing of Ireland, 'arrived in the North part thereof, which is now called *Ulster*, which first inhabiting, and afterwards stretching themselves forth into the Land, as their numbers increased, named it all of themselves *Scuttenland*, which more briefly is called *Scutland*, or *Scotland*.'

This sudden shift from Spain to Scotland in the search for Irish origins takes Eudoxus by surprise: 'I wonder (*Irenaus*) whether you runne so farre astray, for whilest wee talke of *Ireland*, mee thinkes you rippe up the originall of *Scotland*, but what is that to this?' Irenius's response is hardly designed to clear the confusion: 'Surely very much', he tells Eudoxus, 'for *Scotland* and *Ireland* are all one and the same.' Eudoxus is aghast: 'That seemeth more strange; for we all know right well that they are distinguished with a great Sea running between them, or else there are two *Scotlands*.' Irenius reassures Eudoxus, with a mocking and elaborate show of patience, that he is not seeing double:

Never the more are there two *Scotlands*, but two kindes of Scots were indeed (as you may gather out of *Buchanan*) the one *Irin*, or *Irish Scots*, the other *Albin-Scots*; for those *Scots* and *Scythians*, arrived (as I said) in the North parts of *Ireland*, where some of them after passed into the next coast of *Albine*, now called *Scotland*, which (after much trouble) they possessed, & of themselves named *Scotland*; but in processe of time (as it is commonly seene) the dominion of the part prevaileth in the whole, for the *Irish Scots* putting away the name of *Scots*, were called only *Irish*, & the *Albine Scots*, leaving the name of *Albine*, were called only *Scots*. Therefore it commeth thence that of some writers, *Ireland* is called *Scotia major*, and that which now is called *Scotland*, *Scotia minor*. (28)

---

[18] John Breen, 'Imagining voices in *A View of the Present State of Ireland*: a discussion of recent studies concerning Edmund Spenser's Dialogue', *Connotations*, 4:1-2 (1994/5), 126.

Now, in Holinshed's *Chronicles* Richard Stanyhurst had written: 'as
Scotland is named Scotia minor, so Ireland is tearmed Scotia major'.[19]
Another writer that Spenser may have had in mind is Johannes Major,
or John Major (or Mair) of Scotland, author of a *History of Great Britain*
published in Paris in 1521. A key feature of Major's history is his
rejection of the British origin myths being marketed by English historians. Major was particularly keen to scotch the brut that the Scots, like
the Welsh, were descended from Brutus. Indeed, although he styles
himself a 'Scottish Briton', Major insists that 'the Irish are descended
from the Spaniards and the Scottish Britons from the Irish'. Where
Spenser will claim that the Irish are really Scots, Major contends that
the Scots are really Irish.[20] Where the proto-unionist Major seeks the
unification of Britannia Major, the English nationalist Spenser desires
the subordination of Scotia Major and Scotia Minor.[21]

Meanwhile, Eudoxus is now satisfied, and indeed proceeds to recap
and clarify:

I doe now well understand your distinguishing of the two sorts of *Scots*, & two
Scotlands, how that this which is now called *Ireland*, was anciently called *Erin*,
and afterwards of some written *Scotland*, & that which is now called *Scotland* was
formerly called *Albin*, before the comming of the *Scythes* thither; but what other
nation inhabited the other parts of *Ireland*? (28)

Irenius then outlines the other groups in Ireland. Eudoxus summarises,
before going on to praise 'This ripping of Auncestors':

Now thus farre then, I understand your opinion, that the *Scythians* planted in
the north part of *Ireland*: the *Spaniards* (for so we call them, what ever they were
that came from *Spaine*) in the west, the *Gaules* in the south: so that there now
remaineth the east parts towards *England*, which I would be glad to understand
from whence you doe think them peopled.

Irenius replies:

Mary I thinke of the *Brittaines* themselves, of which though there be little
footing now remaining, by reason that the *Saxons* afterwards, and lastly the
English, driving out the Inhabitants thereof, did possesse and people it
themselves. (33)

So, the English drive out the British, and the Irish can with more
justification claim an affinity with the Scots than the Spanish. Moreover,

[19] Richard Stanyhurst, 'The Description of Ireland', in Raphael Holinshed (ed.), *The
Chronicles of England, Scotland, Ireland and Wales* (London, 1586), ii, 52.
[20] John Major, *Historia Majoris Britanniae tam Angliae quam Scotiae* (Paris, 1921), ed. and
trans. Archibald Constable, *John Major's History of Greater Britain*, Scottish History
Society, 1st ser., no. 10 (Edinburgh, 1892).
[21] See Willy Maley, 'Britannia Major: writing and Unionist identity', in Tracey Hill and
William Hughes (eds.), *Contemporary Writing and National Identity* (Bath, 1995),
46–53.

the Old English come in for more severe criticism than the Gaelic Irish. Irenius shocks Eudoxus again by declaring that the chief abuses of the Irish are grown from the English, and indeed that the Old English are more reprehensible than the native Irish, 'which being very wilde at the first, are now become more civill, when as these from civility are growne to be wilde and meere *Irish*' (105). Here, 'Irish' is not simply another word for 'wild', but a term of opposition, in this case opposition to a previous wave of colonisers.

The Old English put out the British and are themselves now 'degenerate'. The Scots, or Scythians, are the other culprits. The Irish customs that Irenius abhors, and which critics often read as evidence of anti-Irish sentiment, are Scythian. Eudoxus speaks of 'the *Scythians*, which you say were the *Scottes*' (34), and Irenius, commencing his account of Irish customs, proposes to begin 'first with the *Scythian* or *Scottish* manners', and with '*Boolying*', the 'pasturing [of cattle] upon the mountaine, and waste wilde places' (35). Also from the Scythians – or Scots – come the '*Mantles*' and '*Glibbes*', and the war-cry '*Ferragh*' (37–9). Of the last, Irenius says:

And here also lyeth open an other manifest proofe, that the *Irish* bee *Scythes* or *Scots*, for in all their incounters they use one very common word, crying *Ferragh*, *Ferragh*, which is a *Scottish* word, to wit, the name of one of the first Kings of *Scotland*, called *Feragus*, or *Fergus*, which fought against the *Pictes*, as you may reade in *Buchanan, de rebus Scoticus*. (39)

The next Scythian or Scottish custom is the use of a short bow. In a helpful marginal note, Sir James Ware tells us: 'The originall of the very name of *Scythians* semeth to come from *shooting*'. Next comes the long shield, the absence of armour and helmet, 'trusting to the thicknes of their glibbs the which (they say) will sometimes beare off a good stroke, is meere *Scythian*, as you may see in the said Images of the old *Scythes* or *Scots*, set forth by *Heriodanus* and others' (40–1). Irenius seals his argument thus: 'By which it may almost infallibly be gathered together, with other circumstances, that the Irish are very Scots or Scythes originally, though sithence intermingled with many other Nations repairing and joyning unto them' (41). Irenius goes on to claim that both the 'wild *Scots*' and the Irish drink blood and swear by their swords (41). They worship the sun (41). A wronged Scythian will sit on an ox hide until others join with him in his quarrel: 'And the same you may likewise reade to have beene the ancient manner of the wilde *Scotts*, which are indeed the very naturall *Irish*' (42). Throughout these passages, Irenius makes it clear time and again that he is speaking of the Irish of the 'North', not the Irish *per se*. Moreover, the whole discussion rests on the assumption that there is no such thing as the Irish as such.

They are a mixture of many nations, and, in the north in particular, are originally Scots. Again, Irenius, having moved on to Gaulish and British customs, says that the use of the long shield, Gaulish as well as Scythian, is something he has observed only in the north: 'But I have not seene such fashioned Targets used in the Southerne parts, but onely amongst the Northerne people, and Irish-*Scottes*, I doe thinke that they were brought in rather by the *Scythians*, then by the *Gaules*' (44).

At this stage, it would be tempting to conclude that Spenser is a proto-unionist who is surreptitiously limiting Ireland's Spanish provenance and strengthening the claim of Scotland, thus anticipating the Ulster plantation of the early seventeenth century that will tie Scotland to England through the colonisation of the north of Ireland. But in fact, Spenser had burned his bridges with Scotland, despite his admiration for Buchanan. *The Faerie Queene*, as I pointed out, had been proscribed in Scotland by the time the *View* was entered in the Stationers Register.

The Scottish Question is posed once more when Irenius outlines the problem of Ulster, the most ungovernable province of Ireland from an English perspective, made manifest in the 1590s with the rebellion of Hugh O'Neill, earl of Tyrone.[22] Various methods of reform are aired, and Eudoxus blithely enquires of Irenius: 'what say you then of that advice . . . which (I heard) was given by some, to draw in Scotts to serve against him? how like you that advice?' This elicits a yelp of protest from Irenius, who harks back to his earlier conflation of the Scots with the Irish of the north:

for who that is experienced in those parts knoweth not that the *ONeales* are neerely allyed unto the *MacNeales* of *Scotland*, and to the Earle of *Argyle*, from whence they use to have all their succours of those *Scottes* and *Redshanckes*. Besides all these *Scottes* are through long continuance intermingled and allyed to all the inhabitants of the north: So as there is no hope that they will ever be wrought to serve faithfully against their old friends and kinsmen: And though they would, how when they have overthrowne him, and the warres are finished, shall they themselves be put out? doe we not all know, that the *Scottes* were the first inhabitants of all the north, and that those which are now called the north *Irish*, are indeed very *Scottes*, which challenge the ancient inheritance and dominion of the Countrey, to be their owne aunciently: This then were but to leap out of the pan into the fire: For the chiefest caveat and provision in reformation of the north, must be keep out those *Scottes*. (79–80)

---

[22] On this topic, see Nicholas Canny, 'Hugh O'Neill, Earl of Tyrone, and the changing face of Gaelic Ulster', *Studia Hibernica*, 10 (1970), 7–35. For the broader context and implications, see Hiram Morgan, 'The end of Gaelic Ulster: a thematic interpretation of events between 1534 and 1610', *Irish Historical Studies*, 26:101 (1988), 8–32. See also Morgan, *Tyrone's Rebellion* (Woodbridge, 1993).

Ware's rather optimistic marginal note at this point reads: 'The causes of these feares have been amputated, since the happy union of *England* and *Scotland*, established by his late Majesty.' This text, one has to remember, was written seven years before the Anglo-Scottish Union of the Crowns and ten years before the Ulster Plantation, and was published in 1633, five years before the Scottish invasion of England. Despite Ware's optimism, the north, and Ulster, continued to be a site of Anglo-*Scottish* conflict, as well as the scene of a complication of interests, from Milton to Maastricht. But it was not the Union alone that allayed Spenser's fears and warded off the awesome spectre of a pan-Celtic alliance against Little England. For the Scots who settled in Ulster after the Anglo-Scottish Union of Crowns in 1603 were not those whom Spenser feared: the Irish Scots, Highlanders and Islanders whom John Major had earlier categorised as 'Wild Scots', and contrasted with the 'domestic' or 'household' variety found in the civilised Lowlands. This is one reason why the term 'Ulster Scots' does not begin to do justice to the subtle nuances of the Scoto-Irish context. Not only does Scotland get lost in the hyphen of 'Anglo-Irish' history but so too does the fact that, as Jenny Wormald has pointed out, the traditional Irish connection with the Western Isles was deliberately superseded as an extension of James VI's policy of planting Lowland Scots in the Western Islands as part of a putative civilising process.[23]

Spenser's injunction not to allow Scots access to the north of Ireland became, within a decade of his prohibitive discourse, an imperative in the interests of solving competing Anglo-Scottish claims to that territory. Henceforth Scotland would shrink to a hyphen, and the English Pale around Dublin would become, in the course of history, and through an act of upward displacement, a British (*née* Scottish) Pale around Belfast. Beyond the English Pale lay the makings of a British polity. The haemorrhage of identity that followed on from the Union – remember that both Scottish and English opponents feared loss of sovereignty – was bandaged up in 'Scotia Major', now 'Britannia Minor'. To scarf up the tender eye of Ireland – the north – was also to blindfold subsequent critics to the part played by Scotland in the reconquest of Ireland.[24]

But why reassert the Scottishness of Ireland/Ulster? It is not in order to promote a singular politics of identity but to advocate an understanding of the multiplicity and confusion of origins that I have tried to

[23] Jenny Wormald, 'The creation of Britain: multiple kingdoms or core and colonies?', *Transactions of the Royal Historical Society*, 6th ser., 2 (1992), 185.

[24] For an intriguing analysis of the Ulster Rising in the context of the 'British Problem', see Michael Perceval-Maxwell, 'Ulster 1641 in the context of political developments in the three kingdoms', in Brian Mac Cuarta (ed.), *Ulster 1641: aspects of the rising* (Belfast, 1993), 93–106.

unravel this Scottish thread in Spenser. Few in Ireland, north or south, have been particularly keen to assert a Scottish dimension. For republicans and nationalists this would be to acknowledge a 'British' stake or investment. James Joyce neatly summed up one Irish perspective on Scotland when he wrote in 'Gas from a Burner' (1907): 'Poor Sister Scotland, her doom is fell! She has no more Stuarts to sell.'

What, finally, are the limits of Anglo-Irish identity? One limit or horizon is that even when this term does not imply a unitary Englishness and a monolithic Irishness, even when one speaks in terms of competing forms of Englishness in early modern Ireland, or varieties of Irishness in modern Ireland, other identities, traditions, histories and ethnicities get left out of the grand oppositional narrative. The example of Scotland is salutary. However, there are others. The term Anglo-Irish is freighted with conflictual histories. Scotland gets lost in the hyphen. Anglo-Irish is used nowadays to refer to relations between England (or, to be precise, Britain) and Ireland (or, to be precise, the Irish Republic). Its other use is to refer to Irish literature in English. And the third meaning, the one that is used in relation to Spenser, denotes the nascent Protestant Ascendancy.

Of course, identity is a minefield. And old workings can yield underfoot, but they can also give rise to an open cast identity in place of ethnic closure. We all know the story of how the Anglo-Normans in Ireland became the Old English after the advent of the post-Reformation protestant planters known as the New English. The Old English became, in the seventeenth century, the New Irish, and the New English became the Old Protestants. In the eighteenth century, the New Irish were simply Catholics and the Old Protestants were the Ascendancy. After partition, the Irish of the Irish Republic contained the Anglo-Normans, Old English, New English *et al.*, all Irish now, while in Northern Ireland, the six counties of Ulster, there were the Nationalists or Republicans – Irish Catholic – and the Ulster Unionists, Loyalists, or British, with the term 'Ulster Scots' sometimes invoked. The Catholics were Irish and the protestants of the south were Anglo-Irish while the settlers in the north went from Ulster Scots to British etc. Finally, after partition, Ulster (or six counties thereof) is British and the other twenty-six are unproblematically Irish. Simple, isn't it? All too simple. It was Joyce who wrote, in 'Ireland, Island of Saints and Sages' (1907):

What race, or what language . . . can boast of being pure today? And no race has less right to utter such a boast than the race now living in Ireland. Nationality (if it really is not a convenient fiction like so many others to which the scalpels of present-day scientists have given the *coup de grâce*) must find its reason for being rooted in something that surpasses or transcends and informs changing things like blood and the human word.

Studies of Spenser and Ireland, largely oblivious to the complexities of the British Problem, have remained within the binaries of Anglo-Irish history. To speak of 'Spenser and Scotland' is to begin to undo such tired oppositions.

II

I turn now to a minor treatise by Francis Bacon which, like the *View*, captures and crystallises some of the complexities of the Irish problem in a British context or, perhaps more accurately, the British Problem in an Irish context. Bacon's *Certain Considerations Touching the Plantation in Ireland* (1609) has received scant notice either from students of Bacon or historians of early modern Ireland. Yet it is arguably one of the most articulate statements, from a nascent British perspective, of the politics of plantation in the period. The *Considerations* is a remarkable display of Bacon's rhetorical brilliance. The text was first published in 1657 as part of the *Resuscitatio, or bringing into publick light several pieces of the works, civil, historical, philosophical & theological, hitherto sleeping; of the right honourable Francis Bacon ... Together with his lordship's life*, edited by his chaplain, William Rawley. Just as Spenser's *View*, written in 1596 but not published until 1633, participated in a later history than that which it described, so Bacon's considerations of the Ulster Plantation under James I became a text of the Cromwellian plantation of the 1650s. I want here to submit it to another resuscitation, to incorporate it into a discussion of British identity formation.

If the accession of James I as king of Britain marks a crucial juncture in relations between the three kingdoms of England, Scotland and Ireland, then one would expect it also to mark a shift in the English discourse on Ireland which henceforth has to accommodate a Scottish perspective. Of course, we have now seen that such a perspective was evident even in Spenser's pre-Union treatise. On one level the Union did not, at least initially, radically alter the colonial make-up of Ireland. The Scots continued to dominate in the north while the English settled primarily in the south. But the kind of Scots who planted themselves in Ulster did change. Highlanders and Islanders had hitherto been the most active settlers there. After 1603 an increasing number of Low-landers began to arrive even before the official plantation was under way. The borders had been a key area of contention throughout the reign of James VI. In 1587 an act was passed 'for the quieting and keping in obedience of the disorderit subjectis inhabitantis of the borders hielandis and Ilis'.[25] On the eve of the Ulster Plantation an instruction was issued that Islanders and Highlanders be excluded.[26] The threat of Irish and Scottish Gaelic Catholics coming together was too great for the government to countenance. Michael Hill has argued in a recent essay against drawing too clear a distinction between Highlanders and Lowlanders, pointing out that some Borderers were Celtic by culture: 'Only by distinguishing between the anglicized Lowlands and the Celtic Borders-Southwest can we understand the significance of a plantation of non-Highland Scots in Ulster from 1609 to 1625.'[27]

The main plank of policy in the Union of the Crowns was the Ulster Plantation, which resolved the competing claims to Ireland put forward by England and Scotland. According to one historian of the Ulster Plantation, Elizabeth had abandoned an English enterprise in Ulster in 1575: 'Instead of advancing the English interest in the north and putting an end to the Scoto-Irish problem, it had only served to irritate the Irish and confirm them in their hostility to England.'[28] After 1603 and the Union of the Crowns the newly formed Stuart state could synchronise its efforts. The objections of some English writers to the Scottish presence in Ulster were stifled. The competing claims to Ireland, centred on its unruly northern province, were resolved, and the foundation-stone of the Protestant Ascendancy was laid.[29] The Scots had made considerable inroads into the eastern counties of Ulster in the sixteenth century. English settlement in the south west had been less successful. The Munster Plantation had been overthrown in 1598.[30]

Contemporary commentators were quick to recognise the advantages of union. Sir Thomas Craig, author of a pro-Union treatise, insisted 'that so long as the union lasts there will be no further trouble in Ireland'.[31] This was of course optimistic. Within a generation the War of the Three Kingdoms would have Ireland as its most fiery theatre. According to David Stevenson: 'Scottish penetration of Ireland,

---

[25] Michael Perceval-Maxwell, *The Scottish Migration to Ulster in the Reign of James I* (London, 1973), 22.

[26] *Ibid.*, 64.

[27] J. Michael Hill, 'The origins of the Scottish plantations in Ulster to 1625: a reinterpretation', *Journal of British Studies*, 32 (January 1993), 25.

[28] Robert Dunlop, 'Sixteenth-century schemes for the Plantation of Ulster', *Scottish Historical Review*, 22:87 (1925), 211.

[29] See Barnard, 'Planters and policies', 33.

[30] On this episode see Michael MacCarthy-Morrogh, *The Munster Plantation: English migration to southern Ireland, 1583–1641* (Oxford, 1986), 130–5; Anthony J. Sheehan, 'The overthrow of the Plantation of Munster in October 1598', *The Irish Sword*, 15:58 (1982), 11–22.

[31] Cited in Perceval-Maxwell, *The Scottish Migration to Ulster*, 11.

although intended to reinforce English interests there, had, by the time the covenanting crisis broke, begun to undermine them.'[32] Stevenson is referring of course to post-Union Scottish penetration since the Scots had long claimed the right to be in Ireland in their own interests.

At the turn of the seventeenth century there was a genuine widespread belief that the Irish problems of England and Scotland were being solved. Michael Perceval-Maxwell points out that 'after Elizabeth's death, the migration of Scots to Ulster became a policy to be encouraged instead of a process to be deplored'.[33] The Flight of the Earls in 1607 left a political vacuum in Irish society. This vacuum was to be filled by an experimental British culture, planted in the wake of a Union that was limited in scope, and largely unforeseen. The Ulster plantation of 1609–10 was a combined Anglo-Scottish project, the word 'Brittish' being used, but with the coda that it included only 'Inland Scottish'.[34] Thus the Ulster Plantation – notwithstanding the Celtic identity of the post-Union planters from the Borders-Southwest – was a blow to Gaelic Ulster in more ways than one. Hiram Morgan has pointed out that with the departure of the Gaelic aristocracy and the Plantation of Ulster 'a new Pale was in the making'.[35] The focus of colonial activity was shifting from an English Pale around Dublin to a British Pale around Belfast. To Morgan's incisive claim that it was the alliance the Ulster lords made with Spain that rung the death knell of Gaelic Ulster, I would add the Union of England and Scotland.[36] As always in a British context one is dealing with 'external' and 'internal' pressures and demands.

What is fascinating about Bacon's text is his conjuncture of union and plantation as complementary processes, and his recognition of the complication of interests in Ireland. Bacon's tract reveals the colonial project that underpins the newly united crowns. Few histories of Anglo-Scottish Union focus on the Ulster Plantation. Few histories of the Ulster Plantation dwell on the Union. Bacon's *Considerations* brings the two together: 'And certainly I reckon this action as a second brother to the Union. For I assure myself that England, Scotland, and Ireland well united is such a trefoil as no prince except yourself (who are the worthiest) weareth in his crown.'[37] It is this 'trefoil' that intrigues me, the trefoil of Anglo-Scottish union and Irish plantation, the three-ply

[32] David Stevenson, 'Ulster 1641 in the context of political developments in the three kingdoms', in Mac Cuarta (ed.), *Ulster 1641*, 94.

[33] Cited in Perceval-Maxwell, *The Scottish Migration to Ulster*, 11.

[34] *Conditions to be Observed by the British Undertakers of the Escheated Lands in Ulster* (London, 1610), 5; Perceval-Maxwell, *The Scottish Migration to Ulster*, 64.

[35] Morgan, 'The end of Gaelic Ulster', 31.   [36] *Ibid.*, 32.

[37] Bacon, *Works* 11:4, 114. Further references to the *Considerations* will be cited by page number in the text.

nature of the British problem in an Irish context, a three-way struggle for sovereignty. The OED defines a 'trefoil' as 'a leguminous plant of genus *Trifolium* with leaves of three leaflets . . . (thing) arranged in three lobes'. One thinks immediately of the shamrock, an ironic, yet far from inappropriate symbol of the Three Kingdoms and British unity. Scotland is the third term that gets lost in the hyphen of 'Anglo-Irish', a term that binds three nations under one heading, the third lobe of a trefoil, recalling a contemporary vision: 'And some I see/ That two-fold balls and treble sceptres carry' (*Macbeth* IV.1.119–20). For Bacon, like Banquo, the future comes in twos and threes. Can Scotland be inserted into a seamless English narrative, or an uninterrupted discourse on Ireland? Revisionist Irish history has not reinscribed Scotland. It remains within an 'Anglo-Irish' problematic. Nor has cultural materialism, Irish revisionism, or the new historicism: all seem content to leave this binary opposition intact. Yet the exclusion of Scotland from discussions of Ireland matters. It is the matter of Britain, the matter of the British problem, the problem of identity and difference in a multination state.

Bacon justifies his intervention in the matter of the Ulster Plantation by adverting to the king's earlier acceptance of his views on the union. Bacon tells the king that 'God hath reserved to your Majesty's times two works, which amongst the acts of kings have the supreme preeminence; the union, and the plantation of kingdoms' (116). In doing so he employs a telling metaphor for the act of founding 'estates or kingdoms': 'for as in arts and sciences, to be the first inventor is more than to illustrate or amplify; and as in the works of God, the creation is greater than the preservation; and as in the works of nature the birth and nativity is more than the continuance; so in kingdoms, the first foundation or plantation is of more noble dignity and merit that all that followeth' (116). For Bacon there are two kinds of foundation, 'the first, that maketh one of more; and the second, that maketh one of none'. These correspond to 'the creation of the world' and 'the edification of the church'. James I can claim 'both these kinds of foundations or regenerations':

The one, in the union of the island of Britain; the other, in the plantation of the great and noble parts of the island of Ireland. Which enterprises happily accomplished, then that which was uttered by one of the best orators, in one of the worst verses, *O fortunatum natam me consule Romam!* may be far more truly and properly applied to your majesty's acts; *natam te rege Britanniam; natam Hiberniam.*

Pursuing the metaphor of creation, of different kinds of creation – artistic, scientific, divine etc. – he declares: 'For indeed unions and

plantations are the very nativities or birth-days of kingdoms.' But there
is a dark side to these birthdays:

For most part of unions and plantations of kingdoms have been founded in the
effusion of blood. But your majesty shall build *in solo puro, et in area pura*, that
shall need no sacrifices expiatory for blood; and therefore, no doubt, under an
higher and more assured blessing. (117)

Bacon is not one of those who see the unification of Britain as a return
to a former state. He does not wholly subscribe to the origin-myths of
Brutus and Arthur: 'It doth not appear by the records and monuments
of any true history, nor scarcely by the fiction and pleasure of any
fabulous narration or tradition of any antiquity, that ever this island of
Great Britain was united under one king before this day.'[38] Yet elsewhere
he alluded to the king's 'heroical desire to reduce these two kingdoms of
England and Scotland into the unity of their ancient mother kingdom of
Britain'.[39] However, this is not necessarily a contradiction. Britain could
be unified in different ways. According to Bacon, there are four parts to
a perfect union: 'Union in Name, Union in Language, Union in Laws,
and Union in Employments.' Asserting that Britain has 'one language,
though of several dialects',[40] he postulates two conditions that will bring
about 'a Perfect mixture': 'Time', and the scientific principle 'that the
greater draw the less': 'So we see when two lights do meet, the greater
doth darken and drown the less. And when a smaller river runs into a
greater, it leeseth both the name and the stream.'[41] In his *History of King
Henry VII*, Bacon records that some of Henry's counsellors cautioned:

that if God should take the King's two sons without issue, that then the
kingdom of England would fall to the King of Scotland, which might prejudice
the monarchy of England. Whereunto the King replied; That if that should be,
Scotland would be but an accession to England, and not England to Scotland;
for the greater would draw the less: and it was a safer union for England than
that of France.[42]

'Scotland', Bacon acknowledges:

is now an ancient and noble realm, substantive of itself: But when this island
shall be made Britain, then Scotland is no more to be considered as Scotland,
but as a part of Britain; no more than England is to be considered as England,
but as a part likewise of Britain; and consequently neither of these are to be
considered as things entire to themselves, but in the proportion that they bear to
the whole. And therefore let us imagine ... that Britain had never been divided,
but had ever been one kingdom: then that part of soil or territory which is
comprehended under the name of Scotland is in quantity (as I have heard it
esteemed, how truly I know not) not past a third part of Britain; and that part of

[38] Bacon, *Life and Letters*, 10:3, 92.   [39] *Ibid.*, 218.   [40] *Ibid.*, 96, 97.
[41] *Ibid.*, 99.   [42] Bacon, *Works* 6, 216.

soil or territory which is comprehended under the name of England is two parts of Britain; leaving to speak of any difference of wealth or population, and speaking only of quantity. So that if, for example, Scotland should bring to parliament as much nobility as England, then a third part should countervail two parts; *nam si inequalibus equalia addas, omnia erunt inequalia.* And this, I speak, not as a man born in England, but as a man born in Britain.[43]

Only in his wildest imagination, of course, was Bacor᾿ ... [illegible] ... [torn] ... Britain'. There was no 'Britain' when Bacon was bor   [illegible]ugh he . certainly, in career terms, a man *made in Britain.*

In the *Considerations* the 'internal' threat to peace through over-population can be warded off through colonial enterprise:

Now what an excellent diversion of this inconvenience is ministred, by God's providence, to your Majesty, in this plantation of Ireland? wherein families may receive sustentations and fortunes, and the discharge of th᾿ out of England and Scotland may prevent many seeds of future perturb᾿   ns. So that it is as if a man were troubled for the avoidance of water from the place where he hath built his house, and afterwards should advise with himself to cast those waters, and to turn them into fair pools or streams, for pleasure, provision, or use. So shall your Majesty in this work have a *double commodity*, in the avoidance of people here, and in making use of them there. (118)

This *double commodity* follows like a second brother. In the speech on naturalisation, Bacon named the benefits as 'surety' and 'greatness':

Touching surety ... it was well said by Titus Quintius the Roman touching the state of Peleponnesus, that the tortoise is safe within her shell ... But if there be any parts that lie open, they endanger all the rest. We know well, that although the state at this time be in a happy peace, yet for the time past, the most ancient enemy to this kingdom hath been the French, and the more late the Spaniard; and both these had as it were their several postern gates, whereby they mought have approach and entrance to annoy us. France had Scotland, and Spain had Ireland.

The conquest of Ireland and the union of crowns had closed those gates, and made England safe:

I think a man may speak it soberly and without bravery, that this kingdom of England, having Scotland united, Ireland reduced, these provinces of the Low countries contracted, and shipping maintained, is one of the greatest monarchies, in forces truly esteemed, that hath been in the world.[44]

He goes on to suggest that the British state is the fulfilment of the imperial 'dream of a Monarchy in the West':[45] ironically, his Irish treatise first saw light under a republic.

---

[43] Bacon, *Life and Letters* 10:3, 228.   [44] *Ibid.*, 322–3.

[45] *Ibid.*, 325. For a perceptive article that draws attention to the emergence of this vision within the Cecilian circle, see Jane E. Dawson, 'William Cecil and the British dimension of early Elizabethan foreign policy', *History*, 74 (1989), 196–216.

Bacon provided three arguments against the English objection that 'sheep or cattle, that if they find a gap or passage open will leave the more barren pasture, and get into the more rich and plentiful'.[46] First, he suggested that Scottish migration would be limited by the fact that 'we see it to be the nature of all men that they will sooner discover poverty abroad, than at home'. So much for Scottish fortune-hunters. Second, he claimed that England was 'not yet peopled to the full', and could thus afford to accommodate any such prospective Scots invasion.[47] Finally, he put his finger on a key feature of the Union, its third term, as it were – the mutually profitable carve-up of Ireland:

there was never any kingdom in the ages of the world had, I think, so fair and happy means to issue and discharge the multitude of their people, if it were too great, as this kingdom hath, in regard of that desolate and wasted kingdom of Ireland; which being a country blessed with almost all the dowries of nature, as rivers, havens, woods, quarries, good soil, and temperate climate, and now at last under his Majesty blessed also with obedience) doth, as it were, continually call unto us for our colonies and plantations.[48]

In the event, the (relative) surplus population of Scotland was planted in Ulster under Anglo-Scottish/British jurisdiction, thus allaying the perception in English minds of Scots massing on the Borders: Ireland earthed the political energy generated by the Union, displaced its tensions and energies.

Another key feature of Bacon's *Considerations* pertains to the security of the British state. The plantation of Ireland would make the new polity safe from the threat of invasion. Bacon uses three examples to illustrate his point:

the tortoise is safe within her shell: but if she put forth any part of her body, then it endangereth not only the part that is so put forth, but all the rest. And so we see in armour, if any part be left naked, it puts in hazard the whole person. And in the natural body of man, if there be any weak or affected part, it is enough to draw rheums or malign humours unto it, to the interruption of the health of the whole body. (119)

He had used the metaphor of the tortoise ten years earlier, in a letter of advice to the earl of Essex, his patron, following the latter's appointment as lord lieutenant of Ireland in March 1599, when he stated that 'there is a great difference, whether the tortoise gather herself within her shell hurt or unhurt'.[49]

Bacon adverts to 'the great profit and strength which is like to redound to your crown, by the working upon this unpolished part

---

[46] Bacon, *Life and Letters* 10:3, 310.   [47] *Ibid.*, 310.
[48] *Ibid.*, 313.   [49] Bacon, *Works* 9, 131.

thereof'. Here, he invokes Ireland as both within and outwith the new united kingdom, 'another Britain' to supplement the first:

For this island being another Britain, as Britain was said to be another world, is endowed with so many dowries of nature, considering the fruitfulness of the soil, the ports, the rivers, the fishings, the quarries, the woods and other materials; and specially the race and generation of men, valiant, hard, and active, as it is not easy, no not upon the continent, to find such confluence of commodities, if the hand of man did join with the hand of nature. (119)

This is of course a characteristic theme of the promotional literature of plantation, but this passage does not quite square with the earlier claim that James had enacted two kinds of foundation, 'the first, that maketh one of more; and the second, that maketh one of none ... The one, in the union of the island of Britain; the other, in the plantation of the great and noble parts of the island of Ireland.' Here, 'another Britain' implies making two of one in the act of making one of none. Bacon's political theory found it difficult to countenance a Britain that appeared virtually *ex nihilo*. He therefore needed 'another Britain', one that was constructed in an active enterprise. The first had arisen through a win on what John Morrill refers to as 'dynastic roulette', namely the accident of James VI succeeding Elizabeth as James I.[50] The second would be a decisive act of social and political engineering, part of the *vita activa*, a programme in which Bacon himself would play such a decisive role. The invention of Britain can be reproduced, patented, multiplied. The use of the term 'mainland Britain' to imply that Ireland is an offshore island is proof of the relevance of Bacon's evocation of another Britain. Geography is political. The 'British Isles' is disputed terminology as well as disputed territory. The north of Ireland is intimately bound up with the beginnings of modern Britishness.

Bacon represented the Ulster Plantation as 'a second brother to the Union'. This recalls that revealing 'textual error' in the first folio edition of *Henry V* (V.ii.12): 'So happy be the issue, brother Ireland', where it has been conjectured that the contemporary preoccupation with the Irish wars led to Ireland being substituted for England. A 'textual error' of greater magnitude has permitted England to stand for Britain, and 'another Britain'. There was always the risk that these two brothers might not agree. Was there room for 'another Britain' so soon after the forging of the first? It is worth recalling that when the Irish officer Macmorris first appears in *Henry V* he is in the company of the Scottish Captain Jamy.

An author writing at the end of that fateful decade had hoped that

---

[50] John Morrill, 'The fashioning of Britain', in Ellis and Barber, *Conquest and Union*, 19.

'her Majesty shall make Ireland profitable unto her as England or mearly a West England'.[51] After the union, it was no longer a question of a west England, or a north England, but of another Britain. Ulster became, not a province like the North of England, but a province in which Highland and Island Scottish settlers were to be displaced by Lowlanders and Borderers, a province which would become a crux of British identity. Sir John Davies, in his *Discovery* (1612), praised the execution of the Ulster Plantation for its creation of national unity: 'his Majesty did not utterly exclude the Natives out of this plantatiõ, with a purpose to roote them out, as the Irish wer excluded out of the first *English* Colonies; but made a mixt plantation of *Brittish and Irish*, that they might grow up togither in one Nation'.[52] But what would that 'one Nation' be? It was the Union that reconciled Anglo-Scottish differences over Ulster, 'the most rude and unreformed part of Ireland, and the *Seat* and *Nest* of the last great Rebellion'.[53] In a letter to Salisbury dated from Coleraine, 28 August 1609, Davies spoke of the welcome the commissioners had received from the Londoners there: 'We all use our best Rhetorick to persuade them to go on wth their plantation; wch will assure this whole Iland to the Crowne of England forever.'[54] The Crown of England? This is the best rhetoric indeed, rhetoric that can speak of 'Brittish' undertakers and yet insist on English sovereignty.

Jenny Wormald notes that the lord chancellor, Ellesmere, Bacon's predecessor in that office, endorsed the latter's letter of April 1605 calling for the writing of a British history, 'Sir Francis Bacon touching the story of *England*', and describes it as 'one of the earliest examples of that habit which infuriates inhabitants of the other parts of the British Isles to this day: the habit of using "England" as synonymous with "Britain".'[55] No less infuriating perhaps as the habit of counting Ireland as part of the 'British Isles' but then, Bacon, in alluding to Ireland as 'another Britain', anticipated that particular habit. The Union of Great Britain and Ireland of 1800 would give way, in time, to a continuing claim to the Six Counties of Ulster, as an exemplary conflictual site of British identity. Bacon's brief treatise is a timely reminder of the way in

---

[51] Cited in D. B. Quinn, '"A Discourse on Ireland (circa 1599)": a sidelight on English colonial policy', *Proceedings of the Royal Irish Academy*, 47, C, 3 (1942), 166.

[52] John Davies, *A Discovery of the True Causes why Ireland was Never Entirely Subdued, nor Brought under Obedience of the Crowne of ENGLAND, untill the Beginning of his Majesties Happie Raigne* (London, 1612), 286.

[53] *Ibid.*, 280.

[54] Davies to Salisbury, Coleraine 28/8/1609, Public Record Office, London, SP 63/227/122.

[55] Wormald, 'The creation of Britain', 180.

which the plantation of Ulster is ultimately bound up with the historical foundations of Britishness.

III

Finally, I turn briefly to my third example of an English tract on Ireland that problematises British identity. Like Spenser's *View*, Milton's *Observations* is a document neglected by both historians of Ireland and English literary critics.[56] However, I propose to show that, like the *View*, it is an exemplary text, one which carries within it a cross-section of views which epitomise the cultural politics of the period. Moreover, just as Bacon's *Considerations* can be read as a prelude to his *Beginnings of Great Britain*, so the attitude to the three kingdoms espoused by Milton in this document anticipate, and rehearse, the anglocentric assumptions implicit in his *History of Britain*.

1649 is a crucial year in English and Irish history. Charles I was executed on 30 January, making it the first year of the English Republic. On 30 March, Oliver Cromwell was approved as commander-in-chief in Ireland. Parliament had already appointed him governor there by 22 June, declaring that 'civil and military power shall be for the present conjoined in one person'. The infamous massacres at Drogheda on 11 September and Wexford on 11 October set the scene for the Cromwellian conquest of Ireland. On 28 March, Cromwell's parliament commissioned John Milton 'to make some observations upon the complication of interests which is now among the several designers against the peace of the Commonwealth. And that it be made ready to be printed with the papers out of Ireland which the House hath ordered to be printed.'[57] His *Observations* duly appeared on 16 May appended to a compilation of documents comprising the articles of peace concluded by James Butler, earl of Ormond, with the Irish confederates (dated 17 January); his proclamation of Charles II as king; the ensuing exchange of letters (9 and 14 March) between Ormond and colonel Michael Jones, governor of Dublin; and an attack on the English republican parliament by the Scottish presbytery at Belfast, 15 February. What Milton has to say about 'the complication of interests' between the Old

---

[56] For contextual approaches to the *Observations*, see Thomas N. Corns, 'Milton's *Observations upon the Articles of Peace*: Ireland under English eyes', in Loewenstein and Turner, *Politics, Poetics, and Hermeneutics*, 123–34; Christopher Hill, 'Seventeenth-century English radicals and Ireland', in Patrick J. Corish (ed.), *Radicals, Rebels and Establishments* (Belfast, 1985), 33–49; M. Y. Hughes, 'The historical setting of Milton's *Observations on the Articles of Peace*, 1649' in *Publications of the Modern Languages Association of America* 64:5 (1949), 1049–73.

[57] Public Record Office, SP 25/62/125.

English, the Irish 'rebels', and the Ulster Presbytery highlights the difficulties attending the representation of Ireland in the period.

The Articles of Peace called for the repeal of Poynings' law which subordinated the sovereignty of the Irish parliament to the will of the executive in England. Ormond's letter to Jones accused Cromwell of trying 'to change the Monarchy of *England* into Anarchy'. The 'Necessary Representation' of the Scottish Presbytery described the trial of the late king as 'against both the Interest and the Protestation of the Kingdome of *Scotland*', and demanded of the English parliament: 'that they doe cordially endeavour the preservation of the Union amongst the well affected in the Kingdomes, not being swayed by any Nationall respect: remembering that part of the Covenant: 'That wee shall not suffer our selves directly, nor indirectly, by whatsoever Combination, perswasion, or terrour, to be divided, or withdrawne from this blessed Union, and Conjunction.'[58] At stake here was more than a conflict between Protestants and Catholics or even a struggle between competing colonial communities. Scottish and Irish Unionists were opposed to English nationalists and republicans.

One way of reading the *Observations* would be to place it within an English colonial ambience: the 'discourse on Ireland'. Here, Milton's text would belong to a genre of political writing about Ireland from an English perspective which stretches from Giraldus Cambrensis to the present day, and tells 'nothing but the same old story'. This would both condemn and exonerate Milton: condemn because he failed to step outside of the conventional discourse, and exonerate because he was not responsible for manufacturing anti-Irish prejudice. He merely imbibed it. According to Don Wolfe, 'John Milton had no more respect for the Irish than Edmund Spenser: 'Both men regarded the Irish as barbarous, savage, uncouth, but, worst of all, papistical in religious beliefs.' But as Norah Carlin has astutely pointed out, there was more than a fear of Catholicism at work in English texts on Ireland in the 1640s, and the old, pre-Reformation ethnography constantly came into play.[59] Milton and Spenser both belonged to a radical Protestant tradition that championed English sovereignty and supremacy within the British Isles.

One advantage of linking Spenser, Bacon and Milton is that it argues a long-term effect of Ireland on England, highlighting three decisive decades of crisis, the 1590s, the 1640s, and the early 1600s. Two entries

---

[58] *John Milton: Complete Prose Works*, ed. M. Y. Hughes (New Haven, 1962), iii, 299.

[59] See Don Wolfe, 'Introduction', *John Milton: collected prose works*, i, ed. D. M. Wolfe (New Haven, 1960), 169; Norah Carlin, 'Extreme or mainstream?: The English Independents and the Cromwellian reconquest of Ireland, 1649–1651' in Bradshaw *et al.* (eds.), *Representing Ireland*, 210.

in Milton's commonplace book show that he had read Ware's 1633 edition of Spenser's *View*.[60] These texts can be discussed both as representations of Ireland and as contributions to the 'British problem'. Milton's targets in the *Observations* are Spenser's targets in the *View* – the native Irish, the Old English and the Scots. Milton is as scathing of the Scots as Spenser. He rails against the Belfast Presbyterians:

who from a ground which is not thir own dare send such defiance to the sovran Magistracy of *England*, by whose autoritie and in whose right they inhabit there. By thir actions we might rather judge them to be a generation of Highland theevs and Redshanks, who beeing neighbourly admitted, not as the *Saxons* by merit of thir warfare, against our enemies, but by the courtesie of *England* to hold possessions in our Province, a Countrey better than thir own, have, with worse faith then those Heathen, prov'd ingratefull and treacherous guests to thir best friends and entertainers.[61]

By characterising them as 'treacherous guests', Milton vindicates Spenser's conviction that the Scots were not to be trusted in Ulster. Milton's theme here in the *Observations*, as in the *History of Britain*, is 'Saxon Agonistes'. The *Observations* is more than a scurrilous polemic defaming the Irish nation. It is a worrisome meditation on the 'complication of interests' that binds England, Scotland and Ireland. Milton's vision may be 'anglocentric' but it is also distinctively British in a way that many critics have overlooked. His view of Ireland was far more complex than any simple opposition model would suggest. Ireland was – and is – a fulcrum of British identity and Milton, perhaps more than any other writer, recognised its unique dual status as a staging-post of empire and a crucible of colonial otherness.

The *Observations* share with Milton's other writings on Ireland a determination to expound his theory of permanent reformation:

But it will here be said that the reformation is a long work, and the miseries of *Ireland* are urgent of a speedy redresse. They be indeed; and how speedy we are, the poore afflicted remnant of our martyr'd countrymen that sit there on the Sea-shore, counting the houres of our delay with their sighs, and the minuts with their falling teares, perhaps with the destilling of their bloody wounds, if they have not quite by this time cast off, and almost curst the vain hope of our founder'd ships, and aids, can best judge how speedy we are to their reliefe.[62]

---

[60] See Willy Maley, 'How Milton and some contemporaries read Spenser's *View*' in Bradshaw *et al.* (eds.), *Representing Ireland*, 191–208. For the relationship between Spenser and Bacon, see Clark Hulse, 'Spenser, Bacon, and the myth of power', in Heather Dubrow and Richard Strier (eds.), *The Historical Renaissance: new essays on Tudor and Stuart literature and culture* (Chicago, 1988), 315–46.

[61] Milton, *Observations*, 333–4.

[62] Milton, *The Reason of Church Government*, in *Complete Prose Works*, i, 799.

For Milton, the Ulster Rising, far from coming out of the blue, provided an indication of the perennial threat of Catholicism:

For it cannot be imaginable that the Irish, guided by so many suttle and *Italian* heads of the Romish party, should so far have lost the use of reason, and indeed of common Sense, as not supported with other strength then thir own, to begin a Warr so desperate and irreconcilable against both England and Scotland at once.[63]

Milton recognises Ireland's unique status as a site of military activity, but places it within a British context: '[Ireland had] the onely army in his [i.e. Charles I's] three kingdoms, till the very burst of that Rebellion [i.e. the Ulster Rising of 1641]'.[64] Milton writes of Charles I's attitude to the Irish: 'He holds them less in fault then the *scots*, as from whom they might *allege* to have fetch'd *thir imitation*; making no difference between men that rose necessarily to defend themselves, which no Protestant Doctrin ever disallow'd, against them who threatn'd Warr, and those who began a voluntary and causeless Rebellion with the Massacher of so many thousands who never meant them harme.'[65] Milton, in the face of royal claims to the contrary, accuses the king of provoking discord in the three kingdoms.[66] He maintains that Ireland constituted a testing ground for tyranny, and says of the king's aborted move to Ireland that it was rightly refused:

For either he had certainly turn'd his rais'd Forces against the Parlament it self, or not gon at all, or had he gon, what work he would have made there, his own following words declare ... he and the Irish Rebels had but one aime, one and the same drift, and would have forthwith joyn'd in one body against us.[67]

As in the *Observations* Milton's aim is to convince his readers that the king's loyalty to his first kingdom of England was in doubt: 'Let men doubt now and dispute to whom the King was a Freind most, to his English Parlament, or to his Irish Rebels.'[68]

Milton repeatedly makes the connection between events in Ireland and royal policy with regard to Scotland.[69] He posits religion as the proper cohesive force to maintain the British state: 'the bishops seek to rouze us up to ... a cursed, a Fraternall *Warre*. ENGLAND and SCOTLAND dearest Brothers both in *Nature*, and in CHRIST must be set to wade in one anothers blood; and IRELAND our free Denizon upon the back of us both.'[70]

It is Milton's anti-Irish sentiment that underpins his belief that England must reign supreme in the three kingdoms:

---

[63] Milton, *Eikonoklastes* (1649), in Hughes (ed.), *Complete Prose Works*, iii, 471–1.
[64] *Ibid.*, 473.   [65] *Ibid.*, 478.   [66] *Ibid.*, 484–5.   [67] *Ibid.*, 482.
[68] *Ibid.*, 483.   [69] *Ibid.*, 580–1.   [70] *Ibid.*, 595–6.

Then you summon to the king's side the villainous and savage scum of Ireland, which in itself shows your criminal madness and how far you surpass most of your fellow men in wicked thoughtless rage, not scrupling to seek the aid and friendship of an accursed race from whose unholy alliance, stained as it is with the blood of so many of our worthiest citizens, even the king himself always drew back, or so pretended.[71]

In a curious turn in *A Defence of the People of England* Milton expands on this theme:

'Never was so much blood spilled, so many families destroyed, under any king'. But all this must be laid to Charles account, not to the English people; he first raised a host of Irishmen against us and by his own warrant bade all Ireland rise against the English. Through their agency some 200,000 English were slain by him in the single province of Ulster, to say nothing of the rest ... Does it matter whether the enemy be foreign or domestic?[72]

He goes so far as to charge Charles with the Ulster Rising. When his Scottish intrigues failed, the king 'gave a certain traitor Dillon secret instructions to the Irish to rise in a sudden attack on all the English settlers in that island'.[73] The *bête noire* of *A Defence of the People of England* is 'Irish butchery'.[74]

With Milton, we are back once more with Spenser, and a vehemently Protestant English nationalism. Between the two, Bacon's modest proposal stands as a breathing space of sorts, a celebratory and conciliatory Unionist hiatus in the midst of a recurrent cycle of war and plantation. If we were simply comparing the pre-Union Spenser with the post-Union Bacon a significant shift in the English discourse on Ireland would be discernible. As it is, Milton's Spenserian polemic returns us to an anglocentric British perspective that is less concerned with confederation than with domination and conquest. These three treatises by arguably the most accomplished prose writers of the English Renaissance amply illustrate the interplay between Albion, Albany and Erin in the early modern period. Viewed from an English historical perspective, Ireland appears to be a side-show as far as questions of sovereignty are concerned. However the struggle between crown and parliament in England cannot be seen outside of the interaction between England, Scotland and Ireland. In this 'British' context, Ireland is not simply a convenient alternative power-base for Essex, Charles I, or Cromwell. It is a crucial site of conflict for competing national identities.

---

[71] *A Defence of the People of England* (24 February 1651), in Wolfe (ed.), *Complete Prose Works*, iv, 323.
[72] *Ibid.*, 431–1.   [73] *Ibid.*, 522–3.   [74] *Ibid.*, 528.

6   James Ussher and the creation of an Irish protestant identity

Alan Ford

History, remembered and forgotten, told and retold, imagined and invented, plays a vital role in forming a people's sense of national identity. Carefully manipulated, it can be used to bring together disparate groups and communities into cohesive nations.[1] The continuing union of Scotland, England and Wales owes much to the shaping of historical memory that produced the binding concept of Britishness.[2] Equally, however, contentious and disputed histories can sometimes split societies and divide their racially distinguishable elements into warring factions, each sustained by distinctive origin myths. One such battleground was, and remains, Ireland: here conflicting identities continue to characterise its culture and frustrate both neat academic labelling and ambitious political panaceas. The aim of this chapter is to outline in some detail the origins, and briefly to analyse the ambiguities, of one skein of Irish identity, the protestant tradition, concentrating upon the way in which in the early modern period it appropriated and developed a particular vision of Ireland's history. This sense of protestant identity was distinguished by its 'doubleness', its ability to face both ways: to reject the blandishments of a wider British consciousness then developing in imperial England and identify with Irish culture and history, whilst at the same time carefully distinguishing themselves from other communities in Ireland.

By 1600 Ireland's confused history of partial colonisation and recolonisation had left a legacy of three contrasting communities: the native Irish, heirs of Ireland's ancient Celtic civilisation; the New English, the

[1] Benedict Anderson, *Imagined Communities: reflections on the origin and spread of nationalism* (London, 1983); J. R. Gillis (ed.), *Commemorations: the politics of national identity* (Princeton, 1994); for a useful discussion of this process in early-modern France, see D. C. Margolf, 'Adjudicating memory: law and religious difference in early seventeenth-century France', *The Sixteenth Century Journal*, 27 (1996), 416–18.

[2] Linda Colley, *Britons: forging the nation 1707–1837* (2nd edn, London, 1994). 367; Colin Kidd, *Subverting Scotland's Past. Scottish Whig historians and the creation of an Anglo-British identity, 1689 – c. 1830* (Cambridge, 1993); P. R. Roberts, 'The union with England and the identity of "Anglican" Wales', *Transactions of the Royal Historical Society*, 5th ser. 22 (1972), 49–70.

most recent wave of settlers and officials sent over by English monarchs anxious to secure their hold on Ireland; and, in between, the Anglo-Irish, the descendants of the twelfth-century Anglo-Norman invaders.[3] Each group had a definite sense of its own cultural and historical roots: the native Irish, suspicious of the imposition of English government and mores, were distinguished by ancient legal, intellectual, political and religious traditions; the New English saw themselves as representatives of a superior civilisation, entrusted with the anglicisation of a backward island; while the Anglo-Irish were convinced that they too were superior – to the native Irish in their espousal of English manners, and to the New English in their knowledge of Ireland. The addition of religion to this ideological cocktail in the sixteenth century both complicated and stimulated the conflict of identities. At either extreme the religious choice offered by the Protestant Reformation was relatively straightforward. The native Irish in general remained wedded to Rome and hostile to the stumbling efforts of the Church of Ireland to convert them to protestantism. The New English were, for the most part, equally committed to the Reformation. But the Anglo-Irish faced a difficult decision, torn between their instinctive loyalty to the English monarch – now the supreme governor of the Church of Ireland – and their desire to remain faithful to their traditional religious allegiance. Though, after some initial hesitation, the vast majority of the Anglo-Irish had, by the end of Elizabeth's reign, opted for Catholicism, and came increasingly to describe themselves as Old English, a small but significant minority chose protestantism. The history of Irish protestantism, therefore, begins with these two contrasting groups – the New English and the protestant Anglo-Irish – and their efforts to construct a coherent identity in the late sixteenth and early seventeenth century.

I

The Reformation posed an obvious historical challenge for all protestants in Europe. How could they justify to an age that viewed the early church and the apostolic succession as vital sources of purity and

---

[3] Precise definition of the term Anglo-Irish is difficult. For the purposes of my argument here, I have used it to denote the descendants of the Anglo-Norman conquerors and of those English families who were well established in Ireland by the sixteenth century, regardless of their religious affiliation. I have used the term Old English to describe those Anglo-Irish who opted for Catholicism after 1600, and retained the term protestant Anglo-Irish to describe those who chose the state religion. The cut off date is, obviously, arguable, but I would suggest not wholly arbitrary. For a brief discussion of nomenclature see T. W. Moody, 'Introduction: early modern Ireland', in T. W. Moody, F. X. Martin and F. J. Byrne, *A New History of Ireland: early modern Ireland* (Oxford, 1976), xii–xliii; Aidan Clarke, *The Old English in Ireland, 1625–42* (London, 1966), 15.

authority, something that shattered the unity of the medieval church and appeared, therefore, to mark a radical new departure? The answer to taunts of novelty was, of course, antiquity. Francis Bacon later claimed that Martin Luther had been 'enforced to awake all antiquity and to call former times to his succours ... so that the ancient authors, both in divinity and humanity, which had long time slept in libraries, began generally to be read'.[4] The first scholars to rise to the challenge were the Magdeburg Centuriators, led by the founding father of protestant historiography, Mathias Flacius Illyricus (1520–75).

They produced between 1559 and 1574, an *Ecclesiastica historia* which covered the history of the church in immense detail from Christ to the thirteenth century. The thrust of the work, which was to be repeated for various national churches throughout Europe, was to demonstrate how the 'protestant' purity of the first centuries of the church had been corrupted by the rise of papal abuses and errors. At the height of this corruption, in the middle ages, the gospel truth was preserved thanks to the brave efforts of small groups such as the Albigensians, the Lollards and the Waldensians, whose credentials were of course confirmed by their persecution at the hand of the papal authorities.[5] This protestant attempt to steal church history initially caught the Catholic side off-guard. It was not till the end of the sixteenth century that their champions, Baronius and Bellarmine, completed their reassertion of ownership.[6]

The argument between these newly created protestant and Catholic schools of historiography was not simply about the discovery and appropriation of favourable historical facts and precedents. Underlying the battle on the protestant side was a theological shift in the way that they saw history. While they shared with their Catholic opponents a conviction that history was the record of God's providence, they differed from them in their belief that God had revealed how his secret will worked in the events of history through the apocalyptic books and passages of the bible. The application of the highly symbolic and mysterious passages of Revelation or Daniel not, as Catholic theologians preferred, to the distant past or far future, but to the whole of human

---

[4] Quoted in T. D. Kendrick, *British Antiquity* (London, 1950), 115.

[5] *Ecclesiastica historia* (13 books, Basle, 1559–74); O. K. Olson, 'Matthias Flacius Illyricus', in Jill Raitt and R. M. Kingdon (eds.), *Shapers of Religious Traditions in Germany, Switzerland and Poland: 1560–1600* (New Haven, 1981), 1–18; R. E. Diener, 'Johann Wigand', in *ibid.*, 19–38; Euan Cameron, *The Reformation of the Heretics. The Waldenses of the Alps 1480–1580* (Oxford, 1984), 243ff.

[6] C. K. Pullapilly, *Caesar Baronius, Counter-Reformation Historian* (Notre Dame, 1975); E. A. Ryan, *The Historical Scholarship of Saint Bellarmine* (Louvain, 1936); James Brodrick, *Robert Bellarmine: saint and scholar* (London, 1961).

history, including the present and the immediate future, offered a powerful incentive for sectarian historical study. By the end of the sixteenth century, the study of history, scripture and theology were inextricably bound together by the overarching framework of apocalyptic. Flacius on the continent, and John Bale and John Foxe in England, had established the idea that history could be interpreted as a conflict between the true and false churches, between Christ and Antichrist, between protestants and proto-protestants on the one hand and the corrupt papalists on the other, between the pure ideals of the early church and the later corruption and abuse introduced by the medieval papacy, or finally, 'in these latter days', the battle between the Reformation and the Counter Reformation. History was divided into ages, each linked to apocalyptic prophecies. In particular, the first 600 years of church history became established as a golden age, and as such a crucial heritage claimed by both protestants and Catholics as their *fons et origo*, fought over by controversial theologians trying to demonstrate that the church fathers had in effect subscribed to the decrees of the Council of Trent or the Thirty Nine Articles.[7]

This was the ground chosen by the leading English controversialist at the start of Elizabeth's reign, John Jewell, in his debate with Thomas Harding and Catholic theologians such as Thomas Stapleton, whom he challenged to prove that transubstantiation, papal supremacy, communion in one kind, and other 'later inventions' had existed before 600. The theme of early purity and freedom from Rome inspired Archbishop Parker's research into the origins of Christianity in England which showed how Joseph of Arimathea and King Lucius had founded a native Christianity well before the despatch of Augustine from Rome in 596.[8] History, in short, through its association with this apocalyptic became a polemical protestant tool.

II

The first hints of these new protestant theological and historical concerns in Ireland came in the later sixteenth century. The dividing line between pre- and post-Reformation historiography runs through that seminal text for sixteenth-century Irish historians, the section on

[7] R. A. Bauckham, *Tudor Apocalypse* (Appleford, 1978); Paul Christianson, *Reformers and Babylon: English apocalyptic visions from the reformation to the eve of the Civil War* (Toronto, 1978); K. R. Firth, *The Apocalyptic Tradition in Reformation Britain 1530–1645* (Oxford, 1979); Glanmor Williams, *Reformation Views of Church History* (London, 1970).

[8] Matthew Parker, *De antiquitate Britannicae ecclesiae ... historia* (Hanover, 1605), 3–5; F. J. Levy, *Tudor Historical Thought* (San Marino, 1967), 117.

Ireland which James Stanyhurst contributed to Holinshed's *Chronicles*, published in 1577.[9] Stanyhurst embodied the sixteenth-century Anglo-Irish establishment. His father had been speaker of Elizabeth's Irish Reformation parliament. He had been educated at Oxford, returning to Ireland to act as tutor to the children of the earl of Kildare.[10] His contribution to the *Chronicles* consisted of two parts: a 'Description' giving an account of Ireland's geography and people; and a 'History' of the country from antiquity to the end of Henry VIII's reign. Though reliant upon the unpublished history of Ireland by the English Jesuit and future martyr, Edmund Campion, Stanyhurst showed little interest in using history as ammunition for confessional warfare: the Reformation and apocalyptic made little impression on his work.

It was only after its publication that the lines of protestant and Catholic historiography in Ireland begin to diverge. Indeed, the first clear evidence for this divergence can be found in the subsequent fate of both the text and its author. For the second edition of 1587 Stanyhurst's contribution was edited and enlarged by an English historian with first-hand experience of Ireland, John Hooker.[11] Hooker added a translation of that classic Anglo-Norman work of history and cultural prejudice, Giraldus Cambrensis's *Expugnatio Hibernica*, thereby symbolising its expropriation by the New English.[12] He placed this within the broader framework of his much more hostile comments about the native Irish and their character – a 'wicked, effrenated, barbarous and unfaithful nation'.[13] The most obvious departure from Stanyhurst lay in Hooker's explicitly protestant and apocalyptic view of history. Thus in his largely faithful translation of Giraldus, Hooker interpolated a typically protestant reference to Thomas Becket as a 'froward and obstinate traitor', complaining about the 'much ado' made of him by the 'Romish or Popish church', and citing as a corrective Foxe's *Book of Martyrs*.[14] He also slanted Giraldus' account of the relations between the English kings and Rome to stress the threat posed by the 'Romish Antichrist' to the freedom of the English monarchy'.[15] But the most revealing innovation was Hooker's apocalyptic verdict upon the savage suppression of the

[9] Raphael Holinshed, *The Chronicles of England, Scotland and Ireland* (2 vols., London, 1577), i, pt. 3.

[10] Colm Lennon, *Richard Stanihurst the Dubliner 1547–1618. A biography with a Stanihurst text 'On Ireland's past'* (Dublin, 1981).

[11] *DNB*; W. T. McCaffrey, *Exeter, 1540–1640. The growth of an English county town* (2nd edn, Cambridge, Mass., 1975), 7, 272.

[12] Raphael Holinshed, *The Chronicles of England, Scotland, and Ireland* (2nd edn, 2 vols., London, 1584–6), ii, 'The Irish history composed and written by Giraldus Cambrensis'.

[13] *Ibid.*, ii, 'The chronicles of Ireland', 133.   [14] *Ibid.*, ii, 'The Irish history', 16.

[15] *Ibid.*, 25; for a more detailed treatment of these points see Andrew Hadfield, 'Briton and Scythian: Tudor representations of Irish origins', *Irish Historical Studies*, 28 (1993), 393–4.

1579 Desmond revolt, which is worth quoting at some length, since it offers a powerful and novel interpretation of the nature and causation of Irish rebellion:

A heavy, but a just judgement of God upon such a Pharoical stiffnecked people, who by no persuasions ... would be reclaimed and reduced to serve God in true religion, and to obey their most lawful prince in dutiful obedience; but made choice of a wicked idol, the God Mazim to honour, and of that wicked antichrist of Rome to obey ... This is the goodness that cometh from that great city upon the seven hills, and that mighty Babylon, the mother of all wickedness and abominations upon the earth. These be the fruits which come from that holy father, master pope, the son of Satan, and the man of sin, and the enemy unto the cross of Christ, whose bloodthirstiness will never be quenched but in the blood of the saints, and the servants of God; and whose ravening guts be never satisfied, but with the death of such as do serve the Lord in all godliness, and who will not be drunk in the cup of his fornications: as it doth appear by the infinite and most horrible massacres, and bloody persecutions, which he daily exerciseth throughout all Christian lands.[16]

In fact, by the time Hooker came to apply his apocalyptic vision to Stanyhurst's history, the original author had already moved decisively into the opposing religious camp, opting for exile in the Spanish Netherlands, where, eventually, he was ordained as a Catholic priest. There, following the examples of Baronius and Bellarmine, he developed some of the essential themes of a new school of Catholic Irish historiography, forged by the experience of exile and the impact of the Counter-Reformation. In his *De rebus in Hibernia gestis*, published in 1584, he moved away from his earlier aspersions on the native Irish, raising the possibility of an Irish Catholic national identity that transcended racial divisions.[17] Three years later his *De vita Sancti Patricii* sought to affirm Patrick's status as the founding father of Irish Catholicism, concluding with a panegyric praising the steadfastness of Irish Catholics in their continuing and unchanging loyalty to the holy Roman see.[18]

[16] *Ibid.*, ii, 'The chronicles of Ireland', 183.

[17] Colm Lennon, 'Richard Stanyhurst (1547–1618) and Old English identity', *Irish Historical Studies*, 21 (1979); Lennon, *Richard Stanihurst*, but see B. I. Bradshaw, *The Irish Constitutional Revolution of the Sixteenth Century* (Cambridge, 1979), 282–4, where it is argued that Stanyhurst's later emphasis upon the common identity of Gaelic Irish and Anglo-Irish represents a development and a refinement rather than a departure from his earlier stance.

[18] Richard Stanyhurst, *De vita S. Patricii libri duo* (Antwerp, 1587), Stanyhurst's sources are more complicated than Lennon, *Richard Stanihurst*, 63, allows: it is not based on Bede' *Ecclesiastical history*, but rather relies upon Probus's Life of St Patrick, which was published erroneously as part of Bede's works in 1563: Bede, *Operum Venerabilis Bedae* (8 vols., Basle, 1563), iii, cols. 311–334; on the Catholic view of St Patrick, see Bernadette Cunningham and Raymond Gillespie, '"The most adaptable of saints": the cult of St Patrick in the seventeenth century', *Archivium Hibernicum*, 49 (1995), 82–104.

The outline for a protestant response was provided by Meredith Hanmer, a Welsh minister who emigrated to Ireland, probably in disgrace, around 1590, where he held numerous benefices until his death in 1604.[19] Hanmer, without ever moving beyond antiquarianism, nevertheless contributed a number of important elements to the apocalyptic study of history. He was firmly protestant, believing the pope to be Antichrist, and wrote a polemical work attacking Campion.[20] He was also a scholar who published an important translation of Eusebius and other early church historians which provided apocalyptic historians with a chronological framework for that vital period, the first 600 years of the church.[21] After his arrival in Ireland, he developed a marked interest in Irish history and the Irish language.[22] Though primarily concerned with secular and political chronology, he did, in contrast to Stanyhurst, seek to win back the Irish apostle for bible-based protestantism: 'The only doctrine Patrick read and expounded unto the people, was the four evangelists, conferred with the Old Testament.'[23] This latter point was taken up by another *émigré* cleric, the Englishman, John Rider, who in 1598 came over from Lancashire to become dean of St Patrick's Cathedral in Dublin.[24] Rider soon became immersed in one of the first public debates in Ireland between protestant and Catholic, clashing with the Jesuit Henry Fitzsimon. Though no copy of Rider's argument survives, Fitzsimon indicated clearly its thrust when he complained about his reliance upon Bale and other 'tainted histories' to prove that the religion first planted in Ireland was the same as protestantism.[25]

---

[19] *DNB*; James B. Leslie, *Ossory Clergy and Parishes* (Enniskillen, 1933), pp. 84–5; in addition to the allegations of misbehaviour detailed in the *DNB*, a Catholic opponent further claimed that Hanmer had to leave his English benefice because he was a 'filthy sodomite': Peter Holmes, *Resistance and Compromise. the political thought of Elizabethan Catholics* (Cambridge, 1982), 56.

[20] Meredith Hanmer, *The Great Brag and Challenge of M. Campion a Jesuit* (London, 1581), sig. 10v; Meredith Hanmer, *The Jesuit's Banner. Displaying their original and success: their vow and oath: their hypocricy and superstition: their doctrine and positions* (London, 1581), sig. A1v; Meredith Hanmer, *The Baptizing of a Turk* (London, [1586]), sig. E4v.

[21] Meredith Hanmer, *The Ancient Ecclesiastical Histories ... written by Eusebius, Socrates and Evagrius. Whereunto is annexed Dorotheus ... Last of all herein is a chronography* (London, 1577, repr. 1585, 1607); V. N. Olsen, *John Foxe and the Elizabethan Church* (Berkeley, 1973), 22–3.

[22] Some of his papers are preserved in the Public Record Office, London, SP 63/214: R. P. Mahaffy (ed.), *Calendar of the State Papers Relating to Ireland* (11 vols., London, 1912), xi, 661–87.

[23] James Ware (ed.), *Ancient Irish Histories. The works of Spenser, Campion, Hanmer and Marlborough* (2 vols., Dublin, 1809), ii, 87.

[24] H. J. Lawlor, *The Fasti of St Patrick's, Dublin* (Dundalk, 1930), 47; R. D. Edwards (ed.), 'Letter-book of Sir Arthur Chichester 1612–1614', *Analecta Hibernica*, 8 (1938), 28. In 1613 Rider became Bishop of Killaloe, a benefice which he held till his death in 1632.

[25] Henry Fitzsimon, *A Catholic Confutation of M. John Riders Claim of Antiquity and a*

Not all the New English took as positive a view of the early Irish church. Indeed, the fact that that church was a Celtic one was, for some writers, a clear sign of its unsuitability as an ancestor for the modern anglicised and anglicising Church of Ireland. Thus Edmund Spenser castigated Irish religion as being 'generally corrupted with ... Popish trumpery' from the very introduction of Christianity by St Patrick.[26] Thomas Haynes in 1600, following Spenser, saw Patrick as the source of the 'blind devotion' of the ignorant Irish.[27] Parr Lane, a soldier who came to Ireland in the 1590s and settled in Munster, questioned whether Ireland had been an island of saints and scholars or an island of swine.[28] Indeed, there was a tendency within the Church of Ireland, especially pronounced in the case of senior clergy recently arrived from England, to ignore completely the possibility of independent Irish roots, and to see it simply as an offshoot of the mother Church of England. The church's lack of missionary success in Ireland, and its slavish copying of the Church of England when it came to liturgy, confession and legislative framework merely added to this temptation.[29]

However, there was still a third strand which, it has been claimed, made a significant contribution to the development of the self-image of Irish protestantism – that of the Anglo-Irish protestants. Nicholas Canny has sought to rescue this often forgotten minority from obscurity. Their indigenous protestantism, he suggests, offered a way forward for the Irish Reformation, away from the stereotypes of Irish Catholic and English protestant. They provided the state Reformation with a 'human face', offering it a real chance of extending its appeal beyond the garrison community: in short, of ensuring that the Reformation succeeded in Ireland.[30] In support of this contention one can point to the existence in the 1570s and 1580s of a group of Anglo-Irish protestant officials and advisers which, though small, was influential both in Dublin and in England: men such as Thomas Cusack (1490–1571), appointed lord chancellor in 1550, removed under Mary and restored

---

Calming Comfort against his Caveat. In which is demonstrated, by assurances, even of Protestants, that all antiquitie, for all points of religion in controversy, is repugnant to Protestancy (Rouen, 1608), sig. A3v–A4r.

[26] Edmund Spenser, *A View of the Present State of Ireland*, ed. W. L. Renwick (Oxford, 1970), 84.

[27] Armagh Public Library: MS stored in ground floor press: Thomas Haynes, 'Certain principal matters concerning the state of Ireland', fo. 11v.

[28] TCD MS 786, fo. 142v.

[29] Alan Ford, 'Dependent or independent: the Church of Ireland and its colonial context, 1536–1647', *Seventeenth Century*, 9 (1995), 163–87.

[30] N. P. Canny, 'Why the reformation failed in Ireland: *une question mal posée*', *The Journal of Ecclesiastical History*, 30 (1979), 437–40.

to the Irish Privy Council by Elizabeth in 1559,[31] Rowland White (d. 1572), a Dublin merchant;[32] Richard Stanyhurst's father James; and Sir Nicholas White (d. 1593), made an Irish privy councillor in 1569 and master of the rolls in 1572.[33] Nor were these Anglo-Irish unreflective about their religious convictions. Canny has highlighted the writings of Rowland White as evidence for the development of a self-consciously Irish protestant tradition which traced the roots of the established church back to the time of St Patrick, and which continued to flourish in the seventeenth century thanks to the efforts of James Ussher.[34]

There are, however, serious problems with the discovery of a continuous and distinctive Anglo-Irish protestant tradition. First, the precise status of these Anglo-Irish church-goers in the later sixteenth century is deeply ambiguous. Historians confidently speak of their 'allegiance to the state religion', or the 'conformity to the established church' of 'reliably protestant' Anglo-Irish families and of 'Anglo-Irish protestant councillors'.[35] But these various terms are not necessarily synonyms. Religious definition from the 1540s to the 1580s is fraught with difficulty, as taxonomy struggles to catch up with the myriad changes in official policy and public response. It is therefore dangerous to lump such officials together as if they constitute a single identifiable religious outlook. In the case of those that have been confidently labelled protestant, doubts can often be cast about the sincerity of their commitment.[36] Where the commitment is unchallenged, as in the case of Rowland White, his protestantism, on closer analysis, appears theologically amorphous, his interest in the history of the early Irish church minimal.[37] Second, the idea that there was a continuous tradition

---

[31] DNB; J. G. Crawford, Anglicizing the Government of Ireland. The Irish Privy Council and the expansion of Tudor rule, 1556–1578 (Dublin, 1993), 449–50; Hubert Gallway, 'The Cusack family of counties Meath and Dublin', The Irish Genealogist, 5 (1974–9), 591–2, 597.

[32] Nicholas Canny (ed.), 'Rowland White's "The dysorders of the Irisshery", 1571', Studia Hibernica, 30 (1979), 147–60; N. P. Canny (ed.), 'Rowland White's "Discors touching Ireland", c. 1569', Irish Historical Studies, 20: 80 (1977), 439–65.

[33] Lennon, Richard Stanyhurst, 19–35; DNB; Crawford, Anglicizing the Government of Ireland, 470–1.

[34] Canny, 'Why the Reformation failed', 439.

[35] Ibid., 451; N. P. Canny, 'Identity formation in Ireland: the emergence of the Anglo-Irish', in N. P. Canny and Anthony Pagden (eds.), Colonial Identity in the Atlantic World, 1500–1800 (Princeton, 1987), 163; Helen Coburn Walsh, 'Enforcing the Elizabethan settlement: the vicissitudes of Hugh Brady, bishop of Meath, 1563–84', Irish Historical Studies, 26: 104 (1989), 366; Crawford, Anglicizing the Government of Ireland, 159.

[36] E.g. Coburn Walsh, 'Enforcing the Elizabethan settlement', 374.

[37] Canny's claim that White was not a Calvinist because he believed in the comprehensive nature of Christ's atonement rests on very slender evidence: the views in the passage in the 'Disorders' (151, 157) are theologically uninformative and unexceptional; moreover Calvin's own position on the extent of the atonement are complex and not

ignores the evidence for a marked disjuncture between sixteenth-century conformists and seventeenth-century Anglo-Irish protestants. The former have left little evidence of an interest in the apocalyptic basis of protestant history or in an anti-papal crusade. Indeed, they continually argued for a moderate approach to Catholicism. On the other hand, Ussher, as we shall see, enthusiastically endorsed the protestant apocalyptic view of Catholicism and its practical enforcement by means of severe measures against recusants.

What was happening during the latter part of the sixteenth century was a redefinition of what it was to be protestant in Ireland. This was part of a wider process of confessional polarisation, as both Catholics and protestants became more aware of their differences, and more determined to distinguish themselves from their opponents. On the Catholic side, seminary priests and Jesuits set about the task of creating a separate Catholic church structure, insisting that their countrymen have nothing to do with protestant heresy, and denouncing the compromises of Anglo-Irish church papists.[38] On the protestant side, Adam Loftus, who combined the key posts of archbishop of Dublin and lord chancellor, sought wherever possible to weed out what he considered 'time-servers' and 'neuters' (often, in fact, Anglo-Irish officials and clergy) and to insist upon enthusiastic adherence to protestantism. He worked to secure the foundation of a new university, Trinity College Dublin in 1592, and helped to ensure that its religious outlook was strongly, indeed fiercely, protestant.[39] Such pressures forced the conformists to identify clearly with one extreme or the other. Consequently,

open to simplistic summaries. See one recent author's misunderstanding of Calvin on this point: R. T. Kendall, *Calvin and English Calvinism to 1649* (Oxford, 1979), corrected in Paul Helm, *Calvin and the Calvinists* (Edinburgh, 1982). As for the succession of the true church in Ireland, a reference in his 'Disorders', 157, to 'converting or rather recovering' lost Irish souls hardly provides sufficient support for the interpretative superstructure that Canny erects on it.

[38] Aidan Clarke, 'Colonial identity in early seventeenth century Ireland', *Historical Studies*, 11 (1978), 57–71; Colm Lennon, 'The Counter-Reformation in Ireland 1542–1641', in C. F. Brady and Raymond Gillespie (eds.), *Natives and Newcomers. Essays on the making of Irish colonial society* (Dublin, 1986), 75–92; Brady and Gillespie, *The Lords of Dublin in the Age of Reformation* (Dublin, 1989), chs. 5, 6; H. H. W. Hammerstein, 'Aspects of the continental education of Irish students in the reign of Queen Elizabeth', *Historical Studies*, 8 (1971), 137–54.

[39] H. H. W. Robinson-Hammerstein, *Erzbischof Adam Loftus und die elizabethanische Reformationspolitik in Irland* (Marburg, 1976), 204–39; Robinson-Hammerstein, *Archbishop Adam Loftus. the first provost of Trinity College, Dublin* (Dublin, 1993); J. P. Mahaffy, *An Epoch in Irish History. Trinity College, Dublin: its foundation and early fortunes, 1591–1660* (London, 1903), ch. 2 (though Mahaffey unjustly plays down the role of Loftus); William Urwick, *The Early History of Trinity College, Dublin 1591–1660 as told in Contemporary Records on the Occasion of its Tercentenary* (London, Dublin, 1892), 1–26.

the new generation of Anglo-Irishmen, whether Catholic or protestant, differed in their outlook and ideology from their fathers and grandfathers. On the one side, the majority were more exclusively Catholic in their loyalties and identity, as in the case of James Stanyhurst's rejection of his father's compromise with the state religion, or Thomas Cusack's grandson who in 1594 founded that bastion of the Irish Counter Reformation, the Irish College at Douai.[40] On the other side, those who opted for the Reformation were expected to abandon their temporising approach to Catholicism and support the rigorous imposition of conformity, as in the case of Walter Ball, a prominent Dublin merchant, who laid down strict conditions in his will to ensure that his children continued 'in that holy religion I have lived and died in', left money to endow scholarships at Trinity, and was even prepared to condemn his own mother to prison (where she died) for recusancy.[41]

The realignment of religious allegiances also raised questions about the nature of political and national loyalties. On the one hand, faith was naturally linked to fatherland. Hugh O'Neill's appeal for Catholic unity in the Nine Years War echoed changing perceptions of Ireland as *patria* or *athardha* bound together by its adherence to Catholicism.[42] Geoffrey Keating, in his history of pre-conquest Ireland, *Foras feasa ar Éirinn*, written in the early 1630s, used the collective term 'Irish' to describe both Anglo-Irish and native Irish.[43] For protestants, allegiance to the supreme governor of the Church of Ireland was political as well as religious, since the English monarch was appointed by God to rule over Ireland. On the other hand, the link between religion and national feeling was deeply troublesome for both sides. Irish Catholics after the

---

[40] John Brady, 'Father Christopher Cusack and the Irish College of Douai, 1594–1624', in Sylvester O'Brien (ed.), *Measgra i gcuimhne Mhichíl Uí Chléirigh. Miscellany of historical and linguistic studies in honour of Brother Michael Ó Cleirigh, O.F.M. chief of the four masters 1643–1943* (Dublin, 1944), 99–100; Gallwey, 'The Cusack family', 597–8.

[41] W. B. Wright, *Ball Family Records. Genealogical memoirs of some Ball families of Great Britain, Ireland, and America* (York, 1908), 21, app., xi; Lennon, *Lords of Dublin*, 156.

[42] Micheál MacCraith, 'The Gaelic reaction to the reformation', in S. G. Ellis and Sarah Barber (ed.), *Conquest and Union. Fashioning a British state, 1485–1725* (London, 1995), 139–61; J. J. Silke, 'Hugh O'Neill, the Catholic question and the papacy', *Irish Ecclesiastical Record*, 5th ser., 104 (1965), 65–79; Hiram Morgan, 'Faith and fatherland or queen and country? An unpublished exchange between O'Neill and the state at the height of the Nine Years War', *Dúiche Néill: Journal of the O'Neill Country Historical Society*, 9 (1994), 9–65.

[43] Geoffrey Keating, *The History of Ireland*, ed., David Comyn (London, 1902); B. I. Bradshaw, 'Geoffrey Keating: apologist of Irish Ireland', in B. I. Bradshaw, Andrew Hadfield and Willy Maley (eds.), *Representing Ireland. Literature and the origins of the conflict, 1534–1660* (Cambridge, 1993), 169; Bernadette Cunningham, 'Seventeenth-century interpretations of the past: the case of Geoffrey Keating', *Irish Historical Studies*, 25 (1986), 116–28.

defeat of O'Neill at Kinsale had to come to terms with the secular reality of English power in Ireland.[44] Irish protestants, if they were to develop a sense of Irish identity or patriotism, had first to reach some agreement over the nature of the *patria* with which they wished to identify – most particularly and obviously concerning those basic building blocks of national consciousness, language and culture: were they, culturally, English, Irish or Anglo-Irish?

III

To speak of an Irish protestant identity or mentality at any time in modern Irish history is tendentious, running the risk of creating an overly neat and coherent synthesis that seriously misrepresents the disparate and complex range of views and assumptions of Irish protestants.[45] At the start of the seventeenth century it is even more dangerous, since what has so far been identified is essentially inchoate – a collection of hints and implications, traversed by conflicting racial, political and cultural assumptions. The task of putting such disparate elements together was therefore always going to be problematic. But the Church of Ireland just happened to produce in the early seventeenth century a figure, James Ussher, whose combined talents as historian, theologian and ecclesiastical leader enabled him to rise to the challenge and create an origin myth for the Church of Ireland which, though not, as we shall see, without its attendant ambiguities and tensions, was nevertheless to exercise a dominant influence upon the way in which Irish protestants saw themselves even down to the twentieth century.

Ussher's career can be summarised briefly. Born in 1581 of a well-established Dublin family, he was educated at the Dublin free school, whence he went to the newly founded Trinity. There he proceeded to the study of theology, gaining an MA, BD and finally a DD. He went on to serve Trinity as professor of Theological Controversies and the Church of Ireland as chancellor of St Patrick's Cathedral. As a member of Irish Convocation he helped to draft the strongly Calvinist Irish Articles of 1615. He was promoted to the see of Meath in 1621 and became archbishop of Armagh in 1625, a post that he held till his death in 1656, though after the 1641 rebellion he remained in exile in

---

[44] J. J. Silke, 'Primate Lombard and James I', *Irish Theological Quarterly*, 22 (1955), 124–50; Breandán Ó Buachalla, 'James our true king: the ideology of Irish royalism in the seventeenth century', in D. G. Boyce, Robert Eccleshall and Vincent Geoghegan (eds.), *Political Thought in Ireland since the Seventeenth Century* (London, 1993), 7–35.

[45] T. C. Barnard, 'Crises of identity among Irish protestants 1641–1685', *Past & Present*, 127 (1990), 39–83.

England.[46] Ussher's early intellectual formation shows how the institutions built up by Loftus could shape the new generation of Irish protestants. He was one of the first students at two new foundations, the Dublin school and Trinity, that were under the control of Scottish and English presbyterians.[47] Their view of protestantism as the pure antithesis of a corrupt Catholicism was easily transmitted to the young Ussher, and was transmuted by him into a lifelong involvement in anti-Catholic theology, always firmly grounded upon an historical framework. His very first venture into the public arena shows how his education had marked him off from the new generation of Anglo-Irish Catholics. At the age of 18 he challenged his relative, Rider's opponent Henry Fitzsimon (then under arrest in Dublin Castle), to a debate on the main issues at stake between Catholics and protestants. Their first topic was reportedly the identification of Antichrist. The resultant discussion contained all the elements that were to become a familiar feature of such encounters in Ireland: unyielding theological confrontation followed by the ritual claim of victory by each side.[48] Starting from the principle 'that the ancientist must needs be the best, as the nearer the fountain, the purer the streams', and inspired by the desire to rebut Stapleton's claims that the beliefs of the early church differed substantially from later protestant doctrine, the 20-year-old Ussher tackled the prodigious (and as it turned out, eighteen-year-long) task of reading the entire corpus of Greek and Latin fathers.[49] As Professor of Theological Controversies from 1607, Ussher was driven by the closely linked and equally Herculean intellectual challenge – the detailed refutation of

---

[46] The standard modern biographical study of Ussher is that of R. B. Knox, *James Ussher Archbishop of Armagh* (Cardiff, 1967). Knox sees him as representative of a rather anachronistic Anglicanism. Useful recent studies include Hugh Trevor-Roper, 'James Ussher, Archbishop of Armagh', in his *Catholics, Anglicans and Puritans* (London, 1989), 120–65; Amanda Capern, '"Slipperye times and dangerous dayes": James Ussher and the Calvinist reformation of Britain, 1560–1660' (unpublished Ph.D. thesis, University of New South Wales, 1991); and Graham Parry, *Trophies of Time, English Antiquarians of the Seventeenth Century* (Oxford, 1995), ch. 5. Older works on Ussher still retain their value, however, especially Elrington's lengthy introduction to Ussher's collected works: James Ussher, *The Whole Works*, ed., C. R. Elrington and J. H. Todd (17 vols., Dublin, London, 1847–64) [hereafter UW], i, 1–324.

[47] Alan Ford, 'The Church of Ireland 1558–1641: a puritan church?' in Alan Ford, James McGuire and Kenneth Milne (eds.), *As by Law Established. The church of Ireland since the Reformation* (Dublin, 1995), 53, 55.

[48] Nicholas Bernard, *The Life and Death of the Most Reverend Father of our Church Dr James Usher* (Dublin, 1656), 31–3; UW, I, 11–14; Edmund Hogan, *Distinguished Irishmen of the Sixteenth Century* (London, 1894), 228–33; Declan Gaffney, 'The practice of religious controversy in Dublin, 1600–1641', in W. J. Sheils and Diana Wood (eds.), *The Churches, Ireland and the Irish*, Studies in Church History, 25 (Oxford, 1989), 152–5.

[49] Bernard, *Life of Usher*, pp. 28–9; UW, xv, 3–4.

Bellarmine's lifetime of anti-protestant labour. Ussher devoted his lectures to a systematic treatment of the main areas of controversy.[50] He continued the battle over the identity of the early church with another Dublin Jesuit, William Malone. His 1619 challenge: 'how can your religion be true, which disalloweth of many chief articles, which the saints and fathers of that primitive Church of Rome did generally hold to be true?'[51] produced Ussher's 1624, *An Answer to a Challenge Made by a Jesuit in Ireland*. This was a massive historical treatise on the protestant purity of the early church and the subsequent introduction of abuses and superstitions by the increasingly corrupt Church of Rome. Ussher's riposte in turn initiated a lengthy series of replies, rejoinders, replications and surreplications to the rejoinders to the replies, which lasted up to 1641.[52]

Ussher's instinctive determination to return *ad fontes*, and to prove that those earliest springs were pure and protestant, was not just a product of his humanist or antiquarian instincts. It sprang directly from his apocalyptic historical vision. This was expounded in his very first published work, his *Gravissimae quaestionis, de Christianarum ecclesiarum, in Occidentis praesertim partibus, ab apostolicis temporibus ad nostram usque aetatem, continua successione et statu, historica explicatio*.[53] It was presented by Ussher as an addendum to that foundation-stone of English anti-papal polemic, Jewell's great controversy with Harding.[54] Thus Ussher sought to analyse the growth of papal corruption after Jewell's first pure 600 years, up to the Reformation. But his work was different from Jewell's both in content and context. Ussher was more concerned with tracing historical developments – in effect with writing a church history which focused upon the succession of the 'true church' through the ages from its foundation. He thus consciously tried to write in an 'objective' style, seeking merely to state facts, and let his sources speak for themselves, unlike Jewell's more overtly polemical approach.[55] Ussher

[50] UW, xiv, 1–197, 199.

[51] UW, iii, 3; see also Bodleian MS Barlow 13 fos. 393r–395v and William O'Sullivan (ed.), 'Correspondence of David Rothe and James Ussher, 1619–23', *Collectanea Hibernica*, 36–37 (1994–5), 10–11.

[52] James Ussher, *An Answer to a Challenge made by a Jesuit in Ireland. Wherein, the judgement of antiquity in the points questioned is truly delivered and the novelty of the now Romish doctrine discovered* (London, 1624); UW, iii; William Malone, *A Reply to Mrs James Ussher his Answer* (s.l., 1627); George Synge, *A Rejoynder to the Reply* (Dublin, 1632); Roger Puttock, *A Rejoinder unto W. Malone's Reply to the First Article* (Dublin, 1632); Joshua Hoyle, *A Rejoinder to the Master Malone's Reply Concerning the Real Presence* (Dublin, 1641).

[53] (London, 1613).

[54] John Jewell, *A Reply unto M. Hardings Answer* (London, 1565); Peter Milward, *Religious Controversies of the Elizabethan Age. A survey of printed sources* (London, 1978), 1–6.

[55] UW, ii, p. vii.

also differed from Jewell in the much more explicitly apocalyptic framework that he used. Repeatedly he sought to relate the events of history to the prophecies contained in the apocalyptic books and passages of the bible, placing himself firmly in the tradition of Bale, Foxe and other exponents of a literal historical interpretation of apocalyptic. In particular he focused upon Chapter 20 of Revelation, with its account of the 1,000 year binding of Satan in the bottomless pit, 'that he should deceive the nations no more'. Thus, though he dates the birth of Antichrist to the year 600, the growth of Antichrist's power was limited by the 1,000-year binding until the year 1000. Three datings of the 1000-year binding are offered: from Christ's incarnation, from his death, and from the destruction of Jerusalem. Each of these Ussher links to events 1,000 years later which he sees as marking the gradual unbinding of Satan and unleashing of Antichrist during the papacies of Sylvester II (998–1003), Benedict IX (1032–44) and Gregory VII (1073–85). As abuses mount in the Roman church, the line of succession of the 'true' (protestant) church has increasingly to rely upon the heroic witness of martyrs condemned by the papacy as heretics – Berengarius, the Waldensians, even the Cathars, and, in the later middle ages, Wyclif and the Hussites.[56]

During the first and second decades of the seventeenth century Ussher was primarily an academic, concerned with assimilating and expounding the standard European Reformation ideas about history, the true church and apocalyptic. In the 1620s, however, he entered the public and political arena with a succession of appointments, to the see of Meath in 1621, the Irish Privy Council in 1623, and finally the metropolitan seat of Armagh in 1625. His entrée into politics was not confined to Ireland: he was favourably received by King James, and invited to preach before the English House of Commons.[57] With this transition he was faced with the challenge of relating his theological convictions and historical interpretations to practical questions of religious and public policy, most notably official policy towards Catholicism. Here Ussher quickly made a name for himself in both Ireland and England by his refusal to accept that the state could or should compromise with an antichristian religion, a stance which culminated in the 1626 statement of the Irish bishops condemning in stark terms the proposal to grant *de facto* toleration to Irish Catholics:

The religion of the papists is superstitious and idolatrous; their faith and doctrine, erroneous and heretical; their church in respect of both, apostatical.

[56] UW, ii, 1–413.   [57] UW, i, 50–64; ii, 415–57.

To give them therefore a toleration, or to consent that they might freely exercise their religion, and profess their faith and doctrine, is a grievous sin ...[58]

In his new public role Ussher also had to confront the increasingly confident claims of Irish Catholicism to represent the true and only religion of the Irish people, claims that had an important historical dimension. From 1616 to 1619 the leading Catholic bishop in Ireland, David Rothe, produced his *Analecta*, a powerful work of what was in effect contemporary history, which, by recording the steadfast and determined sufferings of Irish people under protestant persecution, sought to demonstrate their unbreakable and time-honoured allegiance to the ancient Catholic religion. Rothe's argument that Ireland had always been Catholic – that, indeed, the very soil of Ireland bred loyal Catholics, so that all those who settled there absorbed the true faith – together with his claiming of all the heroic figures of Irish Christianity for Catholicism, including St Patrick and Columbanus, was an obvious attempt to hibernicise the familiar European Catholic challenge to protestants: where was your church before Luther? By the 1620s, however, it had added political and diplomatic resonances, since by then James's pursuit of a Spanish bride for his son had raised the hopes of Irish Catholics that such a marriage would bring them *de facto* toleration. Rothe's work, with its strident assurance of the absolute loyalty of Irish Catholics to their monarch in secular matters, and its confident assertion that history was on the side of Catholicism, was therefore more than just an intellectual challenge to Irish Protestants. It used the lessons of history to prove that contemporary religious policy was wrong and must be changed.[59]

Ussher's response was *A Discourse of the Religion Anciently Professed by the Irish and British*, which brought together all of his historical, polemical, political and apocalyptic concerns of the 1610s and 1620s to produce what became the classic statement of the ancient origins of Irish protestantism. First published in 1622 as an appendix to a work of apocalyptic anti-papist controversial theology by an English-born Irish judge, Sir Christopher Sibthorp, Ussher expanded the treatise and

---

[58] Declaration cited in Bernard, *Life of Usher*, 57–61; Richard Parr, *The life of ... James Ussher* (London, 1686); UW, i, 73f.; Richard Mant, *History of the Church of Ireland* (2 vols., London, 1840), i, 422.

[59] David Rothe, *Analecta sacra nova et mira de rebus Catholicorum in Hibernia. Pro fide et religione gestis, divisa in tres partes* (s.l., 1616, Cologne, 1617); Rothe, *De processv martyriali quonrandam fidei pugilum in Hibernia, pro complemento sacrorum analectorvm. Collectore & relatore T. N. Philadelpho.* (Cologne, 1619); David Rothe, *The Analecta*, ed., P. F. Moran (Dublin, 1884), for background see Ford 'Reforming the Holy Isle: Parr Lane and the conversion of the Irish', forthcoming in T. C. Barnard *et al.*, (eds.), *A miracle of learning': Irish manuscripts, their owners, their uses.*

reprinted it in 1631.[60] The dedication to Sibthorp credits him with the idea that, in addition to the traditional Reformation appeal to *sola scriptura* and the early church fathers, an essential third weapon in Irish protestants' missionary armoury should be the argument from Irish history. 'If unto the authorities drawn out of scripture and the fathers (which are common to us with others) a true discovery were added of that religion which anciently was professed in this kingdom; it might prove a special motive to induce my poor countrymen to consider a little better of the old and true way from whence they have hitherto been misled.'[61] The dedication also identifies clearly Ussher's apocalyptic framework and polemical intent. 'In this country, as well as in others, corruptions did creep in by little and little, before the devil was let loose to procure that seduction which prevailed so generally in these last times.'[62] Prior to this, however, 'the religion professed by the ancient bishops, priests, monks, and other Christians in this land, was for substance the very same with that which now by public authority is maintained therein, against the foreign doctrine brought in thither in latter times by the bishop of Rome's followers'.[63] In short, Ussher sought to apply to Irish church history, and to the Irish church, the same methods that he had used in his earlier work to prove the continual succession of protestantism in the European church.

He started with the bible, endeavouring to show that the early Irish church had relied, not upon the dangerously corrupt Vulgate version, but upon the original Hebrew and Greek texts, and that these were translated into the language of the people so that the ordinary Christians could 'search the knowledge of the highest truth'.[64] He then went on to show that in its doctrine of salvation the Irish church had rejected free will and justification by works, and had instead espoused predestination and justification by faith alone.[65] Nor, he argued, had the Irish church believed in purgatory or used prayers for the dead.[66] Liturgical practice also pointed to the independence of the church from Roman influences. Ussher found many different forms in the Celtic church, and it was not till the arrival of St Malachy in the eleventh century that the Roman rite was imposed.[67] Similarly in relation to the practice of fasting, the Irish initially followed the Grecian rather than the Roman rule.[68] He also seized upon deviations from later Roman practice in relation to baptism,

---

[60] The title of Ussher's piece when first published in 1622 was *An epistle concerning the religion anciently professed by the Irish and Scottish, shewing it to be for substance the same with that which at this day is by public authority established in the Church of England.* Ussher was closely involved in the writing and printing of Sibthorp's work: UW, xv, 62, 72.

[61] UW, iv, 237.   [62] *Ibid.*, 238.   [63] *Ibid.*, 238–9.   [64] *Ibid.*, 243.
[65] *Ibid.*, ch. 2.   [66] *Ibid.*, ch. 3.   [67] *Ibid.*, 273–4.   [68] *Ibid.*, 305.

clerical marriage, confession and penance, and contrasted the deeply religious Celtic monks, with the 'hypocrisy, pride, idleness and uncleanness of those evil beasts and slothful bellies that afterward succeeded in their room'.[69] Even the constitution of the early Irish church seemed closer to the established Church of Ireland, with bishops being nominated not by the pope but by local kings, and the primate at Armagh erecting new sees and consecrating bishops 'without consulting the see of Rome on the matter'.[70] This independence was confirmed for Ussher by his belief that *pallia* for the metropolitan sees of Ireland were not despatched by the papacy until the twelfth century, all of which went to prove 'how averse the British and the Irish were from having any communion with the Roman party'.[71]

IV

Even though Ussher had established to his own satisfaction the existence of a pure, Celtic and protestant Irish church, a number of problems and ambiguities associated with his thesis reflected the wider tensions inherent in his position as an Irish protestant. First he had to deal with the straightforward cussedness of history, resistant as ever to anachronistic straitjackets. St Patrick and the early Irish church, unfortunately, had had sporadic but undeniable links with Rome. Ussher had to try to play down their importance:

That they consulted with the bishop of Rome when difficult questions did arise, we easily grant; but that they thought they were bound in conscience to stand in his judgement ... and to entertain all his resolutions as certain oracles of truth, is a point that we would fain see proved.[72]

Even when history appeared to support him, Ussher was still faced with the charge that the *Discourse* was selective, a careful culling of telling facts and episodes, open to rebuttal through the selection of different topics or the reinterpretation of particular facts form a different perspective. As a result, it invited, and got, a vigorous Catholic response: 'To what times are we reserved when preachers shall not blush both in print and in pulpit to publish that St Patrick the glorious apostle ... was a protestant ...'[73]

Paul Harris, a maverick English priest who had settled in Ireland, in

---

[69] *Ibid.*, 299–300.   [70] *Ibid.*, 322–9.   [71] *Ibid.*, 319–20, 351.

[72] *Ibid.*, 334; Ussher here was arguing against the claims of O'Sullivan-Beare: see Philip O'Sullivan-Beare, *Historiae Catholicae Iberniae compendium, domino Philippo Austriaco III. Hispaniarum, Indiarum, aliorum regnorum atque multarum ditionum regi Catholico monarchaeque potentissimo* (Ulyssippone, 1621), 42 (tom. 1, lib. IV).

[73] NLI, MS 16, 250, fo. 1v.

his 'An answer unto an epistle written by James Usher to Sir Christopher Sibthorp Knight', offered a detailed account of Ussher's mistakes and misinterpretations of Ireland's past.[74] He attacked Ussher's apocalyptic interpretation of the Irish people's refusal to accept the Reformation, specifically criticising the application of 2 Thessalonians 2 to the Irish context, and producing an alternative cause of the decline of the Irish church around the millennium: not antichrist, but the Vikings.[75] He went on to rebut Ussher's theological and historical claims about the early Irish church one by one, repeatedly using the history of what he pointedly called the Church of Ireland to prove the close relationship between Ireland and the holy see from the very moment of Celestine's despatch of St Patrick. Thus, for example, Ussher's claim that the archiepiscopal palls had not been despatched until the twelfth century, which had been based upon the evidence of St Bernard, was countered by another twelfth-century source, Jocelin's *Vita Patricii*, that specifically stated that St Patrick had received the *pallium* from Pope Celestine.[76] Jocelin's *Life* was an important source for Catholic historians. Indeed it could have been designed for them, since it both stressed Patrick's links with Rome and assimilated him to the mores of twelfth-century Catholicism. It was edited and translated in the 1620s, and twice published on the continent together with a preface which hammered home the message that Patrick was Catholic.[77]

The Catholic response highlighted the way in which Ussher in the *Discourse* used history for his specifically protestant purpose. In doing so it pointed to the complex relationship between Ussher the meticulous historian and Ussher the controversialist. As an antiquarian, compiling succession lists, establishing the basic chronologies, discovering and editing the essential primary sources of early Irish history, and attacking the preposterous claims of the Scot Thomas Dempster about Irish history, he happily co-operated with a wide range of Anglo-Irish and native Irish scholars, regardless of religious affiliation.[78] This produced

[74] *Ibid.*, fos. 84r–v.   [75] *Ibid.*, fos. 3r, 178v.   [76] *Ibid.*, fos. 174v–175v.

[77] Jocelin, *The Life of the Glorious Bishop S. Patricke Apostle and Primate of Ireland. Together with the lives of the holy virgin S. Bridgit and of the glorious abbot S. Columb patron of Ireland* (tr. R. Rochfort), (?Rouen, 1625, 2nd edn 1627).

[78] Joseph Leerssen, 'Archbishop Ussher and Gaelic culture', *Studia Hibernica*, 22–23 (1982–3), 52–3; Brendan Jennings, *Michael O Cleirigh, Chief of the Four Masters, and his Associates* (Dublin, 1936), 41ff.; Aubrey Gwynn, 'Archbishop Ussher and Fr Brendan O'Connor', in Franciscan Fathers (ed.), *Father Luke Wadding* (Dublin, 1957), 263–83; Knox, *James Ussher*, 36ff.; O'Sullivan (ed.), 'Correspondence of Rothe and Ussher', 7–49; Richard Sharpe, *Medieval Irish Saints' Lives. An introduction to the Vitae Sanctorum Hiberniae* (Oxford, 1991), 65–7; on the controversy between Irish writers and Dempster, see the bibliography in Paul Grosjean, 'Un soldat de fortune Irlandais au service des *Acta Sanctorum*: Philippe O'Sullivan Beare et Jean Bollard (1634)', *Analecta Bollandiana*, 71 (1963), 436–46.

works such as his monumental *Britannicarum ecclesiarvm antiquitates,* or his pioneering edition of texts about the early Irish church, *Veterum epistolarum hibernicarum sylloge,* which focused upon the establishment of facts and, though still identifiably protestant, were largely free from overt apocalypticism.[79] Ussher himself was not unaware of the problematic of facts, their collation and interpretation, since, in the 1631 edition of the *Discourse* he added a postscript 'To the reader' in which he accepted that

my principal intention in this discourse was to produce such evidences as might shew the agreement that was betwixt our ancestors and us in matter of religion, and to leave the instances which might be alleged for the contrary to them unto whom the maintaining of that part did properly belong ...[80]

Both the power and the vulnerability of Ussher's vision of Ireland's protestant past thus derived from its complex combination of myth, fact and creative interpretation. It was rather too factual to be dismissed purely as an origin myth or an early example of the fabrication of tradition but too anachronistic and polemical to be accepted unquestioningly as straightforward chronology or history.[81]

The final difficulty in Ussher's historical location of Irish protestantism was a product of the cultural tensions between the New English, Anglo-Irish and native Irish. Put bluntly, Ussher found it difficult to create an 'origin myth' that accommodated the assumptions and prejudices of all three communities.[82] In the *Discourse* he made it plain that his primary audience were his fellow Anglo-Irish. He wanted them to 'consider a little better of the old and true way from whence they have hitherto been misled'.[83] He specifically praised their loyalty during the Nine Years War hoping that, if they could reject their priests' demands that they abandon their loyalty to the king as secular governor, they

[79] James Ussher, *Britannicarum ecclesiarvm antiqvitates: Quibus inserta est pestifera adversus Dei gratiam a Pelagio Britanno in ecclesiam inducta hareseos historia* (Dublin, 1639); James Ussher, *Veterum epistolarum hibernicarum sylloge; quae partim ab Hibernis, partim ad Hibernos, partim de Hibernis vel rebus hibernicis sunt conscriptae* (Dublin, 1632). For example see the treatment in the former, UW, vi, 432, of the dating of the palls; Ussher sought to balance the accounts of Jocelin with those of Bernard and other sources such as Roger of Hovenden and the Annals of Melrose, before concluding mildly that 'the credit of latter writers is deficient concerning the ... the bringing of the pall hither'.

[80] UW, iv, 376.

[81] For examples of the invention of historical origins see James Macpherson's discovery of Ossian in Kidd, *Subverting Scotland's Past,* 220–39; E. J. Hobsbawm and T. O. Ranger (eds.), *The Invention of Tradition* (Cambridge, 1983).

[82] Ute Lotz-Heumann, 'The Protestant interpretation of history in Ireland: the case of James Ussher's *Discourse*' in *Protestant Identity and History in Sixteenth-Century Europe,* ed. Bruce Gordon (Aldershot, 1996), ii, 107–21. I am grateful to Ms Lotz-Heumann for allowing me to see this piece in advance of publication.

[83] UW, iv, 237.

might also reject the priests' insistence that they shun the king as supreme ecclesiastical governor.[84] The problem was that his conviction that Antichrist was loosed to wreak havoc in the Irish church from the year 1000 sat uneasily with the contemporaneous arrival of the ancestors of the Anglo-Irish, the Anglo-Normans. Carelessly handled, the co-incidence between their arrival and the submission of the Irish church to Rome could make them and the English crown seem to be agents of Antichrist. As one recent scholar has commented: 'his language was noticeably "neutral" when he described the consequences of the Norman invasion in Ireland, and he struggled not to connect them with the protestant interpretation of history.'[85]

Ussher was in addition torn between his firm belief in the secular loyalty of the Anglo-Irish to their king, and the incontrovertible evidence that they were equally loyal to the pope. As a result, hope and despair were closely allied in the *Discourse*. Almost as soon as he had stated his intention of converting the Anglo-Irish by his treatise, he slipped into apocalyptic pessimism, convinced that Antichrist in the last days would reach such a height of power that he would deceive the people almost entirely. In particular Ussher cited the resonant text of 2 Thessalonians 2.10–11 – 'because they received not the love of the truth, that they might be saved, God shall send them a strong delusion, that they should believe lies' – and went on:

The woeful experience whereof we may see daily before our eyes in this poor nation: where, such as are slow of heart to believe the saving truth of God delivered by the prophets and apostles, do with all greediness embrace ... those lying legends, wherewith their monks and friars in these latter days have polluted the religion and lives of our ancient saints.[86]

Indeed, Ussher's pessimism had a firm basis in experience. His pleas to his fellow Anglo-Irish to think again repeatedly failed. In 1622 he had been summoned by the civil authorities in Dublin in the fruitless hope that he would be able to convince the Old English to accept the oath of supremacy.[87] Again in 1627 Ussher was chosen by the state to try to convince the Old English of the urgent necessity to provide money for the defence of Ireland. Though on this occasion his appeal was purely to their secular loyalty, reminding them of their faithfulness during the Nine Years War and warning them of the inveterate hatred in which they were held by the native Irish, he was equally unsuccessful.[88] Ussher thus

---

[84] *Ibid.*, 373.   [85] Lotz-Heumann, 'Protestant interpretation of history', 117.
[86] UW, iv. 238.   [87] UW, ii, 461–7.
[88] TCD MS 842, fos. 172r–174v; printed with minor differences in UW, i, 79–86; see also Public Record Office, London, SP 63/24/652 (*Calendar of State Papers, Ireland, 1625–32*, 239–40).

had incontrovertible evidence of the reluctance of his fellow countrymen to embrace not just his vision of Anglo-Irish protestantism, but also his assumptions about Anglo-Irish loyalism.

If his appeal to the Anglo-Irish faced apparently overwhelming obstacles, it was far from evident that Ussher would be any more successful with the New English. They, even more than the Anglo-Irish, saw native-Irish culture and civilisation as backward and barbaric. To them protestantism was 'English, moral and civilised', Catholicism 'Irish, immoral and benighted'.[89] Yet Ussher's purpose was to anchor the reformed protestant church firmly to a Gaelic past. This might have been a plausible argument for a reformed Gaelic church in an independent Ireland. It was not wholly satisfactory as a justification for an anglicised church, staffed by New English clergy under the English monarch.[90] The problem was exacerbated by the fact that one of the chief targets for Ussher's invective in the *Discourse* was Philip O'Sullivan Beare, the embodiment of modern Gaelic Catholicism and nationalism, a 'traitor' and 'as egregious a liar as any that this day breatheth in Christendom' according to Ussher.[91] Ussher's ability to face both ways on this issue – to laud Ireland's Gaelic past whilst criticising its Catholic descendants, to identify a Gaelic protestantism while supporting a church formally committed to the use of English – has caused a degree of confusion amongst historians. A number have claimed that Ussher was hostile to the use of Irish in the Church of Ireland, and quarrelled with Bishop Bedell over the latter's championing of the vernacular.[92] Though it has since been convincingly shown that Ussher's differences with Bedell were not directly related to his use of Irish, and that he himself used Irish, believed that it was an elegant and rich language, cooperated with Gaelic scholars, and preserved numerous Irish manuscripts in his library, nevertheless it would be wrong to elide completely the differences between Bedell and Ussher on this subject.[93] The former had an active evangelical approach to the language which contrasted

---

[89] Joseph Leerssen, *Mere Irish and Fíor Gael: studies in the idea of nationality, its development and literary expression prior to the nineteenth century* (Amsterdam and Philadelphia, 1986), 41.

[90] Lotz-Heumann, 'Protestant interpretation of history', 118.

[91] Bodl, Rawl D 1290, fo. 107v; UW, iv, 333.

[92] E.g. UW, i, 118; Norman Sykes, 'James Ussher as churchman', *Theology*, 60 (1957), 104; and most recently Parry, *Trophies of Time*, 151; see Leerssen, 'Ussher and Gaelic culture', 50–1; Norman Vance, *Irish Literature: a social history. Tradition, identity and difference* (Oxford, 1990), 54–5.

[93] William O'Sullivan, review of Knox, *James Ussher*, in *Irish Historical Studies*, 16 (1968–9), 217–18; Leerssen, 'Ussher and Gaelic culture', 52–8; UW, xvi, 25.

sharply with Ussher's primarily academic concerns.[94] Ussher's public reticence on this subject, which is, after all, at the heart of the issue of national consciousness, points to yet another contradiction in his attempt to create a protestant cultural identity.

V

The end result of this historical controversy was two confessionally distinct schools of history, each offering competing accounts of Irish Christianity, each directed towards providing their respective confessions with a legitimate parentage as the one true church of Ireland, each underpinning the growing sectarian divide.[95] Ussher was matched on the Catholic side by Geoffrey Keating, in whose account of the nation's foundations the early Irish church 'was made to assume the lineaments of post-Tridentine Catholicism'.[96] Subsequent protestant historians slavishly followed Ussher's template. Sir Richard Cox's classic seventeenth-century account of Irish history used Ussher to navigate through what he termed the 'foggy dark sea of antiquity'.[97] Thomas Leland's brave (though unsuccessful) attempt to construct an enlightenment history of Ireland free from religious bias similarly followed the primate whose influence persisted into the nineteenth century.[98] To take just one example amongst many: the summary of contents of the first chapter of *The Ecclesiastical History of Ireland* by the presbyterian author, W. D. Killen includes:

Patrick ... in Ireland – No notice taken of him by Pope Leo I – Patrick's confession; his history – Not sent from Rome – Planted in Ireland the ecclesiastical arrangements of Brittany ... – Early Irish church used no images in

---

[94] Alan Ford, 'The reformation in Kilmore to 1641', in Raymond Gillespie (ed.), *Cavan: an Irish county history* (Dublin, 1995), 90, 94; Parr seeks to rescue Ussher's reputation for encouraging Irish speaking clergy: Parr, *The life of... James Ussher*, 90f. But there is a clear contrast between the number of native Irish in Bedell's diocese of Cavan and Ussher's Armagh in the 1634 Regal Visitation: cf. TCD MS 1034, 119–25, 8–24.

[95] I have sketched this development in ' "Standing one's ground": religion, polemic and Irish history since the reformation', in Ford, McGuire and Milne (eds.), *As by Law Established*, 1–14.

[96] B. I. Bradshaw, 'Geoffrey Keating: apologist of Irish Ireland', in B. I. Bradshaw, Andrew Hadfield and Willy Maley (eds.), *Representing Ireland. Literature and the origins of the conflict, 1534–1660* (Cambridge, 1993), 172.

[97] Richard Cox, *Hibernia Anglicana: or, the history of Ireland from the conquest thereof by the English to this present time with an introductory discourse touching the ancient state of that kingdom* (London, 1689): the 'introductory discourse' (sig. E1r–12v) is largely a summary of Ussher's *Discourse*.

[98] Thomas Leland, *The History of Ireland from the Invasion of Henry II* (3 vols., London, 1773); see Ford, 'Standing one's ground', 5.

worship – Did not practice the rite of extreme unction, and knew no purgatory ...[99]

The need for Ussher's historical framework became even more pressing after disestablishment in 1870. The newly independent church required Irish roots, and writers, both popular and academic, set about providing them. Three examples from many will suffice by way of illustration. John Macbeth who was educated at Trinity College, Dublin, and served as a minister in the diocese of Ferns until his death in 1924 wrote *The Story of Ireland and her Church* with the general reader in mind.[100] From Patrick's despatch to Ireland, where the involvement of the papacy is seen as incidental, to the submission to the papacy in the twelfth century, the Irish church is portrayed as 'perfectly independent'.[101]

Though an overt apocalyptic framework had been abandoned, the historical structure that it had supported remained: the 'errors in doctrine and practice' which were 'gradually creeping into the Roman church' began to affect the Church of Ireland from the eighth century onwards, until the imposition of papal rule forced the church to abandon 'the primitive purity of her doctrinal teaching'.[102] In 1933 a comprehensive three-volume history of the Church of Ireland from the time of Patrick was published. Commissioned by the church's General Synod and written by a distinguished team of protestant scholars, it proudly proclaimed itself to be 'a reasoned defence of the claim of the Church of Ireland to be, both institutionally and in all the essential articles of the Catholic faith, the legitimate successor of the Church founded by St Patrick and the early Irish saints'.[103]

By the 1950s, historiography had progressed somewhat: The co-operative *A History of the Church of Ireland*, written by T. J. Johnson, J. L. Robinson and R. Wyse Jackson at least showed an awareness of the dangers of asking anachronistic questions of the early Irish church, but the central thrust remained the same as that of Ussher – to show that the faith of St Patrick 'is in agreement with what is held by the Church of Ireland now ... We have this faith as an inheritance from him.'[104]

[99] W. D. Killen, *The Ecclesiastical History of Ireland. From the earliest period to the present times* (2 vols., London, 1875), i, xi; see also Richard Murray, *Ireland and Her Church* (2nd edn, London, 1845), 20–50; Christopher Wordsworth, *The History of the Church of Ireland in Eight Sermons Preached in Westminster Abbey* (London, 1869), 23–40.

[100] John Macbeth, *The Story of Ireland and Her Church from the Earliest Times to the Present Day* (Dublin, 1899); James B. Leslie, *Ferns Clergy and Parishes: being an account of the clergy of the Church of Ireland in the Diocese of Ferns, from the earliest period, with historical notices of the several parishes, churches, etc.* (Dublin, 1936), 35–6.

[101] *Ibid.*, 89.   [102] *Ibid.*, 97, 107.

[103] W. A. Phillips (ed.), *History of the Church of Ireland from the Earliest Times to the Present Day* (3 vols., Oxford, 1933), i, p. vii.

[104] (Dublin, 1953), 39.

Though on the protestant side Ussher's proved to be a dominant version, the complications and contradictions implicit in this effort to construct an identity continued to haunt his work and his reputation, and the Irish protestant imagination.

The tension was evident in Ussher's inability to carry his historical work forward to its obvious conclusion – the Reformation. In his *De successione* Ussher had ended at the early thirteenth century, and announced that he would bring the story up to the Reformation in a subsequent volume.[105] But it never appeared. Similarly, his *Discourse* stopped short in the twelfth century after the unleashing of Antichrist and the arrival of the Anglo-Normans.

The cultural contradictions implicit in his approach to history created further tensions for Ussher. In his published works he addressed a number of different audiences. He was, first, a cosmopolitan scholar, a member of that unofficial European academy of distinguished researchers who exchanged elaborate Latin greetings, pupils and arcane historical facts. He also, however, played a significant role, in English intellectual and political life. His commitment to protestantism enabled him to do what his fellow Anglo-Irish would have liked to do but could not because of their allegiance to Catholicism – to move in the circles of power and influence in England and be accepted, culturally, as Englishmen. Indeed, in many respects his assimilation was complete. He had an extensive range of English scholarly contacts. He was utterly at home there with important political connections amongst the Calvinist nobility, and would, one sometimes gains the impression, happily have spent much of his time engaged in research in English libraries had he not had ecclesiastical responsibilities in Ireland.[106] He was, in addition, entirely loyal to the English crown, accepted the right of the English parliament to legislate for Ireland as part of the imperial crown of the realm of England, and proved a staunch defender of Charles in the English civil war.[107] Ussher's loyalty to the English monarch and culture thus allied him willy-nilly with those New English who viewed Ireland as a subservient English colony, and who saw the Irish Reformation as little more than an extension of the English one. From this perspective he appears to be the ultimate 'West British' Anglo-Irish who, far from degenerating into Irishness, instead became more English than the English themselves, even securing that ultimate accolade, a burial place in Westminster Abbey.

Yet, if his protestantism drew him inevitably towards England, and

---

[105] UW, ii, p. xi.
[106] Capern, 'James Ussher and the Calvinist reformation' (see n. 46 above), 132–7.
[107] UW, xi, 455f.

meant that, in his views on policy towards Catholicism, he broke sharply with his Anglo-Irish conformist predecessors, it would still be wrong to identify him as little different from the recently arrived New English. For Ussher was distinguished from the New English in one vital respect: by his strong sense of Irish patriotism. He pointedly referred to 'the honour of my country', 'to which, I confess, I am very much devoted'.[108] He appeared to view the Anglo-Norman invasion of Ireland as a loss of Irish independence, subjecting the nation to the rule of 'foreigners'.[109] He stoutly defended the freedom of the Church of Ireland from English interference, even to the extent of clashing with the lord deputy on this issue in 1634.[110] His vision of the early Irish church as free of any overlords implied its independence not only from Rome but also from Canterbury. The suggestion made by Ussher's friend and fellow historian, Sir Henry Spelman, that there had been an early 'British' patriarchate which had ruled over Ireland, as well as England and Scotland, was sharply rejected by Ussher in a revealing response that testifies to his historical patriotism:

> it would be far better to lay down the Irish and Scottish hierarchy apart, without any subordination unto or dependence upon the British or English archbishops, seeing thereby you shall not only avoid the offence of both the nations, but do right also unto the truth itself . . .[111]

Ussher was similarly hostile to later claims of a Canterburian hegemony. While he accepted that some Irish bishops in the eleventh and twelfth centuries had sought consecration from the archbishop of Canterbury, he pointed out that they were foreign Viking prelates, who 'lived as strangers' in Ireland.[112] In this determination to defend the separateness of the early Irish church from 'British' or 'English' influence Ussher had much in common with patriotic Catholic authors. Thus Geoffrey Keating cited Ussher approvingly in seeking to demonstrate that Canterbury had no claims over Ireland.[113]

Such instincts made it difficult for Ussher to build upon his acceptance of royal supremacy in secular matters and develop an inclusivist 'British' ideology that would transcend Irish distinctiveness. For Ussher Britain and Ireland, despite their historical ties, and whatever the confusions of some early writers, remained nevertheless two distinct

---

[108] UW, iv, 370.   [109] UW, xi, 364.
[110] Ford, 'Dependent or independent', 163–87.
[111] TCD MS 3659: photostat of original in Pierpoint Morgan Library, New York, fo. 224r. Spelman's draft translation of this letter into Latin is in BL Add. MS 34,600, 179r–180v.
[112] TCD MS 3659, fo. 225r; UW, iv, 329.
[113] Keating, *History of Ireland*, iii, 300.

entitles.[114] The title of the 1631 edition of his *Discourse* referred
pointedly to the 'Irish and British'. When Ussher used the term British
in relation to inhabitants of Ireland it referred to the recently arrived
Scottish and English planters in Ulster.[115]

However, this Irishness also had its limitations. We are not dealing
here with an all-encompassing protestant nationalism. To put it crudely,
Ussher was more Anglo-Irish than *fíor Gael*. He represented a tradition
in Irish intellectual history which was proud to be both Irish and
anglicised, a tradition which historians and politicians alike have found
confusing and perplexing, especially when it attempted to appropriate
Ireland's Gaelic past. Thus for Seamus Deane, Ussher was a propagandist for 'New English attitudes', with his 'strident Protestant rejection of
anything Catholic'.[116] Norman Vance, more acutely, has identified the
fundamental ambiguity of Ussher's position, seeing him as a writer
whose imaginative and intellectual energies were stimulated by Ireland's
'distinctive problems of allegiance and identity', and who 'held in finally
unresolved tension the multiple identities of the Irish writer, Irish,
British and European'.[117] Though sharply contrasting, indeed apparently conflicting, neither evaluation is necessarily unfair to Ussher. He
wished to assert his Irish protestant identity. However in doing so he
faced the dilemma that the terms Irish and protestant proved difficult to
yoke together, and were even at times contradictory. For in an overwhelmingly Catholic country there was an ineluctable tendency for Irish
and Catholic, on the one hand, and English and protestant, on the
other, to be treated as synonyms. Ussher, then, was forced to confront
in a new form the cultural dilemma of the earlier Anglo-Irish, of trying
to combine the apparently irreconcilable: Irish history and English
culture; an independent Church of Ireland with a church that was in
practice wholly dependent for its survival upon its English links. The
dilemma was a continuing one. The efforts of Irish protestant patriots in
the later eighteenth century to create 'a national ideal of Ireland,
embracing protestant Anglo-Irish and Catholic Gaels alike' exposed
again the inherent cultural contradictions in protestant national feeling,
and produced such juxtapositions as Charles Vallancey, an enthusiastic

---

[114] The confusion is not, of course, confined to medieval writers, see Conrad Russell's
recognition of the problem of using the term Britain to include Ireland: Conrad
Russell, 'Composite monarchies in early modern Europe: the British and Irish
example', in Alexander Grant and K. J. Stringer (eds.), *Uniting the Kingdom? The
making of British history* (London, 1995), 133.

[115] James Ussher to William Hilton, 3 November 1635: Armagh Archiepiscopal records,
Alb No 128, quoted by William Reeves in TCD MS 1073/2, between pp. 10 and 11.

[116] Seamus Deane, *A Short History of Irish Literature* (London, 1986), 17.

[117] Vance, *Irish Literature*, 56–7.

champion of Ireland's Gaelic past, and Edward Ledwich, that arch sceptic and debunker of all things Celtic who doubted the very existence of St Patrick.[118]

Ussher represents, then, the peculiar 'doubleness' that Richard Kearney has identified as a persistent undercurrent in Irish cultural history.[119] Indeed, he can be claimed as the person who first enabled protestants to be Irish, helping to create their idiosyncratic form of national awareness which was identifiably Irish, but not exclusively or straightforwardly so. The historical grounding he provided was, arguably, often achieved by silence and elision, rather than by confronting the centrifugal force of its constituent parts. But it did nevertheless offer an important and continuing refuge not just for those Anglo-Irish who opted to become protestant, but also for those New English who, like Rider and Hanmer, came to identify with their country of adoption, rather than immerse themselves in some broader 'British' identity. Indeed, for later protestants, Ussher's vision of Irish history became almost a reflex assumption. He therefore constitutes a challenge to historians to move beyond exclusive definitions of national identity and 'to rethink borders of the mind and realise that several identities can be reconciled within the self'.[120]

[118] Leerssen, *Mere Irish*, 403–6, 414–26.
[119] Richard Kearney, *Postnationalist Ireland: politics, culture, philosophy* (London, 1997).
[120] Roy Foster, review of Kearney, *Postnationalist Ireland*, in *Times Literary Supplement*, 11 April 1997, 7.

7   Seventeenth-century Wales: definition and identity

Philip Jenkins

In the 1580s a remarkable group of Welsh scholars and ecclesiastics produced a number of books that would have a formative influence on Welsh culture. The translation of the bible (1588) was perhaps the most celebrated.[1] However, another work that emerged from this age deserves equal attention. This was the *Historie of Cambria, now called Wales* ... published in 1584 by David Powell, but drawing on the work of several predecessors lay and clerical. This book became the basis of William Wynne's *History of Wales* (1697) which in turn remained a key text on Welsh history into the present century. The *Historie of Cambria* did much to establish the notion that Wales was enough of a unity to permit statements of the general kind required to write a 'national' history, and many later writers have undertaken comparable surveys. Conversely, English writers tended to avoid discussing Wales precisely because it was felt to be a distinct nation. It is perhaps time to ask whether 'Wales' is indeed a suitable unit for historical analysis and whether this is the most appropriate way of approaching the history of Welsh communities.

The national existence or definition of *Cambria, now called Wales* is clearly important in the light of recent debates about the construction of a 'new British history', which would escape from the anglocentrism of past years.[2] Ideally, such an approach would attempt an integrated comparative study of the diverse regions of the British Isles and the wider British world, 'in the belief that it is only by adopting a "Britannic" approach that historians can make sense of the particular segment in which they may be primarily interested, whether it be "England", "Ireland", "Scotland", "Wales", Cornwall or the Isle of Man ... A "Britannic" framework is an essential starting point for a fuller understanding of those so-called "national" pasts.'[3] The abun-

---

[1] Philip Jenkins, *A History of Modern Wales 1536–1990* (London, 1992), 103–6.

[2] J. G. A. Pocock, 'British history: a plea for a new subject', *Journal of Modern History*, 4 (1975), 601–24; and Pocock, 'The limits and divisions of British history', *American Historical Review*, 87 (1982).

[3] Hugh Kearney, *The British Isles: a history of four nations* (Cambridge, 1989), 1.

dance of quotation marks provided by Professor Kearney is in itself indicative of the serious problems that exist in discussing any of the four later national units as real entities, at least before the late eighteenth or nineteenth centuries. However, even if this is recognised, there are still fundamental differences between the political development of early modern Wales and that of other units such as Scotland and Ireland. In the latter cases, we can find some consistent tradition of 'national' politics from the later middle ages in the sense of political and cultural institutions, as well as patriotic or nationalistic ideologies. If not exactly in a modern sense, it is at least plausible to speak of a distinct tradition of 'Scottish' or 'Irish' politics in the seventeenth century, even if this should be placed to some extent within a 'Britannic' whole.[4] These domestic political traditions would be of great significance for the development of the wider British entity, in providing potential sources of conflict or instability for the emerging British state, and in shaping the attitudes that would have to be overcome or co-opted before inhabitants of all regions could successfully be absorbed as 'Britons'.[5] Understanding the early national development of the different components of the British Isles is the essential prerequisite for addressing the integration of the various regions and populations.

Recent attempts at writing 'British' history have paid far more attention to Ireland and Scotland than to Wales, an allocation of space that is quite understandable in terms of the population or economic significance of the various regions, as well as their relative importance in political developments. However, this last issue raises serious questions about the nature of early national development, as to why Welsh affairs made so little impact on the British whole, and why there is so little evidence for a distinct political tradition here. The position of Wales within the early modern British state can be discussed in terms of negatives. Between about 1560 and 1790, there were no distinctively Welsh risings or insurrections, and nationalism or separatism plays no role in what riots or disturbances did occur.[6] National politics did not emerge during the turmoil of the civil wars or interregnum, nor did they continue a clandestine existence behind the mask of movements like radical puritanism in the seventeenth century or jacobitism in the eight-

---

[4] Linda Colley, 'Britishness and otherness: an argument', *Journal of British Studies* 31; 4 (1992), 315.

[5] Linda Colley, *Britons: forging the nation 1707–1837* (New Haven, 1992).

[6] Among the general histories of Wales used throughout this chapter are Hugh Thomas, *A History of Wales 1485–1660* (Cardiff, 1972); E. D. Evans, *A History of Wales 1660–1815* (Cardiff, 1976); Gareth E. Jones, *Modern Wales: a concise history 1485–1979* (Cambridge, 1984); Gwyn A. Williams, *When was Wales?* (London, 1985); and John Davies, *Hanes Cymru* (London, 1990).

eenth. The citizens of Shrewsbury or Bristol never had cause to fear the assaults of Welsh rebels struggling for their independence, though there might be concern about Welsh soldiers serving the interests of wider British movements, such as the royalist cause in the 1640s. No Georgian fortifications or military roads survive to mark the progress of redcoats on their way to stamp out the last smouldering vestiges of revolt in Snowdonia or the Prescelly hills. The very absurdity of such images suggests the extent to which we take for granted the political integration of Wales into Britain. Even if we put aside such spectacular manifestations of imaginary dissent it is difficult to find early radical pamphleteers urging the creation of a Welsh state or even limited autonomy for Wales within a British entity.[7]

It can be argued that there was.no such thing as Welsh politics in the seventeenth century, at least in the sense of a culture or movement distinct from that of England. Of course there were differences and peculiarities, resulting in large measure from the country's geographical position and economic interests, but it is difficult to discern a 'Welsh political tradition' more distinctive from the English norm as it existed (say) in Norfolk or Lancashire. This is all the more surprising when we take account of linguistic and cultural factors. During the seventeenth and early eighteenth centuries at least 90 per cent of the people of the thirteen traditional counties would have spoken Welsh with some fluency, and the usage spilled over the border into Herefordshire and Shropshire. Not until the present century would the proportion have fallen below 60 per cent, a pattern of survival far superior to that of either Irish or Scottish Gaelic. Until the end of the seventeenth century, Welsh continued to be well known and used at all levels of Welsh society up to the wealthiest aristocrats.[8] Ethnic self-recognition derived from this linguistic unity provided the basis for some kind of national awareness, if not active nationalism, however rudimentary. Historical scholarship in particular provided the potential for a nationalist rhetoric

---

[7] As far as I am aware, the only advocacy for a 'Welsh parliament' in the seventeenth century comes from anti-Welsh satirical tracts like the work of 'Morgan Lloyd', *News from Wales, or the Prittish Parliament. Called and assembled upon many cood reasons and considerations, and for the benefit of her countries to secure them from her round-head, long-tayld enemies, by the crave and politick wisdoms of her Prittish purgesses … newly sent up py her trusty and welbeloved Gousin the Welch embassadour, to give the world notice of her purpose, to call a Welch parliament* (London, 1642: all spellings in this title are *sic*).

[8] Glanmor Williams, *Religion, Language and Nationality in Wales* (Cardiff, 1979); Victor E. Durkacz, *The Decline of the Celtic Languages* (Edinburgh, 1983); Meic Stephens, *Linguistic Minorities in Western Europe* (Llandysul, 1976) offers a European context for the development and decline of the Welsh language. Compare R. Merfyn Jones, 'Beyond identity: the reconstruction of the Welsh', *Journal of British Studies*, 31: 4 (1992), 330–57.

and political culture that could, in theory, have had quite explosive consequences.

The question obviously arises therefore why we do not find 'Wales' or Welshness in seventeenth-century politics. The question is significant for what it implies about the stability of the emerging British state, as the Welsh made up perhaps 8 per cent of the population of 'England-and-Wales' in 1700. If nationalist sentiment had indeed been a significant force in Wales, Stuart regimes might have faced the terrifying pros·····of a hostile and restive colony across a long and indefensible bor‹ with the chance of foreign foes or domestic rebels capitalising on t!. 'nearer Ireland'.[9] In political terms alone, the degree of Welsh cultural assimilation or separateness would seem important. For the social historian, it is remarkable to find that radical cultural dissimilarity can indeed coexist with political stability.[10] Seventeenth-century Wales presents a curious paradox, being perhaps the most thoroughly 'other' and Celtic society in the British Isles, yet one so assimilated in political terms as to be essentially indistinguishable from any English region. The question then arises of how the British state had been so successful, or perhaps so fortunate, in achieving so thorough an integration of England's oldest and oddest colony. It will be suggested here that geographical factors played a critical role in fragmenting the various Welsh regions so thoroughly as to prevent the emergence of any rudimentary national institutions. However, Wales also became the first region of the British Isles to develop an ideology of 'British' unity based on loyalty to the monarchy and the protestant cause. It was the 'Ancient Britons' who were the harbingers of modern 'Britishness'.

I

In the seventeenth century, there was no doubt of Wales's separate existence as a cultural and linguistic entity, and 'Welshness' regularly attracted expressions of pride and loyalty. In contemporary writings Wales was generally recognised as a 'country', though that did not in itself carry the modern implications of nationhood. It might rather suggest the geographical connotations we find in the 'west country'. However, there are cases where 'country' and 'countrymen' are used in the sense of ethnic self-identification, as in 'our Welsh country'.[11] In

---

[9] This Irish analogy would emerge quite strongly in response to the social unrest between about 1830 and 1844: see, for example, Jenkins, *Modern Wales*, 262–73.

[10] Compare Keith Robbins, *Nineteenth-century Britain: integration and diversity* (Oxford, 1988); and Eric Hobsbawm, in *Nations and Nationalism Since 1780* (Cambridge, 1990).

[11] Some of the clearest and most perceptive discussions of Welsh identity in the wider Britain are to be found in the work of A. H. Dodd in the 1940s and 1950s, especially in

1653, John Jones the regicide complained of the spiritual darkness of 'our poor country of Wales', while William Erbery of Cardiff addressed 'his countryman'.[12] Letters between casual acquaintances might well be signed, 'your countryman', indicating that this was hoped to create a sense of good will or solidarity. In 1693, Edward Lhuyd wrote to John Aubrey, noting at the end that 'the bearer is Mr Thomas, a countryman of ours'.[13] The term 'Welsh' is often used with a sense of pride and an apparent recognition of obligations arising from these common origins. Wealthy and sophisticated Glamorgan squires like Sir Edward Mansell of Margam described themselves proudly as 'mountainous Welshmen' while Francis Gwyn spoke of 'my own Welsh country'.[14] Love of one's native soil was at least a familiar literary device, and we frequently find Welsh correspondents in England or overseas pining for their native land, clamouring for one clod of good Welsh earth.[15] In this sense, patriotism was recognised and praiseworthy: as a petty Carmarthenshire landowner wrote in 1656, it was a small sin in a Welshman 'to applaud and commend his own country'. Petitioners to lords or squires expected that these patrons would be especially sympathetic to Welsh people, fellow 'ancient Britons'.[16]

Assertions of pride or patriotism are not surprising in themselves, but it should be emphasised how far these sentiments transcend class boundaries within Wales. In explaining the relative docility of Welsh politics it has been common to suggest that Welsh elites were anglicised at a very early stage, adopting the English language and the cultural beliefs and outlook that went with it. The cooption of the aristocracy and wealthy gentry has been placed in Tudor or early Stuart times, a view expressed by no less an authority than David Williams, who wrote that 'as the [sixteenth] century wore on, the gentry showed a tendency to become anglicized in speech ... the tendency was for the Welsh language to disappear among them, due to their contacts with the English gentry'.[17] 'There thus came about the dichotomy which has

major articles like 'The pattern of politics in Stuart Wales', *Transactions of the Honourable Society of Cymmrodorion* (1948), 8–91; see also his *Studies in Stuart Wales* (1952, rev. edn, 1971). For the use of 'countrymen', W. J. Smith (ed.), *Herbert Correspondence* (Cardiff, 1963), 34.

[12] National Library of Wales, Add. MS 11440D, fos. 139–140; *Milton State Papers*, 88.

[13] Bodl. Aubrey MS 12, fo. 241.

[14] *Calendar of State Papers Domestic*, 513; H.M.C. *Portland MSS*, i, 536; see also Philip Jenkins, *The Making of a Ruling Class: the Glamorgan gentry 1640–1790* (Cambridge, 1983).

[15] Jenkins, *Making of a Ruling Class*, 207–11.

[16] William Williams, *The Mystery of Iniquity, or a Remarkable Relation of a Carmarthenshire Cause* (London, 1656).

[17] David Williams, *A History of Modern Wales* (2nd edn, London, 1977), 87–9.

marred so much of Welsh life.' Among more recent writers, the drift away from Welsh is seen as a decisive event that effectively shaped Welsh social relations into the nineteenth century. Hechter remarks that 'by 1640, the anglicization of the Welsh gentry has reached its final stages'.[18] Kearney speaks of the failure of the 'English-orientated gentry and clergy' in their attempted anglicisation of traditional society, a campaign which he appears to date before the eighteenth century.[19] The new protestant church has also been implicated in this supposed cultural schism. Durkacz' study of *The Decline of the Celtic Languages* comments on the hostility of the established church towards the Welsh language affirming that 'it is a commonplace remark in Welsh historiography that anglican cures were filled with English placemen who disparaged the Welsh language and actively sought to destroy it'.[20] In this view, both lay and clerical elites should by the mid seventeenth century at the latest have been well on the way to abandoning traditional culture and loyalties, and becoming part of a new 'British' society. If true, this view would go far towards explaining the absorption of Wales into Britain, but the account rests on thoroughly unsatisfactory foundations. In part, the idea of a gentry and clergy separated from their tenants and parishioners by language is an extrapolation from nineteenth-century conditions, exacerbated by later non-conformist propaganda against the 'anti-national' character of the Anglican elites. In the ecclesiastical context, the alleged hostility of the clergy to the Welsh language was intended to exaggerate the darkness of the 'long sleep' that preceded the evangelical awakening of the eighteenth century, and to discredit popular support for the established church – which in reality had employed a Welsh bible and liturgy since Elizabethan times.[21]

In contrast to the stereotypes, assertions of Welshness and Welsh loyalty often emanated from gentle and aristocratic families whom one might expect to be thoroughly integrated into English society, including those who lived on or over the border. In 1665, Lord Herbert of Cherbury apologised for writing so long an account of his misfortunes, but explained that 'being a Welshman he must give a pedigree of his sufferings'.[22] Such families were often proud of their knowledge and use of the Welsh language. In 1632 the author of a *Welsh Grammar* referred to the Earl of Worcester as one 'who does not hesitate to speak Welsh

---

[18] Michael Hechter, *Internal Colonialism: the Celtic fringe in British national development* (London, 1975), 111.
[19] Kearney, *Four Nations*, 119.   [20] Durkacz, *Decline*, 7.
[21] Philip Jenkins, 'The Anglican Church and the unity of Britain: the Welsh experience', in Steven Ellis and Sarah Barber (eds.), *Conquest and Union: fashioning a British state 1485–1725* (London, 1995), 115–38.
[22] Smith, *Herbert Correspondence*, 189.

and to cherish and magnify it in a clearly British manner', while Sir Edward Stradling of Glamorgan was perhaps 'the chief cherisher of our Welsh language in south Wales'.[23] Also in Glamorgan during the 1630s the wealthy gentry family of Lewis of Van employed three tutors for their children, one each for the Latin, French and Welsh tongues.[24] Not until the end of the century did the gentry and aristocracy cease to patronise such vehicles of traditional Welsh culture as bardic poetry or the music of the harp.[25]

Throughout the century, ethnic identity and loyalty were most clearly expressed in cultural matters, above all in history and antiquarianism. And as in the case of bardic patronage, the great landed families continued to be deeply involved. To take one example from many, it was in 1661 that Percy Enderbie published *Cambria Triumphans*, which emphasised the ancient Welsh roots both of the British monarchy and of some leading aristocratic families of England.[26] This intensely patriotic work was patronised by an impressive list of magnates from southern Wales and the borders: Lord Powis, Lord Herbert of Cherbury and the later Marquess of Worcester, as well as great gentry like the Monmouthshire Morgans, and the Glamorgan Stradlings and Lewises. A few years later, a similarly prestigious group of west Wales gentry like John Barlow and William Wogan led a campaign to secure the appointment of a royal printer for the Welsh language. These men came from south Pembrokeshire, historically one of the most anglicised parts of Wales, but they joined unequivocally in the movement.[27] At the end of the century, some of the strongest testimony to the strength of Welsh cultural patriotism comes from the correspondence of Edward Lhuyd the antiquary, as he collected Welsh materials for the 1695 revision of the classic text *Britannia*, and sought subscribers for his own *Archaeologia Britannica* (1707).[28] Especially useful is his collection of parochial surveys, the respondents to which were generally clerics and petty gentry far below the social level of those whose voices normally survive from this period. Lhuyd himself was staunchly Welsh, affirming that he was no Englishman 'but an old Briton'.[29] The patriotic agenda in his work was overt, suggested for example in the letter of Archdeacon John Williams, who urged Lhuyd to create a new Welsh history purged from

[23] Roland Mathias, *Whitsun Riot* (London, 1963), 56.
[24] Jenkins, *Making of a Ruling Class*, 222.   [25] Jenkins, *Modern Wales*, 57–77.
[26] Percy Enderbie, *Cambria triumphans* (London, 1661).
[27] Jenkins, *Making of a Ruling Class*, 209.
[28] F. V. Emery, *Edward Lhuyd 1660–1709* (Cardiff, 1971); Brynley F. Roberts, *Edward Lhuyd: the making of a scientist* (Cardiff, 1980); Edward Lhuyd, 'Parochialia', ed. R. H. Morris, *Archaeologia Cambrensis* supplements (1909–11).
[29] National Library of Wales MS 823e.

the 'fabulous traditions of our own countrymen, or the dry partial accounts of the English writers'.[30] Lhuyd's work indicates the existence of real and widespread enthusiasm for Welsh antiquities among large sections of the gentry and clergy. In 1707, the subscription list for his *Archaeologia Britannica* included some 200 of the leading lay magnates in Wales.

II

Historical study had at least the potential for developing a nationalist agenda. 'Welsh' and 'British' featured synonymously in contemporary usage, implying that the Welsh were identical with the 'ancient Britons', with all that implied for their prior rights of occupancy in the island of Britain. Discussing the evolution of 'British' into 'Welsh' also involved exploring the means by which the island had been lost to the English. In the process of historical explanation the antiquaries would produce some remarkably radical manifestations of national resentment, as the story they recounted so often involved the crushing of Welsh national aspirations by English and Norman overlords, generally through deceit and treachery. One of the best known tales concerned the establishment of English power through the entrapment of the fifth-century King Vortigern by the Saxon witch Rowena, and the subsequent massacre of British chieftains at a banquet. Welsh poetry long retained the phrase 'children of Rowena' as a loaded poetic soubriquet for the English, and in the bardic poetry of the fifteenth and sixteenth centuries the legend was often accompanied by hair-raising threats of racial vengeance.[31] The visceral power of such theories often emerges with surprising vigour from Lhuyd's correspondents. In the Neath area, for example, we hear that the abbey was founded in the time of William Rufus who 'treacherously' took the lands of the last native ruler of Morgannwg. The story of the conquest of Breconshire emphasised that the conquering 'twelve knights' slew the 'rightful heir' of the region of Brycheiniog.[32] Also about this time a popular Monmouthshire movement against the duke of Beaufort's land enclosures was justified in terms of ancient Welsh

[30] F. V. Emery, 'Edward Lhuyd and some of his correspondents', *Transactions of the Honourable Society of Cymmrodorion* (1965).
[31] Glanmor Williams, *Recovery, Reorientation and Reformation: Wales c. 1415–1642* (Oxford, 1987), especially 8, 454–5. The story of Rowena originates with Nennius, but it was popularised by Geoffrey of Monmouth. For the frequent accounts of English treachery and oppression in bardic lore, see Rachel Bromwich (ed.), *Trioedd ynys Prydein* (2nd edn, Cardiff, 1978). See also Roberts above, 7.
[32] National Library of Wales, Penrice and Margam MS A92. For the Elizabethan view of the 'twelve knights', see Rice Merrick, *Morganiae Archaiographia*, ed. Brian Ll. James, South Wales Record Society (Cardiff, 1983), 20–30.

(and indeed Romano-British) rights usurped by the Norman conquerors.[33]

The potency of this theme was enhanced by its religious dimension as the invaders had also destroyed the native Celtic church of Wales. This was seen as a primitive lost ideal, the exact nature of which varied according to the interests and predilections of the observer.[34] Recusants naturally saw the early English invasions as precursors of contemporary Anglican usurpations. Protestants like the Elizabethan bishop Richard Davies noted that the apostolic Celtic church had been suppressed by Rome presumably because of its authentic proto-protestantism. In 1662, Fuller's *Worthies* similarly viewed the era of 'Augustine the monk' as a critical time of decline and degeneracy in the face of Catholic intrigue. In 1695 we hear that the Welsh church 'continued 438 years before Austin the monk came to pervert them by introducing Romish ceremonies, superstitions and servitude'.[35] Before this point the British church had recognised no ecclesiastic as superficial to the (mythical) archbishop of Caerleon. In one form or another the malleable notion of the Saxon yoke can be traced as a potent influence in Welsh political culture from the sixteenth century through the nineteenth; though, as we will see below, the nationalistic implications were rarely explored.

We find a definite sense of ethnic self-recognition in seventeenth-century Wales, and this had political ramifications. Moreover, the earlier precedents were quite ominous, and there had been clear expressions of ethnic hatred and overt nationalist politics in earlier years.[36] The Elizabethan antiquary George Owen writes of the early fifteenth century that 'there grew about the time deadly hatred between [the Welsh] and the English nation, insomuch that the name of a Welshman was odious to the Englishman, and the name of Englishman woeful to the Welshman'.[37] In the years before Bosworth Field the nationalism and violent anglophobia of major poets like Guto'r Glyn or Dafydd Llwyd were quite unabashed. Traces of such sentiments continue into the Stuart period. At the simplest level, occasional expressions of xenophobia are found, though it is difficult to know how far this can be described as 'nationalistic'. For example, in 1672 it was assumed that an

---

[33] Nathan Rogers, *Memoirs of Monmouthshire* (London, 1708).
[34] Dodd, 'Pattern of politics'; Glanmor Williams, *Welsh Reformation Essays* (Cardiff, 1967), 207–19; Williams, *Religion, Language and Nationality*; Jenkins, *Making of a Ruling Class*; P. R. Roberts, 'The union with England and the identity of "Anglican" Wales', *Transactions of the Royal Historical Society*, 22 (1972), 65–8; compare Geraint H. Jenkins, *Literature, Religion and Society in Wales 1660–1730* (Cardiff, 1978).
[35] Thomas Fuller, *Worthies of England* (London, 1811), 559; R. Burton, *History of the Principality of Wales* (London, 1695), 157.
[36] Williams, *Recovery, Reorientation and Reformation*, 8, 155, 451–70.
[37] Quoted in *ibid.*, 8.

English lawyer would be anxious to settle a dispute in Denbighshire because of 'the jealousy of a Welsh jury where an Englishman is concerned'.[38] This seems clear enough, though it might be asked whether the hostility involved would be any greater than that of (say) a jury in Kent or Yorkshire hearing the case of a man from another English region. More convincing perhaps is the evidence of genealogy, an art which enjoyed enormous popularity in contemporary Wales.[39] Welsh families assiduously cultivated genealogies and explored distant links with enthusiasm. However, links outside Wales were regarded with little sympathy or interest. It is common to find references to a daughter who 'married in England', without further specification of the individual or family involved.[40] The reason for this lack of interest might have been ethnic coolness or open hostility, as in the case of an amateur Radnorshire genealogist named David Price. At the end of the century he married a Herefordshire woman, but bitterly regretted this action as he thus became the first of his family who ever 'crossed the ancient British strain by a foreigner'.[41]

Hostility was mutual. A long English tradition of writing in the 'taffy' genre depicts a stereotyped and impoverished Wales characterised by steep crags, thorny shrubs and thistles, goats, leeks, and (inevitably) cheese.[42] Wales, after all, was 'where earth was first from chaos formed'. The inhabitants of this landscape spoke a dialect frequently parodied in print with phrases such as 'Taffies was all Shentlemen ...'; or in the title of a 1652 pamphlet, *The Humble Remonstrances of Rice ap Meredith ap Morgan. Shentilman of Wales, with Fery Brave New Ballacks, or Songs ...*[43] Hundreds of such tracts represent the common European tendency to stereotype upland people as primitive or uncivilised: the attitude summarised by the description of Restoration Montgomeryshire as 'very mountainous and rude'.[44] It is debateable how far there was an ethnic agenda to these remarks. The upland–lowland conflict

---

[38] W. J. Smith (ed.), *Calendar of Salusbury Correspondence* (Cardiff, 1954), 207.

[39] Jenkins, *Modern Wales*, 39–40, 65–6.

[40] For an example of the many genealogical tracts which illustrate this hostility to English connections, see Cardiff Central Library MS 4.87.

[41] *Genuine Account of the Life and Transactions of Howell ap David Price, Gentleman of Wales* (London, 1752).

[42] See for example 'W.R.', *Wallography, or the Briton Described* (London, 1682). The genre is discussed in Geraint H. Jenkins, *The Foundations of Modern Wales: Wales 1642–1780* (Oxford, 1987), 213. For the use of the 'Taffy' genre for a political attack on a Welsh politician, see *The Welsh Monster, or the Rise and Downfall of that Late Upstart ...* (Sir John Trevor) (London, 1702).

[43] James O. Halliwell (ed.), *The Humble Remonstrances of Rice ap Meredith ap Morgan, Shentilman of Wales, with fery brave new ballacks, or songs ...* (1652, reprinted London, 1861: privately printed).

[44] *Calendar of State Papers Domestic 1663–64*, 532.

certainly existed between inhabitants of English regions and also within Wales itself. In the eighteenth century there is evidence from church courts in the diocese of Llandaff that the term 'mountainy' was *ipso facto* slanderous.[45]

While ethnic dislike and stereotyping can be easily illustrated, more concrete political manifestations are controversial. In Welsh historical writing numerous retroactive attempts have sought to annex political movements for the cause of nationalism, to see nationalist or separatist motives in the development of groups such as sixteenth-century recusants, seventeenth-century puritans or eighteenth-century jacobites.[46] Few of these attempts can be sustained. Often, such accounts tend to see the history of the movements in Wales as both far more influential and more distinctive than was actually the case. In reality, seventeenth-century Wales was neither a hotbed of recusancy nor of puritanism, and it is quite unacceptable to see either as in any sense a 'national' movement. It is very difficult to find specific incidents (still less whole parties or movements) which can be cited as expressions of nationalistic politics or even Welsh national sentiment. Virtually the only instances in which Welsh politicians acted in harmony involved regional economic interests such as the regulation of the Shrewsbury wool trade, or the importation of Irish cattle.[47] In such cases Welsh MPs struggled vigorously for the economic interests of themselves and their tenants. After the Irish cattle campaign succeeded in 1666, 'Wales' as an entity – even as a region – would be a ghostly presence at Westminster.

One cannot prove a negative, but it is instructive to see how few events lend themselves to a 'nationalistic' interpretation. In the seventeenth century we might expect to find the clearest demonstrations of 'Welsh' politics during the 1650s; and the Commission for the Propagation of the Gospel was the nearest approach to an innovative Welsh national institution from Tudor times through the Victorian era.[48] Conversely, the anglicans and moderate puritans used patriotic arguments against the radicals. Most commonly, it was argued that the long tradition of including Wales as one of the 'dark corners of the realm' was an unfair stereotype which neglected Welsh religious and educational achievements. The country was in fact 'far from that wild heathenism

[45] National Library of Wales. Church in Wales MSS. LL/CC/G 657a.
[46] Nigel Yates, 'The Welsh church and Celtic nationalism', *Journal of Welsh Ecclesiastical History*, 1 (1984), 1–10; Jenkins, *Modern Wales*, 111–17.
[47] A. H. Dodd, *History of Caernarfonshire*, Caernarfonshire Historical Society (Caernarfon, 1968), 166.
[48] A. H. Johnson, 'Wales during the Commonwealth and Protectorate', in D. H. Pennington and Keith Thomas (eds.), *Puritans and Revolutionaries* (Oxford, 1978), 233–56; Dodd, *Studies*.

and brutish ignorance' alleged by the puritans.[49] However, both the creation and eclipse of Propagation owed as much to puritan politics in London as to any putative separatist movement within Wales itself. Other instances of 'nationalism' are equally uncertain. The most spectacular incident occurred in 1592 when the Pembrokeshire magnate Sir John Perrott died in the Tower facing charges involving an alleged plot to secure his power over an autonomous Wales.[50] The background to this affair is extraordinarily controversial. Perrott appears to have fallen victim to rivalries in Dublin, and especially to the hostility of Adam Loftus, so the accuracy of the allegations against him is most improbable. Even if true, the charges would be wildly untypical. Political conspiracy in Wales at this time chiefly involved schemes with Spain and other powers to restore Catholic rule to the wider realm of Britain rather than simply Wales.[51]

In the following century possible examples of nationalism are few and dubious, even at times when we might expect them, such as during the political turmoil of the 1640s. Consider for example the incident in 1645, when Archbishop Ussher of Armagh was one of several distinguished royalist refugees invited to St Donat's castle in Glamorgan. This was an inauspicious time to visit: 'The country thereabouts was up in arms, in a tumultuous manner to the number of ten thousand, as was supposed, who chose themselves officers, to form them into a body pretending for the king but yet would not be governed by English commanders or suffer any English garrisons in the country'.[52] Trying to avoid the main area of conflict, Ussher's party strayed into side-roads in the hill country, but this offered no escape: 'They fell into a straggling party that were scouting thereabouts, who soon led them to their main body, where it was crime enough that they were English.' The 'tumultuous rabble' assaulted the group, plundered Ussher's belongings and scattered his library, though some local gentry soon came to the rescue, and escorted them to Llantrithyd house. The references here to 'English' garrisons might seem to suggest that Ussher's group was attacked because it was English, or at least non-Welsh, but this would be to stretch the evidence. We might equally well suggest that the location of the incident was in a remote hilly area little visited by local gentry, and class motives might have played a role in provoking resentment. Then again, Ussher and his colleagues were clergy, probably passing

[49] *Gemitus Ecclesiae Cambro-Britannicae, or the Candlesticks Removed* (London, 1654).
[50] *Dictionary of Welsh Biography* (Cardiff, 1959).
[51] Williams, *Recovery, Reorientation and Reformation*, 305–56.
[52] Richard Parr, *Life of the Most Reverend Father in God James Ussher, late lord Archbishop of Armagh, primate and metropolitan of All Ireland* (London, 1686), 58–60.

through a region of incipient puritan sentiment, so anti-clerical protestantism might also be considered as a motive for the attack, as might simple banditry. In summary, the popular discontent in 1645 might have had anti-English ramifications but it is more likely to have represented a familiar British pattern of revulsion at outside extremists who were prolonging the savage war.[53] In addition, Glamorgan was in arms in 1645 precisely because parliamentary forces had just captured the regional capital – which was the English city of Bristol.

It might seem excessive to devote so much attention to one minor episode, but similar qualifications face virtually any apparent expression of 'nationalistic' views during this period. In some cases, there are doubts about the accuracy or objectivity of the observer. In others, the political situation suggests a context other than xenophobia. Finally, most such incidents emerge from 'all-British' rather than specifically Welsh political alignments. This is illustrated by another affair which initially seems to suggest vigorous anti-English sentiment in the Welsh political community. In 1684, the high anglican cleric Thomas Godwyn published an account of the series of misfortunes and persecutions which had destroyed his career.[54] After a number of bitter encounters with non-conformists in Bristol and elsewhere he became rector of the parish of Pwllcrochan near Milford Haven in Pembrokeshire, where he was criticised by a local squire named Essex Meyrick. Meyrick was said to lead a strong anti-English party in that area, and had earlier forced the removal of an English merchant as one of 'the strangers who came thither to eat the countrymen's bread out of their mouths'. Godwyn was arrested, jailed and transported to London, where he wrote his tract. Godwyn's work offers a fascinating account of political rivalries in the popish plot years. However, the value of its statements about nationalistic sentiment is negligible. First, the area in question stood in the very anglicised hundred of Castlemartin, the heart of the 'little England beyond Wales', and probably the least likely setting in Wales for the feelings he describes. Also, the very name of 'Essex' Meyrick indicates the family's century-long client relationship to the aristocratic Devereux family. It is likely that the source of Godwyn's difficulties was not Welsh xenophobia so much as the partisan rivalry then at its peak throughout both England and Wales. He was an indiscreet high-flying Tory moving into an area with a strong radical Whig presence, due in large measure to the 'frequent commerce' from Bristol to Milford and Haverfordwest. In fact Godwyn's conflicts in south Pembrokeshire were quite compar-

---

[53] Jenkins, *Making of a Ruling Class*, 104–17.
[54] Thomas Godwyn *Phanatical Tenderness, or the Charity of the Nonconformists Exemplified* ... (London, 1684), 24–6.

able to his repeated battles with his parish in Bristol, where of course he claims no Welsh element. It seems that the whole issue of Meyrick's anglophobia is invented in order to depict him as a thoroughgoing and irrational fanatic.

III

A Welsh political tradition is very difficult to locate; which is not to say that the pursuit of politics was not a lively theme in Stuart Wales. The country produced some leading figures in the national British politics of the day, though the distinctively Welsh component of their careers would be hard to discern. They were significant because their careers achieved an impact in the pan-British arena. This is true whether we think of courtiers like the marquesses of Worcester or earls of Pembroke, parliamentarians like Sir John Trevor or Sir William Williams, puritan activists like William Erbery, John Jones or Christopher Love, tories like Sir Leoline Jenkins, or churchmen like Archbishop John Williams.[55] Welsh political life was wholly oriented to British conditions and realities, a tendency indicated by the terms used for national identification. The same individuals who would proudly describe themselves as 'Welsh' in personal correspondence saw no contradiction in using the word 'English' in any political context, for example, in commending the nation's armed forces during wartime. In 1720, for example, Cardiganshire squire John Barlow urged his neighbour Lewis Pryse to run for parliament 'for the good of England'. Yet both men would undoubtedly have described themselves as 'Welsh' on other occasions, and both worked for the advancement of Welsh cultural projects.[56]

By the seventeenth century the elite political culture of every Welsh region was based on the monarchy and the church and the assumptions and mythology which had developed around these fundamental institutions. Despite some specific regional manifestations Welsh political commonplaces were overwhelmingly those of the wider Britain, epitomised in ideas such as liberty, property and the protestant interest. Suggestive here is the case of Judge David Jenkins, a royalist activist of pure Welsh origins who maintained strong interests in Welsh culture. When imprisoned by parliament he asserted the foundations of his political beliefs when he offered to die with the Bible in one hand and a copy of Magna Carta in the other.[57] While the sentiment was not novel, it probably epitomised the views of the majority of royalist gentry in both Wales and England. In Welsh political correspondence, Magna

[55] Dodd, *Studies.*   [56] National Library of Wales, Nanteos MS 5.
[57] Oliver Lawson Dick (ed.), *Aubrey's Brief Lives* (London, 1972), 333–4.

Carta was cited far more often than any national concept such as the
Celtic church or the Saxon yoke, a remarkable fact when it is considered
how little the actual baronial document had conceded to the Welsh as
such.

When Welshness was employed as a polemical weapon in political and
ideological argument the objective was far more likely to be the assertion
of British unity than Welsh separatism, with the monarchy as the
primary focus of loyalty. Undoubtedly the policies of the Tudor dynasty
had assisted this identification, especially the relief from discriminatory
legislation against the Welsh. The coming of the new dynasty enhanced
still further the already considerable benefits that the Welsh elites were
reaping from the *de facto* union, and the Reformation offered rich
rewards. During the sixteenth century dynastic service and monastic
lands established the fortunes of most of the leaders of county society
throughout Wales.[58] George Owen expressed a commonplace when he
described the first two Tudor monarchs as the 'deliverers' of Wales. It is
not difficult to understand the strong vested interest which Welsh elites
had in the success of the united British monarchy. Meanwhile, neither
the language nor Welsh culture was in any danger under the current
landed elites, who continued the tradition of bardic patronage until the
later seventeenth century; and the Welsh language flourished in the
Stuart church.[59] Conversely, the political events of these years drew
England and Wales together in common fears of outside enemies. Wales
was increasingly seen as a likely target for foreign foes. The exact
content of particular scares might vary but they usually included Irish
invaders allied to a local Catholic fifth column.[60] In understanding this
it is helpful to view the atlas in contemporary terms, placing due
emphasis on the western sea routes as the primary entry way for
continental invaders. The Irish-Catholic threat from the west remained
the chief reality in Welsh politics throughout the century, and this
perception goes far towards explaining the bitter resentment of Catholic

---

[58] P. R. Roberts, 'The acts of union in Welsh history', *Transactions of the Honourable
   Society of Cymmrodorion* (1974). There is a large literature on the development of the
   Welsh elites under the Tudor state. See for example Howell A. Lloyd, *The Gentry of
   South-west Wales 1540–1640* (Cardiff, 1968); Gareth E. Jones, *The Gentry and the
   Elizabethan State* (Swansea, 1977); G. Dyfnallt Owen, *Wales in the Reign of James I*
   (London, 1988); J. Gwynfor Jones, *Wales and the Tudor State* (Cardiff, 1989); and J.
   Gwynfor Jones (ed.), *Class, Community and Culture in Tudor Wales* (Cardiff, 1989).
[59] George Owen's remark is quoted in Williams, *Recovery, Reorientation and Reformation*,
   8. Roberts, 'The union with England and the identity of anglican Wales', 69–70.
   Roberts also suggests that referring to the dynasty as 'Tudor' was a distinctively Welsh
   usage in the sixteenth century (*History Today*, 36 (1986), 7–13). For the church and
   Welsh culture, see Jenkins, 'The Anglican church and the unity of Britain'.
[60] Williams, *Recovery, Reorientation and Reformation*, 358–80.

peers like the marquesses of Worcester and Barons Powis, and the consequent explosions of anti-papist rage and fear in 1641, 1679 and 1688.[61] Against such a background the suggestion that Wales might somehow fare better as an independent entity, thus forfeiting the invaluable defence against maritime danger, would have been unthinkable. As Dr Colley has emphasised, the new Britain was defined in terms of its common religious foes.[62]

Protestant loyalties and self-preservation were inextricably bound up with the fate of the ruling dynasty. Thus both protestantism and the monarchy now became integral components of Welsh political ideology. In the sixteenth century Welsh history and Arthurian precedent were enlisted for the cause of asserting the imperial independence of the Tudor protestant state. The Stuarts likewise presented themselves as legitimate heirs of this 'British' monarchy in which task they were ably supported by courtiers like the Herberts and Somersets. Under James I it was the Welsh squire Sir William Maurice of Clenennau who was credited with establishing the name of 'Great Britain'. Welsh genealogists delighted in exploring the ramifications of royal ancestry, placing Stuart kings firmly in the succession of Welsh monarchs and heroes. Enderbie's *Cambria Triumphans* traced the pedigree of Charles II to the tenth-century law-giver Hywel Dda, source of most of the royal lines of medieval Wales.

The cult of Welshness often focused on the person of the Prince of Wales, a connection at least as old as Henry VII's choice of the name 'Arthur' for his eldest son in 1486. The suggestion was clearly that the 'princes' were successors not just to the independent monarchs of medieval Wales but also to the more speculative predecessors derived from Arthurian romance and Geoffrey of Monmouth (on whom Percy Enderbie drew copiously). The association of the princely title with Welsh identity and tradition is rarely emphasised by historians discussing post-Tudor Wales, but it was critically important during the seventeenth century, especially when James I was anxious to develop the 'British' symbolism to justify his rule over the three kingdoms.[63] He

---

[61] Philip Jenkins, 'Anti-popery on the Welsh marches in the seventeenth century', *Historical Journal* 23: 2 (1980), 275–93; Jenkins, *Modern Wales*, 115–44; *A Great Discovery of a Damnable Plot at Raglan Castle, in Monmouthshire* ... (London, 1641). Welsh–Irish relations are discussed in Dodd, *Studies*, 76–109.

[62] Colley, 'Britishness and otherness'.

[63] For the Welsh aspects of the new monarchy, see the important article by P. R. Roberts on 'The union with England and the identity of "Anglican" Wales'. The institution of the Prince of Wales is discussed in Dodd, *Studies*, 51; Dodd, 'Pattern of politics'. The specifically Welsh national context of the prince's title is suggested by a work like Burton's 1695 *History* of Wales, which includes brief biographical sketches of all those who had held the title from the medieval princes onwards.

successively invested two of his sons as prince of Wales – Henry in 1610, Charles in 1616 – and, on both occasions, the ceremonial drew heavily on Welsh imagery: the mountain of 'Craig-Eriri', a plethora of 'goats and Welsh speeches'. Charles' elevation was marked by a 'solemnity' at Ludlow, the seat of the Council in the Marches and thus the nearest thing available to a 'Welsh capital'. One telling incident occurred in October 1642 at the marquess of Worcester's castle at Raglan, in Monmouthshire, when the twelve-year-old Charles, prince of Wales, arrived to muster support and money for the king's cause from his principality.[64] Surrounded by Worcester's tapestries 'full of lively figures and ancient British stories', the courtiers were presented with the traditional Welsh drink, metheglin. Bardic poetry and Welsh prophecy undoubtedly formed part of the entertainment, as both were especially cultivated in the Somerset household.[65] In this ultra-patriotic atmosphere, Charles heard 'loving and loyal' speeches, asserting that the Britons were 'the true remaining and only one people of this land'. They would therefore do their patriotic duty to help 'upon any lawful design to the maintenance of justice, piety and religion, and defend their persons from all malignants and enemies'. The rhetorical framework appears set to assert nationalism, but the conclusion is resolutely unionist. A similar conclusion emerges from another apparent outbreak of patriotic sentiment, which occurred in 1695 and 1696 following William III's grant of crown lordships in north Wales to his favourite, the earl of Portland. Portland would thus become a 'Dutch prince of Wales', and the issue brought together all shades of anti-court opposition. A particularly daring contribution to the debate was made by Robert Price who was hailed in opposition pamphlets as a 'bold Briton', the 'patriot of his native country', and whose speeches defended *Gloria Cambriae* against a tyrannical monarchy. These texts made frequent reference to Welsh rights and liberties, usurped by the English crown and church over the centuries, and cited a series of historical manifestations of Welsh pride, such as Sir William Williams' remark that 'The Welsh were never subject to any but God and the King, and that none showed their allegiance more than the Welsh.'[66]

---

[64] *A Loving and Loyal Speech Spoken unto the Excellency of our Noble Prince Charles, by Sir Hugh Vaughan the 2 of October at Raglan Castle in Monmouthshire in Wales* ... (London, 1642), 2–4.

[65] It would be noted after the castle's fall in 1646 that 'Never was there an old house so pulled down by prophecies, ushered into its ruin by predictions, and so laid hold upon by signs and tokens': Thomas Bayly, *Worcester's Apothegmes, or Witty Sayings of the Right Honourable Henry late Marquess and Earl of Worcester* (London, 1650), 81.

[66] *Gloria Cambriae, or the Speech of a Bold Briton against a Dutch Prince of Wales* (London, 1702); Edmund Curll, *Life of the Late Right Honourable Robert Price Esq.* (London, 1734), 12–13; see Jenkins, *Foundations of Modern Wales*, 153.

It is tempting to see these outbursts as at least proto-nationalistic –
although even here the boast is that the Welsh are ultra-loyal to the
British monarchy.[67] But once again the rhetoric is misleading, and
Price's lengthy career suggests less the 'bold Briton' than the lifelong
'country' activist who happened to be using a 'patriotic' Welsh stance
which seemed expedient. At another point, he would even remind
William's court that 'I would have you consider we are Englishmen, and
must like patriots stand by our country, and not suffer it to be a tributary
to strangers.' Apparently no contradiction existed in claiming simultaneously to be 'English', 'Welsh', a 'Briton' and a 'patriot', an ideological
contortion that is made possible only by the dynastic loyalty which
subsumed Welshness under 'Britishness'. While the two countries never
approached the structure of a true 'composite monarchy' on Continental lines, at least the princely cult kept a Welsh political identity in
being.[68] The tradition can be traced into the next century in the
opposition 'patriot' propaganda associated with the court of Prince
Frederick in the 1730s.[69]

A similar development can be traced in the 'Saxon yoke' theme
outlined above, which seemed to offer a rhetoric ideally suited to Welsh
patriotic dissidence, if not separatism. However, the idea was generally
employed in 'British' rather than Welsh interests. This is suggested by
the work of John Lewis of Glascrug, Cardiganshire, who in 1646 wrote
the *Parliament Explained to Wales*.[70] This tract strongly asserts Welsh
interests, for example advocating the expansion of higher education in
the country. Lewis also offers a patriotic view of Welsh history and the
superior claims of the Celtic church. Using Bede among other medieval
sources, he depicts the British church standing firm against St Augustine's Roman and Catholic mission, and the ensuing massacre of the
Welsh monks at Bangor. This could be taken to argue for Welsh
ecclesiastical independence. In Lewis' work, however, the primitive
incident is used rather to strike at Catholicism, and to argue for the
propagation of the gospel under the auspices of the British state and its
parliament. Once this was achieved, Wales would regain its early glory;

---

[67] Certainly, gentry correspondence of the time suggests much 'nationalist' hostility to
William III in Wales. Also in 1696, there was a dispute over the Powis lands in
Montgomeryshire which again involved one of William's courtiers; and it was regarded
as desirable to have the case heard by a Middlesex jury, as 'the ancient Britons have no
kindness for the Dutch': Smith, *Herbert Correspondence*, 45.

[68] For European analogies, compare J. H. Elliott, 'A Europe of composite monarchies',
Past & Present, 137 (1992), 48–71.

[69] Philip Jenkins, 'Jacobites and freemasons in eighteenth-century Wales', *Welsh History
Review*, 9 (1979), 391–406.

[70] John Lewis, *Contemplations upon these Times, or, the Parliament explained to Wales ...*
(London, 1646), 27–33.

and in the last days, it was likely that the Welsh 'will be employed to overthrow Antichrist'. The notion of a special eschatological role for the Welsh nation can be traced at least as far back as the Lollards.[71]

This theme of the ancient protestantism of Wales recurs in Whig writings, where it is employed to argue against ecclesiastical hierarchy and 'priestcraft', but again, without a hint of separatism. In the Popish Plot years a radical Whig tract advocated the cause of the duke of Monmouth by emphasising the links of his title with this Welsh setting. Monmouth was 'a town so nearly allied to the most ancient Britons, the first Christians of this island, and is still a very good and true protestant town, much beloved by most people, especially by all loyal protestants, far above the great city of York itself, or any other towns in his majesty's dominions'[72] (critics parodied Monmouth's claim to be 'ap Carlo', the Welsh form of 'son of Charles').[73] The potentially nationalistic rhetoric of the Saxon yoke was thus enlisted for various British parties and causes, and increasingly found itself assimilated to those ideas. This process finds an absurd conclusion in the rhetoric of Robert Price, who wished to apply currently popular Whig contract theory to the Welsh situation. He does indeed claim the existence of a 'Welsh original contract' but this is located in the legendary incident when Edward I raised his infant son to be 'prince of Wales' at Caernarfon Castle.[74]

We will often find this apparent paradox. Welsh patriotism is a theme that occurs in a remarkable variety of political causes, often employing a rhetoric with strong nationalistic undercurrents, but these were ignored in practice. This especially applies to the celebration of the popular holiday of St David's Day, which became the partisan weapon of various British political causes. In the 1640s the feast acquired strongly royalist associations, natural enough in view of the puritan hostility to saints' days of any kind.[75] Later in the century the celebration of 'Wales' became especially attached to the person of the prince of Wales. But who exactly was this prince? Jacobites naturally had their own views on this question after 1688, and held appropriate pro-Stuart celebrations on the first of March.[76] The political rhetoric was predictable, but it is interesting that the jacobites felt that the festival was sufficiently important to be worth stealing. In response Whig groups like the London-based Society of Ancient Britons (1715) held their own

---

[71] Williams, *Recovery, Reorientation and Reformation*, 455.
[72] *Advice to the men of Monmouth Concerning the Present Times* (London, 1681).
[73] Harold Love (ed.), *The Penguin Book of Restoration Verse* (London: Penguin, 1968), 115.
[74] *Gloria Cambriae*.
[75] Thomas Morgan, *The Welchmen's Jubilee to the Honour of Saint David* (London, 1642).
[76] Jenkins, *Making of a Ruling Class*, 210; Jenkins, 'Jacobites and freemasons'.

counter-demonstrations to assert Hanoverian claims. Welsh causes and issues were wholly subsumed under the political divisions of a wider Britain.

IV

Why was cultural distinctiveness not translated into political identity, as had seemed so likely in the fifteenth century? Geography undoubtedly played a role. Throughout its history the centres of wealth and landed power in Wales had especially lain in lowland or coastal areas like the southern parts of Monmouthshire, Pembrokeshire and Glamorgan, or the eastern hundreds of Denbighshire and Montgomeryshire.[77] These were also the regions most accessible to English contacts, and influences had been steadily absorbed over the centuries. They were the areas in which we find a villa economy in the Roman period, manorial farming in the Middle Ages and substantial gentry houses under the Stuarts: it is here that the most influential magnate families had their seats, like the Herberts, Somersets, Mansells, Mostyns and Philipps. Outside these regions, Welsh language and culture might thrive with fewer challenges, but by definition the upland fastnesses were far removed from social or political influence. The potential for anglicisation was therefore enormous, and the Acts of Union represented only one stage in a lengthy process. Already in the fifteenth century, the influence of Bristol and Chester over their Welsh hinterlands was a powerful reality, as was the Welsh presence in London and Oxford.[78] By the 1530s, there had already been a period of over two centuries in which Welsh lords and squires had viewed their political fortunes in an Anglo-Welsh context, with a particular emphasis on military service.

Geography was also crucial in preventing the emergence of any sort of Welsh unification which might have provided a counterbalance to these strong centrifugal trends. It is often assumed, rather than demonstrated, that 'Wales' in a given period represents a distinct unit, and thus an appropriate subject for analysis, whereas it is all but impossible to find unity or consistency beyond that provided by the language. Historically, Wales survives because of difficulties of transportation and communication which make most of the country inaccessible from England; but these same features also create fundamental and quite intractable internal divisions. The most obvious schism is that between north and south, a point clearly indicated by the progress of the civil wars in Wales,

[77] Jenkins, *Modern Wales*, 1–13.
[78] Williams, *Recovery, Reorientation and Reformation*.

which involved two distinct and barely related series of campaigns.[79] The process of industrialisation in Wales involved two quite unrelated centres, one in the south-eastern shires of Glamorgan and Monmouth, and another north-eastern focus in the counties of Denbigh and Flint.[80] Since the eighteenth century every scheme for national structures in Wales has recognised this division. Below this fundamental division Wales was an agglomeration of many different societies and regions which lacked an urban centre to unite disparate areas.[81] Without a Welsh city the country's regions looked towards metropolitan centres across the border – chiefly to Chester, Shrewsbury and Bristol. Marriage trends followed economic links, so that the landed houses of the south became closely intertwined with the gentry of Somerset or Gloucestershire, just as their northern counterparts were forming family ties in Staffordshire and Cheshire. Roughly, this led to the creation of three quite distinct regions, a pattern that can be traced through many aspects of social and cultural life.[82] Even less promising for any prospect of national development, these 'metropolitan' regions were defined and maintained in terms of English towns and trading networks.

Nor were there any 'national' structures or institutions to define or characterise Welshness; nothing which might even hope to overcome the enormous difficulties posed by geography. Henry VIII had formally snuffed out any legal distinctions or peculiarities that Wales might formerly have possessed, leaving a mere component of England, 'incorporated, united and annexed'. There was neither a Welsh parliament nor a separate church, nor even a metropolitan to coordinate the activities of the four Welsh dioceses.[83] Apart from the 'prince of Wales', distinctive institutions were scarce. Though a Council of Wales and the Marches survived until 1689, it impinged little on the everyday affairs of any section of Welsh society after 1640.[84] A Welsh Great Sessions was used by judges as a forum for presenting their views on society and politics, but it never produced a glittering local bar with its attendant culture on the lines of Georgian Dublin or Edinburgh. In education there was from Tudor times something like a Welsh 'university college'; but this was Jesus College, Oxford, rather than any local institution.

---

[79] Norman Tucker, *North Wales in the Civil War* (Denbigh, 1958); Dodd, *Studies*; Jenkins, *Foundations of Modern Wales*, 3–42. For regional divisions, see Kearney, *British Isles*, 117.

[80] Jenkins, *Modern Wales*, 211–56.

[81] *Ibid.*, 34–7.   [82] *Ibid.*, 120–3, 145–8.

[83] David Walker (ed.), *History of the Church in Wales*, Church in Wales (1976). Compare the remarks of Peter Roberts, above, 8–13.

[84] Penry Williams, *The Council in the Marches of Wales under Elizabeth I* (Cardiff, 1958).

Early modern Wales lacked most of the characteristic features of nationhood, even those of a nation in subjection.

The consequence might be suggested by considering the situation of a hypothetical landed family in seventeenth-century Caernarvonshire. It was in the highest degree unlikely that this house would have any relationships whatever, social or kin-based, with any family from the southern half of Wales, while there might be extensive contacts with gentry from Cheshire or Staffordshire. The only likely locations for social interaction with southerners would be in Oxford or London, and in both cases northern and southern Welsh tended to maintain a distance. In addition, the economic fate and political alignments of Chester would be a matter of great moment to the northern house, while the mere existence of Swansea or Brecon was a fact of minimal significance. In political terms, there might be several possible spheres of action, depending on the wealth and aspirations of the house in question, ranging from the parish or hundred, to the county and region, and to the nation at large. There simply was no intermediate 'Welsh dimension'. Perhaps such a thing was not conceivable until the coming of the railways.[85]

V

A number of thoughtful discussions of the state of historical writing in Wales have recently appeared, most of which propose agendas for future research.[86] These articles suggest the distinctive strengths of Welsh historical writing such as its pioneering interest in matters such as labour and social movements, and its exploration of the subtle relationships between class, religion, language and ethnicity. All these issues are critical in their way, but there are still long periods of political history which have not received adequate attention or discussion. Evans, for example, notes that the founders of the Welsh historiographical tradition were rarely comfortable with the political study of this non-nation: 'historians were obsessed with states and the documents that they generated; post-conquest Welsh history was in danger of becoming merely a postscript to a failed instance of state-building.[87] More recently, much excellent work has been done on the political history of Wales from the industrial revolution onwards, but the coverage of the

---

[85] For the revolutionary effects of the railways on Welsh life, see Jenkins, *Modern Wales*, 225–8, 244–6.

[86] See, for example, Neil, Evans, 'Writing the social history of modern Wales', *Social History*, 17: 3 (1992), 479–92; compare Jones, 'Beyond identity'.

[87] Evans, 'Writing', 479.

seventeenth and eighteenth centuries leaves much to be desired, and the period is too often dismissed as a time of sterile feuds between landed families. Elite politics are rarely treated with great sympathy or attention. Much of the work there addresses local communities with little regard for the national context. The ideological assumptions of Welsh political culture are often ignored or taken for granted. One frequent criticism is the lack of comparative study, so that it is difficult to tell whether, for example, the expression of paternalistic ideas by a Welsh figure should be presumed to be distinctively Welsh, or if it merely reflected the commonplaces of the wider British society. Issues of national 'British' politics or ideology, such as attitudes towards the monarchy or the national church, are rarely felt to be sufficiently relevant to Welsh conditions to require comment. The consequence is that political conditions and ideologies in Wales are rarely related to the British situation. This permits quite inaccurate generalisations to be made about the degree of Welsh distinctiveness. For example, it has been argued here that recent scholarly accounts tend greatly to exaggerate the pace of anglicisation among Welsh cultural elites, the degree of the cultural and linguistic gulf between rich and poor in this era, and the hostility of the established church towards the Welsh language. Taken together such convenient myths appear to provide an acceptable explanation for the apparent acquiescence of Celtic Wales under the 'English Yoke'. The resulting picture has achieved acceptance in part because it meshes well with modern nationalistic concerns, and especially because it depicts the common people of Wales as the bearers and guardians of national identity.

However, the reality of seventeenth-century Wales was quite different from this picture in most respects, and other interpretations are required. What is needed above all is an understanding of the political culture of this society, which explains how Welsh elites accepted as their own such emerging British institutions as the church and monarchy, and yet shaped them to fit local concerns and traditions. Only thus can we explain how the 'oldest colony' became so thoroughly integrated into the new nation.

8   Scottish identity in the seventeenth century

Keith M. Brown

The seventeenth century marks a crucial watershed in the long re-drawing of the Scottish identity between the Reformation and the Enlightenment. During that 200 year period, from c. 1560 to c. 1760, the fundamental features of what had been the medieval Scottish identity were given new shape by the changing relationship with England that led to Scotland being assimilated into Great Britain in 1707 and by the process of creating a protestant community. These two factors, statehood and religion, are at the core of all nation-state formation in the early modern period, and each played a considerable part in the forging of national identity. Until the mid sixteenth century, the Scots were Roman Catholic and were loyal to their own Stewart kings who ruled over what was an emerging nation-state. By the latter half of the eighteenth century, the Scots were overwhelmingly protestant, being predominantly Calvinist presbyterians, while their loyalty was now divided between an historic Scottish nation and a new British state with a growing imperial role in the world.[1] These two very profound changes largely took place on either side of the seventeenth-century regal union, the irrevocable shift towards protestantism being made between 1560 and c. 1600, while the successful reorientation towards a unionist and British perspective was completed between 1707 and c. 1760. What existed in the middle of these two fairly distinct phases was the regal union, a period delineated by the union of the crowns in 1603 and the union of the parliaments in 1707.[2]

Seventeenth-century Scots, therefore, inhabited a multi-state aggregate of kingdoms, one they shared with the English, Irish and Welsh.

I would like to thank Brendan Bradshaw, Roger Mason and Colin Kidd for their helpful comments and suggestions in the preparation of this chapter.

[1] L. Colley, *Britons. The forging of the nation, 1707–1832* (New York and London, 1992), and C. Kidd, *Subverting Scotland's Past. Scottish Whig historians and the creation of an Anglo-British identity* (Cambridge, 1993).

[2] The best analysis of the seventeenth-century origins of the British state is B. P. Levack, *The Formation of the British State. England, Scotland, and the Union 1603–1707* (Oxford, 1987).

Unlike the Irish and Welsh, Scots were in no sense subordinate to the English crown, although during the 1650s Scotland was brutally conquered and occupied by English troops.[3] However, while the Scots and English enjoyed equal legal status as free subjects of an imperial monarchy within which the distinct powers of the Scottish and English crowns were entirely separate, the reality was that political independence was compromised in 1603.[4] The king himself moved to England and monarchs made only brief visits to their northern kingdoms in 1617, 1633, 1641 and 1650-1. The royal court also went south, exposing the small Scottish elite to a court culture that increasingly was English in its interests and values. At the same time, the absence of a resident court with a role as a cultural patron meant that the crown was unable to use the court to project its own ideology to much effect within Scotland. Political faction continued to be grounded in the localities and in Edinburgh, but English politicians like the duke of Buckingham in the 1620s, the earl of Clarendon in the 1660s, and Lord Godolphin in the 1700s all became influential players in Scottish affairs. Foreign policy was decided at court by the king and his ministers, most of whom were English, and was shaped largely by English interests like the East India Company and in response to pressures from the English parliament. Thus Scotland found itself at war with Spain in the 1620s as a consequence of a policy pursued by Buckingham and a powerful lobby in the House of Commons, while in the 1690s the Company of Scotland was ruined by a combination of its own incompetence and English strategic and commercial interests. Increasingly, therefore, Scottish trade and diplomacy was twisted into patterns set in London. What this dependence adds up to is something very like a satellite state, or even a province, particularly after 1651 when England imposed itself on Scotland in a way that meant the lesson would not be forgotten even after the occupying garrisons were withdrawn a decade later.[5] The insecurity

[3] F. Dow, *Cromwellian Scotland 1651–1660* (Edinburgh, 1979) adequately describes the occupation as a military and administrative exercise, but further work requires to be done in explaining the effect of conquest on Scottish self-confidence. The shift in the relationship is clear from R. Hutton, *The British Republic 1649–60* (Basingstoke, 1990). The republican experiment of the 1650s left no-one with any enthusiasm for Britain in Scotland or in England, D. Hirst, 'The English republic and the meaning of Britain', in B. Bradshaw and J. Morrill (eds.), *The British Problem c. 1534–1707* (Basingstoke, 1996), 192–219.

[4] Some of the issues arising from the union are discussed in E. J. Cowan, 'The union of the crowns and the crisis of the constitution in 17th century Scotland', in S. Dysvik, K. Mykland and J. Oldervoll (eds.), *The Satellite State* (Bergen, 1979), 121–40.

[5] I have explored most of these issues in K. M. Brown, *Kingdom or Province? Scotland and the Regal Union, 1603–1715* (Basingstoke, 1992); alternatively see W. Ferguson, *Scotland's Relations with England: a survey to 1707* (Edinburgh, 1977), and R. Mitchison, *Lordship to Patronage. Scotland 1603–1745* (London, 1983).

that this appearance of provinciality generated was prevalent among contemporaries. In the 1703 parliamentary session Andrew Fletcher of Saltoun raged against English influence which had blighted the last hundred years, arguing that English ministers 'have had so visible an influence upon our whole administration, that we have from that time appeared to the rest of the world more like a conquered province than a free independent people'.[6] But Scotland was not a satellite state or a province, and it remained an independent kingdom with its own parliament, administration and army. Scots also had influence with their London-based kings, participating in court politics and helping to shape British foreign and commercial policies. It was this ambiguous position within the British multistate system of the seventeenth century that makes it difficult to pin-point the ways in which the Scottish state impinged on national identity. That Scottish state was less tangible than the English state, not only because it was more rudimentary, operating on minimalist principles, but also because the centre was diffuse, lacking a definite locale either physically or intellectually.

Since the fourteenth century the idea of the Scottish nation had been identified with the line of monarchs descended from King Fergus who allegedly founded the kingdom in the fourth century BC. Although subjected to savage criticism in the course of the sixteenth century, the Scots stuck by the legend of their ancient kings throughout the seventeenth century, employing them either to reinforce royalist ideas of authority, or to demonstrate the workings of George Buchanan's 'ancient constitution'. One way or another, the ancient kings continued to have a use as patriotic icons. Yet at the same time, the living monarchy was increasingly distanced from Scotland, and James VI's efforts to fashion a new mythology of British kingship that would embrace the Scots within an enlarged imperium failed. Little attention was devoted to reinterpreting Scottish kingship, and as absentees without a resident court, it was difficult for kings to devise a particularly Scottish royalist image to suit the new circumstances of the regal union.[7] In a sense all that was left was the ancient king lists, and beliefs in their efficacy became something of a test of loyalty in the 1680s among shrill royalists like Sir George Mackenzie of Roeshaugh.[8] However, by the end of the century the Stewart dynasty and the Scots had parted company.

[6] *Andrew Fletcher of Saltoun. Selected political writings and speeches*, ed., D. Daiches (Edinburgh, 1979), 70.

[7] Some of these issues are addressed in K. M. Brown, 'The vanishing emperor. British kingship in the seventeenth century', in R. A. Mason (ed.), *Scots and Britons* (Cambridge, 1994), 58–87.

[8] S. Bruce and S. Yearly, 'The social construction of tradition: the restoration portraits and the kings of Scotland', in D. McCrone, S. Kendrick and P. Straw (eds.), *The Making*

Monarchy remained useful, but monarchs were no longer figures invested with popular notions of nationhood. The divorce between the monarchy and the nation was so complete that parliament was content to offer the crown to a Dutch adventurer in 1689, and recognised the claims of a minor German princeling in 1707. It was in a desperate effort to heal this rupture between the house of Stewart and the Scottish nation that the jacobites reinvented the Stewart dynasty in the eighteenth century, cloaking it in a subversive and patriotic rhetoric that had a degree of popular appeal among sections of the community alienated by the union settlement of 1707.[9] However, the jacobites were an increasingly marginalised group, intellectually and geographically, and the great majority of the population was unmoved by their rhetoric. Insofar as the Stewarts still had an influence in shaping national identity, it was in sowing division and in encouraging the notion of the enemy within. Perhaps the most enduring effect of the survival of jacobitism was to push eighteenth-century Scots, Lowlanders in particular, into a closer sense of identity with the English, and loyalty to the whig regime that governed Britain.[10]

The Scottish parliament has suffered greatly from almost three centuries of unionist propaganda that has portrayed it as a peripheral, unsophisticated, corrupt and subservient body. More recent research is beginning to suggest that the Scottish parliament throughout the later middle ages, and right up until 1707, was not only an effective legislator with increasingly developed procedural mechanisms, but did offer a very real arena for national debate.[11] Successive monarchs found that parliament was not simply an instrument of government, and this was as true for fifteenth-century kings like James I and James III, as for James VI in the late sixteenth century, or James VII and William II in the seventeenth century. It was precisely because Queen Anne's ministers could not control parliament that a means was found to get rid of it in 1707.[12] None of this is to deny that kings were successful at managing parliament, but it required considerable political skill and patronage

of Scotland: nation, culture and social change (Edinburgh, 1989), 175–88; Kidd, Subverting Scotland's Past, 27.

[9] H. M. H. Pittock, The Invention of Tradition. The Stewart myth and the Scottish identity, 1638 to the present (London, 1991); W. Donaldson, The Jacobite Song. Political myth and national identity (Aberdeen, 1988).

[10] Colley, Britons, 71–85.

[11] Most notably J. Goodare, 'Parliament and society in Scotland, 1560–1603' (University of Edinburgh unpublished Ph.D. 1989); and J. R. Young, The Scottish Parliament 1639–1660. A political and constitutional analysis (Edinburgh, 1996).

[12] P. W. J. Riley, The Union of Scotland and England (Manchester, 1978), and for a more extreme view see P. H. Scott, Andrew Fletcher of Saltoun and the Treaty of Union (Edinburgh, 1992).

resources to provide a satisfactory level of control. At moments of particular national resentment against government, management simply broke down: in the Reformation parliament of 1560 and in the 1567 parliament that completed the protestant revolution; in the covenanting parliaments of 1639 through to 1650; in the 1689 and 1690 sessions of the Convention parliament; and between 1702 and 1705.[13] Parliament was able to offer a forum in which the political nation expressed itself, and even the notorious 1633 parliament, when Charles I enforced the strictest form of censorship and control, created an opportunity for men to congregate and discuss their grievances in private, if not within Parliament House.[14] No other institution acted as such a comprehensive point of contact for the political elite. The court no longer fulfilled the role of the principal meeting place for a diverse body of opinion, and the general assembly tended to be geographically unrepresentative, besides which it did not meet at all between 1617 and 1638 nor again between 1653 and 1690. Among the political elite there was widespread recognition that parliament expressed the will of the community, or what in the sixteenth century had been described as the commonweal, while its constitutional role was progressively secured by the revolutionary settlements of 1560, 1567, 1641 and 1689–90. As Andrew Fletcher of Saltoun rightly recognised, it was parliament that lay at the heart of Scotland's political identity in the seventeenth century, hence his identification of patriotism and the struggle against the control of parliament by the crown and its English ministers – 'dare any man say he is a Scotsman, and refuse his consent to reduce the government of this nation?'[15]

Further institutional scaffolding on which to sustain a national identity was provided by the system of courts, a legal profession and Scots law. Around the time of the union of the crowns in 1603, Sir Thomas Craig finished writing *Jus Feudale* in which he argued that Scots law and English common law drew on a similar source in feudal law. He developed his idea in *De Union Regnorum Britanniae*, written in

---

[13] For the 1640s see Young, *The Scottish parliament, 1639–1661*; the uncontrollable nature of the convention parliament is clear from J. Halliday, 'The Club and the revolution in Scotland 1689–90', *Scottish Historical Review*, 45 (1966), 143–59; and the loss of crown control in the sessions of 1703 to 1705 is analysed in Riley, *Union of Scotland and England*. Even Restoration parliaments were far from being entirely supine, see J. Patrick, 'The origins of opposition to Lauderdale in the Scottish parliament of 1673', *Scottish Historical Review*, 53 (1974), 1–21.

[14] The 1633 parliament awaits a close analysis, but there is a brief account in A. I. Macinnes, *Charles I and the Making of the Covenanting Movement, 1625–1641* (Edinburgh, 1991), 86–9; also M. Lee, *The Road to Revolution. Scotland under Charles I, 1625–37* (Edinburgh, 1985), 131–3.

[15] Daiches, *Fletcher of Saltoun*, 73.

1605 when unionist enthusiasm at court remained high, arguing that
legal union was not necessary for political union to succeed since the
two systems of law already were compatible. More than half a century
later James Dalrymple of Stair also recognised that Scots law was
something of a 'mixed system' owing a debt to English common law.
Stair too recognised that 'there exists a fundamental identity between
the principles underlying the legal systems of the two countries', but was
still sufficiently patriotic to be able to boast that the legal process and
the judicial procedure of Scotland were 'better than those used in any
other country I know of'.[16] However, while it is true that certain aspects
of feudal law were common throughout Britain, and even throughout
north-western Europe, English common law was moulded by a curious
blend of quaint customs and idiosyncratic respect for precedent that was
distinct from the Roman law found throughout most of Europe,
including Scotland, where its influence was growing. Scottish lawyers,
therefore, looked to the continent for inspiration. While only a tiny
handful of advocates trained in the English Inns of Court, as many as 40
per cent of the admissions to the faculty of advocates between 1660 and
1750 had studied in Dutch universities.[17] Legal union not only failed to
attract support among Scottish or English lawyers, but the two legal
systems moved further apart over the course of the century.[18] Scottish
legal institutions like the court of session and the court of justiciary grew
in confidence, the faculty of advocates expanded considerably, crown
legal officers like the lord advocate, justice general, justice clerk and
solicitor general became well established, the register of sasines was set
up in 1617, and the advocates library was founded in 1680.[19] Even the

---

[16] Sir Thomas Craig, *The Jus Feudale*, tr. J. A. Clyde (2 vols., Edinburgh, 1934); Sir T.
Craig, *De Unione Regnorum Britanniae Tracttatus*, ed. C. S. Terry, Scottish History
Society, 1st ser., 60 (Edinburgh, 1909), ix; W. D. H. Sellar, 'English law as source', in
Stair's Tercentenary Studies, 140–51.

[17] Only two of the 10,917 entrants to the Inns of Court between 1590 and 1639 were
Scots, W. R. Prest, *The Inns of Court under Elizabeth and the Early Stuarts, 1590–1640*
(London, 1972), 32–3. For the Dutch connection see R. Feenstra, 'Scottish-Dutch
legal relations in the seventeenth and eighteenth centuries', in T. C. Smout (ed.),
Scotland and Europe 1200–1850 (Edinburgh, 1986), 128–42.

[18] The most persuasive discussion of legal union and the problems associated with it is
Levack, *Formation of the British State*, 68–101, and see his 'The proposed union of
English law and Scots law in the seventeenth century', *Juridical Review*, n.s., 20 (1975),
97–115, and 'English law, Scots law and the union, 1603–1707', in A. Harding (ed.),
Lawmaking and Lawmakers in British History (London, 1980), 105–19. Also of use is
B. Galloway, *The Union of England and Scotland 1603–1608* (Edinburgh, 1986), 38–41.

[19] On the development of the legal profession G. Donaldson, 'The legal profession in
Scottish society in the sixteenth and seventeenth centuries', *Juridical Review*, n.s., 21
(1976), 1–19; A. Murdoch, 'The advocates, the law and the nation in early modern
Scotland', in W. Prest (ed.), *Lawyers in Early Modern Europe and America* (London,

increase in the survival of seventeenth-century court records points to better record keeping and an increase in professionalism.[20] At the same time the intensely localised nature of the greater part of judicial administration ensured that the system of justice remained rooted in local communities.[21]

Equally important was the significant advance made in writing down the law. It was not until the first decade of the seventeenth century that Sir John Skene compiled a legal dictionary, *De Verborum Significatione* (1597), and completed editing *Regiam Majestatem* and *Quoniam Attachiamenta* (1609) as well as his edition of statute law.[22] Meanwhile, the collecting and editing of decisions, which Sir James Balfour of Pittendreich began in the later sixteenth century, was continued by Sir Thomas Hope, Charles I's lord advocate.[23] However, it was Stair's *Institutions of the Law of Scotland*, published in 1681, that brought Scots law within a coherent framework. Stair set out to avoid the self-congratulatory insularity of the English common lawyers, writing that 'No man can be a knowing lawyer in any nation, who hath not well pondered and digested in his mind the common law of the world.'[24] It was, therefore, with one eye on the broader European community that Stair sought to provide Scots law with a rational and Calvinist philosophy that was both peculiar to Scotland, for example he retained the ancient constitution, and was linked to mainstream European thought.[25]

Scotland was dominated by its landed aristocracy, the peerage and those armigerous heads of houses who held their land freehold of the king, and it was this group that largely defined the nation's public

1981), 147–63; N. Phillipson, 'The social structure of the faculty of advocates in Scotland, 1661–1840', in Harding (ed.), *Law-making and Law-makers*, 147–63.

[20] *Handlist of Records for the Study of Crime in Early Modern Scotland (to 1747)* compiled by P. Rayner, B. Lenman and G. Parker, List and Index Society, 16 (1982).

[21] S. J. Davies, 'The court and the Scottish legal system 1600–1747: the case of Stirlingshire', in V. A. C. Gatrell, B. Lenman and G. Parker (eds.), *Crime and the Law. The social history of crime in Western Europe since 1500* (London, 1980), 120–54.

[22] *Regiam Majestatem and Quoniam Attachiamenta, Based on the Text of Sir John Skene* (ed.), T. M. Cooper, Stair Society, 11 (Edinburgh, 1947).

[23] *Hope's Major Practicks, 1606–1633* (ed.), J. A. Clyde, 2 vols., Stair Society, ii–iii (Edinburgh, 1937–8). These remained unpublished until the eighteenth century.

[24] Sir James Dalrymple of Stair, *Institutions of the Law of Scotland* (ed.), D. M. Walker (Glasgow and Edinburgh, 1981), 7.

[25] G. M. Hutton, 'Stair's philosophic precursors', and P. G. Stein, 'Stair's general concepts', both in *Stair Tercentenary Studies* (ed.), D. M. Walker, Stair Society, 33 (Edinburgh, 1981), 87–99 and 181–7; P. Stein, 'Law and society in eighteenth-century Scottish thought', in N. Phillipson and R. Mitchinson (eds.), *Scotland in the Age of Improvement. Essays in Scottish history in the eighteenth century* (Edinburgh,, 1970), 148–68; G. Donaldson, 'Stair's Scotland: the intellectual heritage', *Juridical Review* (1981), 128–45.

culture.[26] Englishmen from Sir Anthony Weldon at the beginning of the century to Sir Edward Seton a hundred years later venomously ridiculed the Scots, projecting a caricature image of poor, greedy, uncouth and unwashed petty noblemen who made their way to England in search of rich pickings.[27] Some of these allegations undoubtedly were true, partly because Scottish noblemen were disadvantaged in London by an adverse exchange rate, and also because the disproportionately large Scottish nobility was on average poorer. Yet while noblemen were drawn to London, the Scots proved very resistant to the threat posed by anglicisation.[28] The resilience of a strong Scottish identity among the nobility does not mean they were insular. A university education ensured that they formed a literate and cultured elite with the wealth to travel on the continent, to seek out the latest fashions in architecture for their castles and country houses which were stuffed with imported luxuries (even a remote highland chief like Sir Duncan Campbell of Glenorchy surrounded himself with high quality furnishings),[29] and to investigate and acquire new technology, whether in arms, domestic utensils or in agricultural methods. What this adds up to is an emphatic statement of self-confidence, an assertion that these noblemen shared most of the common cultural assumptions of the European aristocracy. Alongside this cosmopolitan image went a very intense relationship with their own localities. Interest in estate management and the building of country houses, alongside a preference for estate consolidation and the strict entail which was introduced in 1685, indicate a determination to maintain a living presence in the countryside,[30] while the determination to hold onto private jurisdictions suggests that enormous importance remained vested in preserving the enhancing local and private

---

[26] Brown, *Kingdom or Province?*, 33–59 anatomises the political elite.

[27] Sir A. Weldon, 'A perfect description of the people and country of Scotland', in W. Scott (ed.), *The Secret History of the Court of James the First* (2 vols., Edinburgh, 1811), ii, 75–89. G. P. R. James (ed.), *The Vernon Letters* (3 vols., London, 1841), ii, 408.

[28] The interaction of the Scottish nobility with their English counterparts is discussed at greater length in K. M. Brown, 'The Scottish aristocracy, anglicization and the court, 1603–38', *The Historical Journal*, 36 (1993), 543–76; K. M. Brown, 'The origins of a British aristocracy: elite integration and its limitations before the treaty of union', in S. Ellis and S. Barber (eds.), *Conquest and Union. Fashioning a British State, 1485–1725* (Harlow, 1995), 229–49.

[29] *The Black Book of Taymouth with other Papers from the Breadalbane Charter Room* (Edinburgh, 1855), 319–51.

[30] I. Whyte, *Agriculture and Society in Seventeenth-Century Scotland* (Edinburgh, 1979); T. C. Smout, 'Scottish landowners and economic growth, 1650–1850', *Scottish Journal of Political Economy*, 11 (1964), 218–34; T. M. Devine (ed.), *Lairds and Improvement in the Scotland of the Enlightenment* (Glasgow, 1978). For entails see A. W. B. Simpson, 'Entails and perpetuities', *Juridical Review*, 24 (1979), 1–20.

authority.[31] The exploitative aspects of this still largely feudal system were balanced by its strong paternalistic ethos. There is no doubt that even in the Highlands commercial and political forces were instigating changes in the organisation of clan society,[32] but visitors to the Lowlands commented on the relaxed nature of relations between lords and their men, on the 'bountifull entertainment of guests', and provided a flattering description of traditions of hospitality and maintenance at a time when, in England at least, aristocratic life was becoming more private.[33] Aristocratic paternalism was also evidenced in the responsibility placed on noblemen and the wider landed community to provide for the maintenance of the parish ministry and local schools, and, while expectations were never wholly met, conditions did improve, and in comparison to many other countries their attitude was enlightened.[34] Similarly, poor relief, while never adequate, was the business of local landlords whose barony courts cooperated with the hard-pressed kirk sessions in times of dearth to adjust rents in the light of the community's ability to pay.[35] This was not an ideal world of kind lords and deferential men, but the entire late medieval and early modern period does not record a single nobleman attacked by his tenants, or the burning of any castle, and there was no popular rising against the landed aristocracy. Even in 1649–50, a period of great political vulnerability, there was no

[31] The best introduction to the local courts is Davies, 'The court and the Scottish legal system 1600–1747', in Gatrell, Lenman Parker (eds.), *Crime and the Law*, 120–54. Also very useful is P. McIntyre, 'The franchise courts' and C. A. Malcolm, 'The sheriff court: sixteenth century and later', in *An Introduction to Scottish Legal History*, Stair Society, 20 (Edinburgh, 1958), 374–83 and 356–62. The records of a number of these courts have been printed by various historical clubs, for example, *Selections from the Records of the Regality of Melrose, 1605–1661* (ed.) J. Curle, Scottish History Society, 2nd ser. 6, 8, 13 (Edinburgh, 1914–15, 1917).

[32] R. A. Dodgshon, 'West highland chiefdoms, 1500–1745: a study in redistributive exchange', in R. Mitchison and P. Roebuck (eds.), *Economy and Society in Scotland and Ireland 1500–1939* (Edinburgh, 1988), 27–37; R. A. Dodgshon, '"Pretense of blude" and "place of thair dwelling": the nature of Scottish clans 1500–1745', in R. A. Houston and I. D. Whyte (eds.), *Scottish Society 1500–1800* (Cambridge, 1989), 169–98. For a very different perspective see A. I. Macinnes, *Clanship, Commerce and the House of Stuart, 1603–1788* (East Linton, 1996); A. I. Macinnes, 'Scottish Gaeldom, 1638–1651: the vernacular response to the covenanting dynamic', in J. Dwyer, R. A. Mason and A. Murdoch (eds.), *New Perspectives on the Politics and Culture of Early Modern Scotland* (Edinburgh, 1982), 59–94; A. I. Macinnes, 'Crown, clans and *fine*: the "civilising" of Scottish Gaeldom, 1587–1638', *Northern Scotland*, 13 (1993), 31–55.

[33] H. Brown (ed.), *Early Travellers in Scotland* (reprnt. Edinburgh, 1973), 127–8.

[34] Although not sufficiently enlightened to allow the 1646 Education Act requiring landlords to pay for schools and teachers to remain on the statute book. It was repealed in 1662 and it was 1696 before further progress was made in creating a legislative framework for universal education.

[35] R. Mitchison, 'The making of the old Scottish poor law', *Past & Present*, 63 (1974), 58–93, especially 58–80.

general attack on the aristocracy. The first instance of popular insurrection had to wait until the very localised levellers' revolt in Galloway in 1724.[36]

The principal role of the nobility in the medieval period was to provide military leadership and expertise. That was less the case by the beginning of the seventeenth century, partly because of the technological changes in warfare throughout Europe, but also because Scotland experienced very little war between 1560 and 1639. Nevertheless, the Scots retained a reputation for being a martial race, and over the course of the seventeenth century the image of the fighting Scot continued to gain substance. However, there was more than one version of that image. That preferred by the Scots themselves was of the sophisticated gentleman warrior, the 'Admirable Scot' of Sir Thomas Urquhart of Cromartie's *The Jewel* in which the daring of James Crichton was used, with a good deal of self-conscious irony, to demonstrate 'the fidelity, valor and gallantry' of the Scottish nation.[37] Even an Englishman like Sir Andrew Marvell celebrated this aspect of the Scottish identity in his poem *The Loyal Scot*.[38] It is this tradition that inspired Patrick Abercromby to market his 1711 general history of the country, *The Martial Achievements of the Scots Nation*.[39] At the same time the Scots were seen as a quarrelsome, bellicose people, much given to fighting with one another and easily provoked to violence. One English visitor in 1679 thought the Scots 'proud, arrogant and vain-glorious boasters, barbarous, and inhuman butchers', and while this clearly was a case of hyperbole, his observations on the heavily fortified houses, well-stocked armouries, and the omnipresent retainers can be substantiated.[40] In the late sixteenth century this image had been closely associated with the bloodfeud and the toleration of private war, but by c. 1700 the aristocratic duel survived as the only form of semi-legitimate

---

[36] The whiggamore regime certainly proscribed many noblemen from political office, but their offence was specific, the values of aristocratic society were not questioned. However, see C. Whatley, 'How tame were the Scottish lowlanders during the eighteenth century?', in T. M. Devine (ed.), *Conflict and Stability in Scottish Society 1700–1850* (Edinburgh, 1850), 1–30 where he revises the picture of a largely deferential peasantry in the eighteenth century.

[37] *The Jewel. Sir Thomas Urquhart*, ed. R. D. S. Jack and R. J. Lyall (Edinburgh, 1983), 92ff.

[38] *Andrew Marvell. The complete poems*, ed. E. S. Donno (Harmondsworth, 1972), 183–91.

[39] P. Abercromby, *The Martial Achievements of the Scots Nation* (Edinburgh, 1711).

[40] Brown, *Early Travellers*, 259, 261–2. Thomas Kirke's experiences were similar to those of Thomas Morer a decade later, although he commented that fortified houses were rarely used for military reasons, *ibid.*, 274–5.

(but illegal) private violence in Lowland society.[41] In the Highlands the traditional martial identity endured longer, sustained by military tenure, cattle raiding and mercenary service, serving to underline the view of the highlanders as particularly aggressive and bloodthirsty.[42] For their part, Highlanders did nothing to discourage this image. The Maclean bards continued to glorify the martial achievements of their clan, and even the female poet of the Macdonalds, Sileas Nighean Mhic Raghnaill, celebrated the lost opportunity of the battle of Sheriffmuir in 1715 with the memory of 'the hardihood of your hands wielding your blades, chopping off heads to the ground, lopping off ears and splitting skulls, and sending the pursuit after them'.[43]

In spite of this martial tradition, Scottish society was not organised for war, except between 1638 and 1651 when a highly effective war machine was put in place by the covenanters.[44] There was no Scottish army before 1638–9, and the small, professional armies garrisoned in the country after 1660 were really para-military forces that fought no great battles and were widely hated for their predatory activities against the covenanters. The militia too attracted little popular enthusiasm, and became associated with equally oppressive actions such as the overawing of the south west by the Highland host in 1678, or the massacre of Glencoe by the Argyll militia in 1692. The presence of soldiers in Scotland, from the English republican force in the 1650s through to that of the duke of Cumberland and his successors in the mid eighteenth century, created a hostile attitude towards the army. It was essentially an oppressive, and often alien force, suggesting on the one hand a people who live under an authoritarian regime – the view of English whigs in the 1670s – and on the other, a people who could not be trusted by the state. Certainly the latter was the view from London whether the enemy

---

[41] J. M. Wormald, 'Bloodfeud, kindred and government in early modern Scotland', *Past & Present*, 87 (1980), 54–97; K. M. Brown, *Bloodfeud in Scotland, 1573–1625. Violence, Justice and Politics in an Early Modern Society* (Edinburgh, 1986).

[42] The idea that the Highlanders were the victims of bad publicity has been argued in A. I. Macinnes, 'Repression and conciliation: the highland dimension 1660–1688', *Scottish Historical Review*, 66 (1986), 153–74. However, any reading of Highland history in the seventeenth century cannot fail to leave an impression of a society that glorified violence, D. Stevenson, *Alandair Macolla and the Highland Problem in the Seventeenth Century* (Edinburgh, 1980); P. Hopkins, *Glencoe and the End of the Highland War* (Edinburgh, 1986); B. Lenman, *The Jacobite Clans of the Great Glen 1650–1784* (London, 1984).

[43] *Enchann Bacach Agus Baird Eile de Chloinn Ghill-eathain*, ed. C. O. Baoill, The Scottish Gaelic Text Society, 14 (Edinburgh, 1979), 3–4; *Bardachd Shilis Na Ceapaich c. 1660–c. 1729*, ed. C. O. Baoill, Scottish Gaelic Text Society, 13 (Edinburgh, 1972), 29.

[44] For the covenanting army and its reputation, E. Furgol, 'Scotland turned Sweden, 1638–1651', in J. Morrill (ed.), *The Scottish National Covenant in its National Context* (Edinburgh, 1990), 134–54.

in Scotland was covenanters or, after 1689, jacobites. It was 1797 before Westminster felt secure enough to give the Scots their own militia.[45]

Yet in spite of these negative images of the martial Scot, the more positive impression of the Scot as a tough, fighting man survived. Most northern European armies contained large numbers of Scottish companies and officers who were highly prized by employers ranging from Gustav Adolph to Louis XIV and Peter the Great.[46] To a considerable extent this pool of manpower was a response to the lack of opportunities at home, but it also grew out of the continuation of a tradition of military service and a respect for a martial identity that was fostered within Scottish society. The nobility especially found that the expanding armies of the European nation-states offered an opportunity to hold onto vestiges of a military aristocracy. However, after 1688-9, William II brought Britain in from the fringes of European politics, and the vast expansion of the British military establishment over the next twenty years allowed Scottish military expertise and enthusiasm to be harnessed to the needs of the British state rather than to those of its competitors or allies. While British regimental histories begin with the Royal Scots in 1633 and the Scots Guards in 1662, it was the War of the League of Augsburg and the War of the Spanish Succession that laid the foundation of a continuous relationship between Scottish regiments and the crown.[47] Here the Scottish martial spirit was being yoked to the British state, although it was another half century before Highland regiments were regarded with the same degree of trust. If a British identity was fostered, it was on the fields of Flanders, and it is surely no accident that the second duke of Argyll, one of the architects of parliamentary union and one of the leading Scottish politicians of the decades immediately following 1707, was a professional soldier who ended his career as commander-in-chief of the British army.

However, in the seventeenth century it was the Church of Scotland that provided the most effective institutional vehicle for a national identity. The church was the only truly national institution, with personnel representing it in every parish of the kingdom and with a community, district, regional and national framework of courts. The

---

[45] B. P. Lenman, 'Militia, fencible men, and home defence, 1660-1797', in N. Macdougall (ed.), *Scotland and War AD79-1918* (Edinburgh, 1991), 170-92; J. Robertson, *The Scottish Enlightenment and the Militia Issue* (Edinburgh, 1985).

[46] For example see I. R. Bartlett, 'Scottish mercenaries in Europe, 1570-1640: a study in attitudes and politics', *Scottish Tradition*, 13 (1984-5), 15-24; K. M. Brown, 'From Scottish lords to British officers: state building, elite integration, and the army in the seventeenth century', in Macdougall (ed.), *Scotland and War*, 141-2.

[47] Brown, 'From Scottish lords to British officers', in Macdougall (ed.), *Scotland and War*, 133-69.

church also administered poor relief, supervised parish schooling, controlled the universities, and interfered directly in the lives of ordinary people through its parish kirk sessions, punishing drunkenness, investigating paternity or providing a form of marriage counselling. No state agency could possibly compete with such a comprehensive involvement in the lives of ordinary people. However, the church's renowned interest in social control indicates the prevalence of a good deal of sin and crime, while the concerns of ministers at non-church-going and the lack of finance all point to another side of the Scottish identity that struggled against religious restraints.[48] Of course, there were Roman Catholics who did not identity with the church, but increasingly they were a marginalised minority of little significance. Indeed vehement anti-Catholicism was an enduring attribute of the Scottish psyche – an attribute crucially shared with English protestants – throughout the early modern period. Among protestants of whatever hue there was little deviation from classical Calvinist theology, the exceptions being found among certain Arminian communities of the episcopalian north east. Church services emphasised preaching that was long and densely packed with doctrine alongside *ex tempore* prayers rather than music or visual art. In many southern Lowland localities large open-air communions were occasions of extraordinary religious fervour and celebration. Self-examination was encouraged, but so was a kind of communal examination in which the uncovering of sin, confession and repentance all took place in public.[49]

The most divisive debate surrounding the Scottish identity concerned the question of authority in the church. Episcopalians traced a continuity in church government back to the pre-reformed church, preserving the idea of government by a hierarchy of bishops who claimed apostolic jurisdiction, accepted the subordination of the church to the crown, and were inclined towards a degree of congruity, if not conformity, with England.[50] By contrast, the presbyterians emphasised the

[48] For the difficulties in establishing control see G. Parker, 'The "Kirk by Law Established" and the origins of the taming of Scotland', in L. Leneman (ed.), *Perspectives in Scottish Social History* (Aberdeen, 1988), 1–32; B. Lenman, 'The limits of godly discipline in the early modern period with particular reference to England and Scotland', in K. von Greyerz (ed.), *Religion and Society in Early Modern Europe 1500–1800* (London, 1984), 124–45; L. Leneman and R. Mitchison, 'Scottish illegitimacy ratios in the early modern period', *Economic History Review*, 40 (1987), 41–63; R. D. Brackenbridge, 'The enforcement of Sunday observance in post-revolution Scotland, 1689–1733', *RSCHS*, 17 (1969), 33–45.

[49] For the best insight into the internal religion of Scottish presbyterianism see L. E. Schmidt, *Holy Fairs. Scottish communions and American revivals in the early modern period* (Princeton, 1989).

[50] At least this was the case in the early seventeenth century, see D. G. Mullan, *Episcopacy in Scotland. The history of an idea 1560–1638* (Edinburgh, 1986). The episcopal church

revolutionary and popular nature of the Reformation, believed in the equality of ministers and the involvement of lay elders in church government, utterly rejected state interference in church affairs, and dismissed the Church of England as only half reformed.[51] The debate very quickly became an argument about history, about what was the authentically Scottish experience of Reformation.[52] Thus John Spottis-woode for the episcopalians and David Calderwood for the presbyterians, who both wrote their histories in the reign of Charles I, sought to show that they represented the true heirs of 1560.[53] The presbyterians in particular poured out a torrent of histories, and succeeded in creating a national story of a godly and suffering protestant people, whose origins lay in the primitive Culdee church rather than in any relationship with Rome, struggling to overcome the worldly ambitions of autocratic kings, ambitious and greedy lords and interfering Englishmen. The Culdee connection was a curious choice given the negative view many Lowland Scots had of the Highlanders. However, it served the purpose of under-lining the nation's Celtic identity and denying the Romano-British alternative. In spite of the employment of ecclesiastical myths, the presbyterians especially made great use of documentation, rooting their arguments in a real, if controversial, past for which they could provide authentic evidence.[54] Through the popularising media of sermons and pamphlets, the presbyterian apologists were highly successful in en-suring that at least among the southern Lowland population their church and the nation were closely identified. Undergirding this rela-tionship was the idea of the covenant between God and the nation. The

of the Restoration era was less ideologically aware, and its Erastian character was much more obvious, see J. Buckroyd, *Church and State in Scotland 1660–1681* (Edinburgh, 1980).

[51] The most useful and authoritative literature on the origins and early development of presbyterianism in Scotland is J. Kirk, *Patterns of Reform. Continuity and change in the Reformation Kirk* (Edinburgh, 1989). On the covenanting church see W. Makey, *The Church of the Covenant 1637–1651. Revolution and Social Change in Scotland* (Edinburgh, 1979), and I. B. Cowan, *The Scottish Covenanters, 1660–88* (London, 1976). There is no satisfactory history of presbyterianism in the later seventeenth century.

[52] On this debate see A. H. Williamson, *Scottish National Consciousness in the Age of James VI* (Edinburgh, 1979); Mullan, *Episcopacy in Scotland.*

[53] J. Spottiswoode, *The History of the Church of Scotland*, ed., M. Napier and M. Russell, Spottiswoode Society, 6 (3 vols., Edinburgh, 1847–51); D. Calderwood, *The History of the Kirk of Scotland*, ed. T. Thomson, Wodrow Society, 8 (8 vols., Edinburgh, 1842–9).

[54] There are interesting discussions of the writing of history in the seventeenth century in Williamson, *Scottish National Consciousness*, and D. Allan, *Virtue, Learning and the Scottish Enlightenment* (Edinburgh, 1993). For the best examples of this determination to bury the opposition under the weight of documentation see *The Works of John Knox*, ed., D. Laing, Wodrow Society, 12 (6 vols., Edinburgh, 1846–64); D. Calderwood, *The History of the Kirk of Scotland*, ed. T. Thomson and S. Laing, Wodrow Society, 7 (8 vols., Edinburgh, 1842–9); *The Autobiography and Diary of Mr James Melvill*, D. R. Pitcairn, Wodrow Society, 3 (Edinburgh, 1842).

National Covenant of 1638 and the Solemn League and Covenant of 1643 electrified the relationship between local communities and the nation as they entered into a compact with God to defend their church, their king and the godly nation itself.[55] However, even in the midst of apocalyptic ideas of a covenanted nation, the counterpoint to the English concept of an elect nation, there were some more sceptical voices. Sir Thomas Urquhart of Cromartie wrote from prison in the Tower of London in the early 1650s that

> there is under the sun no national fault nor national deserving wherby all merit to be punished or all rewarded because the badness of most in each destroys the universality of vertue, and the good inclination in some in all cuts off the generality of vice.[56]

Yet for most people the idea of God interacting in national history was tied closely to beliefs about the sanctity or otherwise of society. It was this business of purifying the community and of resisting degenerate religion that politicised a great many ordinary people, particularly in presbyterian communities where the individual conscience was placed on a higher plane than obedience to authority.[57] By contrast, episcopalians were less successful in creating a clear and popular sense of identity, being very much subject to the rather more transient interests of the state. An episcopalian church also struggled with the damaging charge that it represented an anglicising influence, and the efforts by some bishops to fashion a Constantinian British image never really recovered from the revolt against this process in the later 1630s. This is not to deny that a great many people were in favour of an episcopalian church. However, their motives appear to have been more secular – obedience to the crown, or dislike of theocratic pretensions – and the

[55] S. A. Burrell, 'The apocalyptic ideas of the early covenanters', *Scottish Historical Review*, 43 (1964), 1–24; J. D. Ford, 'The lawful bonds of Scottish society: the Five Articles of Perth, the Negative Confession and the National Covenant', *Historical Journal*, 37 (1994), 45–64; M. Steele, 'The "Politick Christian": the theological background to the national covenant', in J. Morrill (ed.), *The Scottish National Covenant in its British Context 1638–1651* (Edinburgh, 1990), 31–67; E. J. Cowan, 'The making of the national covenant', in Morrill (ed.), *The Scottish National Covenant*, 68–89; E. J. Cowan, 'The Solemn League and Covenant', in R. A. Mason (ed.), *Scotland and England 1286–1815* (Edinburgh, 1987), 182–202; J. D. Ford, 'Conformity in conscience: the structures of the Perth Articles debate in Scotland', *Journal of Ecclesiastical History*, 46 (1995), 256–77. Still useful is S. A. Burrell, 'The covenant idea as a revolutionary symbol: Scotland 1596–1637', *Church History*, 27 (1958), 338–50.

[56] *The Jewel*, 87–8.

[57] V. G. Kiernan, 'A banner with a strange device: the later covenanters', in T. Brotherstone (ed.), *Covenant, Charter and Party. Traditions of revolt and protest in modern Scottish history* (Aberdeen, 1989), 25–49 makes a somewhat eccentric case for popular political participation. More conventionally see Makey, *Church of the Covenant*, and Cowan, *The Scottish Covenanters*. The later covenanters have not really been subjected to the careful analysis they deserve.

church generated little lay enthusiasm. It was only after 1689 that an episcopalian ideology evolved that was able to arouse a limited degree of popular fervour by linking the episcopal church with the house of Stewart and after 1707 with the alleged loss of Scottish identity.[58] However, in guaranteeing the future of the presbyterian church in 1707, unionists ensured that the Church of Scotland would remain distinct from the Church of England, and in removing parliament to Westminster, they raised the status of the general assembly to that of a quasi-parliament.

One of the great achievements of eighteenth-century Scotland was an educational system that produced a level of literacy not surpassed anywhere else in the world. Recently there has been some debate over how superior and distinctive Scottish education was at this time. Yet even if the 'myth' has been exaggerated, the attainment of a literacy level that was comparable with the best elsewhere was remarkable. Where Scotland was most educationally innovative was in the insistence over a very long period that the whole population be provided with a minimum level of education. That the kingdom already had an impressive network of schools before 1560 has become more apparent in recent years, but it was the Reformation that gave impetus to the idea that every parish should have its own school. The rationale behind this church-led campaign was to enable people to read the bible, thus encouraging family worship and bible study and reinforcing the teaching from the pulpit, but obviously reading did not stop at the bible. That ideal of a network of parish schools was not realised for some 200 years because of a lack of resources, but a series of enactments in 1616, 1633, 1646 (repealed in 1662) and culminating in the important 1696 education act, all tried to place more onus on landlords to fund schools. The result was an astonishingly high number of parish and other types of schools, and an already impressive literacy rate in which the nation was beginning to take some pride. Entirely absent from Scottish education was any sense of identity crisis, and it was confidence in their own educational institutions that led the Scots to insist that the act of Union left them with control over the future education of their country. That confidence was rewarded in the remarkable achievements of the following century.[59]

---

[58] B. Lenman, 'The Scottish episcopal clergy and the ideology of Jacobitism', in E. Cruickshanks (ed.), *Ideology and Conspiracy. Aspects of Jacobitism, 1689–1759* (Edinburgh, 1982), 36–47.

[59] R. A. Houston, *Scottish Literacy and the Scottish Identity. Illiteracy and society in Scotland and northern England, 1600–1800* (Cambridge, 1985). For a more traditional, and by no means discredited view, see J. Scotland, *A History of Scottish Education, Volume I. From the beginning to 1872* (London, 1969).

Scotland's five universities were far less innovative than had been the case in the previous century. The period was largely one of consolidation against a background of political interference. There were no new foundations. Teaching regressed to the regenting system that had been abolished by Andrew Melville in Glasgow and St Andrews. The academically brightest students continued to pursue their studies on the continent. On the other hand, the later seventeenth century saw the emergence in the universities of more critical and investigative inquiry. Academics like James Gregory and his nephew, David Gregory, both of whom were involved in exciting new developments in optics and mathematics, were not working in an intellectual vacuum.[60] Furthermore, the universities produced a steady flow of educated landowners, ministers, lawyers and, increasingly towards the end of the century, doctors, who together constituted a sophisticated and diverse critical public, or what might be described as the chattering classes of the seventeenth century, of whom Sir Robert Sibbald and his circle formed the intellectual apex.[61] Evidence for this cultural life can be seen in the expanding book trade, a distinctive style of Scottish book design having developed by the 1670s, and in the private libraries stocked with the very latest thinking on everything from agriculture to theology.[62]

In contrast to the centuries which preceded and followed it, the seventeenth century is not remembered for its cultural achievements. Certainly the absence of a royal court was a blow to the artistic community. There was no building to rival the Stewart palaces of the fifteenth and early sixteenth centuries, and while a new wing was added to Linlithgow in advance of James VI's visit in 1617, and Holyrood was renovated by Sir William Bruce in the 1670s, the royal residences were on the whole allowed to decay. On the other hand, the construction of Parliament House in the 1630s at royal command, if not royal expense, was a major project that greatly enhanced Edinburgh as the capital city and provided a fine setting for the meeting of the estates. More

---

[60] R. Cant, 'Origins of the Enlightenment in Scotland: the universities', in R. H. Campbell and A. S. Skinner (eds.), *The Origins and Nature of the Scottish Enlightenment* (Edinburgh, 1982), 42–64.

[61] Some indication of the richness of this can be found in H. Ouston, 'Cultural life from the Restoration to the Union', in A. Hook (ed.), *The History of Scottish Literature. Volume 2, 1660–1800* (Aberdeen, 1987 repr. 1989), 11–32; R. L. Emerson, 'Sir Robert Sibbald Kt., the Royal Society of Scotland, and the origins of the Scottish Enlightenment', *Annals of Science*, 45 (1988), 41–72.

[62] An indication of Scottish publishing can be glimpsed from H. G. Aldis, *A List of Books Printed in Scotland before 1700* (Edinburgh, 1970). On design see J. Morris, 'Scottish design and the art of the book 1500–1800', in W. Kaplan (ed.), *Scotland Creates. 5000 years of art design* (London, 1990), 84–5. For individual libraries see, for example, R. H. MacDonald (ed.), *The Library of Drummond of Hawthornden* (Edinburgh, 1971).

damaging, perhaps, was the withdrawal of crown patronage for Scottish writers, painters and musicians who had provided the entertainment at James VI's court before 1603. This distancing of the crown from Scottish cultural life was not immediate, since James took a number of Scottish poets including Sir William Alexander, John Murray and Sir Robert Aytoun with him to London. However, by the 1630s the gap between court culture and Scotland was clear to see.[63] That the Scottish public and Scottish artists remained hungry for royal cultural patronage was evident briefly in 1679–81 when the duke of York was resident in the country, but this transient episode served only to highlight the gap in Scottish public life.[64] Possibly the most deleterious effect of this divorce from the point of view of Scottish culture was that there was no resident court to counter the church's disapproval of the theatre which had to struggle to survive at all throughout the seventeenth century.[65]

However, the impact of the absence of the court on Scottish culture has been overstated. The aristocracy formed an enormous reservoir of patronage that was collectively wealthier than the crown, and the idea that after 1603 Scottish noblemen headed south in droves, neglecting their own country, can now be dismissed.[66] To imagine that these well-educated and refined noblemen spent months on end in Scotland deprived of all cultural pursuits while they saved up for another trip to London is nonsense. Baronial or country house culture sustained a great body of Gaelic bards, family historians, architects, craftsmen, musicians and painters that has been overlooked. The product of seventeenth-century aristocratic patronage was a clear statement of confidence and pride in their status as Scottish noblemen, albeit noblemen with aspirations to be recognised on a wider European stage. This confidence is evident above all else in their castles and houses. The early-seventeenth-century building boom saw heavy investment in splendid renaissance castles like Strathbogie Castle which was rebuilt and Carlaverock which was remodelled. It also indicates more innovative styles such as those introduced by Sir William Alexander in his town house at Stirling or by the first earl of Dunfermline in his many building projects which were

---

[63] H. M. Shire, *Song, Dance and Poetry of the Court of Scotland under James VI* (Cambridge, 1969). The shift from royal to aristocratic patronage is discussed briefly on pp. 207–59. Even royalist writers were out of tune with the court, see D. Reid, 'Royalty and self-absorption in Drummond's poetry', *Studies in Scottish Literature*, 22 (1987), 115–31.

[64] H. Ouston, 'York in Edinburgh: James VII and the patronage of learning in Scotland, 1679–1688', in J. Dwyer, R. A. Mason and A. Murdoch (eds.), *New Perspectives on the Politics and Culture of Early Modern Scotland* (Edinburgh, 1982), 133–55.

[65] A. Cameron, 'Theatre in Scotland', in Hook (ed.), *History of Scottish Literature*, 191–205.

[66] Brown, 'The Scottish aristocracy, anglicization and the court'; Brown, 'The origins of a British aristocracy'.

designed to reflect a more peaceful age. Even more extensive building took place after c. 1670. Native baronial influences continued to be popular such as in the third earl of Strathmore and Kinghorn's extraordinary alterations to Glamis Castle. At Thirlstane the first duke of Lauderdale employed a Scot, Sir William Bruce, as his architect, and he combined classical ideas from Italy, drawing chiefly on Sebastiano Serlio, with the employment of Dutch painters and joiners and English plasterers. At Drumlanrig the first duke of Queensberry's architect, James Smith, remained closer to the non-classical French style, but also built the very English Melville House in Fife for the first earl of Melville. Between 1698 and 1703 Hopetoun House, that massive Palladian mansion on the south shores of the Forth estuary, was erected for the first earl of Hopetoun, while Daniel Defoe's reaction to Hamilton Palace, finished by the fourth duke of Hamilton, was that it was 'fit rather for the Court of a Prince than the Palace or House of a Subject'.[67] Decorating these buildings ensured a steady flow of work for painters, both native and imported. The later sixteenth and early seventeenth centuries were marked by a great enthusiasm among noblemen and wealthy merchants for the peculiarly Scottish fashion of painted ceilings, over 100 of which survive today in a range of realist and abstract styles. Scotland's first known portrait painter, George Jamesone, was a pupil of John Anderson, the best known of these craftsmen-artists. He was followed by a line of portraitists including David Scougall, David Paton and the Flemish artist, Sir John Baptist de Medina, who on a brief visit to Scotland to complete a handful of commissions found himself in such demand that he stayed on and was naturalised. Meanwhile picture collecting also grew in popularity, beginning with the first duke of Hamilton in the 1630s and the third earl of Lothian in the 1640s, while in 1703 one finds the first earl of Hopetoun paying the Dutch artist, Philip Tideman, for thirty-seven allegorical paintings.[68] Musical developments were hampered by church disapproval, although most towns retained music teachers. Meanwhile the glittering musical tradition of the Scottish court struggled to survive after 1603 in the castles and country houses of the nobility, many of whom had musicians among their household. But in a country where no public recitals were held until 1693, when they first became fashionable

[67] J. Macaulay, *The Classical Country House in Scotland 1660–1800* (London, 1987), 1–38; D. Howard, *Scottish Architecture from the Reformation to the Restoration, 1560–1660* (Edinburgh, 1995).

[68] D. Macmillan, *Scottish Art 1460–1990* (Edinburgh, 1990); J. Holloway (ed.), *Patrons and Painters in Scotland. Art in Scotland 1650–1760* (Scottish National Portrait Gallery, 1989).

in Edinburgh society, it is not surprising to find no new composition, no notable artists. This is not to say that the Scottish people were not musical. Popular music flourished and it is perhaps a comment on it that the face Scottish music presented to the outside world was that of the Scotch songs, those slightly risqué airs thought by John Dryden to contain a 'rude sweetness' so appealing to English audiences from the Restoration.[69] Family histories like Sir Robert Gordon of Gordonstoun's history on the earls of Sutherland, David Hume of Godscroft's history of the Douglas earls of Angus, and Gilbert Burnet's history of the duke of Hamilton relate a powerful national history through the eyes of particular families. The Gordon historians of the period emphasised the family's origins in Macedonia and their French ancestry, while quickly passing over their arrival in Scotland from England in the twelfth century, preferring to dwell on the tradition that it was a Bertram Gordon who slew Richard I.[70] Furthermore, while the aristocracy was the driving force in shaping Scottish culture, there was some indication towards the end of the century that in Edinburgh the professions and the merchant community were also supportive of artistic and intellectual pursuits, and that Edinburgh as a city had retained its position as a strong centre of national culture. Even the much maligned clergy were not averse to acting as cultural patrons. One of the most sensitive portraits of the century is an anonymous portrait of Alexander Henderson. Meanwhile, the structures of Scottish society, and those modes of thought formed since the Reformation, already had created the kind of environment in which scientific investigation and philosophical inquiry flourished in the decades before 1707.[71]

Those who have sought for cultural dysfunction have most readily found it in both the dearth of literature and the trend towards writing in English. While the latter did indicate some uncertainty over how Scots should best express themselves, in opting for a language that guaranteed

---

[69] D. Johnson, *Music and Society in Lowland Scotland in the Eighteenth Century* (London, 1972), 9–11, 25–6, 32–3; R. Fiske, *Scotland in Music. A European enthusiasm* (Cambridge, 1983), 1–30; D. J. Ross, *Musick Fyne. Robert Carver and the art of music in sixteenth-century Scotland* (Edinburgh, 1993).

[70] Sir Robert Gordon, *A Genealogical History of the Earldom of Sutherland* (Edinburgh, 1813); *The House of Gordon* (ed.), J. M. Bulloch, New Spalding Club, 26 (2 vols., Aberdeen, 1903–7), ii, 11–12, 35–75; David Hume of Godscroft, *The History of The Houses of Douglas and Angus* (Edinburgh, 1644); G. Burnet, *Memoires of the Lives and Actions of James and William Dukes of Hamilton* (London, 1677). Even relatively insignificant families patronised family histories, see *Genealogy of the Lairds of Ednem and Duntreth* (Edinburgh, 1679).

[71] J. R. R. Christie, 'The origins and development of the Scottish scientific community 1680–1760', *History and Science*, 12 (1974), 122–45; A. C. Chitnis, 'Provost Drummond and the origins of Edinburgh medicine', in Campbell and Skinner (eds.), *Origins and Nature of the Enlightenment*, 86–97.

a wider audience, writers were not necessarily betraying their own culture any more than those writers who expressed themselves in Latin. They were adapting to a changing world, and that process of adaptation can as easily be interpreted as a sign of confidence in their identity. In commenting on seventeenth-century literature there has also been a tendency to overstate the importance of poetry and drama in contrast to other forms of literature. Certainly relatively little good poetry was composed, although William Drummond of Hawthornden was as good as any English cavalier poet.[72] Neither was there much imaginative prose other than Sir Thomas Urquhart's idiosyncratic *The Jewel*. Furthermore, only two plays were written in Scotland between 1660 and 1700 of which William Clarke's *Marciano, or the Discovery* was performed in 1663, but Archibald Pitcairn's *The Assembly* had to wait until 1722 before being published.[73] However, the period did see an outpouring of prose in the form of history, sermons, polemic, legal treatises and scientific works which form a broad corpus of writings that ought not to be disparaged. Indeed in the 1650s Sir Thomas Urquhart of Cromartie boasted of Scotland's impressive literary contribution to European culture in the first half of the seventeenth century.[74] A canon of works that includes Drummond's verse alongside the Gaelic poetry of Cathal MacMhuirich, Sir Thomas Craig's *Scotland's Soveraignty Asserted*, John Napier of Merchiston's *Mirifici Logarithmorum Canonis Constructio*, Samuel Rutherford's 'Letters', Archibald Johnston's diary, David Calderwood's *History of the Kirk of Scotland*, Robert Gordon of Straloch's cartography, Stair's *Institutions of the Law of Scotland*, Sir Robert Sibbald's *Scotia Illustrata*, Andrew Fletcher of Saltoun's writings, and the speeches of John Hamilton, second lord Belhaven, is impressive by any standard.[75] As aspects of cultural history they provide clear testament to the Scots' deep desire to understand and explain their society, and to investigate it with a scientific rigour that sprang from the cerebral nature of Calvinism. It is also worth drawing attention to patriotic works like John Barbour's *Brus* and Blind Harry's *Wallace* which remained very popular, the latter being republished eight times between 1661 and 1707.[76] Cosmopolitan ideas existed side by side with deeply rooted patriotic sentiments, emphasising that the Scots remained

---

[72] R. H. MacDonald, *William Drummond of Hawthornden. Poems and prose* (Edinburgh and London, 1976).
[73] T. Tobin, *Plays by Scots 1660–1800* (Iowa, 1974).   [74] Urquhart, *The Jewel*, 149–74.
[75] For a useful selection of the more political prose of the period see D. Reid, *The Party-Coloured Mind* (Edinburgh, 1982) which includes some of the above.
[76] I. Ross and S. Scobie, 'Patriotic publishing as a response to union', in T. I. Rae (ed.), *The Union of 1707* (Glasgow, 1974), 94–119; Kidd, *Subverting Scotland's Past*, 76–7.

rooted in their historic past while engaging with the European world to which they were determined to remain firmly anchored.

Finally, the negative aspects of Calvinism on artistic and intellectual expression have been greatly exaggerated. There is no doubt that the Scottish church, like that elsewhere, exercised what amounted to informal censorship of thought and expression. However, in raising standards of education, providing a professional ministry and in adhering to a rigorously Calvinist theology that was taught to local congregations through the medium of long and difficult sermons, the church encouraged critical thought. Furthermore, for most of the century the presbyterian clergy inspired political and religious dissent. Ordinary Scottish people might not have been able to see satirical Restoration comedies on the stage, but the church provoked them into thinking for themselves. Again, while the seventeenth century left little in terms of an artistic legacy of church decoration, and even continued the iconoclastic process of removing evidence of earlier religious art, the plain, simple church buildings of the period are in themselves embodiments of the very powerful and distinct cultural values of the people who worshipped in them. The ordered, patriotic Calvinist mind can also be seen at work in the collection of historical documents and in Stair's codification of the law, just as the concern to understand man's social needs encouraged the beginnings of medical research in Edinburgh. The seventeenth-century church stimulated cultural values that were serious and intellectual, values that demanded individual accountability alongside responsibility to and for the community. Perhaps more than anything else it was these values that served to reorientate Scottish identity and to lay the foundations for the eighteenth-century Scottish Enlightenment.[77]

Seventeenth-century Scots had no identity problems in spite of living in a multi-kingdom state in which they were a minority people. When an external threat to that identity loomed in the 1630s the national response was emphatic, leaving the crown and English politicians wary of repeating the experiment. The survival and ongoing development of vigorous national institutions, elites and cultural values all ensured that Scotland was not anglicised. In 1707 Scottish politicians made a hardheaded decision about the nation's future based on political and economic considerations. Critics at the time suggested that in doing so

[77] Cameron, 'Theological controversy: a factor in the origins of the Enlightenment', in Campbell and Skinner (eds.), *Origins and Nature of the Scottish Enlightenment*, 116–30; S. Sutherland, 'The presbyterian inheritance of Hume and Reid', in Campbell and Skinner (eds.), *Origins and Nature of the Scottish Enlightenment*, 131–49; R. Sher, *Church and University in the Scottish Enlightenment. The moderate Literati of Edinburgh* (Princeton, 1985).

they were undermining the nation, and Lord Belhaven's observation that, 'I think I see a free and independent kingdom delivering up that which all the world hath been fighting for since the days of Nimrod' articulated the genuine frustration and puzzlement of that majority of the population not panicked by the recent economic crisis.[78] Yet while the debate over the long-term effect of the union on Scottish identity continues, there is little evidence of an identity crisis over the course of the eighteenth century, unless one thinks that the likes of James Boswell spoke for anyone other than himself.[79] Those who framed the union made sure that while parliament might be lost, the church, the law, the universities, and the privileges of the aristocracy and royal burghs, would all remain. The challenge of becoming British without ceasing to be Scottish was one that the Scots of the eighteenth century were well equipped to meet, and their success in doing so was very largely due to the powerful sense of nationhood bequeathed them by their seventeenth-century ancestors.

[78] For Belhaven see D. Defoe, *The History of the Union of Scotland and England* (London, 1796), 317–28.

[79] The idea of a dual identity leading to some kind of national nervous breakdown is fashionable among literary critics. For an example see K. Simpson, *The Protean Scot. The crisis of identity in eighteenth-century literature* (Aberdeen, 1989).

9   The Gaidhealtachd and the emergence of the Scottish Highlands

Jane Dawson

During the early modern period the patterns of identity and consciousness found within Scottish Gaeldom underwent a major transformation.
This was an extended but ultimately overwhelming, process which
involved two interlocking developments. The first took place within
Scotland's Gaidhealtachd. There a gradual shift occurred which gave
much greater prominence to the Scottish elements within a broader
Gaelic consciousness. The evolution was mirrored in Ireland by a
corresponding emphasis upon the Irish dimensions of being a Gael. By
the end of the early modern period separate and distinctive Scottish and
Irish identities had emerged within the Gaelic world, although the
consciousness of sharing a common culture and language and of being
branches of the same people was never entirely lost. The internal
awareness of a specifically Scottish Gaelic identity was joined to an
external shift in the way in which a Gael was perceived by his fellow
Scots. This second development was the consequence of a change in the
relationship between Scotland's Gaelic heartlands and the rest of the
Stewart kingdom. That process was accelerated by the adoption of a
novel and simplistic analysis which divided Scotland into two starkly
contrasting regions, the Highlands and the Lowlands. The Highland/
Lowland boundary which was drawn in the early modern period was a
matter of perception, not precision. It produced a single division which
overrode the previous regional diversities to be found throughout
Scotland and neatly filed all the inhabitants of the kingdom under two
simplistic labels: 'Highlander' or 'Lowlander'. To outsiders, the Scottish
Gael became a 'Highlander'. This designation was applied to everyone
who inhabited a specific geographical area, the northern and western
mainland and the Hebrides; spoke a different language, Gaelic, and
followed increasingly alien social customs, the Gaelic social system. The
external label of the 'Highlander' reinforced the shift in internal aware-

I am most grateful to Professor Geoffrey Barrow, Professor Donald Meek and Dr Roger
Mason for their helpful comments on a draft of this chapter.

ness within the Gaidhealtachd. Together these two developments combined to produce a new Scottish Gaelic identity for the Highlands and Islands.

I

During the medieval period Gaelic consciousness had existed at two distinct levels. The first was an awareness of being a Gael. This was based upon linguistic, cultural, social and ethnic categories. 'Gaels' were all those people who spoke the Gaelic language; lived within Gaeldom; were members of the Gaelic societies within Scotland or Ireland; and in myth, if not in fact, were descended from the heroes of early Irish history. This produced a broad and inclusive group bound together by a shared language and a common value system. The community of Gaeldom was asserted most forcefully through a shared culture, especially in the bardic poetry written by professional poets of the Gaelic learned orders. A Gael was a member of a heroic society joined through his culture and language to the glories of the past. In the idealised version portrayed by the poets, Gaelic society embodied the traditional virtues and honour code of the ancient Irish warrior-heroes. Conforming to these patterns of behaviour was more important than simply conversing in the same tongue. Being a 'true' Gael was judged first by deeds and only second by ancestry and language. Even though it focused most strongly on the values of the elite of male fighting-men, the ideal picture of Gaelic society was broad enough to include non-warriors and women. This traditional and static ideal encompassing the whole of Gaelic society underpinned a firmly rooted, common consciousness. Its strength and emotional appeal offered members of the wider Gaelic community in Scotland and Ireland pride in their common identity as Gaels whatever their social status and irrespective of gender.[1]

The second level of Gaelic consciousness was located in a Gael's personal identity and his relation to the society in which he lived his daily life. There were three interlocking dimensions to that personal identity: the individual, the ancestral and the collective. These can be seen most clearly in the different categories of Gaelic personal names. They fulfilled a dual function. On the one hand they distinguished the individual from the rest of his immediate community. On the other, they indicated both his precise place within that community and within the

[1] J. MacInnes, 'The Panegyric code in Gaelic poetry and its historical background', *Transactions of the Gaelic Society of Inverness*, 51 (1978–80), 435–98; 'Gaelic poetry and historical tradition', in L. MacLean (ed.), *The Middle Ages in the Highlands* (Inverness, 1981), 142–63.

wider groups of which he was also a member. In Gaelic society an individual was personally identified by a Christian or forename to which was frequently added a descriptive nickname.[2] The person was also named in relation to his ancestral kin, usually represented by the names of his father and grandfather.[3] Another form of name positioned the individual in geographical terms giving either his place of residence or origin or, for a member of the upper levels of Gaelic society, his territorial title or jurisdiction.[4] As well as by patronymic and place, a person was identified according to the other communities within which he moved. This could include naming by profession or occupation,[5] though for most Gaels the third strand of identity was indicated by the collective name of their kindred or clan.[6] Such a variety of personal names gave both flexibility and precision. It allowed an individual to identify himself accurately and appropriately in all circumstances and in a manner most readily comprehensible to his Gaelic listeners. This worked well within the kin-based society of the Gaidhealtachd. The world outside was characterised by the straightforward designation of *Gall* [foreigner] which included all who were not Gaels. The basic general identity of the Gael and the individual's complex particular identity combined to produce traditional Gaelic consciousness.

By the early modern period, these two levels of Gaelic consciousness were no longer adequate by themselves. At the general level, the awareness of being a Gael resting upon a common language, culture and ancestry proved too nebulous and increasingly divorced from contemporary political realities to provide a firm, corporate solidarity which spanned the whole Gaidhealtachd. At the particular level, strong personal identities were located in groups, such as the farm township, the kin, profession and clan, which were too small to offer more than a

[2] E.g. 'Donnachadh Dubh' or Black Duncan, the designation of Duncan Campbell, sixth Laird of Glenorchy, with his black hair and beard and even darker reputation.

[3] E.g. as Iain mac Dhomhnaill mhic Aonghuis [John, son of Donald, son of Angus]. In Gaelic society women did not normally adopt their husband's name but retained their patronymic using the female form 'nic' instead of 'mac'.

[4] E.g. the seventeenth-century poet, Fear na Pàirce or MacCulloch of Park in Ross-shire.

[5] E.g. An Clàrsair Dall or Roderick Morison, the Blind Harper, one of the most famous Scottish Gaelic poets who was also a harper. These semi-professional names remained in the family even when the occupation was no longer pursued, e.g. Gille-Chriosd [Servant of Christ] became the surname Gilchrist after the ecclesiastical connection was ended and Gobha [Smith] became Gow or was directly anglicised into the surname Smith.

[6] A kindred or clan was usually known by the patronymic of the founder of the clan, e.g. all the members of Clann Griogair adopted the patronymic of their founder Eoin mac Griogair, making Gregor their eponymous ancestor and using the collective designation of the MacGregors. For an illuminating analysis of the various kindreds within Clan Gregor and of their history, see M. MacGregor, 'A political history of the MacGregors before 1571' (Ph.D. thesis, University of Edinburgh, 1989).

localised cohesion. A middle identity was needed to fill the gap between the two levels. It was found by splitting apart the single consciousness of Gaeldom and concentrating upon separate Scottish and Irish Gaelic identities.

The Gaelic societies of Ireland and Scotland had been linked since the fifth and sixth centuries when the Dalriadic settlers began to migrate across the North Channel from northern Ireland to Argyll. The racial, cultural and linguistic ties had been reinforced by a network of seaborne communications which connected the constituent parts of the Gaelic world: the Hebrides, the west coast of Scotland, the northern and western coasts of Ireland and the Isle of Man. At the close of the middle ages, the vessels which plied back and forth between these regions carried far more than trade. They brought the political, military, social and cultural influences which linked the Scottish and Irish sections of Gaeldom. The pan-Gaelic world of the late medieval centuries was undermined and finally rent asunder by a combination of pressures during the early modern period.[7] Gaeldom was gradually divided into two separate worlds. The sixteenth and seventeenth centuries brought a dramatic political splintering, but even before this the Scottish and Irish Gaels had already moved apart in more subtle cultural ways. Within the common culture of Gaeldom a recognisably 'Scottish' component developed. The Scottish Gaidhealtachd became much more aware of its own distinctive identity.[8] Rather than any overt declaration of difference from their fellow Gaels in Ireland, this was a reflection of growing Scottish self-confidence. Tradition was such an important element within Gaelic ideology that innovation was not valued for its own sake. In 1532 a royal letter explained this conservative attitude:

The people are tenacious of old custom, traditional manners and rites: they cannot tolerate the introduction of anything which menaces ancestral practice, and if any man ... fails in a matter of accepted custom, they consider it an imperfection or it fills them with aversion and contempt.[9]

---

[7] For a comprehensive, penetrating and extremely detailed examination of all the links between the north of Ireland and the West Highlands and Islands, see F. A. Macdonald, 'Ireland and Scotland: historical perspectives on the Gaelic dimension, 1560–1760' (Ph.D. thesis, 2 vols., University of Glasgow, 1994). I am most grateful to Ms Macdonald for her helpful comments on a number of the points raised in this article and for permission to cite her thesis.

[8] For an illuminating discussion of these issues from a different perspective, M. Lynch, 'National identity in Ireland and Scotland, 1500–1640', in C. Bjørn, A. Grant and K. Stringer (eds.), *Nations, Nationalism and Patriotism in the European Past* (Copenhagen, 1994), 109–36; J. Watt, 'Gaelic polity and cultural identity', in A. Cosgrove (ed.), *New History of Ireland*, ii (Dublin, 1993), 314–51.

[9] Cited in J. Bannerman, 'The Lordship of the Isles', in J. Brown (ed.), *Scottish Society in the Fifteenth Century* (London, 1977), 239.

Scottish distinctiveness was first and most fully apparent within the artistic field. The schools of Scottish craftsmen producing monumental sculpture from the fourteenth to the sixteenth centuries achieved a high artistic standard and evolved their own unique style. The magnificent tombstones and crosses can be found throughout the Western Highlands and Islands.[10] Significantly, the sculptors did not practise their craft in Ireland nor send their products there. This was especially remarkable since the Glens and the Route in County Antrim had been extensively settled by the same Clan Donald South who held the Lordship of the Isles in Scotland within which most of the schools were located. Despite the presence of the same patron, the ease of communications and the political links between the Islands and the northern and western coast of Ireland, West Highland monumental sculpture did not cross the North Channel. In Ireland sculpture developed along independent lines leaving a sharp and clear break between Scotland and Ireland.[11]

In addition to the artistic split, the spoken languages of the Gaels within Ireland and Scotland also grew apart during the later medieval period. The emergence of a separate cultural consciousness for Scottish Gaeldom was encouraged by the divergence of the Gaelic vernaculars. Scottish vernacular developed its own linguistic character, separating itself from Manx and Irish Gaelic. Although important regional variations remained, the Scottish family of Gaelic dialects had separated itself from those which flourished in Ireland.[12] Change was also apparent in the written form of the language. The Gaelic poems of the *Book of the Dean of Lismore*, collected at the beginning of the sixteenth century, demonstrate that the learned orders in Scotland were not afraid to experiment. Located at Fortingall in Perthshire in the centre of Scotland close to the linguistic boundaries between Gaelic and Scots, James MacGregor, the dean of Lismore, and his fellow scribes, were acutely conscious of their role as a bridge between the different languages of Scotland. These members of the Gaelic learned orders spanned the three cultural worlds of Latin, Gaelic and Scots. In the *Book of the Dean of Lismore* they attempted to fit Scottish Gaelic into a Scottish context by producing a very distinctive orthography based on the phonological system of the Scots tongue. Although this particular style

[10] K. A. Steer and J. Bannerman (eds.), *Late Medieval Monumental Sculpture in the West Highlands* (Edinburgh, 1977), Distribution map, 3, 1–6.

[11] *Ibid.*, 43.

[12] R. L. Thomson, 'The emergence of Scottish Gaelic', in A. Aitken, M. McDiarmid and D. S. Thomson (eds.), *Bards and Makars* (Glasgow, 1977), 127–35; D. S. Thomson (ed.), *The Companion to Gaelic Scotland* (1987), 91–6; C. J. Withers, *Gaelic in Scotland 1698–1981* (Edinburgh, 1984); C. J. Withers, *Gaelic Scotland* (London, 1988); V. Durkacz, *The Decline of the Celtic Languages* (Edinburgh, 1983).

of Gaelic orthography did not take root, it offered a guide to contemporary patterns of Gaelic pronunciation and indicated the growing importance of links with Scots, the other vernacular of Scotland.[13]

It is understandable that a separate Scottish Gaelic culture took longest to spread into the field of classical literary composition where the cultural dominance of the Irish had been greatest. Scottish Gaels had felt themselves to be the apprentices of their i. literary matters. Most of the bardic schools, including all . prestigious ones, were to be found in Ireland, the fountain-head of traditional skills in classical common Gaelic. In poetry, law, medicine and music, Scottish Gaels looked to Ireland for their lead and frequently travelled there for instruction.[14] The shared literary and linguistic heritage remained an important emotive force linking the Gaelic communities on either side of the North Channel.[15] Regarding itself as the guardian of traditional cultural values, especially in bardic literature, the world of Irish Gaeldom did not welcome innovation. Although a Scottish Gaelic literature did emerge, the highly prestigious literary core of Gaeldom was one of the last areas where the cultural diversification took root. During the sixteenth and seventeenth centuries the status of Scottish vernacular rose until it came to be recognised as a suitable literary language as well as a spoken one. All composition had previously been undertaken in classical common Gaelic and had been governed by a complex set of rules, with standard metres and traditional bardic forms permitting strictly limited variations.[16] However, a growing number of Scottish authors of poetry and prose did not feel it necessary to adhere strictly to all the old canons. They were also prepared to abandon classical common Gaelic in favour of Scottish vernacular. By the seventeenth century at the latest, a variety of new forms had emerged, especially in the song tradition. Two of the important Scottish developments, the waulking songs and strophic verse, were not exported

[13] D. Meek, 'The Scots-Gaelic scribes of medieval Perthshire: an overview of the orthography and contents of the Book of the Dean of Lismore', in J. D. McClure and M. Spiller, *Bryght Lanternis* (Aberdeen, 1989), 387–404; R. Black, 'The Gaelic manuscripts of Scotland', in W. Gillies (ed.), *Gaelic and Scotland* (Edinburgh, 1989), 151–60.

[14] D. S. Thomson, *An Introduction to Gaelic Poetry* (Edinburgh, 1990 edn) ch. 1; 'Gaelic learned orders and literati', *Scottish Studies*, 12 (1968), 57–78; W. Gillies, 'Gaelic: the classical tradition', in R. D. Jack (ed.), *History of Scottish Literature* (Aberdeen, 1988), i, 245–61.

[15] For example, John Carswell in 1567 referred to, 'we, the Gaels of Scotland and Ireland' in his Epistle to the Reader of his translation into Gaelic of the *Book of Common Order*, *Foirm na N'Urrnuidheadh*, ed. R. L. Thomson, Scottish Gaelic Text Society, 11 (Edinburgh, 1970), 179.

[16] Thomson, *Introduction*, ch. 1; C. O'Baoill (ed.), *Gàir nan Clàrsach: The Harps' Cry* (Edinburgh, 1994), 19–23.

to Ireland. Both the content of the sixteenth and seventeenth-century poems and songs collected in the Fernaig Manuscript and its distinctive orthography demonstrated an increasing confidence in a Scottish Gaelic identity and in its own vernacular.[17]

A parallel rise in confidence can be seen in the development of Scottish piping.[18] In the Gaidhealtachd of Scotland the harp was gradually replaced by the bagpipe, particularly in the general military context and especially in the incitement to battle.[19] In the Lowlands the harp was virtually disowned and became despised, possibly because of its earlier Gaelic associations.[20] From the sixteenth century onwards the Highland bagpipe rapidly established itself as the characteristic musical instrument of the Scottish Gael. *Ceòl mòr*, the 'great music' of the bagpipe was developed in this period by the specialist pipers who taught their compositions and style of playing and transmitted them aurally to their pupils. The most celebrated were the MacCrimmon family, hereditary pipers to the MacLeods of Dunvegan from the sixteenth to the nineteenth centuries, with their school of piping on Skye. Their style of piping did not take firm root in Ireland, though pipes similar to the Highland bagpipe were played there until the end of the seventeenth century, at which point the 'irish' or 'uillean' pipes replaced them.[21] The musical expression of a distinctively Scottish Gaelic culture was clearly revealed in the *Piobaireachd* and the waulking songs developed in the early modern period. In each of the cultural achievements produced by the Scottish Gaels they demonstrated that they could create lively and mature artistic traditions which were independent and separate from the culture of Irish Gaeldom.

These distinctively Scottish elements were highlighted because the pan-Gaelic unity between Scotland and Ireland was crumbling during the sixteenth century. The Gaelic societies on both sides of the North Channel faced increasing external pressures. The governments in London and Edinburgh were both anxious to exert maximum control over their Gaelic chiefs. In Ireland the offensive took the more direct and aggressive form of the Tudor military conquest and colonisation. Inevitably, Gaelic Ireland became focused primarily upon the English

---

[17] *Gàir nan Clàrsach*, 23–5; Thomson, *Introduction*, chs. 2 and 3; D. Meek, 'The Gaelic ballads of medieval Scotland', *Transactions of the Gaelic Society of Inverness*, 55 (1986–8), 47–72.

[18] F. Collinson, *The Bagpipe: the history of a musical instrument* (London, 1975), 125–41; R. D. Cannon, *The Highland Bagpipe and its Music* (Edinburgh, 1988), 6–9.

[19] J. Mackenzie, 'The Clàrsach', in Maclean, *The Middle Ages in the Highlands*, 101–2.

[20] Although Mary Queen of Scots could play the harp she did not seem to have used this skill when she was in Scotland, D. James Ross, *Musyck Fine* (Edinburgh, 1993), 128.

[21] Cannon, *Highland Bagpipe*, 21.

threat. In a similar, though less dramatic way the political turmoil of the *Linn nan Creach* (Age of Forays) which followed the suppression of the Lordship of the Isles in 1493, kept the attention of Scottish Gaels on domestic concerns throughout the sixteenth century. The conclusion of the Nine Years War in 1603 following the defeat at Kinsale marked the end of the military and political independence of the Irish Gaelic lords. The accession of James VI to the English throne in the same year signalled a new relationship between the constituent realms of the 'King of Greater Britain'. The final and complete destruction of the political and social power of the Irish Gaelic lords after the Flight of the Earls in 1607, and the subsequent Plantation of Ulster, had major social as well as economic consequences for the Scottish Highlands, particularly the Hebrides.[22] It brought an abrupt end to the well-established and lucrative mercenary trade. Scottish mercenaries had served the Irish Gaelic chiefs since the end of the thirteenth century and the trade had been extremely important to the way in which each society evolved. The employment of mercenaries permitted the intense militarisation of the Gaelic lordships of Ireland during the fifteenth and sixteenth centuries, turning them into formidable opponents of the Tudor conquest.[23] In addition, by occupying a sizeable number of Scottish warriors elsewhere, the trade had probably reduced the level of armed conflict within the Islands and Western Highlands. It had also substantially eased the burden upon the resources of their clan bases since the mercenaries were billeted, fed and paid within Ireland, largely in kind. The collapse of the mercenary trade removed one of the most important links which had connected the two sides of the North Channel. It also highlighted the contrasting fortunes of the Gaelic chiefs in Scotland and Ireland: the ruthless destruction of their political and social influence in Ireland but, within Scotland, an attempt to incorporate them into national politics.[24]

By the beginning of the seventeenth century religion provided another

---

[22] For an extended discussion of the military links between Scotland and Ireland from the sixteenth to eighteenth centuries which documents the continuities as well as the breaks see, Macdonald, 'Ireland and Scotland', i, chs. 1–4.

[23] K. Simms, *From Kings to Warlords: the changing political structure of Gaelic Ireland in the later middle ages* (Woodbridge, 1987); 'Warfare in the Medieval Gaelic Lordships', *Irish Sword*, 12 (1975–6), 98–108.

[24] N. Canny, 'Celtic responses to English centralisation: from 1530 to the 1640s', in A. Grant and K. Stringer (eds.), *The Formation of the United Kingdom* (London, 1995); A. I. Macinnes, 'Crown, clan and fine: the civilizing of Scottish Gaeldom, 1587–1638', *Northern Scotland*, 13 (1994), 31–55; A. I. Macinnes, 'Gaelic culture in the seventeenth century: polarization and assimilation', in S. Barber and S. Ellis (eds.), *Conquest and Union* (London, 1995), 162–94. I am grateful to Professor Canny and Professor Macinnes for allowing me to consult their papers prior to publication.

major difference between the two Gaelic societies. Within Ireland, Counter Reformation Roman Catholicism had become a key focus for Irish opposition to the 'New English' colonisers and the political and religious control which London endeavoured to exert over the whole island. A shared commitment to the Catholic cause helped to minimise the old, bitter, racial division between Anglo-Irish and Irish Gaels.[25] The lack of tight government control permitted Catholic priests and practices to operate openly and without serious hindrance within the Gaelic areas of Ireland. This was definitely not the case in Scotland, as the Gaelic-speaking Irish Franciscans, who were sent on mission to the West Highlands and Islands in the 1620s and 1630s, discovered to their cost.[26] Scotland's Gaidhealtachd was sufficiently under the control of the protestant Kirk for the practice of Roman Catholicism to be essentially a clandestine matter. Many of the members of the Scottish Gaelic learned orders used their skills to spread the protestant message within the Highlands and Islands through the medium of the Gaelic language. The Gaelic ministers of Scotland were able to create their own 'Gaelic Calvinism' which survived until 1690. In that year presbyterianism was re-established in the national church and the episcopalians became a separate denomination, a process which had a disproportionately severe effect upon the Kirk in the Highlands.[27]

All of these factors, political, economic and religious, combined with the artistic, linguistic and cultural diversification, underlined the increasing differences between the two parts of Gaeldom. The Irish and Scottish Gaels had been forced to travel down different roads. They were being drawn into separate identities based upon political or geographical units, above all the kingdoms of Scotland and of Ireland. Each group was beginning to think of itself as primarily 'Irish' or 'Scottish' Gaels. In this way the normal meaning of 'Gael' was silently narrowed down to represent the Gaelic speaking area within Scotland or Ireland in the first instance and only secondly the wider community of Gaeldom. The continuous pressure of stronger state structures forced the adoption of a national political boundary which overlaid the traditional cultural and linguistic contours of one Gaeldom. However,

[25] For a discussion of the emergence of an 'Irish' identity see above Bradshaw, 43–111 and Caball, 112–39.

[26] Macdonald 'Ireland and Scotland', i, ch. 6 and other religious contacts across the North Channel, i, & ii, chs. 5, 7–10; P. Holt, 'Irish Franciscan Mission', (M. Th. thesis, University of Edinburgh, 1994).

[27] J. Dawson, 'Calvinism and the Gaidhealtachd in Scotland', in A. Pettegree, A. Duke and G. Lewis (eds.), *Calvinism in Europe, 1540–1620* (Cambridge, 1994), 231–53; T. P. McCaughey, 'Protestantism and Scottish Highland culture', in J. P. Mackey (ed.), *An Introduction to Celtic Christianity* (Edinburgh, 1989), 172–205.

the new national identities did not destroy the broader Gaelic conscious-ness. If anything, they increased the celebration of the common heritage. The careful preservation by many Scottish chiefs of their elaborate genealogies stretching back to the Milesian heroes of Ireland demon-strated the value which was still placed upon descent from the one Gaelic race. The manufacture of pedigrees, whether true or false, remained a thriving business during the early modern period and tracing one's origins back to Ireland remained one of the most prestigious ancestries for a Scottish Gael.[28] The appeal to a single Gaeldom became a fond recollection of past unity rather than a call for a common front to face present troubles together. In the warm glow of hindsight the reality of a common language, culture and ancestry was elevated into an affinity which was more substantial than any which had actually existed. It produced the myth of a 'golden age' of unity and cooperation among the Gaels of Scotland and Ireland.

II

The internal changes on both sides of the North Channel which produced a distinct Scottish Gaelic identity were reinforced by a parallel development within the Stewart kingdom. This produced a shift in the external perception of the Gael and created the new image of a 'High-lander'. That label rested upon the assumption that Scotland could be divided in two: on the one side, the Highlands and Islands, and on the other, the Lowlands. Contrary to popular opinion, Scotland's Highland/ Lowland divide is not inherent nor has it existed from time immemorial. As Professor Barrow had emphasised, 'the very terms "Highlands" and "Lowlands" have no place in the considerable body of written evidence surviving from the period before 1300. "Ye hielans and lawlans, oh whaur hae ye been?" The plain answer is that they do not seem to have been anywhere: in those terms, they had simply not entered the minds of men.'[29] The 'creation' of the Highlands was a protracted historical process which has continued down to the present day.[30] The notion of a distinct and separate Highland region became fixed in the consciousness of Scotsmen during the later medieval and early modern centuries. It was the result of two developments: a major series of changes brought

[28] W. H. D. Sellar, 'Highland family origins – pedigree making and pedigree faking' in *The Middle Ages in the Highlands*, 103–16.

[29] G. W. S. Barrow, 'The Highlands in the lifetime of Robert the Bruce', in *The Kingdom of the Scots* (London, 1973), 362–83 on which the following discussion depends, quotation 362.

[30] C. Withers, 'The historical creation of the Scottish Highlands', in I. Donnachie and C. Whatley (eds.), *The Manufacture of Scottish History* (Edinburgh, 1992), 143–56.

together the Islands and the Highlands; second, the Gaelic-speaking area within Scotland underwent a notable contraction. The fusion of these two processes produced a decisive and enduring convergence between a geographically defined region, the lands beyond the Highland Boundary Fault, with a linguistically defined area, the Scottish Gaidhealtachd. The new region of the Highlands was regarded by Lowlanders as possessing not only its own language, but also a distinct society and culture which were assumed to be radically different from their own. This simplistic partition of Scotland focused upon three categories: geography, language and culture.

The mental map of the kingdom of Scotland was redrawn and came to be divided into two distinct parts: Lowlands and Highlands, Scots and Gaelic, civilised and barbaric.[31] This involved a major shift in perception which began during the later middle ages and was completed by the end of the sixteenth century. It was essentially a change in Lowland rather than Highland attitudes and it reflected the new facts of political geography during the fourteenth and fifteenth centuries. An earlier division of the kingdom into four regions disappeared because it no longer corresponded to the map of Scottish political power. The drive by the Stewart kings to gain greater control over their entire realm neatly divided the country in two. The Lowlands where, it was assumed royal power and the 'rule of law' had already been established were separated from the Highlands where these still needed to be asserted. Lowlanders were not above using the Scots spelling of their region in a word play to emphasise that they lived in the 'law-land'.[32] These were statements of political intention and not examples of royal achievement, and they represented an underlying, long-term policy by the Scottish crown rather than an immediate political goal. The aim of bringing unity, uniformity and the benefits of 'civility', to all parts of the kingdom was embraced by the majority of the political nation within the Lowlands. Dividing the country between the 'barbaric' Highlands and the 'civilised' Lowlands gave geographical expression to this aim.

The close association between the need to bring 'law and order' and the creation of the 'Highland problem' was reflected in the usage of the actual words 'heland' and 'lawland' in the Scots tongue. Although it is difficult to establish the archaeology of individual words and trace the shifts in their usage with chronological precision, a linguistic trend can be identified. The term 'heland' and its derivatives, meaning the region

---

[31] For a recent discussion of the use of the concept of civility in the same period in Ireland, see J. Leerssen, 'Wildness, wilderness and Ireland: medieval and early-modern patterns in the demarcation of civility', *Journal of the History of Ideas*, 56 (1995), 25–39.

[32] 'Lawland', in *Dictionary of the Older Scottish Tongue*, iii, 611–12.

of the Highlands and Islands and its inhabitants, appeared first in the fifteenth century, took root in the sixteenth and by the seventeenth century had become a commonplace. The word 'helandman' was coupled with acts of disorder in the parliament in 1449. An act was passed urging, 'That consideracione be had of the helandemen the quhilikis ... commonly reft and slew ilk ane uthers'. In 1503 the earl of Argyll was given a commission to hold a court in Perth 'sa that everlik heland man and lawland mane may have justice'.[33] By the middle of the sixteenth century the words had become an established part of the Scots language and were most frequently employed in discussions concerning justice or the lack of it. The existence of the two regions had also become an accepted fact of life in the Highlands. This was clearly demonstrated in the terminology employed in the bonds of manrent made by the Campbells of Glenorchy. These bonds were written in Scots, although they were agreed between two parties who spoke Gaelic, the Glenorchy Campbells and Gaelic kin-groups in the Breadalbane district of western Perthshire. In the bonds of manrent the Highland/ Lowland boundary was used as a marker dividing the different obli- gations owed to a clan chief. On 2 June 1547 the McGillekyrs accepted John Campbell of Glenorchy as their chief in the expectation that he would protect them in all their just actions, 'as anye cheyf dois in the contreis of the helandis'. Service to the chief was due in return and, on 10 July 1550, Alexander McPatrick VcCondoqhuy promised Colin Campbell of Glenorchy, 'till ryd and gang on horss and on futt in Heland and Lawland'. It was more usual to distinguish between the duties owed in the two regions, particularly in relation to who bore the cost of the service. Donald Beg McAcrom and his kin promised on 9 September 1552 to serve Glenorchy, 'in the lawlands upon the expenses of the said Colyne and in the helands upon their own expenses, as gentlemen of the country do'.[34]

By the middle of the sixteenth century the existence of the Highland Line, which separated two societies and their customs, had become firmly entrenched in the thinking of these Breadalbane men on the frontiers between the Highlands and Lowlands. It took longer to spread

---

[33] 'Heland' etc. in *Dictionary of the Older Scottish Tongue*, iii, 88–9; and see n. 32 above. The editors do not appear to have noticed the earlier reference in Andrew Wyntoun's *Orygynale Chronykil of Scotland* written in the 1420s. Wyntoun described the burning of Elgin Cathedral in 1390 by the 'Wolf of Badenoch' and 'wyld wykkyd Helandmen', which again associates disorder with the Highlanders, cited in A. Grant, *Independence and Nationhood* (London, 1984), 208.

[34] Quotations from *Black Book of Taymouth* (ed.) C. Innes (Edinburgh, 1855), 185–6; 189–90; 196. The Glenorchy bonds are in the Scottish Record Office, GD 112/1/ 64;76;90.

into the farther reaches of the Highlands and Islands, but was present by the beginning of the next century. A description of 'The Ewill Trowbles of the Lewes' probably written in the reign of James VI, spoke of 'all those Ilanders and Lykewise the hylanders ar by nature most bent and pron to adventur themsleves ther liwes and all they hawe for ther masters and chiefes yea beyond any other people'.[35] Not only was the region itself recognised but all its inhabitants were being credited with 'Highland' virtues.

The geographical boundary between the two regions was provided by the Highland Line. Very roughly, it ran down the geological Highland Boundary Fault which almost completely traverses mainland Scotland, from Stonehaven on the North Sea coast to the Firth of Clyde at the foot of Loch Lomond. The lands to the north and west were labelled the 'Highlands' and those below the fault to the south and east were referred to as the 'Lowlands'. It was a remarkably imprecise frontier, particularly at its northern end. Aberdeen and the Moray coast lie to the north of Stonehaven but by cultural, linguistic and agricultural standards, they were within the Lowlands. Uncertainty persisted about the status of the far northern mainland of Scotland, and whether or not Sutherland and Caithness with their strong Norse tradition formed part of the Highlands. The even stronger Scandinavian links found within the Northern Isles of Orkney and Shetland made them radically different from the Highlands in both language and customs. This was recognised and the Northern Isles were normally treated as a separate unit. The Borders were also treated as a special case, though they lay within the Lowlands. Borderers displayed many of the same 'barbaric' characteristics as the Highlanders and, in Lowlanders' minds, the two groups were often bracketed together as exemplars of lawlessness and incivility. However, Borderers could be excused on the grounds that they bore the permanent defence of the realm against the English threat. When such military necessity was removed by the growth of Anglo-Scottish friendship during the sixteenth century and the subsequent union of the crowns in 1603, it was blithely assumed that in time the lawlessness would also disappear. Crucially, the Borders shared the same language and culture as the Lowlands. Rather than having to 'civilise' them completely, the 'roughness' of the Borderers could be smoothed away. The existence of these other areas within Scotland did not detract from the simple division into Highlands and Lowlands. Geographical precision was never of prime concern when determining the line between the two

[35] *Highland Papers* (ed.) J. Macphail, Scottish History Society (Edinburgh, 4 vols., 1914–34), ii, 271.

regions, allowing certain areas to be included or removed according to the particular subject under discussion or the personal opinion of the observer. What mattered was not its exact boundary, but the existence of the division itself.

In 1300 popular and official accounts had commonly divided the country into four main regions (Map 9.1). These were 'Scotland, north of the Forth'; 'Scotland, south of the Forth'; 'Galloway', that is, the south west of the kingdom including the district of Carrick; and 'the Isles', the Hebrides stretching from the Calf of Man in the south to Sula Sgier and North Rona, 50 miles north west of Cape Wrath in the extreme north. In this period 'Scotland, north of Forth' itself had two subdivisions, north and south of the Mounth. The boundary followed the Mounth, the mountain plateau within the Grampians which stretches from Ben Alder to the east coast at Stonehaven. In addition, the region of 'the Isles' included not simply the Hebridean Islands but also a large mainland section from the western seaboard as far east as the Drumalban range. This is the watershed which separates the long rivers which flow east into the North Sea from the short, westward-flowing rivers which empty into the Atlantic. The main regions, together with their own subdivisions which had both been clearly recognisable in 1300, were submerged during the early modern period. Part of the traditional region of 'Scotland, north of the Forth' along with the whole of 'the Isles' were fused into a single entity styled the Highlands and Islands. The new region covered more than half of the Scottish mainland and all the western islands.

The new bonds between the Hebrides and the northern and western mainland were the product of protracted, multifaceted developments. They encompassed extensive political and economic changes along with a quite fundamental reorientation of Scotland's communications network. The first stage in that long process was the destruction of the pre-existing regions. Within 'Scotland, north of Forth' this happened slowly and quietly. The physical barrier of the Mounth continued to influence lines of communication, but it ceased to hold much political significance. The main development was the separation of the mountainous upland terrain beyond the Firth of Forth from the lower lying and coastal areas in the east. The Forth and Tay valleys, Fife, Clackmannan, Kinross, eastern Perthshire, Angus and the Mearns along with the north-east salient by Aberdeen and the coast around the Moray and Cromarty Firths, all became absorbed into the politics and culture of the Lowlands. The gradual loss of Gaelic speech in the eastern and north-eastern parts of Scotland from the twelfth century onwards was a symptom of the ascendancy of Anglo-Norman, and later Scots, culture

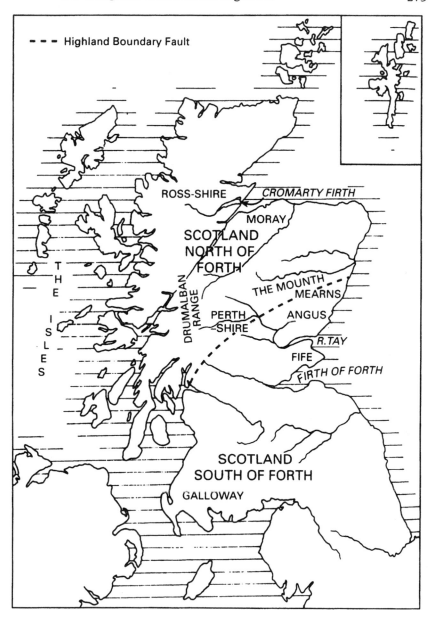

9.1 Territorial division of Scotland c. 1300
Source: M. Lynch, *Scotland: a new history* (London, 1991), 20.

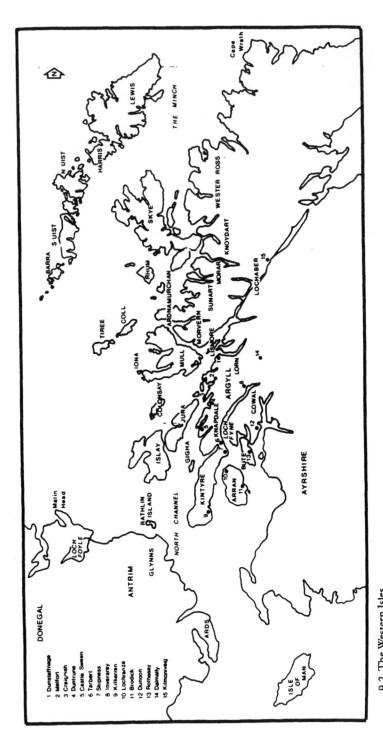

9.2 The Western Isles
Source: J. Dawson, 'The origin of the "Road to the Isles"', in R. Mason and N. MacDougall (eds.), *People and Power in Scotland* (Edinburgh, 1992), 76.

1 Dunstaffnage
2 Melfort
3 Craignish
4 Duntrune
5 Castle Sween
6 Tarbert
7 Skipness
8 Inveraray
9 Killkerran
10 Lochranza
11 Brodick
12 Dunoon
13 Rothesay
14 Dalmally
15 Kilmonivaig

DONEGAL

ARDS

ANTRIM

GLYNNS

LOCH FOYLE

Malin Head

RATHLIN ISLAND

NORTH CHANNEL

ISLE OF MAN

AYRSHIRE

KINTYRE

GIGHA

ISLAY

JURA

COLONSAY

IONA

MULL

COLL

TIREE

ARRAN

BUTE

COWAL

LORN

ARGYLL

KNAPDALE

LOCH FYNE

LISMORE

MORVERN

SUNART

ARDNAMURCHAN

RHUM

SKYE

BARRA

S UIST

N UIST

HARRIS

LEWIS

THE MINCH

WESTER ROSS

MORAR

KNOYDART

LOCHABER

Cape Wrath

N

and attitudes as well as the encroachment of its language.[36] The region 'Scotland, north of the Forth' had been replaced by a basic separation between mountain and valley or coastal plain. In its most literal sense a highland line had been drawn across the northern section of the kingdom marking the difference between the uplands and the lowlands. The new boundary within mainland Scotland had been drawn by c. 1400 and provided the first stage of the broader process. The second stage required the linkage between the old region of the 'Isles' and the newly created 'Highlands'.

By contrast to the quiet demise of the region of 'Scotland north of Forth', the political importance of the 'Isles' increased during the later medieval period (Map 9.2). The Hebrides had been under the jurisdiction of the kings of Norway until 1266, when they were ceded to the Scottish crown. Rather than increasing royal control, this diplomatic exchange consolidated the power of the family of Somerled, who had led the fight against Norse overlordship from the middle of the twelfth century. Somerled's descendants ruled over most of the Hebrides and the many parts of the western coastal areas of the mainland. By the middle of the fourteenth century Clan Donald had emerged as the dominant branch of Somerled's kin and took the title Lord of the Isles, only losing it when the Lordship was suppressed by James IV. The Lords of the Isles tended to pursue their own policies and, when it suited them, were prepared to ally with England, the 'auld enemy' of the Scots. Although still part of the kingdom of Scotland, the Lordship became more detached from national affairs than other regions[37] while the political and geographical cohesiveness provided by Clan Donald emphasised its distinctiveness. There was never a clear-cut frontier to be found on the map but respective areas of influence were apparent and acknowledged. The invisible boundary was most noticeable within the cultural sphere. The magnificent monumental sculpture of the late medieval period found in the West Highlands and Islands did not penetrate into southern or eastern Scotland in the same way, as was noted earlier, it did not spread into Ireland. Sea communications held the region together which, in addition to the islands, included the mainland's western coastline and its sea lochs around into the Firth of Clyde. Constant travel along the

---

[36] G. W. S. Barrow, 'The lost Gaidhealtachd of medieval Scotland', and C. W. J. Withers, 'On the geography and social history of Gaelic', in *Gaelic and Scotland*, 67–88, 101–30. The Gaelic notes in the *Book of Deer* indicated that in the first half of the twelfth century Gaelic was still spoken in the north east of Scotland, Withers, 103.

[37] Grant, *Independence and Nationhood*, ch. 8; and see the subsequent more assertive interpretation found in his 'Scotland's "Celtic Fringe" in the late middle ages: the MacDonald Lords of the Isles and the Kingdom of Scotland', in R. R. Davies (ed.), *The British Isles, 1100–1500* (Edinburgh, 1988), 118–41.

sea-lanes, in the birlinns, galleys and other boats, produced a water network of trade and communications. These veins and arteries of the region's life gave it a solid economic and geographical coherence and provided its distinctive maritime character. The importance of the sea was graphically illustrated by the galley which was the main feature displayed on the arms of the MacDonalds and it was also frequently depicted on the graveslabs of the West Highlands. Though the geographical extent of the region of the 'Isles' which had existed in 1300 had been retained, it had developed a different relationship to the rest of the realm. The semi-independent stance of the Isles divided the kingdom of Scotland along an east–west axis running roughly down the Drumalban watershed. The fourteenth and fifteenth centuries had witnessed the demise of 'Scotland north of Forth' and the semi-detachment of the 'Isles' from the rest of the realm.

The next stage in the creation of the new composite region of the Highlands and Islands was the disintegration of the unity of the Western Isles. It was eroded by three factors, two of which were the direct consequence of the actions of the MacDonalds themselves and particularly of their efforts to expand. In the north the MacDonalds claimed the earldom of Ross whose lands spanned mainland Scotland from the west coast opposite Skye to the east at the Moray and Cromarty Firths. The claim was based on the marriage of Donald, Lord of the Isles to Mariota Leslie, daughter of the last earl of Ross, at some point before 1403.[38] The MacDonalds clashed directly with the Stewart kings over the earldom and were drawn a long way east in pursuit of their Ross title. In 1411 they fought royal forces at the Battle of Harlaw, by Inverurie, in the north-east corner of Scotland (Map 9.3). Although they were not able to secure a lasting hold upon the earldom, in their struggle over Ross-shire the lords of the Isles had plainly demonstrated their military power to the Scottish crown. Throughout the fifteenth and well into the sixteenth century the Stewart kings could scarcely avoid regarding the MacDonalds as a potential threat to their royal position and authority.

The unity of the isles was also undermined by MacDonald expansion to the south into Ireland. Through marriage to the Bisset heiress, the MacDonalds acquired territory in Antrim and during the fifteenth century steadily expanded into the Glens and Route. Inevitably this drew them even deeper into the struggles for power within Ulster and, to a lesser extent, the whole of Ireland. This involvement was reinforced by the increased use among the Irish Gaelic chiefs of Scottish mercenary soldiers. The gallowglasses who were permanent, resident mercenaries,

[38] J. Bannerman, 'The Lordship of the Isles', in Steer and Bannerman, 205.

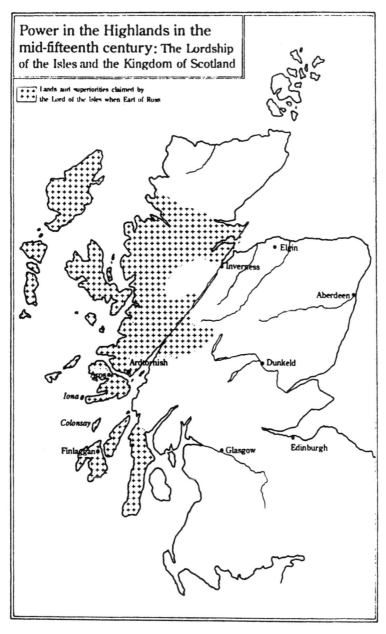

Power in the Highlands in the mid-fifteenth century: The Lordship of the Isles and the Kingdom of Scotland

Lands and superiorities claimed by the Lord of the Isles when Earl of Ross

Elgin

Inverness

Aberdeen

Ardtornish

Dunkeld

Iona

Colonsay

Finlaggan

Glasgow

Edinburgh

9.3 Power in the Highlands in the mid-fifteenth century
Source: C. Bingham, *Beyond the Highland line* (London, 1991), 72.

and the redshanks who fought only for the summer season, were primarily recruited from the isles. The economic and political pull to the south provided by the mercenary trade and their own territorial expansion into mainland Ireland shifted the focus of MacDonald power further south. The very success of Clan Donald's Irish ventures threatened to overextend their power at the Lordship's periphery and draw them away from its centre. This became fully apparent only during the sixteenth century when the southern branch of the MacDonalds concentrated upon Antrim rather than the southern Hebrides.

The regional unity of the Isles, already undermined by these pressures from the north and south, suffered a fatal blow with the formal suppression of the Lordship in 1493. Despite a series of rebellions by the MacDonalds, the subsequent enforcement of this edict both by James IV during the 1490s and by his successors throughout the sixteenth century prevented any permanent re-establishment of the Lordship. The Scottish crown was not able to take full control of the Isles but it could ensure that the previous political unity disintegrated. In the ensuing fight over the spoils no single victor emerged to replace the MacDonalds. The Lordship had provided a necessary coherence. Its collapse destroyed the integrity of the Isles as a region, creating the political conflicts and instability of the sixteenth-century 'Age of Forays'. The two main beneficiaries were, in the south the Campbells, led by the earls of Argyll, and in the north the Mackenzies, whose chief was later ennobled as the earl of Seaforth. The chiefs of the Campbells, and to a lesser extent the Mackenzies, had deliberately involved themselves in Scottish national politics and reaped the rewards of their integration into the Lowland aristocracy. Both clans remained in royal favour throughout the early modern period and gained considerable power from their position as government agents in the Highlands and Islands where royal authority was weak and, as a result, control tended to be informal and indirect. This was in addition to the great territorial strength they drew from their own formidable power bases located within the southern and northern Highlands. Each clan had been firmly rooted on the Scottish mainland and only later sought to expand into the Islands when favourable opportunities presented themselves. This was in direct contrast to the MacDonalds whose Lordship had been centred upon the islands themselves.

The political changes which followed the breakup of the lordship were central to the emergence of a new alignment within the Highland region. The east–west line between 'the Isles' and the mainland east of Drumalban disappeared to be replaced by a weaker north–south dividing line running across both the mainland and the islands. The disintegration of the region of 'the Isles' brought a return to the situation as it had been before 1300 and reattached the Hebrides to the mainland. The separate islands became bonded to their nearest section of mainland coastline. The Outer Isles of Lewis, Harris, the Uists and Barra were anchored to Ross and Sutherland in the north-west of the kingdom. Skye, with its own satellite islands, was firmly bound to Lochalsh and Knoydart; Canna, Rhum and Eigg to Arisaig and Moidart; Mull, Coll and Tiree were linked to Ardnamurchan, Morvern and Lorn, whilst Islay, Jura and Colonsay, together with the smaller islands from Seil down to Gigha were attached to southern Lorn, Mid-Argyll, Knapdale and Kintyre.

The political realignment was part of a much wider process which created a composite region covering both the Western Isles and all the Highlands. The links between the Hebrides and the whole of the northern and north-western mainland were cemented by economic developments and by the evolution of a different pattern of communications within Scotland. Previously the communications network had been dominated by sea travel, but during the early modern period continuous land routes which traversed mainland Scotland came into use. They started from the Lowlands, passed through the Highlands and finally made the short sea crossings to the islands themselves. They served a significant economic function especially for the all-important droving trade in cattle and horses (Map 9.4). These changes in the network of communications did not bring about an immediate transformation in the forms of transport. Road communications became more important, but many people continued to make the entire journey to the Western Isles or the neighbouring mainland coast by boat. Sea transport remained absolutely essential for certain purposes, especially the movement of bulky goods. The key feature to emerge in the early modern period was that for the first time it became common to travel most of the distance to the Hebrides by land with only a brief sea crossing at the end of the journey. The 'Road to the Isles' had been created.[39] Communications played a crucial role in defining Scotland's geographical divisions. Whilst the Western Isles had been held together by its seaways, the Highlands and Islands gained their coherence from the land route which crossed them and linked them to the Lowlands. The network of land communications encouraged more frequent travel across the Highland Line but the roads were primarily utilised by Highlanders coming to and

[39] J. Dawson, 'The origin of the "Road to the Isles": trade, communications and Campbell power in early modern Scotland', in R. Mason and N. Macdougall (eds.), *People and Power in Scotland: essays in honour of T. C. Smout* (Edinburgh, 1992), 74–103.

from the lowlands rather than Lowlanders travelling north. The routes did little to increase the level of accurate geographical knowledge or encourage sympathetic understanding of the inhabitants of the Highlands and Islands by their Lowland compatriots. Instead it meant that a greater number of Lowlanders, particularly those who lived in 'frontier' areas, had dealings with Highlandmen. Rather than removing the established stereotypes, the development of the 'Road to the Isles' perpetuated and probably encouraged them.

III

The new pattern of communications revolutionised the mental map of Scotland. The relative location of the Isles within the kingdom underwent a dramatic alteration. Rather than being a sea voyage away the Hebrides were placed at the end of an arduous land route. The journey now carried the traveller through the heart of the Highland mountains instead of avoiding them altogether by travelling by boat. The Isles were perceived to be beyond the mountains. To the Lowlander they appeared to lie literally and metaphorically 'at the back of beyond'. On the new mental reconstruction of their country Lowlanders relegated the Hebrides to its outer edge. 'The Isles' had lost their separate identity and had been reduced to one element within the composite region of the Highlands and Islands. In the minds of Lowland contemporaries they had been incorporated into the Scottish kingdom. When placed in relation to the Lowland 'core' of the realm the Hebridean islands were a distant periphery at the very edge of Scotland. As one seventeenth-century commentator described them, the Isles had been reduced to 'the barbarous appendices of the Scottish continent'.[40] Even Martin Martin in the Address to his *Description of the Western Islands of Scotland c. 1695* had to admit 'that it is owing to their great distance from the imperial seat, rather than their want of native worth, that their [Western] islands have been so little regarded'. He added sadly that the Isles were 'but little known or considered, not only by strangers, but even by those under the same government and climate'.[41]

The communications network bound together the new composite region of the Highlands and Islands. Its shared Gaelic language and

[40] Cited in G. A. Hayes-McCoy, *Scots Mercenary Forces in Ireland, 1565–1603* (Dublin, 1937), 86.

[41] M. Martin, *A Description of the Western Islands of Scotland c. 1695*, ed. D. J. Macleod (Edinburgh, 1994 edn), 59, 62. The Address was made to His Royal Highness Prince George of Denmark, lord high admiral of England and Ireland, and played upon the previous links between Denmark and the Hebrides in an attempt to secure the patronage of Prince George.

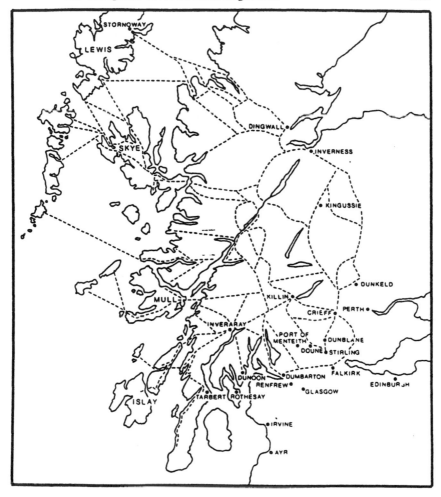

9.4 Drove routes through the Highlands
Source: As for Map 9.2.

culture provided a further strong adhesive. Gaelic had been spoken throughout much of the Western Isles and the Highlands since the eighth and ninth centuries but the linguistic tie assumed far greater significance from the later medieval period onwards. The shrinkage of Scotland's Gaelic-speaking area meant that the Gaelic heartlands now coincided with the new geographical region of the Highlands and Islands. Very soon they were regarded as synonymous. The linguistic map of medieval Scotland revealed a complex situation which only

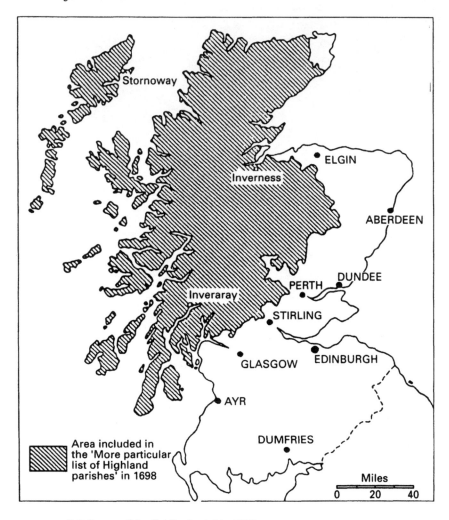

9.5 Extent of the Gaidhealtachd in 1698
Source: J. Dawson, 'Calvinism and the Gaidhealtachd in Scotland', in A. Duke,
G. Lewis and A. Pettegree (eds.), *Calvinism in Europe, 1540–1620* (Cambridge,
1994), 232.

slowly resolved itself into the two components of Gaelic and Scots-
speaking areas. In the period of its formation the kingdom of the Scots
had been created from a number of different peoples speaking a variety
of tongues. As the annalist recorded, David I (1124–53) had led into the
Battle of the Standard in 1138 an army composed of 'Normans,
Germans, English, Northumbrians and Cumbrians, men of Teviotdale

and Lothian, Galwegians, and Scots'.[42] Through much of this hetero-
geneous kingdom Gaelic was spoken. The dialect of Middle English
which became known as Scots gradually gained ground at the expense of
Gaelic and Norn, the dialect of Norse spoken in the Northern Isles and
Caithness. Even at the royal court where Anglo-Norman influence was
strong and linguistic fashion changed more quickly than in the countryside, Gaelic continued to be one of the languages spoken during the
twelfth and thirteenth centuries. At the inauguration of Alexander III on
13 July 1249, the ceremonies included the full recitation in Gaelic of the
king's pedigree by the royal sennachie or historian.[43] By the end of the
fifteenth century, however, a knowledge of Gaelic was no longer necessary at court and the vernacular of Scots had largely replaced the
international languages of Latin and aristocratic French. James IV's
careful efforts when he was king to learn Gaelic during his trips to the
Western Highlands and Islands were unusual enough to be remarked
upon by a contemporary observer.[44] During the later medieval period,
when there was a strong Gaelic revival in Ireland, the same language was
being forced into retreat within Scotland. It is not clear precisely why
Gaelic lost so much ground to Scots particularly in the east and north
east of the country.[45] The linguistic boundaries remained blurred with
many bilingual areas along the 'frontier'. By the beginning of the early
modern period it is probable that Gaelic speaking had shrunk to a pocket
in the south-west of Scotland in Galloway and to its main heartland
north of the Highland Boundary Fault (Map 9.5). By ignoring the Gaelic
spoken in the south-west it was possible to identify the Highlands and
Islands as the sole Gaelic-speaking area of Scotland. With such blinkered
vision the complex linguistic frontier between Scots and Gaelic could be
simplified and clarified. The regional and linguistic diversity present and
acknowledged within Scotland in 1300 was abandoned in favour of two
alternatives – Gaelic or Scots. Any exceptions or anomalies, such as
Norn spoken in the Northern Isles, were simply ignored.

A straightforward and simplistic identification was then made linking
a single geographical area to a single language and culture. This can be
perceived in the successive changes to the nomenclature applied to the
different vernaculars within Scotland. Until the end of the fourteenth

---

[42] Cited in M. Lynch, *Scotland: a new history* (Edinburgh, 1991), 53.

[43] J. Bannerman, 'The King's poet and the inauguration of Alexander III', *Scottish
Historical Review*, 68 (1989), 120–49.

[44] Don Pedro de Ayala, the Spanish ambassador, noted that James could speak, 'the
language of the savages who live in some parts of Scotland and on the islands': N.
Macdougall, *James IV* (Edinburgh, 1989), 283, 285.

[45] Barrow, 'The lost Gaidhealtachd' and Withers, 'On the geography and social history of
Gaelic'.

century the Latin terms 'Scotice, lingua Scotica' were regularly applied to the Gaelic language. By c. 1450 that language was referred to as 'Hibernice', 'Erse' or 'Irish', though the speech of the Lowlands continued to be known as 'Inglis'. Significantly, by the end of the fifteenth century the term 'Scottis' was used to describe Lowland speech. The Lowlanders had appropriated the name of the whole kingdom for their own tongue. In addition, by labelling Gaelic 'Irish' they associated that language and culture with a foreign realm.[46] The division into 'us' and 'them' had been made.

The congruity between the linguistic and geographical boundaries enabled the region of the Highlands and Islands to acquire a vital third characteristic. The distinctive Gaelic way of life provided the final ingredient in the stark contrast between Highlander and Lowlander. By the sixteenth century the lifestyle found within the Lowlands had diverged sufficiently from the social customs and the culture of the Gaels to create two separate societies. Both communities became increasingly convinced that Scotland was deeply divided by a cultural barrier. The tradition of vilification of the Gael which had developed in colonial Ireland had not previously been found within Scotland.[47] The composite origins of the medieval Scottish monarchy and kingdom meant that it had been impossible to treat the Gaelic element within Scotland as totally alien. This did not preclude an awareness of cultural and linguistic divisions within Scotland. The Lowlander's belief that the whole of Highland society and Gaelic culture were radically different from his own was the first move in a new direction. In the 1380s the chronicler John of Fordun had written:

The manners and customs of the Scots vary with the diversity of their speech. For two languages are spoken amongst them, the Scottish and the Teutonic; the latter of which is the language of those who occupy the seaboard and plains, while the race of Scottish speech inhabits the highlands and outlying islands. The people of the coast are of domestic and civilized habits, trusty, patient, and urbane, decent in their attire, affable, and peaceful, devout in Divine worship, yet always ready to resist a wrong at the hands of their enemies. The highlanders and people of the islands, on the other hand, are a savage and untamed nation, rude and independent, given to rapine, ease-loving, clever and quick to learn, comely in person, but unsightly in dress, hostile to the English people and language, and, owing to diversity of speech, even to their own nation, and exceedingly cruel. They are, however, faithful and obedient to their king and country, and easily made to submit to law, if properly governed.[48]

[46] D. Murison, 'Linguistic relationships in medieval Scotland' in G. W. S. Barrow (ed.), *The Scottish Tradition* (Edinburgh, 1974), 71–83.

[47] B. Bradshaw (ed.), *Representing Ireland* (Cambridge, 1993).

[48] Cited in Grant, *Independence and Nationhood*, 201.

For literary effect, Fordun was oversimplyfying a complex situation and exaggerating the differences in language and culture which existed in his day. He gave a foretaste of many of the later Lowland prejudices about Highlanders but ended on a remarkably optimistic note. He believed that, if properly governed, the Gaels would be peaceful and civilised. By using 'Scottish' as the term to describe the Gaelic language Fordun indicated that he still viewed Gaelic Scotland as an integral part of the realm. At the end of the fourteenth century there was a marked difference between the seaboard and plains and the highlands and islands but this had not yet developed into a radical split into separate regions.

By the sixteenth century it was assumed that Highlanders and Lowlanders could be distinguished not simply by where they lived, or by the language they spoke, but by the manner in which they went about their daily lives. In 1521 John Mair in his *History of Greater Britain* explained:

Among the Scots we find two distinct tongues, so we likewise find two different ways of life and conduct. For some are born in the forests and mountains of the north, and these we call men of the Highland, but the others men of the Lowland. By foreigners the former are called Wild Scots, the latter householding Scots. The Irish tongue is in use among the former, the English tongue among the latter. One half of Scotland speaks Irish, and all these as well as the Islanders we reckon to belong to the Wild Scots. In dress, in the manner of their outward life, and in good morals, for example, these come behind the householding Scots – yet they are not less, but rather much more, prompt to fight; and this both because they dwell towards the north, and because, born as they are in the mountains, and dwellers in forests, their very nature is more combative ... One part of the Wild Scots have a wealth of cattle, sheep, and horses, and these, with a thought for the possible loss of their possessions yield more obedience to the courts of law and the king. The other part of these people delight in the chase and a life of indolence; their chiefs eagerly follow bad men if only they may not have the need to labour, taking no pains to earn their own livelihood, they live upon others, and follow their own worthless and savage chief in all evil courses sooner than they pursue an honest industry. They are full of natural dissensions, and war rather than peace is their normal condition.[49]

As with the geographical and linguistic boundaries, there was sufficient basis in reality to give substance to this belief in two lifestyles. The two areas did differ significantly in their methods of farming which was the basis of their economic systems and social organisation. Though there were numerous exceptions in both Highlands and Lowlands, it remained broadly the case that the generally poor quality of the lands found in the Highlands made it a primarily pastoral region whilst the

[49] *Scotland before 1700 from Contemporary Documents*, ed. P. Hume Brown (Edinburgh, 1893), 60.

richer soils found in the Lowlands permitted arable or mixed agriculture.[50] In this respect at least the Highland Boundary Fault did mark a genuine boundary because above it lie the acid rocks which dominate the geological composition of the Highlands. The Fault line separates the poorer soils of the upland areas to the north and west from the more productive agricultural regions of the eastern littoral and the south. Arable farming is impossible across much of the Highlands with its large tracts of moorland and peat bogs. The wet climate generally brings milder temperatures than the east of Scotland but at the high altitudes, such as the Cairngorms or Ben Nevis range, full Arctic conditions are found in winter.

Although they have different soils and climatic conditions the productivity of the Islands is also generally low with one or two exceptions, notably Tiree and Islay where the land is remarkably fertile and sizeable quantities of grain can be grown. During the medieval and early modern periods the Highlands and Islands had a predominantly pastoral economy with the population engaged in tending herds of cattle and horses. The extra food essential to maintain subsistence was produced by hunting and fishing. This pattern of existence imposed a different set of seasonal rhythms to those generated by the more settled, agricultural life which predominated across much of the Lowlands. During the summer months there was a noticeable variation in lifestyle. In the Highlands it was common for communities to transfer themselves and their herds to the shielings on the upland pastures. The practice, known as transhumance, was dying out in the Lowlands although it continued to be followed in the Borders and other parts of the southern uplands until the seventeenth century.

These different farming patterns produced misunderstandings and conflict. This was particularly apparent in the contrasting attitudes towards the ubiquitous Highland practice of cattle-raiding. The very idea horrified many settled Lowlanders, who were often its victims, but within Gaelic society it was an accepted custom which was carefully regulated by its own set of rules. Raiding served the important economic function of redistributing livestock, the main means of subsistence, and had a role in the long-term survival of Highland society.[51] Cattle-raiding was also endemic in the Borders where it provoked equally adverse comment. Lowlanders occasionally excused such reiving as a form of

[50] See the Soil Survey of Scotland Maps (The Macaulay Institute for Soil Research, Aberdeen).

[51] R. Dodghson, 'West Highland chiefdoms, 1500–1745: a study in redistributive exchange', in R. Mitchison and P. Roebuck (eds.), *Economy and Society in Scotland and Ireland* (Edinburgh, 1988), 27–37.

Border warfare which, when it became overenthusiastic, failed to restrict itself to its 'legitimate' English targets.

The different rhythms of life imposed by the terrain of the Highlands and Islands were reflected in Gaelic literary culture. With the food and cattle 'wealth' from the hunt or the raid providing an important contribution to a community's resources, it was not surprising that the qualities needed by a good huntsman or the leader of a raiding band were so consistently celebrated in Gaelic poetry. The highly stylised literature of classical common Gaelic perpetuated the illusion of a static society which adhered to the traditional values of a heroic warrior caste. It praised the fighting, raiding, hunting and feasting which were supported by the region's pastoral economy.[52] These same cultural values were, however, viewed in the Lowlands as, at best, archaic and, at worst, positively barbaric. Such an attitude reflected the growing sophistication and complexity of Lowland society and its own divergence from those values previously shared with Gaelic society. Lowlanders strove to identify with, and emulate, the attitudes of mainland Europe with which they were increasingly in contact. Their diplomatic, trading and cultural links across the North Sea, especially with the old ally France and with the Low Countries, reinforced their consciousness of being part of the civilisation of Renaissance Europe and so different from the 'primitive barbarism' of the Highlands. The parallel concepts of 'civility' and 'barbarism' brought with them a moral dimension to the geographical, cultural and linguistic divisions.[53] At the beginning of the sixteenth century, as Louise Frandenburg has noted, 'the Lowlands "discovered" ideologically speaking the wildness of the north at the moment of its own attempts at consolidation'.[54]

The tensions of this Lowland view of Gaeldom and particularly the ambiguity of the use of the image of the 'wild man' were most clearly displayed within the court culture of James IV's reign. As has been noted above, the king learnt Gaelic himself, was appreciative of other aspects of Gaelic literary and musical culture and spent considerable time in the Highlands on hunting, devotional and amorous expeditions. Yet he was also active as a military campaigner in the Isles, particularly after the forfeiture of the Lordship in 1497. The suppression of the revolt of Donald Dubh MacDonald and his recapture in 1505 led the court poet, William Dunbar, to write his 'Epetaphe for Donald Oure'

[52] MacInnes, 'Panegyric code'.

[53] H. White, 'The forms of wildness: the archaeology of an idea', in *Tropics of Discourse* (Baltimore, 1978), 150–82; J. Leerssen, *Mere Irish and Fior-Ghael: studies in the idea of Irish Nationality* (Amsterdam, 1986) and above n. 31.

[54] L. G. Frandenburg, *City, Marriage, Tournament: arts of rule in late medieval Scotland* (Madison, Wis., 1991), 239.

(Donald Dubh).[55] The poem attempted to criminalise not simply Donald Dubh but his fellow Gaels as well by emphasising their treachery and linking it to the natural violence and even bestiality of their 'wildness'. The poem also tacitly criticised James' leniency towards MacDonald, suggesting that the king should have executed rather than imprisoned him.[56] The resolution of the conflict produced by James IV's contrasting responses to Gaelic Scotland, his deep attraction to its 'wildness' and his firm desire to order and civilise the region, formed the central motif within the spectacular tournament he held in June 1507 which was repeated with even greater grandeur in May 1508. The tournament's theme was the wild knight and the black lady and it celebrated both the king's recent victories over Donald Dubh and his marriage to Margaret Tudor in 1503. James himself took the role of the black knight with his troupe of 'wild men' who in the minds of the onlookers would have been associated with Highlanders. The king had taken the black 'colours' of Donald Dubh and in his own royal person resolved the tension by civilising the wildness. The tournament reflected the choices facing the Stewart kingdom at the start of the sixteenth century both in its internal and external relations. Although it was focused upon

the problem of intimate violence, of the foreigner within, and the marriage with the problem of the foreigner without, both marriage and tournament took place in the context of a whole array of challenges to and possibilities for the formation of national identity. The Scottish 'wildmen' of the later fifteenth century and early sixteenth centuries highlighted the problem and opportunity of rivalry within and between national boundaries, and between sovereign and (aristocratic) subject.[57]

Although always viewed as alien and 'wild', the 'primitive native' could sometimes be seen pursuing his life in a rural idyll. This could produce a benign if patronising interest in native customs which was found at the Stewart court when Gaelic dress was sometimes employed to evoke a rustic setting. As has recently been recognised, the distinctive 'saffron shirt' of the Highlander was depicted in an illumination in the Edinburgh *Aeneid*, probably painted for a royal wedding in 1449. The figure of Hercules on one of the carved roundels made in 1540–2 for the Presence Chamber at Stirling Castle was also shown dressed in a full saffron shirt. A few years earlier in 1538 James V had a suit of Highland

---

[55] Donald 'Oure' from the Gaelic *odhar* dun or brown, more commonly known as Donald Dubh [black]. Dunbar's famous *Flyting of Dunbar and Kennedy* attacked the Gaelic language and generally ridiculed its customs when pursuing his quarrel in verse against the Gaelic-speaking Kennedy, a poet from Carrick in the south west.

[56] Frandenburg, *City*, 167–8.   [57] *Ibid.*, 238.

clothes made for him, consisting of a long linen shirt, a short Highland jacket of variecoloured velvet and 'Heland tertane' hose or trews.[58] A similar attitude towards Scotland's 'natives' flourished in the French court of Francis I and Henry II and almost certainly helped to mould Mary Queen of Scots' own view of Highland society. It included an appreciation and adaptation of the 'rustic' music of Scotland which was often played for the young queen.[59]

During her personal rule Mary Queen of Scots followed in her father's footsteps by seeking to dress as a Highlander. In 1563 she made her only visit to the region, travelling through Cowal to Inveraray in Argyll. Before leaving Edinburgh the queen had decided that everyone who accompanied her on her royal progress should wear native costume. She was presented with a 'Highland' dress by Agnes Campbell, Lady Kintyre, wife of James Macdonald of Dunyveg and the Glens, and was probably loaned other garments by her half-sister, Jean Stewart, the countess of Argyll, when she stayed at Inveraray. In addition, the queen firmly instructed all the male members of her entourage to wear Highland attire. The English ambassador, Thomas Randolph, complained bitterly to William Cecil that, unless he were recalled to London in time, he would be forced to traipse the country in 'a safferon shyrte or a Hylande pladde'.[60] This episode might reflect a serious attempt by the Scottish queen to identify with her Highland subjects or might be just another example of Mary's great delight in dressing up. It did demonstrate in graphic manner that a cultural gap was believed to exist between the Highlands and Lowlands which needed special bridges to cross. Three years later little consideration was given to Highland sensibilities during the celebrations surrounding the baptism of James VI in December 1566. Reflecting similar themes to those present in James IV's tournament, the Renaissance triumph performed for the baptism featured a mock castle, representing the power of the monarchy, which repulsed the forces of war and chaos, dressed as Moors and 'wyld Hieland men'.[61] As his subsequent policies demonstrated, the Stewarts' mission to keep the barbarism and disorder of the Highlands at bay was one which the infant James seemed to have taken very much to heart!

Most sixteenth-century commentators either failed to recognise or chose not to emphasise the similarities between the societies on either side of Scotland's great divide. These could be found, for example, in

[58] D. G. Adams, 'Some unrecognised depictions of the saffron shirt in Scotland', *Northern Studies*, 30 (1993), 63–70.
[59] For example, 'Branles D'Escosse', *Mary's Music*, Scottish Early Music Consort (1984).
[60] PRO, SP 52/8 ff. 80r–v, *Calendar of State Papers, Scottish*, ed. J. Bain *et al.* (Edinburgh, 1898–1903), ii, 13. Randolph gained his recall!
[61] Lynch, *Scotland*, 215–16.

the Gaelic and Scots forms of praise poetry and the ideals of nobility they articulated and defended. The idealisation of the warrior elite of the clan, which comprised one of the main elements in Gaelic eulogies, was regarded by Lowlanders as very different from their own traditions of lauding chivalry and knightly virtue. However, it is interesting that 'clanship', which today would be identified as the key feature of Highland society, was not regarded as distinctive by Lowlanders in the early modern period.[62] They recognised that they shared with the Highlanders a strong sense of loyalty to the head of a 'name' or a clan chief. Their perception in this instance was the exception. The close parallels between the two regions as well as the large number of social customs which they held in common were ignored.[63] Instead of emphasising their shared heritage and experience as subjects within the same realm, the whole of Gaelic society became suspect to Lowlanders.

The Lowland assumption that Highland society was barbaric stood in marked contrast to the more measured view taken of the Northern Isles of Orkney and Shetland. The linguistic, cultural and communication problems which accompanied their assimilation into the Scottish kingdom were remarkably similar to those encountered in the Hebrides. The Northern Isles had also been part of the kingdom of Norway with Orkney and Shetland only finally being ceded to Scotland in 1468-9 and 'annexed' in 1472.[64] Within the Shetland islands and to a lesser extent in Orkney Norn remained the vernacular for the majority of the population and a different legal system based on Norse customs was practised until well into the seventeenth century. Although Orkney had come under the increasing influence of Scots language and customs from the fifteenth century Shetland remained at least as alien as the Hebrides in its cultural and linguistic outlook. It did not, however, attract the same kind of opprobrium with which Lowlanders viewed the Highlands and Islands. The Northern Isles were ruled by a branch of the Stewart royal family which made them appear to be more integrated and less of a threat to the Scottish kingdom. Their geographical location meant that they also had far greater contacts with other European countries than the relatively remote Western Isles. Orkney and Shetland traded extensively with the other countries bordering the North Sea and the Baltic.[65] In a Scottish context the Northern Isles suffered more from

---

[62] T. M. Devine, *Clanship to Crofters' War* (Manchester, 1994), 5.
[63] J. Bannerman, 'The Scots Language and the Kin-Based Society', in D. S. Thomson (ed.), *Gaelic and Scots in Harmony* (Glasgow, 1990), 1–19; W. H. D. Sellar, 'Celtic law and Scots law', *Scottish Studies*, 29 (1986), 1–27.
[64] T. M. Y. Manson, 'Shetland in the sixteenth century' in I. B. Cowan and D. Shaw (eds.), *The Renaissance and Reformation in Scotland* (Edinburgh, 1983), 200–13.
[65] G. Donaldson, *Shetland Life under Earl Patrick* (Edinburgh, 1958).

neglect than the outright hostility directed at the inhabitants of the Highlands and Western Isles. The Borders were regarded as somewhere in between the peace and civility of the 'true' Lowlands and the lawlessness and barbarism of the Highlands. As has been noted above, although they were treated as a 'problem', there was greater optimism that a solution could be found particularly after 1603. By sharing the same language and culture as other Lowlanders the Borderers were still within the charmed circle of 'Scots civilisation'.

The cultural superiority felt by Lowlanders manufactured a stereotype of the 'Highlander' which concentrated solely upon those elements which made him less 'civilised' and more 'inferior'. The catalogue of indictments had not changed a great deal from Fordun's list of unpleasant characteristics. It included the Gaelic language itself, the whole social system which revolved around the clan chief, the 'lawlessness' of Highland military, feuding and raiding activities, disobedience to the crown and, after the Reformation, a lack of religion or continued adherence to Roman Catholicism. Finally, the very appearance of the Highlander with his distinctive dress and hairstyle[66] was a visual demonstration of barbarity. James VI's Instructions to the Commission to Improve the Isles, 8 December 1608, expressed Lowland fear and distrust of the Highlands and particularly the Islands:

First in the cair we haif of planting of the Gospell amang these rude barbarous and uncivill people the want whairof these yeiris past no doubt hes bene to the grite hazard of mony poore soulis being ignorant of their awne salvatioun. Nixt we desire to remove all such scandalous reproches aganis that state [of Scotland], in suffering a pairt of it to be possessed with suche wilde savaiges voide of Godis feare and our obedience, and heirwith the losse we have in nocht ressaving the dew rentis addebtit to us furth of those Ylis, being of the patrimonie of that our crowne.[67]

The king seemed to find no incongruity in the fact that he proudly proclaimed his lineal descent from the Gaelic king Fergus whilst he lambasted Gaelic culture as uncivilised and regarded his Gaelic subjects as 'wilde savaiges voide of Godis feare and our obedience'.[68] The resulting Statutes of Iona of 1609 reflected the latter view of the Highlands and Islands. They attempted to solve the Highland problem by bringing 'civility', by changing the 'Irish' habits and customs of its people.[69] The more drastic method of planting Lowland civilisation

---

[66] In particular the Highlandman's 'glib' or long hair at the front of the head which often hung over his face.

[67] *Collectanea de Rebus Albanicis* (Iona Club, 1847), 115.

[68] I am grateful to Dr Roger Mason for drawing my attention to this irony.

[69] G. Donaldson, *Scottish Historical Documents* (Edinburgh, 1970), 174–5; Macinnes, 'Crown, clans and fine'.

directly had already failed in Scotland though this did not prevent the experiment being repeated in Ulster. The Fife Adventurers' efforts to colonise the island of Lewis at the close of the sixteenth century had been successfully resisted. This, however, merely confirmed for Lowlanders their stereotype of the 'barbarous Highlander' in sore need of lessons in civility and true religion. For nearly all Lowlanders the manners of the Gael had become a matter of comment, joke and suspicion. The Ayrshire poet Alexander Montgomerie, writing at the end of the sixteenth century, had himself spent some considerable time in Argyll. This personal acquaintance with the Highlands did not prevent him gathering together most Lowland prejudices about Highlanders. He wove them into his humourous account:

> *How the first Helandman, of God was maid*
> *Of ane horss turd, in Argylle, as is said.*
>
> God and Sanct Petir was gangand be the way,
> Heiche up in Ardgyle, quhair their gait lay.
> Sanct Petir said to God in a sport word,
> 'Can ze nocht mak a Heilandman of this horss tord?'
> God turned owre the horss turd with his pykit staff,
> And up start a Helandman blak as ony draff.
> Quod God to the Helandman 'Quhair wilt thow now?'
> 'I will down to the Lawland, Lord, and their steill a kow.'
> 'And thow steill a cow, cairle, their they will hang the.'
> 'Quattrack, Lord, of that? For anis mon I die.'
> God then he leuch and owre the dyk lap,
> And owt of his scheith his gowly owtgatt.
> Sanct Petir socht this gowlly fast up and doun,
> Zit could not find it in all that braid rownn.
> 'Now', quod God, 'heir a mervell! how can this be
> That I sowld want my gowly, and we heir bot thre?'
> 'Humff!' quod the Helandman, and turned him abowt,
> And at his plaid nuk the guly fell owt.
> 'Fy', quod Sanct Petir, 'thow sill neuir do weill'
> And thow bot new maid sa sone gais to steill.'
> 'Umph!' quo the Helandman, and swere be yon Kirk,
> 'Sa lang as I may geir get will I nevir work.'[70]

IV

The image of the 'Highlander' was largely (though not entirely) imposed upon Gaelic society from outside. It was mirrored by a subtle change in the self-identification of the Scottish Gael. The Gaelic

[70] *The Poems of Alexander Montgomerie*, J. Cranstoun (ed.), Scottish Text Society (1885–7), 280–1.

language does not contain specific terms for either 'Highlands' or 'Lowlands'.[71] In the eyes of the Gaels, the Scottish Gaidhealtachd remained essentially a cultural and linguistic region, not a geographical one. Its inhabitants thought of themselves first and foremost as Gaels, speaking the same language and sharing one culture, and when using their own language Scotland's Gaels did not need the term Highlander at all. However, it was difficult for them to remain immune to the stark contrasts made between Highlanders and Lowlanders and so the internal awareness of being a Scottish Gael became linked to the external categorisation as a Highlander.

When Scottish Gaels wrote in Scots or English they used the word Highlander to mean a Gaelic speaker. In his *History of the Macdonalds*, probably composed in the reign of Charles II, Hugh MacDonald severely criticised the sixteenth-century historians, Hector Boece and George Buchanan, 'these partial pickers of Scottish chronology and history never spoke a favourable word of the Highlanders, much less of the Islanders and Macdonalds'. He singled out Buchanan who 'knew very well that his last writing would not relish with Highlanders, calling them all *Fures et Latrones* when he treats of them, when it is well known that he himself was a Highlander'. Macdonald was referring to the fact that Buchanan, having been born in Killearn, Stirlingshire, spoke Gaelic as his native tongue. Macdonald was disgusted that Buchanan totally failed to exhibit any sense of solidarity with his fellow Gaelic-speakers. For Macdonald, speaking Gaelic and being a Highlander were one and the same thing and should have evoked a loyalty to the region and its inhabitants.[72]

Despite the new presence of a regional loyalty, a Gael's name and kin group continued to form the core of his personal identity. Clan rivalries and feuds remained important in the Highlands and Islands and provided the inspiration and focus for much of Gaelic culture. Local issues rather than national ones dominated the lives of most of the population of the region. But as contact with the Lowlands increased, so did an awareness of their common identity as Scottish Gaels or Highlanders. The Scottish Gaidhealtachd received much sharper definition because it was compared to the Galldachd, the Scots-speaking Lowlands. Although the Gaels in Scotland stuck firmly to a linguistic and cultural description of themselves, it tended to be defined within the political boundaries of the state. Gaeldom was contrasted with Lowland language, culture and society.

The growing polarisation between the different regions of Scotland

---

[71] MacInnes, 'Gaelic perception', 89–90.   [72] *Highland Papers*, i, 10–11.

was a two-way process as suspicion and mistrust of the Lowland lifestyle simultaneously grew among Highlanders. There was no attempt to highjack the terms 'Scots' and 'Scottish' to represent Gaelic language and culture. The Gaelic word for Scotland was *Alba* and both High-landers and Lowlanders were *Albannach*. Though the Gaels were willing to acknowledge that both groups remained part of the same kingdom, their perceptions of the Lowlanders were far from complimentary. The difference between the two societies was portrayed primarily as a clash of cultural values. In Gaelic praise poetry Lowlanders were called *bodaich Ghallda* or peasants who dug the earth, in contrast to Highland warriors who would not soil their hands with manual labour. In a poem describing the Battle of Killiecrankie the poet was furious that tradi-tional Gaelic fighting skills were negated by Lowland guns, complaining that warriors were 'Being felled with lead – when even cowherds can throw it'. A series of contrasts were drawn between the noble lifestyle of the Gaelic warrior and that of the Lowlander. The Gael ate venison, beef and pork and drank red wine; the Lowlander ate kail and drank whisky.[73] The new military roads through the Highlands constructed in the middle of the eighteenth century by General Wade and his succes-sors were regarded by the Gaels as Lowland devices built for Lowland purposes. Their main aim was indeed to provide fast and easy commu-nications between the bases of the British army and so impose military control over the Highland region. Many of the Highlanders who travelled the roads refused to use the new bridges, fording the streams instead, so that they would not lose their hardiness and courage by following such pampered, Lowland ways![74] The strong sense of the Gaidhealtachd's cultural superiority more than matched that felt by Lowlanders. Edmund Burt in a letter written during his travels in the north of Scotland about 1730 observed of the Gaels, 'They have an adherence to one another as Highlanders, in opposition to the people of the Low-Country, whom they despise as inferior to them in Courage, and believe they have a right to plunder them whenever it is in their Power. This last arises from a Tradition, that the Lowlands, in old Times were the possession of their Ancestors.'[75] Instead of the outright denigration practised by Lowlanders, Highland cultural superiority was more introspective. Its keynote was a marked lack of interest in the fate of Lowlanders, a disdain which was summed up in the traditional

---

[73] Not the drinks now associated with the respective regions!

[74] A. Ross, 'Old Highland roads', *Transactions of the Gaelic Society of Inverness*, 14 (1887–8), 181, 185.

[75] J. MacInnes, 'The Gaelic perception of the Lowlands', in *Gaelic and Scotland*, 89–100; quotations, 93–5.

Highland verse: 'Have you heard what I have heard, that a Lowlander [foreigner] was drowned in Inverness?' 'Tut! I am quite indifferent, I had no kinship with him.'[76]

Highlanders might wish to deny any affinity with Lowlanders but the early modern period witnessed a steady increase in contact between the two societies. In the minds of Lowlanders Gaels were all lumped together as Highlanders and their important kin relationships were largely ignored. This practice was reflected most graphically in the manner in which Lowlanders systematised Gaelic personal names. In their dealings with Lowlanders, Gaels commonly used their patronymics and clan or area names. By the early modern period the meaning of the different types of name had ceased to be properly understood and Lowlanders treated them all indiscriminately as surnames. The careful distinctions of the highly stratified Gaelic society with its numerous divisions into separate kin-groups were misunderstood or ignored by Lowlanders.[77] The very different Highland and Lowland methods of identifying individuals indicated the cultural chasm which had opened up between the two societies. This was starkly illustrated by James VI's notorious Privy Council Act of April 3rd 1603 which ordained that:

the name MacGregoure suld be altogidder abolished, and that the haill persounes of that Clan sulde renounce thair name, and tak them some other name, and that thai nor nane of their posteritie sulde call thame selffis Gregoure or M'Gregoure thair efter under paine of deade.[78]

The act was essentially a piece of propaganda rather than of seriously intended legislation. It attempted a blanket condemnation of all the kin-groups of Clan Gregor with no regard for whether they had been involved in the fighting and raiding which it was devised to end. The act propounded a simple-minded approach to the complexities of Highland society and Gaelic nomenclature and revealed how little was understood in distant Edinburgh. It followed the simplistic logic that since the Macgregors were the source of the current disorder in the Central Highlands, the problem could be solved by disposing of the Macgregors. Many Macgregors had been dispossessed of their lands and followed the lead of their chiefs, the Macgregors of Glenstrae, in fighting to recover them. But some of the Macgregor kin-groups had adopted other survival tactics by seeking the protection of other chiefs and clans.

The hounding of the Macgregors in the Central Highlands was

---

[76] Cited in MacInnes, 'Gaelic perception', 100.
[77] The transliteration of names into Latin, Scots or later English and the assumption that these names could be treated as surnames produced considerable ambiguity and error: see *Companion to Gaelic Scotland*, 210–11.
[78] Cited in W. Gillies, *In Famed Breadalbane* (Perth, 1980 edn), 133.

successful because it was enforced by the Campbells, acting as the main government agents. That clan was effective because it had been feuding with parts of Clan Gregor for nearly fifty years. This ensured that the Campbells knew precisely whom they were chasing and where they might be found. Not surprisingly, they generally caught their quarry. Other MacGregors, particularly those who had been 'adopted' by other clans, stopped using one of the available forms of Gaelic personal names and changed their clan designation. Even the famous Rob Roy Macgregor (1671–1734) could occasionally sign himself Campbell without any sense of betrayal or incongruity.[79] In the Highlands, surnames or even clan names did not provide an infallible guide to a person's allegiances.[80]

One of the key elements within the new Scottish Gaelic identity was the profound sense of belonging to the kingdom of Scotland. This was rooted in the conviction that the Gaidhealtachd had once covered the whole realm. The Gaels cherished the memory that their own language had been spoken over much of Scotland and that large sections of that former Gaidhealtachd were now irretrievably lost. This produced a feeling of dispossession and of regret for the lands which had previously supported Gaelic society and culture. It also encouraged the belief that the Gaels were the true founders and heirs of the kingdom of the Scots.[81] By the seventeenth century this notion had been subtly transformed into the assumption that Scottish Gaeldom had always been deeply committed to the Scottish crown and the kingdom. Such an interpretation of a loyal past could be sustained because throughout the middle ages the Gaelic chiefs of Scotland had acknowledged the king of the Scots as their overlord. Indeed, the royal line, coming in direct descent from the kings of Dalriada, was felt by Gaels to be still essentially their own.[82] Problems had only arisen when the Scottish kings took direct measures against the Gaelic chiefs to ensure that royal authority was fully recognised. The king's commands were disobeyed in specific instances. This certainly generated clashes but such conflict was of an entirely different nature to that encountered in Ireland during the

---

[79] Rob Roy's mother was Margaret Campbell, a member of the Glenlyon branch of the Campbells who had maintained close ties with the Macgregors throughout the preceding two centuries.

[80] The modern practice of providing lists of surnames which 'belong' to particular clans is of great importance to the tourist industry but bears no relation whatsoever to the kin-groups of early modern Gaelic society.

[81] MacInnes, 'Gaelic perception', 96–9.

[82] J. Bannerman, *Studies in the History of Dalriada* (Edinburgh, 1974); A. Macinnes, 'Scottish Gaeldom, 1638–1661: the vernacular response to the covenanting dynamic', in J. Dwyer, R. Mason and A. Murdoch (eds.), *New Perspectives on the Politics and Culture of Early Modern Scotland* (Edinburgh, 1982), 59–94.

medieval and early modern periods. The struggle of Irish Gaelic society against the imperial expansion of the English state had no equivalent on the other side of the North Channel. No war of subjugation and destruction was launched from Edinburgh against the Scottish Gaels. By contrast the stormy relations between the Stewart kings and their Gaelic-speaking subjects were regarded in the same light as quarrels between clans or kin-groups which themselves could easily turn bitter and bloody. Though they might portray themselves as sorely oppressed, Scottish Gaels could not convincingly ascribe their predicament to an alien power which sought to conquer their lands. The ideological context of warfare was radically different for the two Gaelic societies within Ireland and Scotland.[83]

The theme of loyalty to the Stewart monarchy and to the Scottish kingdom was strongly cultivated during the seventeenth and eighteenth centuries. It became a key component in the royalist and Jacobite sentiment found throughout much of the Highlands and Islands. Although it furnished a single common cause which could bind together large numbers of clans, it offered a confusing and ambiguous identity for Scottish Gaels. This first became apparent during the civil wars of the 1640s. The royalist banner raised by Montrose and MacColla provided an ideology which appeared to surmount the petty clan rivalries and feuds which had kept the Scottish Gaidhealtachd disunited.[84] But it could only do so because it rested upon a deeper antagonism: the call to fight for king and country coincided with the hatred of Clan Campbell and its chief the marquis of Argyll, the leader of the Covenanting Party.

Throughout the Islands and Western Highlands hostility to the House of Argyll brought a new unity to many of the clans and was the prime motivation of their notorious military leader, Alasdair MacColla. It brought some spectacular victories for Montrose's army, particularly the defeat of Argyll and his Campbells at the battle of Inverlochy on 2 February 1645. The price of such victories was high and Montrose himself, as well as the whole Royalist cause, suffered because MacColla

---

[83] Cf. the Irish native reaction, B. Bradshaw, 'Native reaction to the Westward Enterprise', in K. Andrews, N. Canny and P. Hair (eds.), *The Westward Enterprise* (Liverpool, 1978), 66–80; N. Canny, 'The formation of the Irish mind', *Past & Present*, 95 (1982), 91–116; 'Identity formation in Ireland', in N. Canny and A. Pagden (eds.), *Colonial Identity in the Atlantic World, 1500–1800* (Princeton, 1987), 159–212; T. Dunne, 'The Gaelic response to conquest and colonisation', *Studia Hibernica*, 20 (1980), 7–30; B. Cunningham, 'Native culture and political change in Ireland, 1580–1640', in C. Brady and R. Gillespie (eds.), *Natives and Newcomers* (Dublin, 1986), 148–70.

[84] E. J. Cowan, *Montrose for Covenant and King* (London, 1977); D. Stevenson, *Alasdair MacColla and the Highland Problem in the Seventeenth Century* (Edinburgh, 1980).

was more concerned to recover the ancestral MacDonald lands of Kintyre and the southern Hebrides from the Campbells and pursue his vendetta against them. Clan loyalties and hatreds had ultimately proved a more potent force for both MacColla and the majority of his soldiers than their commitment to the Stewart sovereign of the Three Kingdoms. When seeking the support of the Gaidhealtachd the Royalist cause had further problems to face. By its very nature, Royalist propaganda could not characterise the king's cause as a straightforward fight between the Highlands and the Lowlands of Scotland.[85] Even if Charles I or Charles II had been willing to concentrate on their Scottish kingdom alone, they would still have wanted to rule the whole realm and not one region within it. Even in their rousing incitements to battle, the Gaelic poets were not able to repudiate the association with the Lowlands or speak of the creation of a separate Gaelic state. The commitment to the whole kingdom of Scotland guaranteed that the propaganda campaign against the Lowlands could not go too far. A vision of a final victory had to include a reconciliation between the Highlands and Lowlands living in a united Scottish realm under the rule of their king.

Even had it been attainable, such an ideal Scottish solution ignored the wider British context. As long as the crown of Scotland remained joined to those of England and Ireland, support for a royalist position would also include a commitment to a form of British identity. The precise nature of that identity varied as the plans and fortunes of the royalist cause fluctuated. However, because the later Stewarts showed no sign whatsoever of abandoning their claims to any of their three kingdoms, a British dimension remained an integral part of royalism. In this respect, Scottish and Irish Gaels faced an identical dilemma. If they supported their king they could not adopt an exclusively Gaelic ideology, whether in an Irish context or in the setting of the Highlands.[86] The Stewarts might occasionally flaunt their Gaelic ancestry but they were never prepared to become kings solely of the Gaidhealtachd. The Scottish Gaels carried the same contradictions into their support of the Jacobite rebellions.[87] The problems and dangers of being tied to the political agenda of the Stewarts were revealed all too clearly in the

[85] In the same way, Ian Lom and the other Gaelic poets could not convincingly portray the Campbells and their allies as Lowlanders or non-Gaels, A. Macinnes, 'Gaelic culture' and 'Scottish Gaeldom'; *Gàir nan Clàrsach*; *The Seventeenth Century in the Highlands*.

[86] Breandàn O Buachalla, 'James our true king: the ideology of Irish royalism in the seventeenth century' in D. G. Boyce (ed.), *Political Thought in Ireland since the seventeenth century* (London, 1993), 7–35.

[87] B. P. Lenman, *The Jacobite Clans of the Great Glen, 1650–1784* (London, 1984); *The Jacobite Risings in Britain 1689–1746* (London, 1980); P. Hopkins, *Glencoe and the End of the Highland War* (Edinburgh, 1986).

aftermath of the 1745 rebellion. When the Highlands became too closely associated with the Jacobite cause, it brought retribution upon the whole of Scottish Gaelic culture and language. The defeat at Culloden led to a concerted military, political and judicial campaign against Gaelic society. In the event, these punitive measures were less effective in altering Highland life than the long-term economic and social factors which led to the transformation of the Gaidhealtachd during the eighteenth century.[88] However, they represented the triumph of the Lowland view that Gaelic culture and society were barbaric and a threat to the country's security. Such an attitude had been readily adopted by the British state because it appeared to fit so accurately with the earlier English experience of the conquest of Ireland.

Significantly, it was only after the Gaels had been subdued and civilised that Highland scenery, society and culture could be 'discovered' by the Lowlanders.[89] The warlike Highlander could then be turned into the key fighting man of the British army.[90] After the assimilation of the Highlands, a place could be found for Scottish Gaels within the British imperial state. The Gaelic diaspora created by the flow of civilian emigrants from the eighteenth to the twentieth centuries along with the military might of the Highland regiments helped to extend and preserve the British empire throughout the world. Within the British Isles the sustained attention created by Queen Victoria and her devotion to Balmoral, coupled with the Romantic Movement's positive evaluation of the region and its culture, completed the transformation of the image of the Highlands. The region became an attractive wilderness of mountain, glen and loch. It was peopled with loyal natives clad in curious attire. Highland dress, especially the kilt and clan tartans which today form the most familiar badges of the Highland heritage, were a product of this imaginative nineteenth-century re-creation. The tame, tartan image of the Highlander was invented.[91] The assumptions which accompany that image have a profound effect upon the current debate concerning the future of the Highlands today and of its 'natural environment'.[92]

However this romantic perception is a far cry from the medieval Scottish Gael's view of his own identity. The changes of the early modern period within the Gaidhealtachd had destroyed the old patterns of consciousness. The emergence of the Highlands and the label of

[88] Devine, chs. 2–3.
[89] T. C. Smout, 'Tours in the Scottish Highlands from the eighteenth to the twentieth centuries', *Northern Scotland*, 5 (1983), 99–121.
[90] Lenman, *Jacobite Clans*, chs. 9–10.
[91] Withers, 'Historical creation of the Scottish Highlands'.
[92] J. Hunter, *On the Other Side of Sorrow: nature and people in the Scottish Highlands* (Edinburgh, 1995).

Highlanders had forced Gaels within Scotland to think of themselves increasingly as Scottish Gaels. They retained their localised personal and clan identities and their general attachment to a common Gaeldom. Although the Scottish element of their identity remained of great significance in Gaelic consciousness, the Highland Line now seemed to divide them from their fellow Scots. This left a contradiction within the Highlanders' self-identity: it was distinct from that of the Lowlander but could not be conceived of as entirely separate from them. By contrast, Lowlanders had succeeded in excluding the Gaidhealtachd from their mental map of the realm. They had appropriated the name of 'Scots' for their own language and culture and at the same time, by labelling Gaelic 'Irish', had indicated that it was foreign to Scotland. By the sixteenth century Lowlanders believed that Scotland should be a monocultural kingdom and that the culture should be their own. The Highland/Lowland divide was the geographical expression of this attitude. It constituted the boundary between Lowland civilisation and Gaelic barbarity.

Scottish Gaels could find no way to counter this Lowland exclusivity. They were left with an extremely strong linguistic and cultural identity but one which could find no permanent political expression of its own. The British dimension of their royalist and Jacobite ideologies did not bring any clear political goals for the Gaidhealtachd itself. With the Scottish element of their identity blocked by Lowland attitudes, and the British element remaining vague and insubstantial, Highland consciousness was forced to become more introspective. The concentration upon Gaelic language and culture produced a renewed emphasis upon the glories of the past and the Gaelic unity which had previously existed. But the early modern period witnessed the separation of Gaeldom into Scottish and Irish worlds. It left the Scottish Gaels, though fortified by their own remarkable cultural achievements, on their own, coping with their new label of Highlanders. They were able to reshape that image to suit the Gaidhealtachd but they were not able to forge all the components of a complete identity. The lack of a clear political goal left the Scottish Gaels vulnerable to the resulting contradictions. The tensions between being Scottish, being a Gael, and being a Highlander could not easily be resolved. The legacies of these competing elements within the Scottish Gaelic identity were to have a profound and lasting impact upon the history of the Highlands, Scotland and the whole British archipelago. They remain with us to this day.

10　'No remedy more proper': Anglo-Irish unionism before 1707

Jim Smyth

Can the divergent political and cultural experience of eighteenth-century Scotland and Ireland be traced to the 1707 act of Union? The great Victorian historians James Froude and William Lecky thought so. In their view Scotland's prosperity and stability, and Ireland's poverty and discontent, were rooted in the former's admission to, and the latter's exclusion from, full partnership with England in the new British empire. While that interpretation is, to say the least, debatable, the insight on which it is predicated is suggestive; namely that the Anglo-Scottish union constitutes an event in Irish history. Certainly it had an impact at the time. Irish readers could follow the Anglo-Scottish stand-off in 1704–5 in the pages of the Dublin-published *Impartial Occurrences*, just as they were later furnished with detailed reports of the negotiations leading to the union, 'this great and glorious work', by the *Dublin Gazette*.[1] And during these tense years the authorities kept a close watch on northern presbyterians, fearful that they were conspiring with their Scottish brethren to oppose the treaty. In 1759 the mere rumour of an intended union between Britain and Ireland sparked off rioting in Dublin, but in 1707, outside Ulster, public (that is Anglican) opinion ran in precisely the opposite direction. It seems that Jonathan Swift's protests at Ireland's exclusion from the Union, his 'Verses said to be composed upon the union' and the better known *The Story of the Injured Lady* – though published posthumously – reflected public concerns.

Swift scholars usually relate the *Injured Lady* back to William Molyneux's *The Case of Ireland Being Bound by Acts of Parliament in England, Stated* (1698) and forward to his own *Drapier's Letters* in the 1720s. The 1707 disquisition – his first pamphlet on Irish affairs – is thus firmly located within a discourse, or 'tradition', which used to be called

---

An earlier version of this chapter appeared in *Bullán. An Irish Studies Journal*, 2:1 (1995).

[1] E.g. *Impartial Occurrences*, 26 Dec. 1704, 6 Jan., 23 Jan., 27 Jan., 3 July, 7 Aug., 9 Aug., and 5 Oct. 1705. *Dublin Gazette*, nos. 164–91, 12 Nov. 1706–18 Feb. 1707. The quotation is from the Irish parliament's address published in the *Gazette* no. 236, 22–26 July 1707.

'colonial', and is now called protestant or Anglo-Irish, nationalism. It is true that the author of the *Injured Lady* advocates economic self-sufficiency for the poor and slighted kingdom of Ireland and that, in this sense, he anticipates the patriotic self-help literature, some of it by his own hand, of eighteenth-century protestant Ireland. But it is worth restating the obvious: that the pamphlet was inspired as much by a sense of disappointed unionism, as by 'national' pride. In this respect *The Injured Lady* relates to another, lesser known, Anglo-Irish discourse.

In the persona of the patriotic Drapier, Swift's position in the canon of eighteenth-century Anglo-Irish nationalism (so awkwardly at variance with his self-proclaimed Englishness), owes much to the venerable governing paradigm of Irish eighteenth-century historiography: the formation of an Irish identity among protestants and, partly as an outcome of that process, the assertion by the protestant elite of Ireland's status as a distinct kingdom with an autonomous parliament. As J. C. Beckett put it, 'the only continuing theme' [of Irish political history in this period, is that] 'of conflict over the constitutional relations between Ireland and England'.[2] This history of conflict had a recognisable starting point with the 'startling assertion of independence' by the Irish general convention held at Dublin in 1660. Sir William Domville prepared a 'disquisition' for the convention which marshalled historical precedent to demonstrate the autonomy of the Irish parliament, thereby 'anticipating' by thirty-eight years his son-in-law, William Molyneux's, *Case of Ireland*.[3] The case in turn served as the foundation text of 'colonial nationalist' aspiration and argument: an aspiration realised, or so it seemed, by the 'constitution of 1782'.

Clearly, identity formation and issues of constitutional status are important dynamics of Irish politics and society during the 'long eighteenth century', but the road to 1782 was neither straight nor narrow. T. C. Barnard and David Hayton have shown that protestant senses of identity in the century after 1660 were variegated, mutable and ambivalent. Similarly, while Irish protestant unionist sentiment before 1707 is often dismissed as near irrelevant,[4] recent explorations of unionist

[2] J. C. Beckett, *The Anglo-Irish Tradition* (London, 1975), 47. Strictly speaking, after 1707 constitutional relations subsisted between Ireland and Great Britain.
[3] T. C. Barnard, 'Planters and politics in Cromwellian Ireland', *Past & Present*, 61 (1973), 60–1, 66. More recently Dr Barnard has argued that it is wrong to view either the convention, Domville or Molyneux as proto-nationalist: see his contributions to J. H. Ohlmeyer (ed.), *Ireland, from Independence to Occupation 1641–1660* (Cambridge, 1995), at 239, 288.
[4] David Hayton describes the Irish commons' 1703 unionist address as a 'footnote': Hayton and Daniel Szechni, 'John Bull's other kingdoms: the English government of Scotland and Ireland', in C. Jones (ed.), *Britain in the First Age of Party, 1680–1750: essays presented to Geoffrey Holmes* (London, 1987), 268.

opinion suggest otherwise.[5] The traditional emphasis on Irish identity and on the politics of legislative independence can be explained in part – drawing an analogy with classic historiography of pre-revolutionary America – by the search for the ideological origins of the 'revolution' of 1782, and, indeed, of the separatism of the United Irish movement in the 1790s. Non-origins, false starts or failed projects – such as early Irish unionism – are sidelined by an indifferent hindsight. Imaginative reconstructions of the range of alternative possibilities available to contemporaries are thus inhibited. Yet like the once little-heeded English Jacobites, colonial American loyalists or E. P. Thompson's handloom weavers, the early Irish unionists are entitled to their say.

In the late nineteenth century both Lecky and Froude – and they agreed on very little – treated pre-1707 Irish union proposals seriously.[6] As unionists, writing at a time when the union was being called into question by the home rule movement, their position is understandable. They may have worried about the future of the union, but they never doubted its legitimacy or desirability; nor did they assume that it would break up. For both, the centripetal impulses at work in Anglo-Irish relations were as significant and as revealing as the centrifugal. In contrast, Hibernocentric history focuses more on divergence than on convergence. It seems likely, however, that as the Irish experience is re-examined from the vantage point of the new three-kingdom 'British' history, so the centripetal and integrative factors at work in Anglo-Irish relations will again become more visible. Caroline Robbins, a pre-Pocockian practitioner of these islands' history, identified federal unionism as a shared tenet of the Scottish and Irish 'eighteenth-century commonwealthmen', Andrew Fletcher, Robert Molesworth and Henry Maxwell.[7]

I

If Anglo-Irish relations represent the master theme of eighteenth-century politics, the 'Catholic Question' runs a close second. The Catholic presence raised problems for advocates of parliamentary

[5] J. Kelly, 'The origins of the act of union: an examination of unionist opinion in Britain and Ireland, 1650–1800', *Irish Historical Studies*, 99 (1987), 236–63; J. Smyth, '"Like amphibious animals": Irish Protestants, ancient Britons 1691–1707', *Historical Journal*, 36 (1993), 785–97.

[6] J. A. Froude, *The English in Ireland in the Eighteenth Century* (3 vols, London, 1872), i, 285–7, 303–4; W. E. H. Lecky, *England in the Eighteenth Century* (8 vols, London, 1878–90), ii, n.p. 416, viii, 266, 268–9.

[7] C. Robbins, *The Eighteenth-Century Commonwealthman* (Cambridge, Mass., 1959), 6, 9–10, 20, 147–9, 183–4.

sovereignty and of union alike. The first insisted that the realm of Ireland was a 'sister kingdom' to the realm of England and that the king's loyal subjects in Ireland enjoyed their own ancient constitution and all the rights and privileges of free-born Englishmen. The second insisted that, as free-born Englishmen, the protestants of Ireland were as entitled to representation at Westminster as the inhabitants of Hampshire or Essex. Both schools – and they overlapped – insisted upon equality of treatment. But if Ireland was a conquered country, and it was obvious to protestants on either side of the Irish Sea in 1659 or 1692 that the Catholics were a conquered people, then surely Ireland could not be an equal partner of England. Was it not, rather, a colony, or province, subject to the laws of conquest?

Seventeenth-century Englishmen assumed that Ireland was a conquered country and rebutted Irish protestant claims to legislative independence or requests for union accordingly. When the anti-protectorate republicans – the commonwealthmen – challenged the right of Scottish and Irish MPs to sit in Richard Cromwell's parliament in 1659, they argued that Scotland, and Ireland even more so, were but 'provinces at best'.[8] Since the conquest of Catholic Ireland was not disputed, the 'Irish' MPs and the court party, to which most of them belonged, drew a distinction, which would later become familiar, between the 'political nation' comprising English protestants, and the subjugated popish natives. As Dr Clarges declared, 'For Ireland, they have as good a foot as any. They are united to you, and have always had an equal right with you ... those that sit for them are not Irish Teagues, but faithful persons.'[9] Sir Thomas Stanley, the member for Tipperary and Waterford, did not equivocate: 'I am not to speak for Ireland' he announced, 'but for the English of Ireland ... the members for Ireland and their electors are all English who naturally claim the right to have votes in making laws by which they must be governed.'[10] During the restoration period protestants acknowledged the conquest but denied that it applied to them. In fact, they had themselves carried out the conquest under the 'commission of royal authority'.[11] Entering a protest against the restrictions placed on the Irish cattle trade by Westminster in 1667, Arthur Annesley, earl of Anglesey, conceded that 'Ireland is a conquered nation' but warned that it 'must not be so treated, for the conquerers inhabit there'.[12]

[8] J. T. Rutt (ed.), *Diary of Thomas Burton* (4 vols., London, 1828), iv, 130, 229.
[9] *Ibid.*, 174.   [10] *Ibid.*, 114, 239.
[11] Roger Boyle, Earl of Orrery, *An Answer to a Scandalous Letter Lately Printed and Subscribed by Peter Walsh* (Dublin, 1662), 10; Richard Lawrence, *The Interest of Ireland in its trade and Wealth Stated* (Dublin, 1682), 118.
[12] *Cal. S.P. Ire 1667*, 539.

Paradoxically, in 1698, seven years after the Williamite reconquest, Molyneux's *Case* did not concede even that much, positing instead the voluntary submission of the native nobility to Henry II as the contractual basis for the continuing sovereign status of the kingdom of Ireland. But, as one of his English critics, Simon Clement, was quick to point out, that theory was critically flawed: the constitutional inheritance to which he laid claim had (Old English) Catholic antecedents. Molyneux's solution to the problem – he wished the Catholic majority away – is unsatisfactory, patently inaccurate, and has achieved notoriety among twentieth-century historians.[13] It was not, however, without precedent. Like Stanley before him, he spoke only for the English of Ireland. The 'natives' could be discounted because 'the present people of Ireland are the progeny of the English and Britains, that from time to time came over into this kingdom, and there remain but a mere handful of the ancient Irish at this day; I may say, not one in a thousand'.[14] Insofar as he silently conflated 'ancient Irish' with 'Catholic', and implied that 'Old English' somehow equalled New English protestant, Molyneux does indeed stand guilty of the evasion of which he is accused. As Clement responded 'he takes no notice of the distinctions that ought to be made ... but that he might carry his point, blends and confounds them together, as if they were to be considered alike, as one entire people established and continuing upon the same bottom'.[15] On the other hand, those Englishmen who described Ireland as a conquered nation, colony or province, were likewise guilty of 'blending and confounding' protestant and Catholic.

Molyneux and others were anxious not only to make a distinction between the political nation, 'the present people of Ireland', and the native Catholic inhabitants, but, by understating Catholic numbers, to exclude them from the constitutional agenda. This conjuring trick was performed by a surreptitious transfusion of 'Old English' blood. 'So many English colonies [have been] planted in Ireland', wrote a pamphleteer in 1673, 'that if the people had been numbered by poll, such as were descended of English race, would have been more in number, than the ancient natives.' Moreover, the 'first inhabitants' almost certainly came 'out of Britain'.[16] Both these arguments were recycled by Sir

---

[13] Smyth, 'Like amphibious animals', 789–90.

[14] William Molyneux, *The Case of Ireland being Bound by Acts of Parliament in England, Stated* (Dublin, 1698), 20.

[15] Simon Clement, *An Answer to Mr Molyneux his Case of Ireland ... Stated: and his dangerous notion of Ireland's being under no subordination to the parliamentary authority of England refuted* (London, 1698), 4.

[16] *The Present State of Ireland, Together with Some Remarques upon the Ancient State Thereof* (London, 1673), A3, 2.

Richard Cox in 1698; both were disingenuous. The 'British' and 'English' majority constructed by Molyneux, Cox and earlier pamphleteers implied a protestant majority. The Old English unilaterally recruited to make up the numbers were, however, incorrigibly Catholic.

The Catholic Question shaped Anglo-Irish constitutional debates in other, sometimes contradictory, ways. Unionists who wished to stress Ireland's affinities with, and therefore its assimilability to, England, stressed the protestantism and Englishness of the political nation and minimised the Catholic presence. In 1703 Henry Maxwell reassured his English audience that 'the number of protestants are much increased of late' and that there 'is no danger to be apprehended' from the defeated, disarmed and leaderless 'popish Irish'. All that was now required were 'some foot and dragoons, to scour the bogs and mountains, and keep the raparees in order'. Five years later Swift made a similar argument, albeit for different purposes. The Catholics, he maintained, had been successfully subdued by the penal laws: 'some of the most considerable among them are already turned protestants, and so, in all probability, will many more ... and, in the mean time, the common people without leaders, without discipline, or natural courage, being little better than *Hewers of Wood, and Drawers of Water*, are out of all capacity of doing any mischief'. Nevertheless the English government must not be complacent. If it continued to exclude Ireland from the commercial benefits of union, Maxwell warned, then the British protestant merchants and manufacturers, 'the only sure pledge we have for the security of our government', would be 'driven away [and] Ireland must necessarily, in the course of a few years, return into the possession of its old proprietors'. Also in 1703 the Irish parliament's address calling for union declared that 'the number of and power of the papists is very formidable'. Great danger was to be apprehended from the Catholics after all.[17]

II

England and the 'English interest' in Ireland needed each other. The protestants garrisoned hostile territory on England's exposed western flank. Ultimately protestant security in Ireland rested on English arms. The Catholic threat thus set limits to protestant ambitions and they always denied any intention of 'setting up for themselves'. The contrast

---

[17] Henry Maxwell, *An Essay towards an Union Between England and Ireland* (London, 1703), 20–1, 32, 34. Swift, *A letter from a member of the house of commons in Ireland to a member of the house of commons in England* in J. McMinn (ed.), *Swift's Irish Pamphlets, an Introductory Selection* (Geralds Cross, 1991), 41; *Commons Journal Ireland*, ii, 341–2.

with Scotland is illuminating. Whereas the Scottish parliament precipitated the political crisis which led to the 1707 act of Union by
threatening to opt out of the Hanoverian succession, in 1703 the Irish
parliament declared any 'impeachment' of the English act fixing the
succession treasonable. They dared not challenge it. The alleged self-
confidence and self-reliance of the post-Boyne elite[18] must have looked
rather tame when viewed from Edinburgh.

Technically Irish protestants also had less space to manoeuvre than
the Scots. The British monarchy had been created by the union of the
Scottish and English crowns in 1603; the 1703 Scottish act of security
seemed to presage the dissolution of that union. The Irish 'crown' was
created by the 1541 act for kingly title, whereby the kingdom of Ireland
was 'annex'd' to the king of England. The king of England was therefore
de jure and *de facto* king of Ireland. The difference between the Scottish
and Irish crowns was vividly demonstrated on 17 March 1649, by the
act for 'abolishing the kingly office of England and Ireland'. The English
parliament treated the English and Irish crowns as indivisible, but, while
it was prepared to execute the king of Scotland, it did not presume to
abolish the Scottish crown.[19] Similarly, in 1689 Westminster confirmed
William and Mary as king and queen of England and Ireland but not of
Scotland, which titles the Scots conferred themselves. The protestant
community in Ireland was tied to England by the imperatives of security
and statute. The separation of the Irish from the English crown was not,
even in constitutional theory, an option.

Anglo-Irish and Anglo-Scottish relations differed in another important respect. The Anglo-Scottish union was a self-consciously 'British'
project. The Scots thought of themselves as Scots or as north Britons
but never, no matter how anglicised, as north English. With the notable
exception of the Scots presbyterians in Ulster, protestants in Ireland –
arrivistes or second, third or fourth generation settlers – considered
themselves English. This was a function of custom, language, in a word,
of 'culture' and of descent. As the first duke of Ormond remarked in
1667, 'I have been strongly mistaken these forty years and upwards, if I
am not by birth, education, religion and affection a perfect Englishman.'[20] The inclusive term 'British' tended to emerge only at those rare

---

[18] N. Canny, *Kingdom or Colony, Ireland in the Atlantic world 1560–1800* (Baltimore and
London, 1988), 116.

[19] C. H. Firth and R. S. Rait (eds.), *Acts and Ordinances of the Interregnum, 1642–1660*
(London, 1911), iii, 18–20. This act refers to 'the said crowns of England and Ireland'.
I am grateful to Dr John Robertson for alerting me to the significance of this act in its
three kingdom context.

[20] Ormond to Ossory 21 Jan. 1667: Bodl. Carte MS 70 ff. 415–18.

moments of pan-protestant solidarity, such as the Jacobite war. As soon as the Catholic enemy was defeated the old church–presbyterian animosities resurfaced, and along with them the old distinction between English and Scots. The construction of a new 'British' identity has little or no place in an Anglo-Irish unionist discourse predicated upon the inalienability of English liberties. Protestants bristled at the inferior status implied by their being bound by laws, usually restricting trade, to which they had not consented. Were they not 'one people, sometimes dwelling here ' [in Ireland], sometimes there [in England]', 'bone of their bone and flesh of their flesh'?[21]

The closeness of settler identification with the 'mother country' is worth underlining, not least because in the headlong pursuit of the 'ideological origins' of protestant nationalism it is perhaps too easily lost sight of; more so because it set limits to the aspiration to legislative 'independence' – separatism was not envisaged – and helps to explain the seeming ambivalence of their constitutional posturing. In the course of his defence of Irish parliamentary sovereignty, Molyneux lamented the fact that union was not on offer. In 1703 the Irish commons advocated either annual parliaments or a union as appropriate remedies for Irish grievances. The contradiction is only apparent. The champions of parliamentary sovereignty did not aim at national self-determination but government by consent and economic prosperity, and to these ends 'independence' or union represented equally valid means. In the later eighteenth century when the protestant community had come to define itself as 'the Irish nation', that sense of identity precluded the unionist option. Earlier generations of English–Irish protestants entertained no such qualms.

Many of the theoretical and practical issues raised by union were first aired in a sustained and public fashion during the debates in Richard Cromwell's parliament on whether or not Scottish and Irish members should be allowed to sit. The inspiration of these debates was short term and party political. The anti-protectorate, commonwealth opposition targeted the thirty 'Scottish' and thirty 'Irish' members as a fairly solid phalanx of 'court' placemen, and hoped to reduce or eliminate the court majority by expelling them. The arguments, 'prudential, political,

---

[21] Sir Francis Brewster, *A Discourse Concerning Ireland and the Different Interests Thereof, in Answer to the Exon and Barstaple Petitions; shewing that if a law were enacted to prevent the exportation of woollen manufactures from Ireland to foreign parts, what the consequences thereof would be both to England and Ireland* (London, 1698), 50; J. Hovell, *A Discourse on the Woollen Manufacture of Ireland and the Consequences of Prohibiting its Exportation* (Dublin, 1698), 41; Annesley in *Diary of Thomas Burton*, 225, *Declaration of Sir Charles Coote* (Dublin, 1660), 7; *A Declaration of the General Convention of Ireland* (London, 1660), 5.

equitable and legal' (as James Harrington summarised them[22]) were driven more by immediate tactical considerations than by ideological conviction. None the less, real issues of principle were at stake. Harrington, for example, had earlier addressed the problem of provincial dependencies in his *Oceana*, published in 1656. He also tackled these issues, including the dangers of the Anglo-Scottish union, in his *Political Aphorisms*, published in 1659, when, after the demise of Richard's parliament, tactical considerations no longer applied. The principal objection of the commonwealthmen, that the 'Scots' and 'Irish' were mere voting fodder jobbed in by Whitehall, was both genuine and prescient. It has been argued that the primary motive, on the English side, for the Anglo-Scottish union initiatives of 1668–70 and 1702–7, was precisely the prospect of augmenting the court's parliamentary majority, and that the forty-five closely 'managed' Scottish members returned to Westminster after 1 May 1707 did generally live down to expectation.[23] With very few exceptions English statesmen were either indifferent or hostile to Anglo-Irish union in this period. Significantly, on one of the few occasions when it does appear to have been actively considered, once again Westminster arithmetic provided the spur.[24]

A point that the 1659 opposition repeatedly hammered home was that the 'Scottish' and 'Irish' members were neither Scottish nor Irish. This was particularly true of the Scottish representatives, many of whom, as an irate commonwealth supporter afterwards noted, had never got further north than Gray's Inn.[25] The accusation was less grounded in the case of the Irish representatives who did, at least (insofar as seventeenth-century MPs represented anyone) represent the protestant interest in Ireland. There were however, two kinds of protestant: the Cromwellian newcomers and those born in Ireland, or established there before 1641 – the old protestants. This division probably accounts for the differing positions adopted by the Irish contingent during the debates. Stanley, a Cromwellian, speaking for 'the English in Ireland', insisted that 'Ireland is naturally and inseparably' united to England by language, habit, laws and interest, and should remain so on grounds of equity and government by consent. Arthur Annesley, Irish by birth, and interestingly a supporter of Anglo-Scottish

---

[22] *Diary of Thomas Burton*, 143.

[23] P. W. J. Riley, *The Union of England and Scotland: a study in Anglo-Scottish politics of the eighteenth century* (Manchester, 1978), 5–6, 241, 314; Hayton and Szechni, 'John Bull's other kingdoms', 247.

[24] Hayton and Szechni, 'John Bull's other kingdoms', 268.

[25] Slingsby Barthall, *A Narrative of the Most Material Debates and Passages in the Late Parliament* (1659), 484, in *Somers Tracts* (London, 1811), vi.

union, reminded the house that the Irish 'are your own flesh', before proceeding the next day to call for an Irish parliament: 'That was the old constitution ... as you are reducing yourselves to your ancient constitutions why not Ireland the same? Why not lords and commons there?'[26] As events soon showed, Annesley spoke for the old protestants.

The centre could not hold. The political destablisation which followed the fall of the protectorate led to the collapse of London-based authority. And as authority at the centre disintegrated, the Cromwellian settlements in Scotland and Ireland began to unravel. Up in Edinburgh General Monck, fearful that the withdrawal of English troops would expose his rear to a national or royalist uprising, cannily delayed his march south until he had reached an understanding with the Scottish estates. In Dublin on 13 December 1659 a group of army officers, with old protestant support, seized Dublin Castle, and the political initiative, from the republican faction then in control. The old protestants, led by Lord Broghill and Sir Charles Coote, declared for the Long Parliament in February 1660, denouncing the Rump for, among its other transgressions, assuming authority over Scotland and Ireland 'without precedent or example in any former age'.[27] The Cromwellian union was dead.

Disproportionate taxation and the denial of free trade have been cited as the chief causes of old protestant disenchantment with the union; a disenchantment which, James Kelly suggests, explains why the 1660 Dublin Convention opted for a 'domestic parliament' under a restored monarchy, as well as the absence of pro-unionist rhetoric during the following decades.[28] The recovery of the ancient constitution and the redress of economic grievances converged. The Convention 'declared and asserted':

> that as for several hundred years last past, by the laws and laudable customs and constitution of the nation, parliament has been usually held in Ireland and that those parliaments' laws have been enacted, and laws repealed, and subsidy's granted ... so that right of having parliaments held in Ireland, is still justly and lawfully due and belonging to Ireland, and that the parliament of England never charged Ireland in any age with any subsidies, or other public taxes or assessments, until the violence offered in December 1648.[29]

[26] *Diary of Thomas Burton*, 225, 239, 241–2.
[27] Cited by A. Clarke in 'Colonial constitutional attitudes in Ireland, 1640–1660', *Proceedings of the Royal Irish Academy*, 90, C (1990), 372.
[28] Kelly, 'Origins of the act of union', 238; Barnard, *Cromwellian Ireland: English government and reform in Ireland 1649–1660* (Oxford, 1975), 29, 34; 'Planters and politics', 60–2, 65.
[29] *Declaration of the General Convention of Ireland*, 4.

That protestant assertion of independence is, indeed, as has been said, 'startling', especially when we note the Old English Catholic sources of the constitutional tradition it invoked.[30]

Yet the Convention's declaration was heavily qualified. 'The people of Ireland' it stated, 'are so far from designing or intending to divide or separate from England, as they conclude such a division or separation would be absolutely destructive to the nation, and that there is nothing that Ireland more abhors, they being generally bone of their bone and flesh of their flesh.' Moreover, an appendix to the published text reported that a 'common theme' of the Convention was that 'the benefit of Ireland is chiefly contained in *a subordination to the authority of the parliament now sitting in England*'.[31] These assurances answered explicitly the rumours then circulating in England that the protestants in Ireland wished to 'set up for themselves'. Yet even in that context this affirmation of loyalty and of English identity by 'the people of Ireland' rings true.

The comparatively muted opposition of the political elite to the mercantilist restrictions imposed on Ireland in 1663, 1667 and 1671 indicate the lower profile of constitutional debate in the restoration era. Protestants had other, more pressing concerns: the halting, but unmistakable and deeply worrying revival of Catholic Ireland. Sir William Petty offered a novel, if wildly impractical, solution to the Catholic problem by proposing a union accompanied by population transfers, of Catholics to England and protestants to Ireland, thereby rendering Catholics a minority on both islands.[32] It is no coincidence either, that constitutional controversy reappeared in the 1690s. At a time when the Catholics were as firmly subjugated as in 1659–60, protestant Ireland could once again indulge the luxury of straining the English leash.

III

The revolution settlement of 1689 effected a transition in Anglo-Irish relations. The location of sovereignty in the crown-in-[the Westminster] parliament challenged a fundamental tenet of the 'sister kingdom' proposition. According to the theory elaborated by the Old English lawyer, Patrick Darcy, by Domville and by Molyneux, Ireland and England were distinct kingdoms each with their own courts, parliament,

[30] Clarke, 'Colonial constitutional attitudes'.
[31] *Declaration*, 5, 10. Italics added.
[32] Kelly, 'Origins of the act of union', 238–40. Petty's proposals are perhaps less extravagant that James Harrington's suggestion that Ireland in the 1650s offered an ideal site for a Jewish homeland! John Toland (ed.), *The Oceana of James Harrington and his Other Works* (London, 1700), 35–6.

and ancient constitution. They shared the same king, but the English parliament had no more right to meddle in the affairs of the Irish kingdom than in those of the Scottish one. According to the new post-revolution doctrine of sovereignty it was not simply the crown's, but the crown-in-parliament's authority which extended to Ireland. In short, Westminster claimed the right to legislate for the sister kingdom. Molyneux's *Case* entered a protest against Westminster's intention of prohibiting the export of Irish wool. It restated and updated traditional constitutional arguments, it denied that Ireland was a colony and the conquest on which that colonial status was premised. It also marked an intellectual advance on previous precedent-based defences of Irish sovereignty by appealing to Lockean principles of natural right and consent.

Both the contents of the *Case* and the wider controversy in which it intervened are well known. While Molyneux occupied the high ground of constitutional theory, others attacked the proposed woollen act as economic and political folly. As members of a single community, the same people 'sometimes residing here, sometimes there', the rights of protestants, as free-born Englishmen, to trade freely and to be governed by laws to which they had given their consent, were being infringed. Moreover, as the wool trades generally belonged to the 'English interest' in Ireland, their destruction would destroy the livelihoods of loyal protestant subjects, stimulate the growth of the dissenter-dominated linen industry in Ulster, and undermine England's first line of defence against the Catholic natives. The argument that the protestant community formed part of a larger, indivisible and interdependent English community was marshalled to promote equality of treatment and, as such, was perfectly congruent with the existence of an autonomous parliament. Precisely the same argument could be used, of course (as it soon would be) to promote union. It was later suggested, in fact, that as Englishmen the protestants of Ireland had a stronger claim to be admitted into a union than either the Scots or the Welsh.[33]

Molyneux's reputation rests on the influence which the *Case* exercised amongst eighteenth-century Irish and American patriots[34] and on its

---

[33] Maxwell, *Essay Towards an Union*, 12; Ezekiel Burridge, *A Short View of the Present State of Ireland* (Dublin, 1708), anonymous preface.

[34] J. G. Simms, *William Molyneux of Dublin, a life of the Seventeenth-century Writer and Scientist*, ed. P. H. Kelly (Dublin, 1982), 116–17; Simms, *Colonial Nationalism*, 9; Robbins, *Eighteenth-century Commonwealthman*, 138; C. H. McIlwain, *The American Revolution: a constitutional interpretation* (New York, 1923), 35–6, 55–6. For a contrary view denying that the writings of Molyneux and others had a significant impact in pre-revolutionary America see J. C. D. Clark, *The Language of Liberty 1660–1832: political discourse and social dynamics in the Anglo-American world* (Cambridge, 1994), 25–6.

contribution to the history of political thought. But, as a canonical, free-standing text, the *Case* presents certain puzzles, notably the stray single-sentence endorsement of union and the rhetorical near-elimination of the Catholic population. Placed in context, it is clear that union as a means to an end did not necessarily conflict with the defence of the Irish parliament, viewed as a means to the same end. It is equally clear that the minimising of Catholic numbers was not quite a 'bare-faced' 'evasion', or at least not an original or even an unusual one. Molyneux's reputation also owes a great deal to the controversy which the *Case* provoked in England, where it was condemned by Westminster and elicited at least four replies.

Ironically, Molyneux's critics, such as William Atwood, were whig champions of parliamentary supremacy, who drew different conclusions from the same assumptions, principles and libertarian rhetoric.[35] Simon Clement nimbly turned the proclaimed Englishness of Molyneux and his fellow protestants back on them. Membership of a community, he reminded them, entailed responsibilities as well as rights and privileges. Selfish, sectional or merely local interests – such as the Irish wool trade – must be subordinated to the 'well-being of the whole community'.[36] Molyneux's English adversaries refused to concede that Ireland was a distinct kingdom. As Clement tellingly riposted to the observation that Ireland, unlike the Maryland or Virginia colonies, was styled a 'kingdom', so too were the conquered and annexed dependencies of imperial Spain, Mexico and Peru. What's in a name? These critics sought to demonstrate that Ireland had been conquered (and reconquered) and was therefore annexed to, and dependent upon, the imperial crown of England.

Clement drew a distinction between 'colonies', consisting of the conquerers and settlers drawn from the mother country, and 'provinces' – subordinate imperial territories occupied by those colonists. Citing the Roman example, he argued that there were a range of possible relationships between the imperial centre and its outlying provinces, with the colonists being granted more or less autonomy as circumstances demanded. The deployment of classical analogies against the case for Irish liberty highlights a central problem of republican political theory:

[35] The work of William Petyt has been identified as a 'conjoint' influence on Molyneux's theory of conquest. William Atwood, the author of *The History and Reasons for the Dependency of Ireland upon the Imperial Crown of England, Rectifying Mr Molyneux's State of the Case of Ireland's Being Bound by Acts of Parliament in England, Stated* (1698), was a protégé of Petyt's: J. G. A. Pocock, *The Feudal Law and the Ancient Constitution* (Cambridge, 1957), 188, 196, 238.

[36] Clement, *An Answer*, p. xxxii; Kelly, 'Molyneux and Locke, the anatomy of a friendship', *Hermanthena*, 126 (1979), 50–1.

the proper relationship between a commonwealth and its dependencies. Republicans like Machiavelli, and his English heirs Henry Neville and James Harrington, discussed 'provinces' almost exclusively in terms of conquest and containment. Like the late seventeenth-century whigs, Atwood and Clement, they were no more troubled by the inconsistency of excluding the colonists (or natives) from the liberties which they claimed for themselves, than was Molyneux by the inconsistency of excluding Catholics from the liberties which he claimed for all mankind. Colonies were perceived as a potential threat. In *Plato redivivus* Neville endorsed the Cromwellian conquest of Ireland and generalised that 'provincial governments, if they be wisely ordered, no more must have any the least share in managing the affairs of state, but strangers, or such as have no share or part in the possessions there, for else they will have a very good opportunity of shaking off their yoak'.[37]

Harrington was equally, one might say refreshingly, frank in the true Machiavellian style. Subordination, if not always direct coercion, was necessary, he believed, because over-mighty provinces endangered the state; after all 'the acquisition of provinces devour'd the commonwealth of Rome'. It was a mistake to devolve authority. Rome had been careful not to plant colonies 'without the bounds of Italy' because that 'would have alienated the citizens and given root to liberty abroad that might have sprung up foren, or savage, and hostile to her'. What is more, the 'military colonys' which she did plant provided a springboard for the overthrow of the republic and the imposition of military dictatorship. Neither the 'natives' nor the colonists, who, he wrote, 'like flowers or roots being transplanted, take after the soil wherein they grow', could be trusted with power or arms.[38]

IV

Harrington's *Oceana* first published in 1656 was republished by John Toland in 1700. Along with the 1694 edition of Neville's translations of Machiavelli and Robert Molesworth's 1693 *Account of Denmark*, it has been identified as one of the key ideological resources of the whig–radical paper war on standing armies in England.[39] Several of the opponents of standing armies and arbitrary power – John Trenchard, Molesworth and Toland – were Irish born and formed part of an intellectual, political and social nexus, variously described as common-

---

[37] Cited by Robbins, *Eighteenth-century Commonwealthman*, 40.
[38] Toland (ed.), *The Oceana of James Harrington*, 43, 62, 250, 456.
[39] L. Schwoerer, *No Standing Armies! The anti-army ideology in seventeenth-century England* (Baltimore and London, 1974), 173–5.

wealthmen or neo-Harringtonian. Henry Maxwell, who sat for Bangor, county Down, in the Irish parliament, was connected to this group through Molesworth[40] and his *Essay Towards an Union of Ireland with England* (1703) can be read as an intervention in – or skilful exploitation of – the standing army controversy, and as a refutation of Harrington's theory of provinces, so recently made accessible by Toland.

In striking contrast to Molyneux's often cited and much analysed *Case*, Maxwell's *Essay*, though well known to Irish historians of the period, has enjoyed little other historiographical afterlife.[41] Maxwell's pamphlet slipped from view not because the quality of argument is inferior to Molyneux's, but because it had no political impact at the time or later. As a contribution to the history of Anglo-Irish political thought, however, as a contribution to a British Isles wide debate on the nature of government, and as an example of early Irish unionist opinion, the *Essay* is as deserving of attention as the *Case*.

Maxwell briskly disposed of Molyneux's elaborate defence of legislative autonomy at the outset. 'It is not the design of this discourse', he writes, 'to examine whether laws made in England ought to bind Ireland, it being sufficient for those of that nation [Ireland] to know that this is a power which England claims, and is able to vindicate.' Although he had no quarrel with English jurisdiction *per se*, in practice England's treatment of her province had, he believed, generated a justifiable sense of grievance. In a clear echo of Harrington, Ireland is depicted as being 'in an unnatural state, which implies force, and an unwilling obedience'.[42] But whereas Harrington advocated subordination as the surest way of safeguarding the commonwealth from rebellious provinces, Maxwell warned that the means of subordination – a standing army – posed an even greater threat to English liberty. In his view, the Romans had permitted their colonies to make their own laws and choose their own magistrates 'and for these reasons the Romans were always most faithfully serv'd by their colonies'. Governing 'provinces, or annex'd states, by force' entailed 'maintaining a constant standing force' ultimately destructive of freedom. And if Ireland were held in subjection 'by a constant force' it 'must sometime destroy the liberty of England'.[43] Recent history furnished examples. Both Strafford, under Charles I, and

---

[40] Robbins, *Eighteenth-century Commonwealthman*, 147.

[41] For example, Maxwell's pamphlet is not included by Schwoerer in her discussion of eighteenth-century pamphlets on the theme of standing armies: *No Standing Armies*, 188–200. The *Essay towards Union* is discussed by Caroline Robbins, of course, and by John Robertson in 'Union, state and empire, the Britain of 1707 in its European setting', in L. Stone (ed.), *An Imperial State at War, Britain from 1689 to 1815* (London and New York, 1994), 244.

[42] Maxwell, *Essay Towards an Union*, 3.   [43] *Ibid.*, 5–8.

Tyrconnell, under James II, had recruited papist armies and 'a standing army and arbitrary power never took root in Ireland, but the next step was to transplant themselves into England'.[44]

Maxwell's solution to the problem of provincial government was an incorporating union of the kingdom of Ireland 'into the kingdom of England, upon the same foot with Wales'.[45] This made sense on grounds of equity, justice, religion, race, trade and *England*'s security. Most of the *Essay* consists of an extended, detailed discussion of the advantages for both kingdoms of free trade between them. Yet even that wound its way back to the security issue. Since Irish manufactures were concentrated in the hands of the English protestants this was the group which would continue to suffer from trade restrictions, such as the 1699 woollen act, imposed by England. If, in the absence of union and free trade, they were 'driven away', then 'Ireland must necessarily, in the course of a few years, return to the possession of its old proprietors.'[46]

Maxwell's manipulation of the standing army scare in his discourse on union places him squarely in the neo-Harringtonian school (the defence of *Oceana* fell to a citizen militia), even if he used it to turn Harrington's theory of provinces neatly on its head. Caroline Robbins placed him, along with Molesworth and Andrew Fletcher, on the Hiberno-Scots wing of radical whiggery, and the affinities are obvious enough. Fletcher, for instance, anticipated Maxwell by four years when in his *Discourse on Government with Relation to Militias* he observed that 'it is not very suitable to [our rights and privileges] that any standing forces be kept up in Britain: or that there should be any Scots, English, or Irish regiments maintained in Ireland, or anywhere abroad ... we all know with what expedition the Irish mercenary forces were brought into Britain to oppose his present majesty in that glorious enterprise for our deliverance'.[47] Robbins was wrong, however, in classifying Maxwell with Molesworth and Fletcher as a federal unionist. As we have seen, he favoured an incorporating union. Irish and Scottish commonwealthmen followed Molyneux in seeking to retain their national parliaments, albeit within a unionist framework, as the best means of securing the liberties of the king's subjects in each of his three kingdoms, and it might be interesting to speculate on why Maxwell parted company with them on that score.

One explanation may be that although a whig he was also, in his own words, 'always a churchman'. In 1703 he opposed renewing the *regium*

---

[44] *Ibid.*, 12.   [45] *Ibid.*, 17.   [46] *Ibid.*, 34.

[47] D. Daiches (ed.), *Andrew Fletcher of Saltoun, selected political writings and speeches* (Edinburgh, 1979), 14–15.

donum to the Irish presbyterian clergy.[48] Molesworth, on the other hand, though nominally a churchman too, consistently championed toleration for dissenters. Irish opposition to the Anglo-Scottish union stemmed mainly from the high church party, notably Jonathan Swift and the attorney general, Sir Richard Cox, who feared that it would strengthen the position of presbyterianism within the new British state and, by extension, in Scotland's presbyterian colony, Ulster. Even if Maxwell did not have that dire prospect in mind, it is clear from the *Essay* that he spoke for the 'English interest' in Ireland. His union was an English protestant not – despite his occasional use of the term – a 'British' project.

Maxwell differed from Fletcher in other respects too. Most of the *Essay*, like most of Fletcher's *An Account of a Conversation Concerning a Right Regulation of Government* (1704) concerns the predicted economic consequences of union. Maxwell argued that by eliminating English restrictions on Irish trade, union would stimulate a free market led commercial expansion beneficial to both partners. Fletcher, while he believed that 'Britain' and Ireland seemed 'conveniently situated for one government',[49] contended that an incorporating union which concentrated political power would concentrate economic power as well. Contradicting the orthodoxy, accepted by Maxwell, that the union with Wales had been wholly successful, Fletcher pointed to the comparative poverty of post-union Wales despite its proximity to London and its ideally located ports, as a warning of Scotland's fate should it be swallowed up by its larger neighbour. Ireland's experience offered a similar cautionary tale: 'though the native Irish were conquered' he wrote, England's 'colony was not; which yet you [England] favoured no longer till you saw them begin to flourish and grow rich. And to show what we are to expect, if ever beginning to thrive, though never so long after our union, I shall give some instance of our conduct towards Ireland in relation to trade.'[50]

Maxwell's *Essay* made nothing happen. Harsh political realities, not political ideas, however finely wrought, or 'public opinion', however forcefully articulated, shaped the English government's choices. And as the dominant partner in the union courtship England's attitude counted for most. Take, for example, the issue of trade to which Maxwell devoted so much space. Fletcher maintained that 'trade is the constant stumbling block and ball of contention'. Maxwell held up the prospect of an Anglo-Irish union increasing *English* prosperity, while Lecky and

---

[48] D. Hayton, 'A debate in the Irish house of commons in 1703: a whiff of Tory grapeshot', *Parliamentary History*, 10, pt. 2 (1991), 157, 161.
[49] Daiches, *Andrew Fletcher*, 127.   [50] *Ibid.*, 120–1.

Froude later attributed England's opposition to union with Ireland to a spirit of commercial monopoly. But for the Namierite historian of the Anglo-Scottish union, P. J. W. Riley, public discussion of trade issues before the treaty only enters the equation as diversionary propagandist froth.[51] With the single exception of Fletcher, to whom he grants an ideological dispensation (or fool's pardon), Riley casts all the players in the union debates as a calculating 'parcel of rogues'. According to this reductionist analysis, court whigs and their Scottish clients pushed through the union, as much for immediate factional advantage – Westminster party political arithmetic again – as to secure the Hanoverian succession. Since the Irish political elite dared not even bluff on the succession question, for the English government the possibility of an Anglo-Irish union simply did not arise.

Maxwell's *Essay* is addressed to an English audience. He tried to surmount English indifference (or hostility) to union by warning his imagined audience that doing nothing jeopardised English liberty. However, although Irish pro-unionist advocacy was ultimately ignored, and although the Anglo-Scottish union was imposed regardless of popular opposition, it would be unsafe to conclude with Riley that 'public opinion' remained irrelevant. In fact recent studies of the 1707 union emphasise its broadly ideological dimensions. Brian Levack sees the treaty as 'as much a product of the century-old union debate as [of] the immediate needs and relative bargaining strength' of its negotiaters. The ideas and attitudes shaped by that debate 'defined the limits within which compromises could be made and helped to define many of the features' of the newly united kingdom. And, in John Robertson's view, the union 'should be understood within an intellectual as well as a political and economic context'.[52]

Despite initial Scots hostility, historians were once generally agreed that on balance the 1707 union was 'successful'. During the eighteenth century 'intelligent Scots', it has been claimed, happily seized on the rich opportunities opened up to them 'within the empire'.[53] Moreover, as net beneficiaries of the union they increasingly came to share in a non-contentious sense of Britishness, which overlay, but did not oblit-

---

[51] Lecky, *England in the Eighteenth Century*, viii, 269; Froude, *The English in Ireland*, i, 303–4; Riley, *Union of England and Scotland*, 7, 201; I. Hont, 'Free trade and the economic limits to national politics: neo-Machiavellian political economy reconsidered', in J. Dunn (ed.), *The Economic Limits of Modern Politics* (Cambridge, 1990), 78–89.

[52] Brian P. Levack, *The Formation of the British State, England, Scotland, and the Union, 1603–1707* (Oxford, 1987), 16; John Robertson (ed.), *A Union for Empire, Political Thought and the British Union of 1707* (Cambridge, 1995), xiii.

[53] H. Trevor-Roper, 'The Anglo-Scottish Union', in *From Counter-Reformation to Revolution* (London, 1992), 296.

erate, older national allegiances. To Lecky and Froude Scots prosperity
under the union and the formation of an inclusive British identity
contrasted bitterly with the discordance of Anglo-Irish relations and the
blight of an antipathetic (Catholic) Irish nationalism. If only, they
mused, those 'thoughtful' and 'enlightened' Irishmen who had advocated union in the first years of the eighteenth century had been listened
to, how different, how much better, Irish history might have been! From
today's post-imperial perspective, however, when many astute commentators discern the impending 'break-up of Britain', the unalloyed
success of the 1707 union on which the Lecky–Froude contrapuntal
conjecture rested no longer appears self-evident.

In one sense the British experiment began in 1707, but by choosing
1707 as the starting point of her study of British identities, *Britons*,
Linda Colley introduces the union as a *fait accompli*. Her 'success
school' analysis is thus skewed at the outset towards the integrative
processes she goes on to explore so expertly. Her chronology inevitably
elides the tensions which preceded the passing of the Act of Union;
tensions subsequently submerged but never quite resolved. Shortly after
the Union Defoe recalled popular resistance to the notion of Britishness:
'The people cryed out they were Scots Men, and they would be Scots
Men still; they condemn'd the name of Britains, fit for the Welsh Men,
who were made the scoff of the English after they had reduc'd them.'[54]
In other words, pro-union polemicists like Defoe enjoyed less than
complete success in the paper war which accompanied the negotiation
of the treaty. Colley acknowledges that old national identities were not
'supplanted'; she is less clear that the superimposition (or forging) of a
British identity was a project (or process) flawed at its inception. As
another historian remarks, the union was not 'accompanied by any
ideological consensus ... there was no real attempt to build a bridge
between the Scottish and English political nations to create a common
British revolution culture'.[55] South of the border the English clung to a
'tenacious sense of [their] peculiarity' sustained by 'simple Scoto-
phobia'.[56] And if presbyterian Scotland failed, or refused, to lose its
distinctiveness within a protestant United Kingdom, what were the
prospects of Catholic Ireland doing so?

There is some evidence to support the view that in the early eighteenth century Irish Catholics would have welcomed a union because
that wider constitutional arrangement might have provided more dis-
interested government than the face-to-face oppression which Catholics

---

[54] D. Defoe, *The History of the Union of Great Britain* (Edinburgh, 1709), ch. 3, 17.
[55] C. Kidd, *Subverting Scotland's Past* (Cambridge, 1993), 50.
[56] Robertson, 'Union, state and empire', in Stone (ed.), *An Imperial State at War*, 248.

suffered at the hands of the local protestant elite.[57] As we have seen, protestants at the time attempted to resolve the Catholic problem by writing that unwanted group out of the script. The Catholics thus disposed of, it was the very Englishness of the political nation which, many protestants felt, made Ireland a more worthy and logical candidate for union than either Wales or Scotland. Like the church whig, Maxwell, the church tory, Sir Richard Cox, envisaged an English protestant, not a British, union. There was, he insisted, 'no remedy so proper'; it would 'enrich and strengthen England' and induce the 'Irish' and the 'British' (i.e. the Ulster Scots) to become good Englishmen.[58]

Cox saw himself – to borrow Jonathan Swift's description of William Molyneux – as an 'English gentleman born in Ireland' and, like many of his contemporaries, 'never grew tired of proclaiming the fact'.[59] His sense of identity and his unionist opinions seem a long way indeed from the proto-nationalist aspirations so often detected in this period. That English/Irish polarity arises because there is evidence to support both interpretations. Clearly, after 1691 protestant senses of identity were in transition. But, because those processes culminated in a variety of early Irish nationalism, historians have concentrated on digging for the cultural and political roots of that later eighteenth-century protestant allegiance. Other possible outcomes of those processes of transition – the inclusive Britishness imagined by Froude, for example – have received less attention. Yet only by reimagining the range of possibilities open to contemporaries do figures like Cox or Maxwell, or the pro-union Irish parliaments of 1703, 1707 and 1709, make sense. Lecky understood that. Firmly linking the question of identity formation to its political framework, he argued that an Anglo-(or British-)Irish union at this juncture had every chance of success because 'the protestants had as yet no distinctively national feeling' and because the Irish constitution was then in such a 'pliant, plastic condition'.[60] And so the great mythologiser of Grattanite patriotism got behind hindsight and restored to the English–Irish political elite of the early eighteenth century the uncertain and contingent future into which it faced.

[57] T. B. Macaulay, *The History of England from the Accession of James II* (1936 edn), iii, n.p. 569; Lecky, 'Ireland in the light of history', *Historical and Political Essays* (London, 1910 edn), 67–8.

[58] Cox to Nottingham 13 Feb. 1704, *Cal. S.P. (Dom), 1703–4*, 531.

[59] J. T. Leerssen, *Mere Irish and Fior-Ghael, Studies in the Idea of Irish Nationality, its Development and Literary Expression Prior to the Nineteenth Century* (Amsterdam and Philadelphia, 1986), 340.

[60] Lecky, 'Ireland in the light of history', 67–8; *England in the Eighteenth Century*, viii, 269.

11   Protestantism, constitutionalism and British identity under the later Stuarts

Colin Kidd

Throughout the later Stuart period the nations of the British Isles became increasingly aware that their political, economic and religious interests were interdependent. The British wars of religion of 1639 to 1651, the union of England, Scotland and Ireland under the Commonwealth, the anti-Jacobite wars in Scotland and Ireland which followed and secured the Glorious Revolution in England, and the union of the English and Scottish kingdoms of 1707, ensured that the subjects of the seventeenth-century Stuart multiple monarchy[1] became conscious of their dependence on the workings of a 'British' three-kingdom system.[2] However, it will be argued here that the sense that the Stuarts' British dominions comprised more than a dynastic ensemble was not reflected in the emergence of a common British identity during this period. First, the existing national traditions of England, Scotland and Ireland proved too resilient to be easily fused beneath an overarching pan-Britannic identity. Moreover, it will be suggested, these identities found expression in three incompatible discourses. The conflicting regnal claims and counter-claims which constituted the principal expression of English, Scottish and Irish national identities were exacerbated by the politics of the composite state. For instance, in the century after the union of the crowns, Scottish churchmen, Episcopalians as well as presbyterians, were particularly prone to fears of Anglican ecclesiastical imperialism. Such jurisdictional anxieties added to the more obvious confessional divisions which plagued British protestantism.

It will be clear from the analysis that follows, therefore, that no plausible British identity capable of engaging the affections of the various British peoples emerged under the Stuart dynasty. The central

I wish to thank Brendan Bradshaw, Brian Young, John Robertson, Charles Webster and Scott Mandelbrote for comments and suggestions.

[1] For the concept of multiple monarchies or composite states, see H. G. Koenigsberger, '*Dominium politicum* or *dominium politicum et regale*: monarchies and parliaments in early modern Europe', in Koenigsberger, *Politicians and virtuosi* (London, 1986).

[2] C. Russell, *The Causes of the English Civil War* (Oxford, 1990); Russell, *The Fall of the British Monarchies 1637–42* (Oxford, 1991).

problem was the lack of a suitable 'matter of Britain'. What emerged instead were a number of competing sub-traditions of Britishness, none of which was definitive, and some of which were either of declining ideological effectiveness or of limited appeal. Some had pronounced Cambro-British[3] or Scoto-British[4] biases which tended to alienate or exclude other British nations. The Cambro-British identity was championed by the English as well as by the Welsh. The Welsh took pride in their biological descent from the island's British 'aborigines'. On the other hand, the English claimed to be the heirs of the original political institutions and Christian church established on English soil by the ancient Britons.[5] However, the British myth of origins constructed by Geoffrey of Monmouth in the twelfth century had long been viewed in Scotland and Ireland as a cover for English imperialism. Similarly, English propagandists had used Galfridian arguments, including Brutus's division of the island or the Arthurian conquest of the entire British Isles, to advance claims to a pan-Britannic suzerainty.[6] By contrast, the Scoto-British presbyterian ideal of an Anglo-Scottish union on the basis of the Solemn League and Covenant of 1643 was anathema to the great majority of Anglican churchmen and Scots episcopalians alike.

Nevertheless, early modern identities were far from exclusive, unlike many modern ethnic-nationalist solidarities. The existence of concentric loyalties compensated for the lack of a common British history, ethnic identity or confessional commitment. Basic yearnings for mixed constitutionalism, for the triumph of the broader protestant movement over the forces of the Counter Reformation and for the quashing of Bourbon aspirations to universal monarchy, welded together a minimalist Britishness which transcended the frequent collisions of national shibboleths. Eighteenth-century Britons were to inherit a very qualified sense of British identity which had no powerful ideological source. Indeed it had emerged in spite of well-known tensions among the British political nations. Nevertheless, space was to be found for the development of a vague compound of Hanoverian loyalism, whiggery and protestantism.[7]

---

[3] T. D. Kendrick, *British Antiquity* (New York and London, 1970, 1st edn 1950).

[4] A. Williamson, 'Scotland, Antichrist and the invention of Great Britain', in J. Dwyer, R. A. Mason and A. Murdoch (eds.), *New Perspectives on the Politics and Culture of Early Modern Scotland* (Edinburgh, 1982); B. Galloway, *The Union of England and Scotland 1603–1608* (Edinburgh, 1986), 33–4, 43, 51–2.

[5] G. Williams, 'Some Protestant views of early British church history', in Williams, *Welsh Reformation Essays* (Cardiff, 1967), 212–13.

[6] Scots were keenly aware that Galfridianism had been used to justify Edward I's claim to overlordship of their realm. See e.g. R. A. Mason, 'Scotching the Brut: politics, history and national myth in sixteenth-century Britain', in Mason (ed.), *Scotland and England 1286–1815* (Edinburgh, 1987).

[7] L. Colley, *Britons: forging the nation 1707–1837* (New Haven, 1992).

I

The Restoration of the Stuarts in 1660 involved a return not only to traditional institutions but also to historic national communities. The centralised Cromwellian union was dissolved in 1659. Known as the Commonwealth of England, Scotland and Ireland, it had been an experiment in expansionist English republicanism, rather than a serious attempt at British nation-building.[8] At the Restoration, England, Scotland and Ireland again enjoyed their traditional domestic constitutions within the loose framework of a composite monarchy. There was now considerable ambivalence about Britishness. Although there were to be further court-inspired attempts at commercial and political union between England and Scotland in 1668 and 1670,[9] union was implicated in the demonology of the restored regime. It was associated not only with an imperialist republicanism, but also with the presbyterian Solemn League and Covenant.

The loosely defined and largely customary web of relationships which once again enmeshed the nations of the Stuart multiple monarchy provoked status anxieties about national honour, independence and civility. This sensitivity found expression in chauvinistic boasting conducted through the medium of patriotic histories. For Britishness was not reducible to an identity or aspiration. Rather it was a theatre of multipolar ideological conflict about regnal and ecclesiastical autonomy, national precedence and antiquity. Uncertainty about the place of the nations and kingdoms of Scotland and Ireland[10] within what was

[8] For an English republican imperialism inspired by the Roman model and the Machiavellian idea of militant expansion, see B. Worden, 'Classical republicanism and the Puritan revolution', in H. Lloyd-Jones, V. Pearl and B. Worden (eds.), *History and Imagination: essays in honour of H. R. Trevor-Roper* (London, 1981), 196–9; B. Worden, 'English republicanism', in J. H. Burns and M. Goldie (eds.), *The Cambridge History of Political Thought 1450–1700* (Cambridge, 1991), 466–7; J. Scott, *Algernon Sidney and the English Republic 1623–1677* (Cambridge, 1988), 105, 111. Recent research offers a warning against an anachronistic assumption that the British Isles were the exclusive focus of republican aspirations; for the vision of a union between the protestant maritime commonwealths of England and the United Provinces, see S. Pincus, *Protestantism and patriotism: ideologies and the making of English foreign policy 1650–1668* (Cambridge, 1996).

[9] B. Levack, *The Formation of the British State: England, Scotland and the Union 1603–1707* (Oxford, 1987), 10–11.

[10] It is important to note that for this period Irish identities and their relationships to some wider British allegiance are peculiarly difficult to parse. The very language of identification was in flux. The tripartite ethnic categories of Old Irish (or Gaelic), Old English (or Norman-Irish) and New English (the planters of the early modern period) which prevailed in the first half of the seventeenth century were giving way to a binary division into Catholic and protestant confessions (though there were at first considerable differences between the Tridentine reform Catholicism which gained hold more quickly among the Old English and the more traditional religion which long survived

becoming *de facto* an English empire aroused peripheral defensiveness. In addition, the historical experiences of the four nations, three kingdoms and various ethnic groups of different languages, cultures and confessions, had bequeathed a mosaic of particularist battles. Any commonality arising out of shared allegiances was overwhelmed by a culture of patriotic contestation. Some disputes concerned petty affronts to national pride. Others had serious implications for constitutional and ecclesiastical arrangements. Each nation defended its own historical myths while dismissing the allegedly ridiculous claims of the others. Within English patriotic discourse, the 'British' past, including myths of Arthurian conquests or the history of the ancient British church, was bent to suit English needs, in particular the claim to a British *imperium* and a parallel metropolitan authority in the ecclesiastical sphere.[11] Scottish historians continued to be on their guard against any suggestion that the kings of Scotland had ever done homage to the kings of England for any part of what was modern Scottish territory, and to refute any suggestion that the Scottish church, whose first archbishoprics were created in the fifteenth century, had ever been subject to the metropolitan authority of the archbishops of York.[12] Irish scholars continued to reject suggestions that King Arthur had ever exacted tribute from Ireland as a suzerain.[13] The Gaels of Ireland and the hibernicised Old

among the Old Irish). Each community was committed, with different emphases, to the idea of an Irish *regnum*. On the other hand, while the protestants saw themselves as the English nation in Ireland, it is unclear whether the emerging Catholic community (despite the former self-image the Old English had of themselves as Anglo-Irish) maintained a sense of Britishness which extended beyond its vexed loyalty to the Stuart dynasty. See A. Clarke, 'Colonial identity in early seventeenth-century Ireland', in T. W. Moody (ed.), *Nationality and the Pursuit of National Independence*, Historical Studies, 11 (Belfast, 1978), esp. 58–60, 69–71; A. Clarke, 'Colonial constitutional attitudes in Ireland, 1640–60', *Proceedings of the Royal Irish Academy*, 90, C, no. 11 (1990), 357–75; S. J. Connolly, *Religion, Law and Power: the making of Protestant Ireland, 1660–1760* (Oxford, 1992), 114–15; B. Ó Buachalla, 'James our true king: the ideology of Irish royalism in the seventeenth century', in D. G. Boyce, R. Eccleshall and V. Geoghegan (eds.), *Political Thought in Ireland Since the Seventeenth Century* (London, 1993), 7–35.

[11] Peter Heylin, *Cosmographie* (London, 1652), 298, 305–6; John Milton, *History of Britain* (London, 1677, 1st edn 1670), 259, 275; Thomas Rymer, *Edgar, or the English Monarch: an heroick tragedy* (London, 1678), 10–12.

[12] George Mackenzie, 'A discourse concerning the three unions betwixt Scotland and England', National Library of Scotland Adv. MS 31.7.7, fos. 6–8; Mackenzie, *Observations upon the Laws and Customs of Nations as to Precedency* (1680), in Mackenzie, *Works* (2 vols., Edinburgh, 1716–22), ii, 520–9; Robert Sibbald, 'A defence or vindication of the Scottish history and of the Scottish historians' (c. 1685), National Library of Scotland Adv. MS 15.1.3, fos. 1, 167.

[13] John Lynch, *Cambrensis eversus* (1662: trans. M. Kelly, 3 vols., Dublin, 1848–51), ii, 81–5; Peter Walsh, *A Prospect of the State of Ireland* (London, 1682), 342, 396. These scholars were building on a critique launched in the early seventeenth century by the Old English antiquary Geoffrey Keating. See B. Bradshaw, 'Geoffrey Keating: apologist

English continued to repudiate the charges of barbarism which had first been heaped on their culture by the Norman-Welsh cleric Giraldus Cambrensis and which were later reprised by sixteenth- and seventeenth-century New English colonisers.[14] There was also a dispute between Scottish and Irish historians as to whether the Scots colony of Dalriada had acknowledged a tributary status to the Milesian kingdom of the Irish motherland.[15]

Despite the potential institutional backbone inherent in the multiple monarchy, no serious attempt was made to construct a comprehensively British strain of Stuart dynasticism. Rather, royalist ideology was grounded in a collection of distinct national traditions of discourse which did not serve to integrate the peoples subject to the Stuarts. Indeed, Welsh, Scots and Irish royalists vied with one another in claiming that it was from their respective ancient monarchies that the Stuarts derived their high precedence among the monarchs of Europe. Percy Enderbie propounded a Galfridian royalism, tracing the descent of Charles II from the ancient British royal line through the daughter of Griffith ap Llewelyn, the Princess Nest, who, it was claimed, had married a Scottish noble, Fleance, son of Banquo.[16] The Gaelic antiquary and champion of Irish royalism, Roderic O'Flaherty (1629–1718), reiterating the argument earlier adumbrated by Geoffrey Keating, boasted in his *Ogygia* (1685) that the Stuarts derived their greatest glory from their Milesian ancestry. Accordingly he trumpeted the superior antiquity of the kingdom of Ireland to the kingdoms of England and Scotland. O'Flaherty argued that only with the elevation of a descendant of the Irish Milesian line, James VI of Scotland, to the thrones of England and Ireland in 1603, was Ireland formally subordinated to a mainland-based monarchy. Significantly, like Keating, he insisted that Ireland had never submitted to the English nation or legislature.[17] There was also a distinct culture of Scottish royalism whose most magnificent expression was the series of 111 portraits of the kings of Scotland, beginning with the mythical Fergus MacFerqhard, by the Dutch artist Jacob De Wet, commissioned for the royal palace of Holyroodhouse. Sir George Mackenzie of Rosehaugh (1636–91), Scotland's lord advocate, argued that it was *lèse-majesté* for a subject of any

---

of Irish Ireland', in B. Bradshaw, A. Hadfield and W. Maley (eds.), *Representing Ireland: literature and the origins of conflict, 1534–1660* (Cambridge, 1993), 171–2.

[14] Lynch, *Cambrensis eversus*, i, 191, 429, ii, 166–93, 272–9, 362–87.

[15] Walsh, *Prospect*, 23–4, 393.

[16] Percy Enderbie, *Cambria triumphans* (London, 1661), 'The genealogy of Charles II'.

[17] Roderic O'Flaherty, *Ogygia* (2 vols., Dublin, 1793, 1st edn 1685), trans. J. Hely, i, xiv, 414–18. See also Lynch, *Cambrensis eversus*, iii, ch. xxvii. For the original exposition of such arguments, see Bradshaw, 'Geoffrey Keating', 170–1.

of the Stuart realms to question the veracity of the ancient Fergusian line whose historicity was central to the official doctrine of Scottish absolutism.[18] Nevertheless, patriotic scholars from the other nations of the British Isles openly scoffed at this Scottish legend.[19]

The most spectacular clash of conflicting patriotisms to occur during the Restoration era took place in the mid-1680s. It arose out of Anglican concern about the Scottish ecclesiological supports of English presbyterian dissent, and culminated in a prominent Scottish episcopalian defending the antiquity of Scotland's past against English, Anglo-Welsh and Gaelic assaults. Scots presbyterians claimed that there had been an ancient non-episcopal Christian church in Scotland from around AD 200. However, English, Welsh and Irish scholars argued that the history of the Scots in Scotland before AD 500 was a figment of chauvinistic imagination. For centuries after the conversion of the shadowy King Donald I, so the Scots presbyterians claimed, the church in Scotland had been governed without bishops. Instead there had been government by colleges of monks or Culdees without any episcopal supervision. This ancient presbyterian constitution of the Scottish church had been seized upon with relish by the French Huguenot scholar David Blondel (1590–1655) as a vital example from the primitive era of a non-episcopal church. The argument also offered succour to English Dissenters such as Richard Baxter (1615–91) who desired a non-prelatical Church of England. The appearance in England of the dangerous Scots presbyterian precedent of rule by Culdees seemed to undermine the patristic case for primitive episcopacy and it was answered by the Anglo-Welsh scholar William Lloyd (1627–1717), bishop of St Asaph. Lloyd challenged the authenticity not only of anti-episcopal interpretations of Scotland's past, but of the whole farrago of legends which comprised Scottish antiquity. Lloyd's argument was met by Mackenzie of Rosehaugh who, while sympathetic to the bishop's ecclesiological position, argued that he had undermined the monarchy whose glorious genealogy stretched back to King Fergus MacFerquhard in 330 BC. This position was rejected in turn by Edward Stillingfleet, later bishop of Worcester, and by O'Flaherty.[20]

[18] S. Bruce and S. Yearley, 'The social construction of tradition: the Restoration portraits and the kings of Scotland', in D. McCrone *et al.* (eds.), *The Making of Scotland: nation, culture and social change* (Edinburgh, 1989); George Mackenzie, *A Defence of the Antiquity of the Royal Line of Scotland* (1685), in *Works*, II, 358; Mackenzie, *Precedency*, in *Works*, II, 516–20; G. Donaldson (ed.), *Scottish Historical Documents* (Edinburgh, 1970), 247–8.

[19] O'Flaherty, *Ogygia*, I, xix, lvii–lxvi, 225–92; Edward Stillingfleet, 'Preface', in *Origines Britannicae* (London, 1685), iii–xvii, xlii–xlix, lix–lxiv.

[20] David Blondel, *Apologia pro sententia Hieronymi de episcopis et presbyteris* (Amsterdam, 1646), 314–15, 375; Richard Baxter, *A Treatise on Episcopacy* (London, 1681), 224–5; William Lloyd, *An Historical Account of Church-Government* (London, 1684); A. Tindal

It is clear that well-established regnal and particularist ideologies predominated in political discourse over any ideology of Britishness. Moreover, these various national traditions had developed as a system of competing claims. Thus their necessary irreconcilability in itself constituted a hindrance to a common Britishness. In other words, a British historical identity could not be composed simply by combining material from the variety of well-established patriotic myths which traditionally defined the nations of England, Scotland, Ireland and Wales.

This posed a particular obstacle, as has been noted, for the Cambro-British tradition which also had to struggle throughout the Restoration era with several other major problems. Most seriously, only a few scholars continued to treat Geoffrey of Monmouth as a reliable historian. The Galfridian *mythistoire*, the tradition derived from the chronicle of Geoffrey of Monmouth, had originally been debunked by Polydore Vergil and, though resilient, was of declining influence in seventeenth-century England.[21] Geoffrey of Monmouth's influential account of the origins of Britain was increasingly disregarded as a worthless heap of fables in spite of the efforts of a loyal core of defenders. However, the loyalists included the distinguished Cambridge orientalist Robert Sheringham (1602–78) and his fellow Cantabrigian Daniel Langhorne (d. 1681).[22] Geoffrey's legends continued to be used in historical politics, though as much concerning domestic constitutional and legal debates as in constructing a British consciousness. For example, Silas Taylor suggested that Geoffrey's account of the division of Britain among the sons of Brutus was the origin of partible gavelkind inheritance.[23] Nevertheless, some components of the Galfridian tradition, such as the legend of King Arthur, retained a firmer foothold in English culture than the shaky foundation myth of the Trojan–British monarchy.[24] Further, shorn of its Galfridian elements, the ancient British tradition retained a significant currency. In particular, the descent claimed by the Church of England from the apostolic church of the ancient Britons remained crucial to the

Hart, *William Lloyd 1627–1717* (London, 1952), 92–3, 229; Mackenzie, *Defence* and *The Antiquity of the Royal Line of Scotland Further Cleared and Defended* (1686), both in *Works*, II, 356–9, 397–401; Stillingfleet, *Origines Britannicae*, iv; Roderic O'Flaherty, *Ogygia Vindicated* (Dublin, 1775), 209–17, 223–36.

[21] In his *History of Britain* Milton utilised Galfridian material, only to question its authenticity.

[22] Robert Sheringham, *De Anglorum gentis origine disceptatio* (Cambridge, 1670), 9; Daniel Langhorne, *An Introduction to the History of England* (London, 1676), 'To the Reader' and 5–6; Kendrick, *British Antiquity*, 101–2.

[23] Silas Taylor, *The History of Gavel-Kind* (London, 1663), 85–6.

[24] R. F. Brinkley, *Arthurian Legend in the Seventeenth Century* (Baltimore, 1932).

defence of Anglican legitimacy.[25] However, the other major problem with the Cambro-British tradition lay in the rise of a potent alternative identity drawn from England's Gothic past.[26] Not only did the emergence of Anglo-Saxonism displace former associations with the ancient Britons (in the political sphere especially), but the inconsistencies between these two identities also limited the potential for a shared Anglo-Welsh origin myth. The existence of a Welsh critique of the Saxon yoke meant that the rise of the more pronounced Saxonist strain in English historiography led, in spite of the growing anglicisation of Welsh society, to an increasing divergence between the historical identities of the English and Welsh peoples. However, at this stage, ethnic classifications remained sufficiently fluid for some measure of reconciliation between the British and the Gothic traditions. Sheringham somehow managed to combine enthusiasm for both Galfridian and Saxon origins without any trace of discomfiture.[27] The English antiquary Aylette Sammes (1636?–79?) fused Saxon and British identities by tracing the ethnic genealogies of both Welsh and English peoples through descent from Magog. In addition, the myth of a common origin for Briton and Saxon was reinforced by the frequent conflation of the Cymri with the Teutonic tribe of Cimbri.[28] Nevertheless, the growing ascendancy of Gothicism in English discourse restricted the scope for an Anglo-Welsh umbrella identity. The Galfridian and ancient-British traditions were to become increasingly particularistic. However, confined to Welsh patriotic discourse, they survived long after they had been sublimated in English culture into imaginative literature.[29]

By the late seventeenth century, Britain had also loosened its grasp on the religious imagination. The apocalyptic vision of Britain's divine mission, an influential ideological tradition since the Reformation, had begun to be diluted into a more prosaic image of a providentially insular bulwark against popery. In Scotland the ideology of Reformed unionism was in decline, and was, under the episcopalian establishment of the Restoration era, increasingly confined to the Covenanting extremes of the nation. By the late seventeenth century, the mainstream of even

[25] Stillingfleet, *Origines Britannicae*.

[26] S. Kliger, *The Goths in England* (Cambridge, Mass., 1952); D. C. Douglas, *English Scholars* (1939: London, 1943), chs. 2 and 3; H. MacDougall, *Racial Myth in English History* (Montreal and Hanover, NH, 1982), 46–50, 56–70.

[27] Despite its Galfridianism, the main theme of Sheringham's *De Anglorum gentis origine* was the origin of the Goths. On the anglicisation of Welsh society see Philip Jenkins above, 213–35.

[28] Aylette Sammes, *Britannia antiqua illustrata* (London, 1676), 10–12, 15, 423; Langhorne, *Introduction*, 17, 22, 26–7, 32; Kliger, *Goths*, 291–2.

[29] G. Jenkins, *The Foundations of Modern Wales 1642–1780* (1987, Oxford, 1993), 246–7, 406–7.

Scottish presbyterian discourse had become more particularistic. A pragmatic concern to preserve presbyterianism-in-one-nation dulled the zeal formerly associated with the covenanted commitment to export Scots presbyterian forms throughout the British Isles.[30] In England the exegesis of millennialist prophecy remained a vigorous theological current,[31] and the pope continued to be depicted as the Antichrist. However, critiques of Catholicism couched in a temporal rhetoric of political liberty and the national interest began to predominate in the mainstream of political culture.[32] Condemnations of 'popery and arbitrary rule' and fears of a Bourbon universal monarchy forcibly reintegrating the nations of Christendom under its aegis would begin to resonate throughout the British protestant nations from the 1690s, offering at a very basic level a common identity – if only in opposition to a Catholic 'other'.[33]

II

From 1689 the governments of both England and Scotland stood on a Revolution footing, a situation pregnant with potential for a common British Revolution identity. England, Scotland and Ireland boasted distinct political cultures, each with its own set of Revolution principles and particular form of anti-Revolutionary ideology. English Revolution culture was a minefield of ambiguity at the heart of which was the legal fiction of James II's abdication. Tories tended to justify the Revolution as a providential deliverance, and mainstream whigs as the restoration of the ancient constitution; Lockean contractarianism and resistance were on the radical margins of political culture.[34] In Scotland there was no

---

[30] S. A. Burrell, 'The apocalyptic vision of the early covenanters', *Scottish Historical Review*, 43 (1964), 20–4.

[31] See e.g. S. Mandelbrote, '"A duty of the greatest moment": Isaac Newton and the writing of Biblical criticism', *British Journal of the History of Science*, 26 (1993), 281–302.

[32] C. Hill, *Antichrist in Seventeenth-Century England* (1971: London, 1990), 146–54, 159–60; John Miller has argued that Hill exaggerates the case for the decline of the English identification of a papal Antichrist; nevertheless, Miller himself points to the emergence of a more directly political critique of Catholicism. J. Miller, *Popery and Politics 1660–1688* (Cambridge, 1973), 88–90, 148–50. The classic example of the new strain of political anti-Catholicism is Andrew Marvell, *An Account of the Growth of Popery and Arbitrary Government* (Amsterdam, 1677).

[33] See e.g. [Charles Davenant], *Essays upon I. The balance of power. II. The right of making war, peace and alliances. III. Universal monarch* (London, 1701).

[34] G. M. Straka, *Anglican reaction to the Revolution of 1688* (Madison, Wis., 1962), 65–79; J. P. Kenyon, *Revolution Principles* (Cambridge, 1977), 24–6, 29; J. G. A. Pocock, *The Ancient Constitution and the Feudal Law* (1957: Cambridge, 1988), 188, 227, 229–30; M. P. Thompson, 'The reception of Locke's *Two treatises of government* 1690–1705', *Political Studies*, 24 (1976), 184–91; M. Goldie, 'The Revolution of 1689 and the

such ambiguity about Revolution principles. The only concession to English susceptibilities was the offer of the throne *jointly* to William and Mary. Otherwise in Scotland there was none of the embarrassment about resistance found in English Revolution culture. The Scottish Claim of Right clearly stated that James VII had 'forefaulted' the throne.[35] Lacking the potential for vagueness and compromise provided by English triadic constitutionalism, Scottish political culture was rigidly divided. The Scottish Calvinist theory of resistance developed by George Buchanan (1506–82) dominated Scottish whig–presbyterian political and historical treatises, and provoked in response an intransigent tradition of absolutism.[36] In Ireland (1691) the key document of the Revolution was the Treaty of Limerick which generated quite different tensions in political culture. Moreover, Anglo-Irish tories, largely for fear of upsetting the land settlement and the privileges of Ireland's Anglican elite, were more clearly committed to the Revolution than were their brethren on the British mainland.[37] Despite these major variations in glossing the discontinuities of 1688–91, the events themselves created a Revolutionary community of interest in the Williamite realms. A basic constitutionalism, and a desire to promote the protestant interest in the wider European sphere, constituted common ground. Moreover, there was a recognition of the crucial transnational British dimension of post-Revolution politics: that the overturning of the Revolution in Scotland might well prove a back-door route to a Jacobite restoration in England.

However, the Revolution also exacerbated the existing regnal anxieties in Ireland and Scotland about their status within the multiple Stuart monarchy. These anxieties were compounded by serious economic tensions with England. As a result, in the 1690s the multipolar conflicts of the British nations tended to become more of a clash between an English core and an economically underdeveloped and constitutionally exposed Scottish and Irish periphery. The Glorious Revolution had transformed the context in which the Anglo-Scottish regal union and the Anglo-Irish Poynings' Law procedures operated. Under Poynings' Law, Ireland was governed by the English king and council through the Irish parliament. The question then arose did the authority of the English king-in-council over the Irish parliament devolve upon the English crown-in-parliament? There were fears that the rise of parlia-

---

structure of political argument', *Bulletin of Research in the Humanities*, 84 (1980), esp. 508, 516–18.

[35] Donaldson (ed.), *Scottish Historical Documents*, 255.

[36] I. D. McFarlane, *Buchanan* (London, 1981), 392–440.

[37] P. Kelly, 'Ireland and the Glorious Revolution: from kingdom to colony', in R. Beddard (ed.), *The Revolutions of 1688* (Oxford, 1991), 163, 178, 180–4.

ment in the English Revolution of 1688–9 had led English politicians to assume that the powers of king and council now belonged to the English parliament. The Irish acknowledged subjection to the Stuart monarchy but not to the English nation. The protestant patriot William Molyneux (1656–98), reiterating an argument of an Old English mid-century patriot, Patrick Darcy, claimed that Ireland was an independent kingdom, and that the English colonists who composed the Irish political nation were an unconquered free people who by right ought to enjoy the privileges and freedoms of Englishmen.[38] In particular, the Irish political nation was concerned that its entitlement to government by consent in the economic sphere was being frustrated by mercantilist restrictions imposed by the English parliament.[39]

In Scotland, too, there were grumblings that the regal union of 1603 was turning into a *de facto* subordination of Scotland to the English political nation. In practice the Scottish court had been absorbed within the metropolitan English court and, as a result, English politicians meddled in Scottish affairs as if Scotland were simply a troublesome distant province of England, its independence nominal since 1603. The most common argument in Scottish political culture between 1689 and 1707 – a prominent feature of the ideology of both whigs and Jacobites, and of separatists, federalists and incorporationists – concerned a demand for the rectification of the union of the crowns, an imperfect conjunction which had corrupted the Scottish constitution. Indeed a feature of Scottish whig culture was an ambivalence on the subject of the Revolution of 1689, a feeling that, whereas the Revolution of 1638–41 had led to the imposition of limitations on the Scottish monarch in London, the Revolution of 1689 had produced no fundamental improvement in Scotland's constitutional situation within the multiple monarchy. Economic developments in the 1690s brought matters to a head. The Company of Scotland established in 1695 was an attempt by the Scots, excluded by the Navigation Acts from the fruits of English imperial expansion, to obtain an overseas trade of their own. The English court used its influence to frustrate the centrepiece of the company's activities, the Darien venture, provoking a widespread sense of betrayal in Scotland, a sense that William had abused his position as

---

[38] William Molyneux, *The case of Ireland's being bound by acts of parliament in England, stated* (Dublin, 1698). Molyneux was developing an argument which had been put forward earlier by the Old English lawyer Patrick Darcy in 1643; see Clarke, 'Colonial constitutional attitudes', 358–9.

[39] I. Hont, 'Free trade and the economic limits to national politics: neo-Machiavellian political economy reconsidered', in J. Dunn (ed.), *The Economic Limits to Modern Politics* (Cambridge, 1990), 78–89.

dual monarch by sacrificing the interests of Scotland to those of England. Scots argued that there was now a pressing need to reorder the constitutional relationship of England, Scotland and the monarchy. Potential solutions included independence under a different monarch from that of England, a treaty giving Scots access to English trade, and a system of limitations on the powers of the monarch unevenly shared by Scotland with England.[40]

The succession crisis attendant on the death of Anne's last surviving child, the duke of Gloucester, in 1700, raised the stakes of Anglo-Scottish differences. Scottish suspicions that the English political nation took the independent sovereign kingdom of Scotland for granted as an appendage of the English monarchy appeared to be confirmed by the English resolution of the succession crisis, the Act of Settlement (1701). The English legislature had assumed without consulting the Scottish parliament that the entail of the crown of England on the Hanoverian line at the death of Anne would automatically follow in Scotland. Occurring so soon after the Darien episode, this outraged the Scottish political nation, whig and Jacobite. Patriotic frustrations were now freely manipulated by unscrupulous magnate politicians in the Scots parliament as a means of ousting their rivals. The Act of Security (1704) was a dramatic display of national assertion. Under the terms of the act, Scotland would not, on Anne's death, choose the same successor as England, unless the regal union was substantially reformed. The English parliament responded by passing the Alien Act (1705) under which Scots would be treated as aliens and their exports excluded from the English market unless they embarked on negotiations for union or accepted the Hanoverian succession. The Scots parliament of 1705 was cajoled into negotiations, and that of 1706 eventually induced to accept an incorporating union.[41]

However, the threat of an English military conquest to secure Scotland in the Revolution interest was to hang over the whole proceedings.[42] In addition, the succession crisis also spawned a new round of Anglo-Scottish historical argument over the question of whether the

[40] [George Ridpath], *A Discourse upon the Union of Scotland and England* (1702), ch. 3; [George Mackenzie, Early of Cromarty], *Paraneisis Pacifica* (London, 1702); *A Speech in Parliament by the Lord Belhaven upon the Act for Security of the Kingdom* (Edinburgh, 1703); [James Hodges], *The Rights and Interests of the two British Monarchies ... Treatise I* (London, 1703).

[41] W. Ferguson, *Scotland's Relations with England: a survey to 1707* (Edinburgh, 1977), chs. 9–14; P. W. J. Riley, *The Union of England and Scotland* (Manchester, 1978); Riley, 'The Scottish parliament of 1703', *Scottish Historical Review*, 47 (1968).

[42] [George Ridpath], *The Reducing of Scotland by Arms, and Annexing it to England as a Province Considered* (London, 1705?); James Hodges, *War Betwixt the two British Kingdoms Considered* (London, 1705).

English crown comprehended a suzerain authority over the whole island of Britain, including a dependent Scottish nation whose kings before the regal union, it was alleged, had been homagers of their English overlords.[43] The argument that Scotland had never been *de iure* a legitimate independent and sovereign kingdom was led by William Atwood (c. 1650–1712),[44] described by one Scottish commentator as 'hackney-state-scribbler in ordinary to Old England'.[45] Atwood's works were burnt on the authority of the Scottish parliament which also commissioned the antiquarian James Anderson (1662–1728) to answer these slurs.[46] The assertion of Scotland's historic independence, always a staple of patriotic historiography, was a prominent aspect of Scottish discourse of all stripes, including unionist, in the run-up to union.[47] Indeed it was vital to the Scottish unionist case that incorporation with England was taking place on the right terms – a treaty between sovereign crowns. Although some English commentators, such as William Nicolson (1655–1727), bishop of Carlisle, disagreed with Atwood, and acknowledged Scottish sovereignty,[48] in general the imperial crown controversy overshadowed attempts to find a common ground, especially a common history, for the future British nation.

English political culture featured no strong commitment to Britishness, merely a recognition of its international strategic necessity and domestic tactical utility. Although union was eventually to become a shibboleth of English whiggism, in the first decade of the eighteenth century English party culture was not rigidly divided between pro-British whigs and narrowly xenophobic tories, though there is an element of truth in this caricature. The flux of politics and the demands of party strategy dictated that around 1699–1700 the whigs supported union as a tactical diversion; that Nottingham and the court tories supported union in 1702–3, a measure opposed by the whig junto; and that by 1706 union had become a whig measure, with opposition in the English parliament tending to be high-church tory.[49]

The Union of 1707 did not arise out of a sense of shared Britishness.

[43] W. Ferguson, 'Imperial crowns: a neglected facet of the Union of 1707', *Scottish Historical Review*, 53 (1974), 22–44.
[44] [William Atwood], *The Superiority and Direct Dominion of the Imperial Crown of England over the Crown and Kingdom of Scotland* (London, 1704); Atwood, *The Superiority and Direct Dominion . . . Reasserted* (London, 1705).
[45] *A Pil for Pork-eaters: or a Scots lancet for an English swelling* (Edinburgh, 1705), 3.
[46] James Anderson, *An Historical Essay shewing that the Crown and Kingdom of Scotland is Imperial and Independent* (Edinburgh, 1705).
[47] For the Scottish reply to Atwood, see C. Kidd, *Subverting Scotland's Past* (Cambridge, 1993), 46 n.
[48] William Nicolson (ed.), 'Preface' in *Leges Marchiarum, or border-laws* (London, 1705).
[49] Riley, *Union*, 23–5, 48, 163–71.

It emerged as a solution to the problem of managing the Scottish parliament. A crucial by-product of the Revolution in Scotland had been the liberation of Scottish parliamentary procedure from the shackles of the Lords of the Articles. This committee whose composition had been determined in large part by the bishops, who were themselves often royal poodles, had enjoyed control over the agenda for each parliamentary session. The abolition of the Articles and the disappearance of the estate of bishops meant that the court had lost its traditional instruments of management, and the rejuvenated legislature proceeded to spin out of control. From the Revolution to 1705 the Scots parliament was a refractory institution whose mulish assertiveness indirectly threatened both the anti-Bourbon war effort and the security of the protestant succession. It eventually became apparent that the easiest way to secure the Hanoverian succession in England's backyard was by incorporating Scotland and its parliament within the institutions of a new 'British' state, effectively creating an enlarged realm of England. Only in the Scottish parliamentary sessions of 1705 and 1706 did the court begin to master the arts of post-Revolutionary Scottish parliamentary management, but by then Anne's ministers had already resorted to the strategy of an Anglo-Scottish treaty.[50] This treaty acknowledged the creation of a multicultural state, with distinct church establishments and legal systems, rather than a monolithic British nation.

Ironically, the English enjoyed a far greater affinity with the Anglican and 'Gothic' Anglo-Irish political nation created by the plantations, than with the Scots whose post-Revolutionary nationhood was based largely on presbyterianism, a radical Buchananite whiggism and a Gaelic *mythos*.[51] It would be a teleological error to view Britishness in terms of the *union achieved* to the exclusion of the *union denied*. The vague sense of a shared Britishness in this period tended to be archipelagic, embracing Ireland, and was not narrowly confined to the nations of mainland Britain.[52] The Irish political nation was Anglican and believed itself heir to English liberties and laws. When patriots such as Molyneux vaunted Ireland's regnal status, they did so largely in reaction to a perceived denial of their historic rights as the English

---

[50] *Ibid.*

[51] See the remarks made about the greater proximity of the English to the Anglo-Irish than to the Welsh with whom they were already united in [Henry Maxwell], *An Essay towards an Union of Ireland with England* (London, 1703), 19.

[52] See e.g. *The Queen an Empress, and her Three Kingdoms one Empire* (London, 1706), 9–10 and Edmund Gibson's 1695 edition of Camden's *Britannia*. In Ireland the sense of Britishness was confined to the New English minority who had by now largely dispossessed the old political elite, Old English and native Irish alike.

nation in Ireland.[53] Several Anglo-Irish politicians and pamphleteers promoted the idea of union with England, and there was a spurned Irish attempt at union with England in 1703.[54] The Anglo-Irish political nation was almost certainly keener than its Scottish counterpart on a union with a kindred nation whose values it shared. Hence Jonathan Swift's lament in 1707 (though not published till 1746) on the injury done to a noble lady – Ireland – jilted by her paramour in favour of a rival mistress – Scotland – who was known to be nothing but trouble, having once already set a gang of scoundrels – Scots Covenanting rebels – to invade and ravage her misguided lover's property. An infuriated Swift went on to argue in the *Publick Spirit of the Whigs* (1714) that England should have conquered Scotland.[55] Why was the protestant political nation in Ireland, more temperamentally suited to assume a British identity, rejected for the Scots, with their presbyterianism and their distinctively anglophobic identity? Crucially, there was no succession crisis in Ireland. The Irish kingdom was annexed to the crown of England. Second, developments in the arts of Irish parliamentary management prevented the sort of crisis of governance which had necessitated Westminster's *de facto* absorption of the Scottish legislature. Although, in the immediate aftermath of the Treaty of Limerick the Irish parliament had been unwilling to ratify an agreement viewed as a betrayal of protestant interests and security, this unruliness was moderated from the mid 1690s by the development of political management by 'undertakers'.[56]

Unsurprisingly the union of Anglo-Scottish incompatibles was not accompanied by the emergence of a new matter of Britain. Britain remained an uninspiringly underimagined community. Contemporary construction of British nationhood lacked a compelling ethnic or historical vision. Instead of a hegemonic British identity, there remained the existing national traditions and a few areas which permitted a degree of common identification. The Union of 1707 was celebrated in terms

53 Molyneux, *Case of Ireland*, 97–8. For an earlier statement of the case by an Old English Catholic patriot see Patrick Darcy, 'A declaration how and by what means, the laws and statutes of England from time to time came to be of force in Ireland', in Walter Harris (ed.), *Hibernica* (Dublin 1747–50), part II, 1–21. See also Clarke, 'Colonial constitutional attitudes', 357–75. See also Smyth above, ch. 10.

54 [Maxwell], *Essay towards an union*; J. Kelly, 'The origins of the Act of Union: an examination of unionist opinion in Britain and Ireland, 1650–1800', *Irish Historical Studies*, 25 (1987), 238–44.

55 Jonathan Swift, *The Story of the Injured Lady* (1707: published 1746), in J. McMinn (ed.), *Swift's Irish Pamphlets* (Gerrards Cross, 1991), 23–8; [Swift], *The Publick Spirit of the Whigs* (London, 1714), 22–3.

56 D. Hayton, 'The beginnings of the "undertaker system"', in T. Bartlett and D. Hayton (eds.), *Penal Era and Golden Age: Essays in Irish history, 1690–1800* (Belfast, 1979), 32–41.

of a very weak milk-and-water Britishness. The thanksgiving sermons delivered in England on the occasion of union hardly convey a widespread sense of enthusiasm for the new nation. Many of the sermons which found their way into print were those of dissenters, especially presbyterians,[57] Calvinist Anglicans,[58] and latitudinarians.[59] The history of Britain was of little account in these sermons except as a past, now discontinued, of intestine broils. Instead, Scripture was pressed into service, the kindred Old Testament kingdoms of Israel and Judah standing proxy for the real or imagined history of the British peoples. The sermons contained little suggestion of authentic British ideological integration and were devoid of positive national themes. Instead they stressed the glory of Queen Anne in achieving union: a cult of monarchy substituted for any convincing sense of nationhood.

What united Britons above all was a sense of a national interest, a set of similar British concerns threatened by a common enemy. Many contemporaries subscribed to an instrumentalist view of Britishness: that the new nation had been created as an anti-Jacobite and anti-Bourbon device. According to the Scottish federalist pamphleteer Andrew Brown, a firmer (though not necessarily incorporating) union was 'no improper expedient for the security of the protestant religion, general liberty, and for the keeping even the balance of Europe'.[60] Strategic theorists on both sides of the border, such as Peter Paxton (d. 1711) and the earl of Cromarty (1630–1714), had argued that the reality of power politics in Europe, and particularly the threat of a Franco-Spanish Bourbon monolith, dictated the necessity of forging a new British entity as a counterweight.[61] However, the notion of a shared interest scarcely sufficed as the basis for a convincing national identity.

---

[57] Giles Dent, *A Thanksgiving Sermon Preached on the 1st day of May, 1707 on Occasion of the happy Union between England and Scotland* (London, 1707); Christopher Taylor, *A Thanksgiving Sermon 1st May 1707 on Occasion of the Happy Union . . .* (London, 1707); Joshua Oldfield, *Israel and Judah Made One Kingdom* (London, 1707); Thomas Freke, *Union the Strength of a People* (London, 1707); Daniel Williams, *A Thanksgiving Sermon Occasioned by the Union of England and Scotland* (London, 1707).

[58] John Edwards, *One Nation, and One King* (London, 1707).

[59] John Ollyffe, *A Sermon Preached May 4th 1707 at Uxbridge upon Occasion of the Late Day of Thanksgiving for the Union of the Two Kingdoms of England and Scotland* (London, 1707); N. Brady, *A Sermon Preached at Richmond in Surrey, on Thursday the first of May, 1707* (London, 1707); Thomas Manningham, *A Sermon upon the Union of the two Kingdoms* (London, 1707).

[60] [Andrew Brown], *Some Very Weighty and Seasonable Considerations Tending to Dispose . . . the nation for the more effectual treating with England* (n.p., 1703), 4.

[61] Peter Paxton, *A Scheme of Union between England and Scotland with Advantages to Both Kingdoms* (London and Edinburgh, 1705); Cromarty, *Paraneisis pacifica*; Cromarty, *Trialogus* (1706).

Necessity and communal self-interest were compelling arguments for uniting but did little to generate a sense of British nationhood.

The lack of an inspiring British identity was not simply a matter of English indifference or of the continuity of a strong sense of Englishness deriving from the ancient constitution and the common law. There were English writers and historians sympathetic to the British idea. However, they appear to have been handicapped by a poverty of materials. Even where resources did exist for the construction of a British identity, there tended to be limits to their potential for further development, or problems with their direct applicability to the Anglo-Scottish Union.

The new revised English edition of William Camden's *Britannia* published in 1695 was the outcome of a genuinely British project. Edmund Gibson (1669–1748) had overall control but there were important contributions by men of learning from the various nations of the British Isles, including the Scottish antiquary Sir Robert Sibbald (1641–1722) and the Welsh polymath Edward Lhuyd (1660–1709). However, the *Britannia* was of limited use for the construction of a British identity. As the late Stuart Piggott observed, the original *Britannia* had been strongly humanist in its patriotism, focusing both on the Roman province of Britannia, and on the 'Celtic tribal areas of Britain as recorded in the classical geographers'. The territories of these various local tribes were assumed to coincide with the borders of the later shire system. This chorographical orientation meant that the tradition established by Camden, which was continued by Gibson's team and by individuals such as Robert Plot (1640–96) and John Aubrey (1626–97), was as much localist as pan-Britannic in perspective. The emphasis was on such historic 'county communities' as the Attrebatii of Berkshire, the Trinobantes of Middlesex and the Coritani of Northamptonshire, or in Scotland on regional identities associated with such tribes as the Selgovae, Damnii, Gadeni and Novantes. The concept of Britannia was less engaging than the curious diversity of its parts.[62]

The English Dissenter and ministerial hack Daniel Defoe (1661?–1731) was keenly aware that the formation of a British national consciousness would be a piecemeal operation and, such were the strengths of existing English and Scottish identities, that the eradication of existing 'national aversions' and 'immortal prejudices' had to take

[62] S. Piggott, 'William Camden and the *Britannia*', *Proceedings of the British Academy*, 37 (1951), 208; S. Mendyk, 'Scottish regional natural historians and the *Britannia* Project', *Scottish Geographical Magazine*, 101 (1985), 165–73; G. Walters and F. Emergy, 'Edward Lhuyd, Edmund Gibson, and the printing of Camden's *Britannia*, 1695', *The Library*, 5th ser., 32 (1977), 109–37; Robert Plot, *The Natural History of Stafford-shire* (Oxford, 1686), esp. 392–3; M. Hunter, *John Aubrey and the Realm of Learning* (London, 1975), esp. 69–70.

place before any positive identity-formation. Defoe's principal contribution to the union debate was a series of six *Essays at Removing National Prejudices* (1706–7), while his poem *Caledonia* was an attempt 'to rescue Scotland out of the jaws of slander'. Defoe was refreshingly free of chauvinism, and of an appropriate disposition to create a British identity. However, he lacked ingenuity and resources to construct anything more compelling than a case based on a weak providentialism and the need to pool resources in the face of the Bourbon leviathan. Defoe had cleverly exposed the flawed historical basis of English xenophobia in his *True-Born Englishman* (1701), noting the various successful invasions which forged out of 'Roman-Saxon-Danish-Norman English' blood that 'Het'rogeneous Thing, an Englishman'. However, in *The True-Born Britain* (1707), Defoe had much more difficulty in the obverse task of creating a positive British identity, and was reduced to an unconvincing Galfridianism: 'Our Liniage we derive from antient Brute.'[63] Similarly, William Nicolson contributed to an understanding of the history of Scotland with his *Scots Historical Library* (1702). Nicolson had an empathetic vision of the British nations, recognising Scotland's historical independence, and, as a Borderer, lamenting the deleterious effects of Anglo-Scottish warfare on marcher life. Nevertheless, despite Nicolson's good intentions, his work indicates the difficulties facing an English historian attempting to create an acceptable British history. For instance, a tory-turning-conservative-whig, Nicolson was appalled by the resistance-oriented radicalism of the Scottish whig tradition.[64]

III

Despite the hegemony of pre-existent national and regnal affiliations, and the lack of a convincing British identity, certain overarching loyalties furthered the process of ideological integration. Protestantism, a basic commitment to civil and political liberty, and a sense of having common roots in a Gothic racial stock which manifested itself historically in the evolution of similar mixed constitutions, together constituted a bedrock of common Britishness.

[63] Daniel Defoe, *The True-born Englishman* (10th edn, 1701), 6, 10; Defoe, *The True-born Britain* (London, 1707), 2; Defoe, 'Dedication' in *Caledonia, A Poem in the Honour of Scotland and the Scots Nation* (Edinburgh, 1706).

[64] William Nicolson, *The Blessings of the Sixth Year. A sermon preach'd before the Queen at St. James's Chappel, on Saturday the eighth of March, 1706/7* (London, 1707), esp. 24–5; Nicolson, *The Scottish Historical Library* (London, 1702), 18, 37–8, 114–15; F. G. James, *North Country Bishop: a biography of William Nicolson* (New Haven and London, 1956), 87, 170–85.

Protestantism was a crucial integrative factor, though there were considerable tensions within British protestantism which qualified this tendency. The decline of both the apocalyptic and covenanting visions of Britain, and the substitution of a diffuse anti-Catholicism in their stead, contributed indirectly to the formation of a united kingdom. The weakening of two of the most potent early modern conceptions of Britishness created the ideological space for the lame Erastian compromise of 1707 – a multiconfessional British state. Nevertheless, significant confessional and sectarian divisions hampered the British idea. The compromise of 1707 did not foreclose on Anglican support for Scotland's disestablished and (until 1712) untolerated episcopalian community. Even within the same confession there could be difficulties, sharp divisions surfacing during the union debates between English and Scottish presbyterians. James Webster, an uncompromising Scots presbyterian, argued that English Baxterian presbyterians were unprincipled accommodationist trimmers.[65] In general, however, the wider protestant cause threatened by the menace of Catholic France, operated as a force for cohesion.

One of the hallmarks of religious life in the late seventeenth and early eighteenth centuries was the sudden upsurge in voluntary religious societies. The causes of this phenomenon were various. They included a recognition that moral vigilantism was more likely to eradicate immorality in the populace at large than the tired juridical procedures of the church courts, a desire to recreate through small-group spirituality the vitality of primitive Christianity, and a growing receptivity to the precepts of German Pietism. From the 1690s societies for the reformation of manners proliferated throughout the British Isles, promoting a shared set of ethical and cultural standards. Moreover, bodies such as the Welsh Trust (1674–81), the charity schools in Wales established by the Society for the Promotion of Christian Knowledge, and the Society in Scotland for Propagating Christian Knowledge (established in 1709), campaigned for the anglicisation of the Celtic peripheries, balancing a drive for cultural homogenisation with a strategic awareness of the utility of evangelising in the local vernacular where necessary. Though anti-Catholic and, in several respects, hostile to particularism, pietistic activism had a tendency to blur denominational and ethnic divisions, and contributed to the formation of a common culture of British protestantism.[66]

---

[65] [James Webster], *Lawful Prejudices against an Incorporating Union with England* (Edinburgh, 1707), 8.

[66] See e.g. D. Bahlman, *The Moral Revolution of 1688* (New Haven, 1957); Jenkins, *Foundations of Modern Wales*, 198–205; C. W. J. Withers, *Gaelic Scotland: the*

Britons were also united by a basic commitment to liberty, embracing both civil freedoms and constitutional government. Hugh Chamberlen (c. 1630–1720?), an English unionist and economic projector described the Scots and English as 'both a free people by their laws'.[67] Proponents of union argued that a strong united British parliament would strengthen the liberties of the people against the ambitions of the crown and that future monarchs, unlike the Stuarts, would be unable to become absolute monarchs 'by playing one of the kingdoms against the other, making use of each (by turns) to oppress and enslave the other, whilst a formidable body of troops was always ready in Scotland to invade the liberties of England, and the riches of England [were] made use of to destroy both church and state in Scotland'.[68] This sense of a common British libertarianism was intertwined with the rising tradition of Gothicism.

The complex of ideas which comprised the Gothic version of historical politics, Gothicism has often been unfairly reduced to Anglo-Saxonism and interpreted as a crucial ideological prop of English chauvinism. Yet it also had the potential to support a common British political identity based on a shared history of similar Gothic mixed constitutions. Political commentators, particularly those of a whiggish or republican bent, became increasingly aware from the mid-seventeenth century that the mixed constitutional governments created by the Gothic peoples of medieval Europe were collapsing and that absolute monarchies were rising in their stead. There was a growing recognition that the three kingdoms of the British Isles had been unusually successful in their avoidance of despotism: 'Our King's Dominions are the only Supporters of this noble Gothick Constitution, save only what little remains may be found thereof in Poland', concluded Molyneux.[69] This awareness provoked a double-edged Gothic identity, a triumphalist exceptionalism checked by concern that the British constitutions would be the next to fall. Expressions of anxiety about the fate of Gothic institutions came from all corners of the British Isles: from the Anglo-Irish commonwealthman, Robert Molesworth (1656–1725), the Scottish republican visionary, Andrew Fletcher of Saltoun (1655–1716) and the Cornish 'real whig', Walter Moyle (1672–1721). Fletcher, who should not be pigeonholed as a straightforward defender of Scottish independence, recognised a basis for

transformation of a culture region (London, 1988), 122; T. C. Barnard, 'Reforming Irish manners: the religious societies in Dublin during the 1690s', *Historical Journal*, 35 (1992), 805–38.

[67] Hugh Camberlen, *The Great Advantages to both Kingdoms of Scotland and England by an Union* (1702), 12.

[68] Taylor, *Thanksgiving sermon*, 14.   [69] Molyneux, *Case of Ireland*, 174.

Britishness in the preservation of a shared Gothic inheritance.[70] Michael Geddes (1650?–1713), an Anglican divine of Scottish birth and early education who later became chancellor of Salisbury after the elevation of another Anglo-Scot, Gilbert Burnet, to that see, was a proponent of a shared Anglo-Scottish Gothic identity. Geddes noted that 'the Lowland Scots do seem to have been a Saxon, or German, and not an Irish nation', a fact confirmed in their libertarian mixed institutions: 'in England and Scotland that German form of government remains to this day'.[71] However, the Scottish political nation was as yet only experiencing the first stirrings of a Gothicism which had not yet displaced the traditional Gaelic association with the ancient west Highland kingdom of Dalriada. Ironically, Gothicism had at this stage a greater potential to cement bonds between the English and Anglo-Irish political nations. As an English identification with the Gothic Angles, Saxons and Jutes replaced older versions of English ethnic origins such as the myths of Geoffrey, so this identity became also the badge of the emergent Protestant nation in Ireland. These were intensely conscious of their separateness from Gaeldom, and, given their exclusion from the new British state, keen to remind the metropolitan authorities of their inherited rights as Englishmen.[72] The ideology of Gothic constitutionalism exhibits in microcosm the limitations inherent in the various elements of later-Stuart Britishness.

The strength of existing national identities suggests that any convincing British identity would have to have been multicultural, fusing existing national shibboleths. Yet these were by their very nature incompatible, indeed had evolved in opposition. In the early eighteenth century Britishness comprehended a considerable degree of conflicting pluralism. English political culture remained dominated by debates over the continuity and applicability of its ancient Saxon constitution.[73] The Welsh resumed the process of shaping their residual British *mythos* into a vivid cultural particularism.[74] In Scotland a large investment of patriotic capital in the ancient constitution and deeds of the Gaelic Scots of

---

[70] Andrew Fletcher, *A Discourse of Government with Relation to Militias* (1698), in Fletcher, *Political Works* (Glasgow, 1749), 5–20, 26–7; Robert Molesworth, *An Account of Denmark* (London, 1694); [Walter Moyle and John Trenchard], *An Argument, Shewing, that a Standing Army is Inconsistent with a Free Government, and Absolutely Destructive to the Constitution of the English Monarchy* (London, 1697).

[71] Michael Geddes, *An Essay on the Countries, Religion, Learning, Numbers, Forms of Government, and the Chief Cause of the Successes of the Nations by which the Roman Empire was Pulled Down*, in Geddes, *Miscellaneous Tracts III* (London, 1706), 3, 19.

[72] D. G. Boyce, *Nationalism in Ireland* (1982: London, 1991), ch. 4.

[73] R. J. Smith, *The Gothic Bequest* (Cambridge, 1987).

[74] P. Morgan, *The Eighteenth-Century Renaissance* (Llandybie, 1981). For the earlier phase of the process see Bradshaw, above 43–111 *passim* and Roberts, 8–42.

Dalriada persisted until the mid eighteenth century.[75] An increasingly distinctive and hibernocentric Anglo-Irish patriotism evolved in reaction to a frustrated Englishness.[76] Yet these identities continued to overlap with certain elements of a core British identity.

Nevertheless an authentic 'matter of Britain' would not be available until the Seven Years War and the Napoleonic Wars yielded a cornucopia of 'British' achievements and heroes – the elder Pitt, Wolfe, Nelson and Wellington. And even then this modern pantheon did not provide the definitive solution to the ideological problems of British nation-building. Lacking any sustenance from an historic British ethnic identity, it seems not to have met deeper atavistic needs.

[75] Kidd, *Subverting Scotland's Past*, ch. 5.
[76] D. Hayton, 'Anglo-Irish attitudes: changing perceptions of national identity among the Protestant ascendancy in Ireland, ca. 1690–1750', *Studies in Eighteenth-Century Culture*, 17 (1987), 145–57.

Index

Lightning Source UK Ltd.
Milton Keynes UK
UKOW050627041011

179731UK00001B/152/A